Stonewall Jackson's Men

General T J "Stonewall" Jackson

Stonewall Jackson's Men
The Personal Experiences and Letters of Three Confederate Soldiers of the Stonewall Brigade during the American Civil War

Four Years in the Stonewall Brigade

John O. Casler

Sketches of the Life of Captain Hugh A. White of Stonewall's Brigade by His Father

A Sketch of the Life of Randolf Fairfax by Philip Slaughter

Stonewall Jackson's Men
The Personal Experiences and Letters of Three Confederate Soldiers
of the Stonewall Brigade during the American Civil War
Four Years in the Stonewall Brigade
by John O. Casler
Sketches of the Life of Captain Hugh White of Stonewall's Brigade
by His Father
and
A Sketch of the Life of Randolf Fairfax
by Philip Slaughter

FIRST EDITION

Leonaur is an imprint of Oakpast Ltd
Copyright in this form © 2019 Oakpast Ltd

ISBN: 978-1-78282-826-6 (hardcover)
ISBN: 978-1-78282-827-3 (softcover)

http://www.leonaur.com

Publisher's Notes

The views expressed in this book are not necessarily those of the publisher.

Contents

First Edition Preface	7
Introductory	9
Enters the Army	12
First Battle of Bull Run	19
Letters	26
Gets in the Guardhouse	37
Midwinter Campaign of '62	49
Up the Shenandoah	56
Death of Ashby	64
Battle of Malvern Hill	70
General Winder	77
On the Rappahannock	82
Lee Crosses into Maryland	90
Start Back to Lee's Army	99
At Imboden's Camp	110
Battle of Chancellorsville	114
Reorganisation	130
Battle of Gettysburg	141
Interesting Adventures	149

Retreat across the Rapidan	157
Battle of the Snowballs	164
Back in Company A	174
Second Battle of Cold Harbor	182
Skirmish at Winchester	189
Battle of Cedar Creek	195
Attempts to Wade the Potomac	203
On the Road to Prison	212
Prisoners on the March	218
Released from Prison	227
Arrives at Home	235
Justice to Absentees	238
Devotion of the Soldiers	245
Conclusion	250
Appendix	257
Sketches of the Life of Captain Hugh A. White, of the Stonewall Brigade	285
A Sketch of the Life of Randolph Fairfax	353

First Edition Preface

In introducing myself to the public I want it distinctly understood that every word of this history is true. I was an eye witness to, and participated in all I here record, except some few incidents which did not come immediately under my eye, but which I have every reason to believe transpired from conversing with comrades who witnessed them. And I also want it understood that I am neither an author, nor the son of an author; that this is the first time I ever wrote anything of any consequence for publication, and in all probability will be the last. That all who want to criticise are at perfect liberty to do so to their hearts content.

At the commencement of the war, I, like many others in both armies, kept a diary, but did not keep it up continuously, as I had intended and at times some of it was lost, so I am unable to write it in diary form; but will mention days and dates as set down in my old diary. I had no idea then of ever having it published, but kept it more for the benefit of my parents and sisters, in the event I should never return, hoping it might chance to fall into their hands.

But it is now more than a quarter of a century since the war ended, and many of my friends who have seen my old diary have prevailed on me to write it over for publication before is it too late, and while I still retain a vivid recollection of many of the scenes herein recorded.

I will not refer to the causes of the war, as to who were right or who were wrong, but simply relate what I went through as a "high private in the rear rank."

I have seen a great many histories of the war and incidents of battles and campaigns written by officers, but have never seen any extended history from the pen of a private. I have seen treatises on military tactics by men who never fired a gun; but I have never seen a continuous history of incidents as they occurred in the army from day to day through a series of years by any one, much less a soldier in the ranks.

That is what this history purports to be, and I think it will be interesting to the youth of our land, as well as to all others, and particularly to the old soldiers who belonged to the command. To them I refer as corroborating witnesses of the facts herein stated.

The Author.

Oklahoma City. September, 1893.

Dedication

This work is respectfully dedicated to the boys who wore the Gray, and the boys who wore the Blue, and who fought and suffered for what they conceived to be right.

> *No more shall the war cry sever,*
> *Or the winding rivers be red;*
> *They banish our anger forever,*
> *When they laurel the graves of the dead;*
> *Under the sod and dew,*
> *Waiting the judgment day;*
> *Love and tears for the Blue,*
> *Tears and love for the Gray.*

The Author.

John O. Casler, 1863.
"High Private in the rear rank."

CHAPTER 1

Introductory

It is not the purpose of the writer, in giving the events that happened in the four years' struggle between the North and South, to enter into a detailed account of the causes that led up to the war.

These are matters of history, and have gone upon record, according to the prejudices and passions of the contending parties; or they have been given from the different points from which men viewed them.

When the Mason and Dixon line was first blazed out the country was divided into two powerful, distinct and widely diverging factions, differing radically in the policy of the government and financial interests, and these of such magnitude that the casual observer will understand at once they must not only lead to a disruption of the government, but to war and bloodshed.

From that very hour the two factions began forming their ranks for the final conflict; the coming was as fixed as fate itself.

Nor did either think of grounding their arms. True, one was aggressive and the other defensive. But if the aggression was persistent, the defence was determined. In both the North and the South, the worst passions of men were appealed to, and in the name of patriotism each was called upon to stand for their homes, their firesides and their country. South of the Mason and Dixon line were the homes and firesides of the Southerner, and north of it the homes of their former Northern brethren.

True, there was a large element, both North and South, whose patriotism arose above sectional lines, and who looked with dark forebodings upon the coming conflict, and who were ready to interpose in behalf of peace and good government, and whose love of country reached beyond the sectional strife that was raging.

But in the great whirl of passion and prejudice their efforts proved in vain; their voices hushed, and they found themselves powerless to avert the inevitable. The die had been cast; the line drawn; the decree had gone forth, and no mortal hand could stay the tempest or arrest the calamity.

And when, at last, the crash came, even the conservative element had nothing to do but to drop into line, according to their feelings or mutual interests.

There was no half-way ground to occupy; war knows nothing but decision, and if one could not decide for himself there was a fate to decide for him.

"He that is not for me is against me" is an inexorable decree of battle, and to that decree men were compelled to bow, whether they would or not. Thus, as the mighty avalanche, or the terrible cyclone, were they swept on.

America was young, and filled with younger sons, sons each of whom felt himself a king. With him to be an American was to be a freeman, and he stood proudly upon his royal rights; to dare to trample upon these inherent privileges was an insult to his honour, to his Americanism. The fires of seventy-six were rekindled into a blazing, burning flame, as each pictured to himself the long catalogue of grievances.

The cannon of 1812 echoed and re-echoed over the plains of South Carolina, while the defiant tones were hurled back from the mountains of New Hampshire, rousing the young blood of the sons of New England.

The young men, full of martial fire, pictured the American flag borne, with proud, victorious arms, into the very Halls of the Montezumas, showing that our arms had been victorious on every battlefield; that never had we crossed swords with any foe but that victory had followed. The American eagle, proud, victorious bird, belonged to each, and each felt called upon to see that that bird soared unfettered in the clear, bright sunlight of heaven.

Each thought himself the special guardian of freedom and the protector of American liberty. None stopped to ponder the old adage, "*When Greek meets Greek, then comes the tug of war.*"

With such a spirit animating each heart, it was not surprising that, when the bugle sounded to arms, from the prairies of Texas to the cotton and rice fields of South Carolina, and the blue-tinged hills of the Old Dominion, men sprang to arms by the thousands, eager for the battle to begin. If the Southerner felt his arm strengthened and nerved for the conflict, the Northern son as confidently rushed to the front at his country's call.

The muttering thunders of war rolled over the vast sweep of country from the Atlantic to the Pacific, and was echoed back from the Gulf to the Lakes.

The hour for calm, sober reflection had passed; no time to reason now, but from hilltop to valley echoed the tramp of war, till a nation trembled beneath the tread of armies.

As the drunken, frenzied rabble rolls on, moved by they know not what, so the gathering hosts shouted, "To arms! To arms!"

From the time of the election of Abraham Lincoln in November, 1860, until the conflict actually began, the whole country was thrown into a fever of excitement, and this was increased in intensity with every floating breeze. One startling event followed another in quick succession; reason was dethroned, and the great whirlwind of passion and prejudice swept the whole land, kindling the fires of conflict in all the States.

On the 20th of December, 1860, the Legislature of South Carolina unanimously declared that that State no longer belonged to the American Union. In January, 1861, Florida withdrew, followed by Mississippi on the 9th of the same month, Alabama on the 11th, Georgia on the 20th, Louisiana on the 26th, and Texas on February 1st. Thus, in less than three months from the time of the election of Abraham Lincoln to the Presidency, all the cotton states, proper, had, by a unanimous vote, withdrawn from the Union, and had taken possession of all the Federal fortifications except those in Charleston Harbor.

While the sympathies of the people of Virginia were overwhelmingly with the South, yet her condition, adjacent as she was to the border of the Free States, made her hesitate before she took a decided stand. She even tried to throw herself into the breach, and, if possible, heal up the differences and wounds of the past, and thus avert the terrors of war. But her effort was not only in vain, but futile. The storm had already gathered; the dark clouds of passion and hatred had already formed, and each hurled black defiance at the other.

The two volcanoes, one at the South and the other at the North, whose pent-up fires had been hissing and struggling to break loose from their smothered furies, were now belching forth fire and flame, and the burning lava rolling on but mocked the feeble efforts of the Middle States for peace.

Hot blood was up, and the furies were all turned loose, and an inexorable fate led them on. What Virginia could not settle for herself was soon settled for her, and she was compelled, whether she would or not, to action.

CHAPTER 2

Enters the Army

I was born in Frederick County, Virginia nine miles west of Winchester on the 1st day of Dec. 1838. My mother's maiden name was Heironimus an old family of that county, dating back of the revolutionary war. When I was three years old my father removed to Springfield, Hampshire County, (in what is now West Virginia) an adjoining county, where I spent my boyhood days as most other boys do in learning a trade and going to school when I received a fair English education for those days.

In March 1859, when I was in my 21st year, I cut loose from the paternal roof, and took Horace Greely's advice to "go west and grow up with the country" I landed in Cass County Mo., where I remained, living in different counties, until the spring of 1861, when the signs of the times indicated war, and I concluded to go back to old Virginia. I left Sedalia, Mo., the 8th day of April, 1861, and returned to Frederick County, Va., where my father was engaged in farming, having moved back to that county during my absence.

After leaving Sedalia I went to St Louis, and there got on board a steamboat bound for Pittsburg, Pa. After passing Cairo, Ill., we heard of the firing on Fort Sumpter and saw bills posted at the different towns we passed, calling for 75,000 troops for ninety days to protect Washington and put down the rebellion. Then we knew the war had commenced.

Various opinions were indulged in by the passengers, some saying that the north did not need that many troops and that it would all be settled in less than ninety days. But, alas! vain hope! how little we knew of the struggle that was before us. I parted with my fellow passengers at Parkersburg, W Va. Some were going into the Union Army and some of us into the Southern army

I arrived at home and remained there a short time. At that time the governor of Virginia was calling for volunteers. There had been a company raised at Springfield, my native town, and they were in service and camped at Blue's Gap, fifteen miles east of Romney, on the road leading to Winchester. As I had but fifteen miles to go to reach them, I bade farewell to my parents and sisters and went to the company, and arrived that evening in camp.

I met my old schoolmates and acquaintances whom I had parted from two years before in the school room, and now found them in army. I signed my name to the muster-roll, put on the uniform of gray, and was mustered into service for one year. The name of the company was Potomac Guards, Captain P. T Grace, commanding; S. D. Long, 1st Lieutenant; Jacob N. Buzzard, 2nd Lieut.; William Johnson, 3rd Lieut. There was another company camped at that place, the Hampshire Riflemen, Captain Geo. Sheetz. They were doing picket duty, not having yet been assigned to any regiment.

The next morning, which was the 19th of June, we were ordered to fall in, and marched, to Romney. The day was hot and the road dusty, and marching went quite hard with us, especially myself, who had never marched a day in my life; but I kept in ranks, for, "who would not be a soldier, and with the soldiers march." Arriving in Romney about 3 p.m., we quartered in an old building, took a good wash, had some refreshments, and felt like soldiers indeed, with our clothes covered with brass buttons, and the ladies smiling at us and cheering us on.

In the early part of June Colonel A. C. Cummins had been sent from Harper's Ferry to Romney to collect the different companies organising in that and adjacent counties, together, and form a regiment. He had been there but a few days and had three companies—the Potomac Guards, from Springfield, the Hampshire Riflemen, from New Creek, and the Independent Greys, from Moorefield, Hardy County. The Riflemen were a company organised before the war, and were well equipped.

The other two companies came there with nothing but their uniforms, but were given old altered muskets and old flint-lock rifles that had been sent there from Harper's Ferry, and two four-pound cannon that had been sent there during the John Brown raid, but no one to use them. They had a few rounds of ammunition in their coat pockets; no tents, cartridge boxes, or any other equipment.

In order that the reader may more fully understand the organisation of the Southern army, I will explain:

The maximum number of a company was one hundred men, commanded by a captain and three lieutenants, commissioned officers; then there were sergeants and corporals, non-commissioned officers, appointed by the captain.

A regiment was composed of ten companies, making one thousand men. Sometimes there were less, and often a regiment was reduced to two or three hundred able for service.

The field officers of a regiment were a colonel, lieutenant colonel and major. Two or more regiments composed a brigade, generally four or five regiments—sometimes more, sometimes less, according to circumstances—and commanded by a brigadier general.

Two or more brigades (generally four) composed a division, commanded by a major general; two or more divisions (generally three) composed an army corps, commanded by a lieutenant general, who was styled a full general. General R. E. Lee ranked as such. There were five full generals in the Southern army.

Several companies banded together—less than ten—was called a battalion, and commanded by a major. Two companies of cavalry formed a squadron. A company of artillery had four or six cannon, generally four, and one piece was called a section; going into action and unlimbering ready for business was called going into battery.

The Federals were camped at New Creek, about twenty miles from there, and sent a regiment over one morning to capture the whole outfit, and they would have succeeded had it not been for a citizen on the road coming a near way and giving the colonel warning. The consequence was the colonel beat a hasty retreat, taking everything with him.

Talk about your first big battles of the war, that was one of them. There were about a dozen shots exchanged, no one hurt and no one captured; the Southern boys pulling for Winchester and the Federals coming into the town. They remained about an hour and then went back to New Creek—both armies marching from each other all day. As a result, three regiments under Colonel A. P Hill were sent there from Harper's Ferry; the 10th Va., 13th Va., and 3rd Tennessee.

When our companies arrived, we found those regiments there. Our three companies were then formed into a battalion and put in command of Major William Lee and called Lee's Battalion—Colonel Cummins going back to Winchester to recruit more companies.

We remained there until the 24th expecting an attack every night and consequently had plenty of false alarms. We then marched back to Winchester, a distance of 45 miles, leaving some cavalry there under command of Captain Turner Ashby.

As we marched out of town the brass bands were playing, the drums beating, colours flying, and the fair ladies waving their handkerchiefs and cheering us onto "victory or death." Oh! how nice to be a soldier!

On the 27th we went into camp on the Opequon Creek, three miles south of Winchester, remaining several days, cleaning arms, drilling, etc. Our next move was to the Shawnee Springs in the suburbs of Winchester, where we were temporarily attached to General Elzy's brigade. The Hampshire riflemen not numbering enough (only 45) to be mustered in, were transferred to the cavalry and ordered back to Romney to recruit and get horses. How I wished then that I had joined that company, and could have done so only a short time before, but my name was down on the roll and there was no chance to get it off honourably I therefore had to remain in the infantry.

General Elzy was quite fond of a dram as most soldiers are, and one night when he and his staff were drinking quite freely, and feeling very liberal, he called in the sentinel who was on guard at his quarters and gave him a drink, and then went to bed. Now when this same sentinel was on post again, about daylight he put his head in the tent door, and finding the general still asleep, woke him up by exclaiming "General! general! ain't it about time for us to take another drink?"

The general roused up, and not being in as merry a mood as the night before, ordered him to be taken off to the guardhouse for his insolence.

That soldier was greeted for months afterward by the whole command by "General, general, ain't it about time for us to take another drink?"

The Federal general, Patterson, had crossed the Potomac with a considerable force. Our army, under General Joseph E. Johnston, had evacuated Harper's Ferry, and the two armies were close together below Martinsburg. One day our advance had a considerable skirmish with the enemy and captured forty-five prisoners, and then fell back south of town to Darkesville, where our whole force lay in line of battle. They were the first prisoners I had seen. As we were ordered to tear down all fences, it looked like a battle was imminent. We lay in line the next day, which was the 4th of July, but still no fight; and on the 5th we returned to Winchester and went into camp at the "Shawnee Springs."

The boys were all mad because we had no fight and accused General Johnston of being a coward, but they soon found out that he knew his business, and that a braver man never lived. After remaining in this camp three days our battalion was ordered to report to Colonel Cummins, one mile South of Winchester, where we found he had collected five more companies, *viz*: Page Grays, Captain Rippetoe; Shenandoah Riflemen, Captain Gatewood; Emerald Guards, Captain Sibert: (nearly all Irishmen) Mt. Jackson Rifles, Captain Allen; and Brook Company, Captain Crabill.

We remained in this camp several days, and received our equipments from Springfield as our company was equipped by private subscription and they were not ready when we left. Our equipments consisted of knapsacks, blankets, cartridge boxes, canteens and tents.

We had all started out with a carpet sack full of "store clothes, biled shirts and paper collars;" but we loaded them in the wagon and sent them home. We soon found out that we had no use for "store clothes and biled shirts."

On the fifteenth of July our regiment was marched one mile north of Winchester and permanently attached to General T. J. Jackson's brigade, consisting of the 2nd, 4th, 5th and 27th Va. regiments. Ours not being full yet was not numbered but called Colonel Cummins Regiment.

On the 16th the report being that General Patterson was advancing on Winchester, we were rushed out in line of battle, tore down all the fences and lay on our arms ready for action at a moment's warning. The next day passed off in the same way but no enemy appeared and we returned to camp and lay quiet.

Another new company comes to our regiment, the "Shenandoah Sharpshooters," Captain David Walton. They have no arms and are given flint-lock muskets. We are now ordered to cook rations and be ready to march at a moment's warning. Our regiment now has eight companies, and numbers about 650 men; but the measles have been raging in camp and about 200 are sent to the hospital, being unable to march.

July 18th, we marched through Winchester and took the road leading to Berry's Ferry, on the Shenandoah River, about 18 miles distant. The citizens were very much grieved to see us leave for fear the enemy would be in town, as there were no troops left but a few militia and Colonel Turner Ashby's cavalry.

After marching a few miles, we were halted, and the adjutant read us orders that the enemy were about to overpower General Beauregard at Manassas Junction and we would have to make a forced march. It was General Johnston's wish that all the men would keep in ranks, and not straggle, if possible. Then we started on a quick march; marched all day and nearly all night, wading the Shenandoah River about 12 o'clock at night; halted at a small village called Paris about two hours, then resumed the march about daylight and arrived at Piedmont Station on the Manassas Gap railroad.

Our brigade was in the advance on the march, and when we arrived at the station the citizens for miles around came flocking in to

Romney, West Virginia, 1861.

see us, bringing us eatables of all kinds, and we fared sumptuously. There were not trains enough to transport all at once, and our regiment had to remain there until the trains returned, which was about 3 o'clock in the afternoon. We had a regular picnic; plenty to eat, lemonade to drink, and beautiful young ladies to chat with. We finally got aboard, bade the ladies a long farewell, and went flying down the road, arriving at the Junction in the night.

The next day, the 20th of July, we marched about eight miles down Bull Run, to where General Beauregard had engaged the enemy on the 18th, and repulsed their advance. There we joined the brigade. We lay on our arms all night. We tore all the feathers out of our hats because we heard the Yanks had feathers in theirs, and we might be fired on by mistake, as our company was the only one that had black plumes in their hats. We could hear the pickets firing at intervals, and did not know what minute we would be rushed into action.

My particular friend and messmate William I. Blue, and myself, lay down together, throwing a blanket over us, and talked concerning our probable fate the next day. We had been in line of battle several times, and had heard a great many false alarms, but we all knew there was no false alarm this time; that the two armies lay facing each other, and that a big battle would be fought the next day; that we were on the eve of experiencing the realities of war, in its most horrible form—brother against brother, father against son, kindred against kindred and our own country torn to pieces by civil war.

While lying thus, being nearly asleep, he roused me up and said that he wanted to make a bargain with me, which was, if either of us got killed the next day, the one who survived, should see the other buried, if we kept possession of the battlefield.

I told him I would certainly do that, and we pledged ourselves accordingly. I then remarked that perhaps we would escape unhurt or wounded.

He said "no, I don't want to be wounded, if I am shot at all I want to be shot right through the heart."

During the night we heard a gun fire on the left of the regiment and I got up and walked down the line to see what had happened. I found one of the men had shot himself through the foot, supposed to have been done intentionally, to keep out of the fight, but the poor fellow made a miscalculation as to where his toes were, and held the muzzle of the gun too far up and blew off about half of his foot, so it had to be amputated.

CHAPTER 3

First Battle of Bull Run

July 21st dawned clear and bright, (and for the last time, on many a poor soldier), and with it the sharpshooters in front commenced skirmishing. We were ordered to "fall in" and were marched up the run about eight miles and then ordered back to "Blackburn's Ford." Our company and the "Hardy Greys" were thrown out as skirmishers, opposite the ford in a skirt of woods, commanding a full view of the ford, and ordered to fire on the enemy if they attempted to cross the run. While we were lying in that position, heavy firing was heard on our left, both infantry and artillery. In a few moments we were ordered from there to join the regiment and went "double-quick" up the Run to where the fighting was going on. The balance of the brigade was in line of battle behind the brow of a small ridge. We were halted at the foot of this ridge and Colonel Cummins told us that it was General Jackson's command that our regiment should depend principally on the bayonet that day, as it was a musket regiment.

Some of the boys were very keen for a fight, and while we were down the Run, they were afraid it would be over before we got into it. One in particular, Thomas McGraw, was very anxious to get a shot at the "bluecoats," and when the colonel read us the order about the bayonet, I asked Tom how he liked that part of the programme. He said that was closer quarters than he anticipated.

Our regiment marched up the hill, and formed "left in front," on the left of the brigade, and on the entire left of our army. As we passed by the other regiments the shells were bursting and cutting down the pines all around us, and we were shaking hands, and bidding farewell to those we were acquainted with, knowing that in a few moments many of us would be stretched lifeless on the field.

At this time our troops were falling back, but in good order, fighting every inch of the way; but were being overpowered and flanked by superior numbers. They were the 2nd Mississippi and Colonel Evans' 4th Alabama Regiments, General Bees' South Carolina Brigade, Colonel Bartow's 7th and 8th Georgia Regiments, Major Wheat's battalion, (called the Louisiana Tigers,) and Imboden's battery. They had resisted the main portion of the "Federal Army," and had done all that men could do, and had lost severely, but were still holding them in check while we were forming.

It was there and at this time that General Jackson received the name of "Stonewall," and the brigade the ever-memorable name of "Stonewall Brigade." General Barnard E. Bee, riding up to General Jackson, who sat on his horse calm and unmoved, though severely wounded in the hand, exclaimed in a voice of anguish: "General, they are beating us back!"

Turning to General Bee, he said calmly: "Sir, we'll give them the bayonet."

Hastening back to his men, General Bee cried enthusiastically, as he pointed to Jackson: "Look yonder! There is Jackson and his brigade standing like a stone wall. Let us determine to die here and we will conquer. Rally behind them!"

They passed through our brigade and formed in the rear. I knew they were South Carolinians by the "Palmetto tree" on their caps. General Bee and Colonel Bartow fell, mortally wounded. The enemy, flushed with victory pushed on, never dreaming what was lying just behind the brow of the hill in the pines.

There seemed to be a lull in the firing just at this time, and Sergeant James P Daily, of my company, walked up to the brow of the hill, but soon returned with the exclamation: "Boys, there is the prettiest sight from the top of the hill you ever saw; they are coming up on the other side in four ranks and all dressed in red."

When we heard that I, with several others, jumped up and started to see, but Colonel Cummins ordered us to "stay in ranks," and Dailey remarked: "We will see them soon enough." Sure enough, in a few seconds the head of the column made its appearance, with three officers on horseback in front and marching by the flank, with the intention of flanking one of our batteries—the "Rockbridge Artillery," Captain W. N. Pendleton. In a few minutes they spied us lying there, and I heard one of the officers say: "Hello! what men are these?"

At that moment some of our men who, perhaps, had the "buck fever," without orders commenced firing some scattering shots. The enemy then poured a volley into us; but as we were lying down the balls went over our heads, harmless.

That morning we had been given a signal to use in time of battle, to distinguish friend from foe, which was to throw the right hand to the forehead, palm outward, and say, "Sumpter." When this regiment (which was the 14th Brooklyn, N.Y.) appeared in view, Colonel Cummins gave the signal, and it was returned by one of the officers; but how they got it was a mystery. So, when the scattering shots were fired by some of our regiment, Colonel Cummins exclaimed, "cease

33d Virginia Going to Bull Run.

firing, you are firing on friends;" and the volley came from them at the same time, and I know that I remarked, "Friends, hell! that looks like it."

Colonel Cummings, seeing his mistake, and also seeing a battery of artillery taking position and unlimbering, in close proximity and in a place where it could enfilade our troops, determined to capture it before it could do any damage. I don't think he had any orders from any superior officer, but took the responsibility on himself. Then came the command: "Attention! Forward march! Charge bayonets! Double quick!" and away we went, sweeping everything before us; but the enemy broke and fled.

We were soon in possession of the guns, killed nearly all the horses, and a great portion of the men were killed or wounded; and we were none too soon, for one minute more and four guns would have belched forth into our ranks, carrying death and destruction, and perhaps been able to have held their position. As it was, the guns were rendered useless, and were not used any more that day, although we had to give them up temporarily.

We were halted, and one of my company, Thomas Furlough, who had belonged to the artillery in the Mexican war, threw down his musket and said: "Boys, let's turn the guns on them." That was the last sentence that ever passed his lips, for just then he was shot dead.

While this was going on, the enemy were throwing a force on our left flank in the pines, and commenced pouring it into us from the front and an enfilading fire from the flank and were cutting us to pieces, when we were ordered back, and halted at our first position.

Then we were reinforced by our 49th Virginia and the 6th North Carolina regiment, commanded by Colonel Chas. F. Fisher (who was killed a few minutes afterwards) and "Extra Billy" Smith. This made our line longer and we were ordered to charge again. The charge of Jackson's men was terrific. The enemy were swept before them like chaff before a whirlwind. Nothing could resist their impetuosity. The men seemed to have caught the dauntless spirit and determined will of their heroic commander, and nothing could stay them in their onward course. The 33rd Virginia, in its timely charge, saved the day by capturing and disabling Griffin's battery, although they could not hold it just then. The name won that day by the brigade and its general is immortal.

In this action our regiment (the 33rd Virginia), being on the extreme left, was alone, the balance of the brigade not charging until later, and we were terribly cut up and had to fall back. General Jackson said he could afford to sacrifice one regiment to save the day; and it was the first check and first repulse the enemy had received, and during the remainder of the day the battle turned in favour of the Confederates.

We did not follow them far, for fresh troops were coming in all the time, and we had lost severely, and were considerably demoralised. I then took a stroll over the battlefield, to see who of my comrades were dead or wounded, and saw my friend, William I. Blue, lying on his face, dead. I turned him over to see where he was shot. He must have been shot through the heart, the place where he wanted to be shot, if shot at all. He must have been killed instantly, for he was in the act of loading his gun. One hand was grasped around his gun, in the other he held a cartridge, with one end of it in his mouth, in the act of tearing it off. I sat down by him and took a hearty cry, and then, thinks I, "It does not look well for a soldier to cry," but I could not help it. I then stuck his gun in the ground by his side, marked his name, company and regiment on a piece of paper, pinned it on his breast, and went off.

I then saw three field officers a short distance from me looking through a field glass. I very deliberately walked up to them and asked them to let me look through it, and one of them handed it to me. When looking through it I saw, about two miles off, in a large field, what I took to be about 10,000 of the enemy. The field appeared to be black with them. I returned the glass, saying: "My God! have we all of them to fight yet?" Just at that moment "Pendleton's Battery" turned their guns on them and I saw the first shell strike in the field. I don't think it was five minutes until the field was vacant. I felt considerably relieved. I had had enough of fighting for that day. We had gained a great victory. The enemy were completely routed and panic-stricken, and never halted until they arrived at Alexandria and Washington.

My company only numbered fifty-five, rank and file, when we went into service, but, so many having the measles and other ailments, we went into the fight with only twenty-seven men, and out of that number we lost five killed and six wounded. The killed were William I. Blue, Thomas Furlough, James Adams, John W. Marker and Amos Hollenback. The wounded were Sergeant William Montgomery, John Rinehart, Robert C. Grace, Edward Allen, A. A. Young and Joseph Cadwallader.

The regiment went into action with about 450 men, and lost

Scene where the Brigade Received the Name of "Stonewall," July 21, 1861.

forty-three killed and 140 wounded. Our regiment fought the 14th Brooklyn Zouaves and the 1st Michigan, which poured a deadly volley into us. While we were engaged in front. Colonel Cummings ordered the regiment to fall back three times before they did so. All the troops engaged suffered more or less, but the loss in the 33rd Virginia was greater than that of any regiment on either side, as the statistics will show, and it was the smallest regiment, not being full and not numbered.

We worked nearly all night taking care of the wounded, for nearly all of the enemy's wounded were left in our hands. I took a short sleep on the battlefield. The next day was rainy and muddy. The regiment was ordered to "fall in," but not knowing where they were going, I did not want to leave until I had buried my friend, according to promise. When they marched off I hid behind a wagon, and Sergeant Daily, seeing me, ordered me to come on. I told him never would I leave that field until I had buried my friend, unless I was put under arrest. He then left me, and I looked around for some tools to dig a grave. I found an old hoe and spade, and commenced digging the grave under an apple tree in an orchard near the "Henry House."

While I was at work a Georgian came to me and wanted the tools as soon as I was done with them. He said he wanted to bury his brother, and asked if I was burying a brother.

"No," I replied, "but dear as a brother."

"As you have no one to help you," he said, "and I have no one to help me, suppose we dig the grave large enough for both, and we can help one another carry them here."

"All right," I said, "but I want to bury my friend next to the tree, for, perhaps, his father will come after him."

So, we buried them that way and gathered up some old shingles to put over the bodies, and a piece of plank between them. Then I rudely carved his name on the tree.

Captain William Lee, who was acting Lieutenant Colonel, was killed, and our Sergeant Major, Randolph Barton, a cadet from the Virginia Military Institute, was severely wounded.

That evening there was a detail made from each company to bury the dead, and we buried all alike, friend and foe, and thus ended the first battle of "Bull Run," and the first big battle of the war.

There is no doubt but that the timely charge of the 33rd Virginia turned the tide of battle and saved the day for the Confederates. Colonel Cummings took the responsibility upon himself and ordered the charge just in the nick of time, for in five minutes' time the Federals would have had their battery in position and would have had an enfilading fire on the brigade and Pendleton's Battery, and made their position untenable. I herewith in the next chapter append a letter from Colonel Cummings, and one from Captain Randolph Barton, which bear me out in my statement, and more fully explain the situation and results. Also, one that I had written to my parents three days after the battle, and which is still preserved.

CHAPTER 4

Letters

Abington, Va., November 10, 1896.

John O. Casler, Esq.:

My Dear Friend: If you could realise the great pleasure your letter gave me you would not regret the time spent in writing. As you know, the 33rd Regiment, which I organised at Winchester, was made up from Hampshire, one company; Hardy, one; Frederick, one; Rockingham, one; Page, one, and Shenandoah five, and as I have hardly ever been from home for the last fifteen years I rarely meet any of the old regiment, and when I do, or hear from them, it is a source of the greatest pleasure, especially when I learn they are getting on well, as I am sure you are.

As you say, I never had a great deal to say, and am somewhat reserved in my manners, but from my experience as Captain in the Mexican war I found that the greatest service I could render the men under my command was to see they were as well taken care of and provided for as circumstances would permit.

I am pleased to know that you have written your experience of *Four Years in the Stonewall Brigade*, and when your new edition is published, I will certainly procure a copy, as I am sure of being interested in it.

I noticed one slight mistake in your letter with regard to myself, but of no importance. I did not resign, but for what I regarded as sufficient reason (not necessary to state now) was not a candidate for re-election at the reorganisation of the army. Was elected to the Legislature, in which I served the last years of the war, until the surrender; practiced law for some fifteen or more years, since which I have devoted myself to my farm a few miles from Abington.

The law was my profession, which I commenced to practice the year after the close of the Mexican war. I have had two letters from

Randolph Barton recently, whom you may remember, who had for the first time since the close of the war visited the battlefield of the First Manassas, and who seems to be much interested in the part performed by the 33rd and the Stonewall Brigade on that memorable 21st of July, 1861.

Barton was a cadet at the Virginia Military Institute, Lexington, Va., at the commencement of the war; was assigned to the 33rd when I was organising at Winchester in the early part of July. I had no field officer at that time, and made him Sergeant Major. He was a bright young man, an Adjutant General on General Walker's staff, and is now a prominent lawyer in Baltimore. He desired my recollection of the part performed by the 33rd and the Stonewall Brigade, which I furnished him, and which corresponded pretty well with his own, with a few minor exceptions.

Our army left Winchester about 2 o'clock on the 18th of July, the Stonewall Brigade in front. The 33rd did not reach Manassas until a little before daylight on Saturday morning, the 20th. On Saturday morning we marched out and joined the other regiments of the brigade in rear of McLane's Ford, on Bull Run. Our line of battle extended from about Union Mills, on Bull Run, on the right, to the stone bridge. It was expected we would be attacked upon the right and centre, but when it was ascertained early Sunday morning that the enemy was marching in the direction of the stone bridge, with the evident design of turning our left flank and reaching the Manassas Gap railroad, the Stonewall Brigade was moved up Bull Run and somewhat parallel with it (making short stops at intervals), until we reached the brow of the hill in front of the "Henry House," where the brigade was formed in line of battle in a thicket of small pines.

In the meantime, the battle was raging in the direction of the stone bridge, and our forces were being driven back before overpowering numbers. The line of the brigade was formed, with the 5th Regiment on the right, then the 4th and 27th (the latter two supporting Pendleton's Battery), then the 2nd and 33rd.

At that time the brigade was the extreme left of our army, and the 33rd, on the left of the brigade, was ordered to lie down in the edge of the pines, which, aided by the conformation of the ground, at that time concealed us from the sight of the enemy, who, in large numbers, were pressing towards our right.

Our orders were to wait until the enemy were within thirty paces, then to fire and charge with the bayonet. About that time General

Jackson came along the line and directed me to look out for the enemy's artillery. As you are aware, the 33rd had just been organised before we left Winchester, and, with the exception of two or three companies, were perfectly raw troops, and two of those, Captain Holliday's (afterward Governor) and Captain Jones' (afterward Colonel) were left behind, one as guard and one on detached service, and consequently were not in the fight. So, there were but eight companies present, numbering about 400 men, for active duty.

When General Jackson directed me to look out for the enemy's artillery, Captain William Lee, who was acting as Lieutenant Colonel, and a gallant man he was, and I walked out on the plateau and saw the artillery of the enemy moving rapidly up the Sudley road to our front and left, and large bodies of the enemy's infantry moving along the hill towards our left flank, and we returned immediately to the regiment.

There had been some confusion in the regiment, produced by a solid shot being fired towards the regiment and tearing up the ground, together with the appearance of some red-coats on our left. Previous to this time the enemy's artillery fire had been directed towards the regiments of the brigade and at Pendleton's Battery. This little confusion in the regiment, and the fact of the men being raw and undisciplined, made me uncertain as to what would be the result, if I waited, as directed by General Jackson, until the enemy was within thirty paces.

And, therefore, as soon as I returned to the regiment, I ordered the charge, without waiting, as directed, until the enemy was within thirty paces, with the result that the enemy's battery was taken, or rather, as I think, a section of it, without, as I believe, a gun being fired. *No old regulars ever made a more gallant charge, though not a very regular one.* Of course, we could not hold it without support, in the face of such overwhelming numbers, though the horses were shot down, and I have now an artillery bit, cut from one of the horses, which I have used ever since.

The 33rd suffered more in the First Battle of Manassas than any regiment in our army.

I regretted very much Captain Lee's death. My acquaintance with him was short, but I esteemed him very highly. He was a true and gallant man, and being from the old army, and experienced, was of great service to me. My friend Barton is also of the true blue order. I have long cherished the hope of visiting the Valley, where I would meet some of the survivors of the 33rd, but suppose I must be content to remember them with the greatest kindness.

I am now in my 75th year, and feel the heavy weight of years. Very truly your friend,

Arthur C. Cummings,
Colonel 33rd Virginia Infantry.

Manassas Junction, July 24, 1861.

Dear Father and Mother: I seat myself once more to write you a few lines, to let you know where I am and that I am still alive.

Last Sunday was such a day as I had never seen, and I hope to God I never will see another such a time. We had one of the hardest battles that ever was fought in the United States. I have not power to describe the scene. It beggars all description.

We left Winchester on Thursday, and travelled that day and night, and Friday, about 9 o'clock, we arrived at Piedmont Station, and that evening we got on the cars and arrived at the Junction that night. The next morning, we marched about four miles east, where they had had a battle on Thursday. We stayed there all that day and nighty expecting an attack every hour.

On Sunday morning our forces were attacked four miles higher up, and we made a quick march from there to the battlefield, where we arrived about 12. They had been fighting all morning, but about 10 they got at it in earnest. We got there (that is, Jackson's Brigade) just in the heat of the battle, and our regiment was on the extreme left, and the enemy was trying to flank us. They did not see us until they were within fifty yards of us, as we were under the brow of the hill, and they were ordered to fire, but we were too soon for them. We fired first, and advanced, and then they fired.

We then charged bayonets, yelling like savages, and they retreated, and our regiment took their artillery; but they were reinforced, and we had to fall back, exposed to two heavy fires, when we were reinforced by a North Carolina regiment; then we charged again and they retreated, and that part of the field, with the famous Griffin's Battery, was ours. But the battle lasted about one hour longer in another part of the field, when they retreated in great confusion towards Alexandria, and then the cavalry and artillery pursued them about seven miles, killing and wounding a great many, and taking all their artillery and baggage; but the field for five miles around was covered with the dead and the dying.

I cannot tell how many we lost, but we lost a great many. Their loss

Burial of William I. Blue.

was three times as great as ours. Our regiment lost thirty-five killed and over one hundred wounded. Our little company of thirty-two lost five killed and five wounded. Among the killed was poor Will Blue. He was shot dead. Never spoke, shot through the heart. Amos Hollenback, Polk Marker, Tom Furlough and Jim Adams, a fellow that lived with Dr. Moore, were killed. Will Montgomery was badly wounded, but not dangerously. Also, John Rinehart, Bob Grace, Arch Young and Ed Allen were slightly wounded, but are able to go about.

We took seventy-six pieces of cannon and between 1,000 and 2,000 prisoners—several important ones, some of Lincoln's cabinet. Also, General Scott's carriage. He and some of the ladies from Washington came out as far as Centerville to see the *Rebels run*. They saw us running, but it was after the Yankees.

The next morning, I went on their retreat two miles, and the baggage was lying in every direction—coats, cartridge boxes, canteens, guns, blankets, broken-down wagons.

The bombs, cannon balls and musket balls whistled all around my head. I could feel the wind from them in my face, but I was not touched. It is rumoured that we are going to take Washington. Jeff Davis got here just after the battle, and is on his way to Alexandria now.

There were about 40,000 of the enemy engaged in the battle, and 25,000 Confederates.

You must not be surprised to hear of me getting killed, for we don't know when we will be killed. Farewell,

John O. Casler.

Captain Randolph Barton's Letter.

Baltimore, Md., January 15, 1897.

John O. Casler:

Dear Comrade: Our command reached Manassas Junction on the 20th of July, in the morning, I think. We marched during the day to the right of the line, and the next day we marched and countermarched, halted and rushed, as the changing localities of the conflict, as far as our commanders could anticipate, seemed to require. My dinner was made from blackberries, for being outside of the ranks (as Sergeant Major) I could pick them as we passed over the fields. About 1 o'clock our regiment reached the elevation on which is seated the historic Henry house, and took position on the left flank of our brigade, up to that hour known as the 1st Brigade, or Jackson's Brigade, ever afterwards as the Stonewall Brigade.

As we approached our position, we heard for the first time the horrid screaming of hostile shells going over our heads, high up in the air, but not so high as not to be dangerous. I recall now with some amusement the intense gravity and astonishment written upon the faces of the men as these dangerous missiles from the batteries of Rickett and Griffin went hurtling over us; but I recall no signs of timidity. The men kept in their ranks, obeyed orders and moved into position on the left of the 2nd Virginia, of which Brother Strother, my cousin, Willie Barton, and all my Winchester friends were members, with steadiness and resolution. My brother David was in the Rockbridge Battery, which was being supported by our brigade. My uncle, Frank Jones, and my brother-in-law, Thomas Marshall, were on Jackson's staff. I felt the solemnity of the moment, but I recall no disposition whatever to turn and run.

On the other hand, a sense of pride, a desire to emulate the action of the best men on the field possessed me, as it did, I believe, all of our command, except the Adjutant of our regiment. I think I went into that action with less trepidation than into any subsequent one. Inexperience doubtless had much to do with it, but, again, I attribute much of the nerve that sustained me to my year at Lexington. I felt on the field that the orders of our officers were supreme; that come what might, they must be obeyed, and discipline told on me from first to last.

I will not give many details of the battle; they have been told by so many writers that it would prolong this narrative unduly for me to repeat them. I will only say that, after taking our position on the left of the brigade, we laid upon the ground listening to the musketry and cannonading going on to our right, or, rather, somewhat in front of our right, from the Confederate forces, which was being vigorously responded to by the Yankees.

The 'Henry house' was in front of our brigade, over the hill—the upper part of the house visible—and the Robinson house was to the right of that a few hundred yards. Occasional shells would explode over our regiment, and the solemn wonderment written on the faces of the men as they would crane their heads around to look out for falling branches was almost amusing. I was near the left flank of the regiment, a few steps in rear, where, upon the formation of the regiment in line of battle, I belonged. Doubtless I wished I was home, but I had to stick. I remember an elderly man riding leisurely by towards the left, in rear of us, apparently giving orders. Someone, possibly myself, asked him who he was. He turned his horse and said: 'I am Colonel Smith, otherwise Governor Smith, otherwise Extra Billy Smith.' It was, in fact, Colonel Smith, a game old fellow, who, I suppose, was looking over the ground for a position for his regiment, the 49th Virginia, as it subsequently took position on our left, and finally united in one of the charges upon Griffin's Battery.

Colonel Cummings and Lieutenant Colonel Lee were in front of our regiment, perhaps a hundred yards, stooping down, and occasionally standing to get a view over the crest of the hill that rose gently before us for a little over a hundred yards. The musketry kept up on our right, and then Colonels Cummings and Lee were seen to rise and, bending down, to come back with somewhat quickened steps to the regiment. I remember, as Colonel Cummings drew near, he called out: 'Boys, they are coming, now wait until they get close before you fire.'

Almost immediately several pieces of artillery, their horses in front, made their appearance on the hill in front of us, curving as if going into battery, and at the same time I descried the spear-point and upper portion of a United States flag, as it rose in the hands of its bearer over the hill; then I saw the bearer, and the heads of the men composing the line of battle to the right and left of him. At the sight several of our men rose from the ranks, levelled their muskets at the line, and, although I called out, 'Do not fire yet,' it was of no use; they fired and then the shrill cry of Colonel Cummings was heard, 'Charge!' and away the regiment went, firing as they ran, into the ranks of the enemy, and particularly at the battery towards which our line rapidly approached.

Although bearing a non-commissioned officer's sword, I had obtained a cartridge box, belted it on, and had in some way secured a flintlock musket, with which one of our companies was armed. This gun, after two futile efforts, I fired at a man on horseback in the battery, one of the drivers, I think. I got near enough to the battery to see that it was thoroughly disabled, horses and men falling, and our line driving ahead, when I felt the sting of a bullet tearing a, piece from my side, just under my cartridge box, which I had pulled well around on the right and front of my waist. I called out that I was wounded to my uncle, Frank Jones, who helped me up on his horse, and carried me to the rear.

I think it can be demonstrated that the victory of First Manassas is traceable to Colonel Cummings. For fifteen or twenty minutes before, our regiment (the 33rd Virginia) rose and charged Griffin's Battery the men of Bee's and Bartow's (and, I think, Evans') commands were coming back over the hill from the Robinson and Henry houses in the greatest disorder, a flying, panic-stricken mob. The Stonewall Brigade maintained its line with the steadiness of veterans. The Rockbridge Battery, with its little guns, was doing its best. Jackson, about that time, rode along the front of his brigade, waiting for the critical moment to order his men into action.

It was in his efforts to rally his command that the gallant Bee called to them to rally behind the Virginians. Pointing to Jackson, he used the memorable expression, 'Look at Jackson, standing like a stone wall.' The precise expression he used it is impossible to learn. He most probably said, 'Look at Jackson and his men, standing like a stone wall.' He had galloped up to Jackson a moment before, and had said: 'General, they are driving us back,' and Jackson replied, the words snapping from his lips like grape-shot from a gun, 'Then we will give them the bayonet.'

Bee turned to gallop toward his fleeing men, with the inspiration of Jackson possessing him, called out his immortal language, and fell, mortally wounded.

Jackson had, within the half hour before, passed along his brigade the order not to fire until the enemy was within thirty paces, and then charge. So, Colonel Cummings writes to me under date of September 20, 1896. But, says Colonel Cummings, the shells of the enemy had caused some confusion 'with the left company of my regiment,' or, rather, his command, of eight companies, and when Griffin's Battery showed itself on the hill in front of us, and occasional shots began to fall among us from the enemy moving towards our left to flank us, when the tumult of the broken ranks of Bee and Bartow was threatening the steadiness of our right, and the enemy, with exultant shouts, was pressing on.

Colonel Cummings, like a flash, thought if those guns get into battery and pour one discharge of grape and canister into the ranks of my raw recruits the day is gone, and then it was, with splendid discretion, he took the responsibility of changing his orders, with the changed conditions, as Grouchy should have done at Waterloo, and charged the enemy.

The suddenness of our attack, the boldness of it, for our men went over and past the battery, the disabling of the guns, all checked the advancing line. It was immediately followed up by the remainder of the brigade charging, and the troops on our left poured in. The tide of battle turned when it dashed against the farmer boys of the 33rd Virginia. It was the first resistance it had met. The enemy came upon the point of a spear, one small regiment of undisciplined boys and men, not a month from the plough-handle and the mechanic's shop. The point broadened, as to the right and left assistance poured in, until it became a sharp blade against which the enemy could not and dared not rush; but the 33rd led the van of the movement that first arrested McDowell's victorious line, and from that moment the scene changed, and from the brink of disaster our army turned to a great victory. Colonel Cummings changed the life of McDowell by his order, 'Charge!' He may have changed the history of the war. The battle pivoted upon his nerve. It was the turning point in tremendous events.

I visited the Robinson and Henry houses in September, 1861, and again in September, 1896. My last visit caused me to correspond with Colonel Cummings and read every line I could lay my eyes upon, including the reports of officers on both sides, as published in the compilation called the *Rebellion Record*, and I believe what I have attributed to Colonel Cummings cannot be successfully gainsaid. He turned the tide of battle at First Manassas. Instead of the Confederate army flying as a mob to the Rappahannock, the Yankee Army fled as a mob to Washington.

Several days have elapsed since I wrote the above. A day or so ago I accidentally saw in the Mercantile Library the *Recollections of a Private*, by Warren Lee Goss, of the Federal Army. Turning to his narrative of the battle I find a good representation of the Henry house plateau and the confusion in Griffin's Battery following the attack of the 33rd Regiment. I recognise the Sudley mill road, the entrance to the Henry place, on the left of the road, and the fence torn away to allow Griffin's Battery freely to leave the road and go upon the plateau. In September, 1896, I stood on, this very ground, and, observing that between the bed of the road and the fence on the left hand side there was the usual wash, or gutter, I remarked to my companions that no doubt Griffin tore down the fence and filled the wash with the rails, thus making an easy crossing into the field for his artillery. The picture I am looking at shows the fence torn down, and imagination shows the rails placed as I surmised.

And now I quote from the book what seems to me brings the 33rd face to face with the troops Goss writes about. Remember that the Sudley Mills road runs a southeasterly course from the mill to the Henry plateau. Our regiment charged northwesterly. McDowell's line came over the hill supporting Griffin's Battery, at right angles to the Sudley Mills road, advancing southeasterly.

Says Goss: 'About 1 o'clock the fence skirting the road at the foot of the hill was pulled down to let our batteries (Griffin's and Rickett's) pass up to the plateau. The batteries were in the open field near us. We were watching to see what they'd do next, when a terrible volley was poured into them. It was like a pack of Fourth of July firecrackers under a barrel magnified a thousand times. The Rebels had crept upon them unawares and the batteries were all killed and wounded.

'Here,' says Goss, continuing, 'let me interrupt Tinkermann's narrative to say that one of the artillerymen then engaged has since told me that, though he had been in several battles since, he had seldom seen worse destruction in so short a time. He said they saw a regiment advancing, and the natural inference was that they were Rebels. But an officer insisted that it was a New York regiment, which was expected for support, and so no order was given to fire on them. Then came a tremendous explosion of musketry' said the artilleryman, 'and all was confusion; wounded men with dripping wounds were clinging to caissons, to which were attached frightened and wounded horses. Horses attached to caissons rushed through the infantry ranks. I saw three horses galloping off, dragging a fourth, which was dead.

The dead cannoneers lay with the rammers of the guns and the lanyards in their hands. The battery was annihilated by those volleys in a moment. Those who could get away didn't wait. We had no supports near enough to protect us properly, and the enemy was within seventy yards of us when that volley was fired. *Our battery being demolished in that way was the beginning of our* defeat at Bull Run,' says the old regular.

This ends the quotation. I have italicised the words which strike me as a direct confirmation of the claim I make that the 33rd turned the tide, and Colonel Cummings' timely order let loose the 33rd at the very crisis of the battle. I distinctly only claim that with the order and because of the order came the first check McDowell sustained. That other troops immensely aided in forcing back the Yankee line when thus checked, I freely admit. But our regiment called a halt in the victorious advance of the enemy. I dwell upon the circumstance because of the great interest it adds to the engagement to know that you belonged to the regiment that received and repelled the dangerous thrust of the enemy at the nice turning point of the day.

I should think to Colonel Cummings the circumstance would be of extraordinary interest, and that he would time and again reflect how little he thought, when he braced himself to give the order to his regiment, that he was making a long page in history.

Randolph Barton,
Late Staff Officer 2nd Corps, A. N. V.

Chapter 5

Gets in the Guardhouse

The adjutant of our regiment was L. Jacquelin Smith, and the regiment took a dislike to him from the first, for he was a fop in kid gloves, and wanted to be very strict, especially on dress parade. In reading orders, he always pronounced his name as above, and put on more airs than a brigadier general. Some of the boys prophesied that he was a coward. Sure enough, when the battle commenced, he showed the "white feather" and disappeared. In a few days he returned to camp.

When Colonel Cummings saw him, he called out, "Hello. Smith, how did the battle go about Winchester?" and then told him that he had no further use for him. Winchester was about eighty miles to the rear. That was the last we ever heard of "L. Jacquelin Smith, Adjutant."

✶✶✶✶✶✶

Some years after this was written, I met in Texas an old gentleman by the name of Jacquelin Smith, from Fauquier County, Virginia, who, having seen an extract from my diary published in a newspaper, begged of me, if I should ever publish my diary, to leave that part out, as someone might think that it referred to him. He was a true representative of the Virginia gentleman, and I make this statement in justice to the Smith family. It wasn't this Smith.

✶✶✶✶✶✶

We were camped about five miles east of the battlefield, and from the impurity of the water and the stench from the surrounding country the boys gave it the name of "Maggot Camp." A great many were taken sick at this camp, and General Jackson turned the house that he used for his headquarters into a hospital.

While here we received two more companies into our regiment—the "Mountain Rangers," Captain W. F. M. Holliday, from Frederick County, Virginia, and the "Rockingham Confederates," Captain J. E. Jones, from Rockingham County, which made ten companies—the full number for a regiment. We were numbered and lettered, our number being 33rd Virginia Infantry, and my company "A." Therefore I belonged to Company A, 33rd Virginia Infantry, Stonewall Brigade,

General Joseph E. Johnston's Corps, Army of the Potomac, as it was then called.

The regiments which composed the Stonewall Brigade were the 2nd, 4th, 5th, 27th and 33rd Virginia Regiments of Infantry, the Rockridge Artillery, commanded by Captain W. N. Pendleton, and Carpenter's Battery, as it was composed of a company of the "Alleghency Roughs" from the 27th Virginia Infantry. Those five regiments were together in that brigade during the whole war, and no others were attached to it.

It would not be amiss to give here a brief history of the famous Stonewall Brigade Band.

This historic association was organised in 1855, at Staunton, Va., under the name of "The Mountain Sax-Horn Band," which name it retained until the commencement of the Civil War, at which time it mustered in as the "5th Virginia Regiment Band."

Being recognised by General "Stonewall" Jackson, as the best band in the brigade, he appointed it his Brigade Band, hence its present name.

The band served during the entire four years of strife, and the members were often exposed to great danger, as they acted as assistant surgeons, and helped to bear the dead and wounded from the field. They also did hospital duty, and several of them could, in war times, amputate a leg or an arm as well as a regular surgeon. Only two were killed in battle.

At Appomattox General Grant issued an order to allow the members of the band to take their instruments home with them, and they are now on exhibition in their band hall.

******

These instruments, which are probably the only complete set in existence that were used during the entire Civil War, have attracted much attention in Northern cities, and were exhibited by the Band at the World's Columbian Exposition in Chicago.

******

The band occupied a post of honour at the funeral of General Grant, in New York, and has attended nearly all the famous military events in this country. The organisation was incorporated in 1874 under the laws of Virginia.

The present membership (exclusive of honorary war members) is thirty.

There are three original war members still in active service, (as at

1906).

A few days after the battle, Joseph Earsome, of the 2nd Regiment, and myself took a stroll over the battlefield and surrounding country, on the line of retreat as far as Centerville. The whole country was strewn with broken guns, cartridge boxes, canteens, knapsacks, cannon, caissons, broken wagons and the general, baggage of an army.

I must here relate an act of heroism that happened where the battle raged the hottest. There was a small house that stood between the lines of the two armies, and in it lived an old lady of 90 years, and her daughter, who was pretty well advanced in years.

I don't suppose the soldiers of either army knew there was anyone living in the house, for all the other citizens around had fled for safety early in the day. However, be that as it may, they were there. The house was riddled with shot and shell from both sides, and the old lady, being helpless and confined to her bed, was pierced with several bullets and killed, while the daughter, unable to carry her off at the commencement of the fight, remained with her. She had crawled under the bed and escaped unhurt. I conversed with the daughter the next day, when she related what is here recorded. I also saw the corpse of the old lady. Their names were Henry, and this was the since noted "Henry house."

We moved camp the 1st of August, one mile east of Centerville, to a beautiful place where we had good water, which we called "Camp Harman," in honour of Major John A. Harman, our brigade quartermaster, who selected the camp. We remained in this camp one month, nothing of interest transpiring but the usual routine of camp life. We marched three different times down to Fairfax Court House to fight the enemy, but each time it was a false alarm.

Some six or seven of my company, being very anxious to go home on a visit, and not being able to get a furlough, took a "French Furlough" and disappeared one night. What we meant by "French Furlough" was simply "absent without leave," and was not considered desertion. If they returned without being arrested, they were put on extra guard duty for a few nights, but if arrested and brought back they were court-martialled, and had to ride a wooden horse, or wear a barrel shirt, or receive some such punishment.

While here Lieutenant Buzzard, of my company, was detailed to go to Hampshire County and gather up absentees. When he returned be brought back sixteen.

The day before those boys took their "French Furlough" Sergeant James A. Parsons had taken several of them to the surgeon's tent to get some medicine, as they were complaining of being sick. Dr. Nete Baldwin, our surgeon, prescribed for them, and that night they left. The next morning Parsons rushed up to Dr. Baldwin's tent, very much excited, exclaiming: "Doctor! doctor! for God's sake what kind of medicine was that you gave those men yesterday?" The doctor, thinking perhaps he had made some mistake in prescribing, wanted to know what had happened.

Parsons replied that it had had a terrible effect on them, as it had worked them clear out of the county, and to not give the men any more of that kind of medicine. When they returned, we were joking them about it, and they were very much insulted, and talked of whipping Parsons.

While in this camp we received our first pay, and I received some new clothes from home. There were a great many hucksters came to camp, with chickens, butter, eggs, etc., to sell, and always found ready sale. One morning, just after roll call, Mike Dagnon (a messmate) and myself saw a wagon near camp, retailing produce.

"Come," says Mike, "we will have some chickens for breakfast."

When we arrived at the wagon, we found a considerable crowd. So, Mike mounted the wagon, and, selecting two fine chickens, handed them to me, saying: "You hold these until I get my change."

"What change?" says I, "you haven't paid him yet."

"Never mind," says he, "you hold the chickens. Come, old man," turning to the chicken vendor, "give me my change. I'm in a hurry."

The old man, being very busy selling, and confused, says: "How much did you give me?"

"Five dollars," says Mike.

When he handed us the change and we walked off with four dollars and the chickens I told Mike that was too bad. He "allowed" it was good enough for war times.

At this time, we had a cook, Jacob Adams, detailed, who cooked for the whole company, so we repaired to the cook house and wanted him to cook our chickens for us, but he contended that chicken was not on the bill of fare, and refused to do so. Consequently, we took the frying pan from him and proceeded to cook them ourselves. This ended in a skirmish between us and the cook, in which the cook beat a retreat. He went to the captain's tent and reported the state of affairs. The captain ordered the sergeant to take a file of men and conduct us to the guardhouse. By this time the chickens were about cooked, and we took them along. I told Mike that we were getting paid for cheating the old man out of his change and chickens.

Now, this was the brigade guardhouse we were put in, and as it was getting pretty well crowded. Colonel Cummings concluded to have a regimental guardhouse. So, the next day all those who were in the guardhouse from my regiment were taken out and taken to our regimental headquarters and put in charge of an officer and ordered to build a new guardhouse. A guardhouse was simply a large pen of round logs, with no roof on.

Mike and I were ordered to carry up the corners. Some of the logs were crooked, and Mike says to me: "Let's put two of the crooked logs together, so we can creep out some nights."

"All right." says I, and we did so.

We remained in the guardhouse six days, and every night we would slip out that crack and roam around over the brigade, crawling back before day. We did not care if the sentinel did see us coming back, for we would make him believe we got out while he was on duty, and would report him for negligence. So, he would keep mum, and every night there would be a different sentinel. But soldiers had to do some devilment to relieve the monotony of camp life.

On the 1st of September we moved camp to within one mile of Fairfax Court House, about ten miles nearer Alexandria, and our regiment went on picket duty at "Munson's Hill," in sight of Washington City. We remained on picket one week, and had quite a nice time.

My cousin, Smith Casler, of the 1st Kentucky Regiment, came to see me while in this camp. I had not seen him since we were little boys, he living in Louisville, Ky., when the war broke out. I got a pass for a few days and he and I went to the battlefield, and I showed him all about the place, and the ground we fought over. We saw the marble shaft erected to mark the place where General Bee fell.

We then went to the "Henry house," and there accidentally met a son of the old lady who was killed there. He was living in Alexandria, and had slipped through the lines to visit his old home, now desolate and torn to pieces by the ravages of war. He spoke kindly to us, and was much grieved about his mother's death. He gave us a short history of his past life, and entreated us to go forth and avenge his mother's death. He was apparently about 50 years of age, and we parted with him with sad hearts, if not with tears in our eyes. We then went to a house nearby and stayed all night.

The next morning, we went to Manassas Junction and got on the cars and went to Fairfax Station, visited the "Hampshire Guards" in the 13th Virginia, remained two days and then returned to our respective commands. I found my regiment about starting on picket again. This time we went to "Falls Church," which was very close to the enemy. We had very strict orders, for we were expecting an attack from the whole army.

I was on post the first night, and had orders to fire at anything I heard in front that would not "halt" when challenged. I had not been on post long when I heard something walking in the leaves.

"Halt!" I cried, and it stopped.

"Who comes there?"

No answer.

Directly I heard the steps again, and was about to fire, when I heard a hog grunt. By this time the captain had come from the reserve post, having heard my challenge. I felt a little mortified from being deceived by a hog, but he said I did exactly right, for the enemy had killed several of our pickets in that way—by sneaking up on them in the night.

One time, when the 13th Virginia was on picket at "Munson's Hill," near Alexandria, they had thrown up a little earthwork for protection, and the Federal pickets had done the same, as in those days the pickets would fire on each other whenever the opportunity presented itself, but we learned better afterwards. Our pickets had the old smooth-bore altered muskets, and the Federals had longer range guns, and it was soon found that our guns would not reach their lines, while theirs would whistle around, making it very uncomfortable for a fellow to be exposed too much, and they, knowing our bullets could not reach them, took advantage of the situation, and would expose themselves on their works and tantalize our boys.

Lieutenant P. W. Pugh, of the 62nd Virginia, who was then temporarily attached to the 13th Virginia, and another soldier, happened to capture two of the Federal pickets who had these long-range guns. Pugh then remarked that we would pay those pickets back in their own coin.

Consequently, the next day, when the firing and tantalising commenced, Pugh and his partner took deliberate aim at two of the Federals, who were making themselves conspicuous, and fired. The Federals rolled off the bank and disappeared, but whether they were hurt or not was not known. Anyway, they kept concealed after that, but stuck their heads above the works and hallooed over to our boys: "You stole them guns, you d—d Rebel thieves."

They at least found out that our boys had guns that would reach their lines, and kept quiet.

We remained on picket one week, were not attacked, and had plenty to eat. There was a farmhouse nearby, but the family had all left, leaving a fine garden of potatoes and other vegetables behind, which we dug for them and appropriated to our own use. The woods were full of chestnuts and chinquepins, which we gathered when not on duty.

We came back to camp, and after remaining a few days the whole army had orders to fall back to Centerville and commence fortifying. But before leaving this camp the rail fence all around the field we were camped in had disappeared, and we had had strict orders not to burn a rail. But they were gone, and, of course, nobody did it. Colonel Cummings knew that it was done by his regiment, and he made the whole regiment go into the woods, make new rails, and rebuild the fence.

The day we fell back to Centerville we marched very slowly and halted quite often. One time we halted where the 1st Kentucky had been camped, and where they had left some commissary stores behind in charge of the Commissary Sergeant until the wagons returned for them. We had not halted long before we discovered a barrel of whiskey in the lot. To get it out of the bunghole without being discovered was the trouble with us, but one fellow happened to have a long reed pipe-stem that had, never been used. We soon had it in the bunghole, and took turns sucking through it. But that was too slow a process to supply so many, so we got to tilting the barrel over and catching it in our tin cups. But the old Commissary Sergeant discovered us just as we were ordered to "fall in" and march off. He raved and charged and swore that if the 1st Kentucky was there he would make them whip the whole brigade, but it did no good, for we had the whiskey and he had the barrel.

While in this camp near Centerville we had a grand review before Governor John Letcher, then Governor of Virginia, who presented each Virginia regiment with a beautiful state flag, and made us a short speech, in which he told us we had a long and bloody war before us.

It was against orders for anyone to sell whiskey to the soldiers, or bring any into camp; but one day a huckster, more bold than the others, had some five-gallon kegs full of whiskey in the bottom of his wagon, and was selling it on the sly to the soldiers. My mess, some eight in number, concluded to buy a keg, which we did, and smuggled it into the tent and buried it in the ground! under the bunk. We appointed one of the mess to issue it out, as we needed it, but in a few days, we were ordered to get ready to go on picket, none being left in camp but the sick. We therefore detailed one of the mess (who was pretty good at it anyhow) to play off sick, so he would be excused from duty and get to stay in camp and take care of our tent, which he did admirably the next morning. The rest of us went on picket down on the "Little River Turnpike," and remained one week. When we returned, we found him well and the whiskey safe, but each of us had taken his canteen full along on picket for fear of an accident.

On the 4th of October General Jackson was promoted to Major General, and ordered to Winchester, to take command of the forces then in the Shenandoah Valley, and he had his brigade paraded to bid them farewell. We all had the blues, for we did not want to part with him as our commander. Besides, we all wanted to go with him, as nearly all of us came from the different counties in the Shenandoah Valley.

General Jackson and his staff officers rode up in front of the brigade, after we had formed on the hillside, and looked up and down the line. He then slowly raised his cap and said:

> Officers and Soldiers of the First Brigade: I am not here to make a speech, but simply to say farewell. I first met you at Harper's Ferry, in the commencement of this war, and I cannot take leave of you without giving expression to my admiration for your conduct from that day to this, whether on the march, the bivouac, the tented field, or the bloody plains of Manassas, when you gained the well-deserved reputation of having decided the fate of that battle.
>
> Throughout the broad extent of country over which you have marched, by your respect for the rights and property of citizens you have shown that you were soldiers, not only to defend, but able and willing both to defend and protect. You have already gained a brilliant and deservedly high reputation throughout the army and the whole Confederacy, and I trust in the future, by your own deeds on the field, and by the assistance of the same kind Providence who has heretofore favoured our cause, you will gain more victories, and add additional lustre to the reputation you now enjoy.
>
> You have already gained a proud position in the future history of this, our second war of independence. I shall look with great

anxiety to your future movements, and I trust that whenever I shall hear of the 1st Brigade on the field of battle it will be of still nobler deeds achieved and a higher reputation won.

Here he paused and glanced proudly around him. Then, raising himself in his stirrups and throwing the reins on his horse's neck, he exclaimed in a voice of such deep feeling that it thrilled through every heart in the brigade: "In the Army of the Shenandoah you were the *First* Brigade, in the Army of the Potomac you were the *First* Brigade, in the 2nd Corps of this army you are the *First* Brigade; you are *First* Brigade in the affections of your general, and I hope by your future deeds and bearing you will be handed down to posterity as the *First* Brigade in this, our second war of independence. Farewell!"

For a moment there was a pause, and then arose cheer after cheer, so wild and thrilling that the very heavens rang with them. General Jackson waved farewell to his men, and, gathering his reins, rode rapidly away.

This was the only time I ever heard him open his mouth to speak, except once afterwards he spoke a few words in my presence. He was a man who had very little to say.

Now, I don't consider that the "Stonewall Brigade" was better than other brigades, for there were plenty of other brigades that did just as good service as we did, and if any other brigade had been similarly situated at the First Battle of Manassas, I have no doubt they would have done as well as we did, and gained the same reputation.

We had to pay dearly for our reputation afterwards, for whenever there was an extra hard duty to be performed General Jackson always sent his old brigade to that post of duty for fear the other brigades under his command would think and say that he favoured his old command. Consequently, we often had harder duty to perform than the others.

We all returned to camp after his farewell address considerably out of humour, for we wanted to go with him wherever he went, and be immediately under his eye, and especially to the Valley, as our homes were there.

Nothing of interest transpired in camp, except every few days some private belonging to the brigade would come into camp with a long yarn, that he heard such and such officers say that our brigade had orders to report to General Jackson. But they all proved to be "false alarms," until one day, about a month after he left us, such an order did come, and we were ordered to "strike tents" and be ready to march the next morning. Then there was joy in the camp, and the excitement kept up until the next morning, when the 2nd, 6th and 27th Regiments marched off to Manassas Junction and took the cars for Strasburg, about fifty miles away.

For want of transportation, my regiment and the 4th had to wait until the next day. We then marched to the railroad, but the trains had not returned, and we anxiously waited all day. It then commenced raining, but we could not put up our tents, for we did not know what moment the trains would return; so, we had a glorious night in the rain and mud.

About one hour before day the cars came, when we loaded on our baggage, boarded the trains and away we went, as merry a set of fellows as ever rode. We had a gay time that day, waving our hats and cheering every lady we saw, and, in due time, arrived at Strasburg.

Several of our companies were from that neighbourhood, and their friends and relatives came to meet them, and brought them cooked food and many delicacies. It was quite an affecting scene for a short time, for some were overjoyed with meeting their husbands, brothers and lovers, while others were bathed in tears for their husbands, brothers, sons or lovers who had fallen on the bloody plains of Manassas.

We then marched about one mile from town on the road to Winchester, and camped in an old barn.

The next day we marched toward Winchester, eighteen miles distant, and joined the brigade and went into camp near Kernstown, a few miles from Winchester.

Some of the soldiers belonging to the 27th Regiment were determined to go on to Winchester, and they flanked the guard and kept on down the road, but when in sight of town they were halted by the militia picket and were told they could go no farther without a pass.

Now, the militia were never much in the way of volunteers when they had a notion for a raid in town. So, one of the volunteers took command of the squad and ordered them to load their arms and prepare to charge the militia. Then the militia broke and fled as fast as their legs could carry them—the boys yelling and charging until they got to town. Here they scattered, for fear of being arrested by the provost guard.

They all got on a spree, and most of them landed in the guardhouse that night, and were sent to the camp under arrest. We remained in this camp about one week, when my cousin, Smith Casler (who

In the Guard House at Camp Harman.

was on a furlough), and my sister Sallie came in a buggy to see me. They spent a few hours with me and returned home.

I wanted a leave of absence for a few days to go with them, but could not get it. Smith told me to meet him in Winchester the next day and he would let me have the horse and his pass, and I could go home, a distance of fifteen miles. I got a pass the next day from my captain to go to Winchester and meet my cousin. I then changed the date of his pass, got on the horse, and was soon on my way home, as merry as if I had a genuine furlough.

I remained at home seven days, and then returned to camp, and found the brigade had moved camp four miles north of Winchester, near Stephenson's Depot. I was put on double duty for seven nights, as a punishment for my "French Furlough."

We remained at "Camp Stephenson" for some time; had good tents, plenty to eat, and nothing to do but guard duty and drill, with plenty of visitors at our camp every day. While at this camp Brigadier General R. B. Garnett was made Brigadier of our brigade, and we had a review, in order to display our soldierly qualities before our new general and the ladies.

On the 17th day of December we struck tents and marched about fifteen miles towards Martinsburg, and camped within three miles of that place. The next morning, we were on the march, and went through Martinsburg down to Dam No. 5, on the Potomac River—another fifteen miles. We had about twenty flatboats with us, in covered wagons. They were not so much concealed but they could be easily seen by any spies there might be about, and there were plenty of them. This was a ruse to make the Federals think we were going to cross the Potomac, while our object was to destroy the dam, so the Chesapeake and Ohio canal could not be used by the enemy.

Almost everybody thought we were going to invade Maryland, but we halted at the dam and commenced to destroy it. The enemy, on the other side of the river, kept up such a continuous firing that we could not work, so we took the boats up the river opposite Little Georgetown, Md., unloaded them, and made preparations as if we were going to cross. The enemy at once drew all their forces up there in order to intercept us, and left us free to tear open the dam in their absence, which we did. We then returned to our old camp near Winchester, where we remained until January 1, 1862. Thus, ended the first year of the war.

Chapter 6
Midwinter Campaign of '62

On the 1st of January, 1862, we struck tents, marched out of camp, and took the road leading to Bath (now Berkely Springs), Morgan County, Va. (now West Virginia), about forty miles distant, and near the Baltimore and Ohio railroad. It was a very pleasant, warm day for the time of year, and we marched about twenty miles and camped for the night. I went home, as it was near, and stayed all night, and returned to camp next morning, ready for the march. But the weather had changed considerably, and it was cold and rainy. We continued the march, but it snowed that evening, so that our baggage wagons could not get up with us, and we were without tents, blankets and rations.

They came up next morning, when we cooked rations, and were soon on the march again. That evening we entered Bath (now Berkely Springs) and captured some few of the enemy, but the greater portion escaped by running over the militia force that was sent around to cut off their retreat to the Potomac.

The next day we went on to the river, opposite Hancock, Md., and threw a few shells across. We captured some government stores and remained there two days, the weather being very bad all the time—snowing, sleeting, raining and freezing. We would lie down at nights without tents, rolled up head and heels in our blankets, and in the morning would be covered with snow. Every few minutes someone of the party I was sleeping with would poke his head out from under the blankets and let in the snow around our necks, when he would get punched in the ribs until he would "haul in his horns."

We then marched back towards Winchester and camped at Unger's Store. The roads were one glare of ice, and it was very difficult for the wagons and artillery to get along. Four men were detailed to go with each wagon in order to keep it on the road on going around the hillside curves. I was on one detail, and we would tie ropes to the top of the wagon-bed in the rear and all swing to the upper side of the road. The horses were smooth shod, and in going up a little hill I have seen one horse in each team down nearly all the time. As soon as one would get up, another would be down, and sometimes all four at once.

That day I saw General Jackson get down off his horse and put his shoulder to the wheel of a wagon to keep it from sliding back. By slow and tedious work, we arrived at camp after night. The troops were marching in the rear. I had our tent up and a good fire made out of rails by the time they arrived.

We remained at this camp three days, sent all the sick to Winchester, and took up the line of march for Romney, Hampshire County, thirty-five miles west. The first night we camped at the Great Capon river, built a bridge across it and North River, and camped the second night at Slane's Crossroads.

The third day we entered Romney, and found the enemy had evacuated the place on hearing of our approach. The weather was extremely rough. We were all covered over with sleet, and as it would freeze fast to us as it fell, we presented rather an icy appearance.

We remained in Romney several days, when our brigade was ordered back to Winchester, some of General W. W. Loring's command remaining. My company, being from Hampshire County, received ten days' furlough, through the kindness of Lieutenant Colonel J. E. Jones, who pleaded with General Jackson in our behalf. So, we all started off for Springfield, our native town, nine miles north of Romney, in high spirits, and the brigade started for Winchester.

But when we arrived at Springfield we were not as happy as we expected to be, from the fact that we were two miles outside of our pickets, and were constantly in danger of being picked up by a scouting party from the enemy, which came in nearly every day or night. But we managed to dodge them all the time, and enjoyed ourselves hugely with the girls with whom we had spent our schoolboy days. But the last day they came near capturing some of our boys, for they were just starting out of town when the scouts came in, and they ran into the houses and hid until all were safe.

We all met in Romney at the time appointed, and started *en route* for Winchester, leaving Loring's brigade to hold the place, and arrived in Winchester in three days. We found the brigade building winter quarters four miles northwest of town, on the Pughtown road. So, we went to work and did likewise. Thus, ended a severe winter campaign.

We were out nearly one month, and had miserable weather all the time, and did no fighting, except some little skirmishing, but we lost more men from sickness than if we had been engaged in a big battle. We accomplished nothing, for the enemy retreated across the Potomac, only to come back again as soon as we left. Winchester was full of soldiers, sick with the pneumonia, and they died by hundreds.

We lost our Second Lieutenant, Jacob N. Buzzard, who died in Winchester, where our company buried him with the honours of war. It was a very solemn ceremony, as he was greatly beloved by the

Stealing Whiskey from 1st Kentucky Regiment.

whole company.

We finished our quarters the 1st day of February, when I was taken sick and sent to the hospital in Winchester. I remained there until the 11th of March, at which time General Jackson evacuated Winchester, and the boys had to give up their good quarters and take the field for it again. I was sent on to the hospital at Mount Jackson. General Jackson fell back to Rude's Hill, fifty miles from Winchester, and remained there some time. I began to get better, and, being tired of the hospital, I returned to my regiment the 21st of March. That day we started towards Winchester to advance on the enemy. The next day we made a forced march of twenty-eight miles, and I, just getting over my sickness, could hardly make the "riffle," and it was difficult to keep up with the troops. The next day, the 23rd of March, we marched fifteen miles, and met the enemy three miles south of Winchester, near Kernstown, and there fought one of the hardest little battles of the war, and were defeated.

General Jackson attacked 8,000 of the enemy under General Shields, with 2,500 infantry and Ashby's cavalry, and repeatedly charged them, but was driven back, and finally had to give up the field and retreat. Darkness was all that saved us.

As part of our brigade were marching up a hill in the open field, alongside a fence, to take position, at the commencement of the fight, the enemy could see us, and they commenced shelling us from a hill on our right, and killed and wounded several. Just as Elijah Hartley, of my company, was making a step a shell passed between his legs and exploded, literally tearing him to pieces. He fell over in the fence corner, and that was the last we ever saw or heard of him.

We went on and took position, and were soon hotly engaged. A shell struck an artillery horse and exploded inside of him, tearing him to pieces and tearing both legs off of his driver.

There was a stone fence between two fields running parallel with the lines of battle—a Federal regiment on one side, a short distance from it, and the 37th Virginia about the same distance on the other side, advancing towards each other. Both regiments charged for the fence about the same time, and it was "nip and tuck" which would reach it first, but the 37th Virginia got there, and, kneeling down, poured a deadly volley into the other at close quarters, and nearly annihilated it. Such would have been their fate if the Federals had gotten there first.

Our company lost two men killed— Elijah Hartley and Thomas

Gross—three wounded—Sergeant James P. Daily, Robert C. Grace and Mart Miller—and two captured—Mike Bright and Ed. Allen. R. C. Grace was wounded early in the action, and put into an ambulance with other wounded and sent to the rear. The ambulance was fired on by the enemy's cavalry and Grace wounded again, and all captured. He was taken to Winchester, and from there his friends took him home, where he died. Sergeant J. P. Daily was wounded in the leg as we were falling back, and his brother, William Daily, wanted to stay and help him along, but he said, "No, save yourself, and I will do the best I can." He fell into the hands of the enemy, was taken to Winchester, and died. Mart Miller was shot in the back of the neck as we were running down a hill, and the bullet came out in front, near his windpipe; but he kept on running, when a spent ball struck him in his overcoat collar and lodged there. He turned a complete somersault, and we all thought he was dead; but he said he was all right, and was helped up and escaped. He was sent to the hospital, but came back to the company in about six weeks, perfectly well and ready for duty.

Several of us had halted under a tree in the edge of the woods, to see what was best to do, and while there a man on horseback came dashing up to us and asked us what command we belonged to. Seeing that he was a Confederate, we told him. He exclaimed: "We've lost the day; we've lost the day," in the saddest tones I ever heard. He looked all around and then repeated it: "We've lost the day; we've lost the day," and turned his horse toward the battlefield and dashed off at full speed. None of us knew him or his rank, as it was getting too dark to observe him well.

But I thought then, and have since thought, that the man was shocked by a shell passing or exploding near him, for he appeared crazy, or bewildered. We all scattered back as far as Newtown that night, about five miles from the battlefield, and lay along the road, every fellow for himself, building fires out of fence rails, and making ourselves as comfortable as we could after the fatigues of the day. I did not see but one regiment in any kind of order, and that was the 5th Virginia, of our brigade. It had acted as a reserve during the battle, and covered our retreat. There was no attempt to rally us that night, but next morning we were all at our posts in our respective regiments.

We continued to fall back in good order to the south side of Cedar Creek, Ashby's cavalry holding the enemy in check. They did not appear very anxious for another fight. Our loss was not very heavy in that battle. The citizens who gathered up our dead, and buried there, reported eighty-three dead on the field. A greater portion of the wounded fell into the enemy's hands; also a few prisoners.

That was a kind of Virginia fight, for they were all Virginians, except a few Maryland companies, on the Southern side, and there were a good many Virginia regiments on the Federal side; and it was fought in Virginia.

After the fight was over it was a mystery to us why General Jackson would evacuate Winchester and fall back fifty miles, and then turn around with a smaller force than he left Winchester with and go back and attack such a large force, with no chance of success. We had a smaller army, to my certain knowledge, for after we left Winchester there were one or two regiments sent away, and the soldiers were re-enlisting, getting $50 bounty and thirty days furlough; besides, one-fourth or one-third of our command were already absent on furlough. We had also left all the militia behind.

But military men don't tell privates their plans, and General Jackson never told officers his. But we knew it was all right when "Old Bluelight" gave his orders. We found out afterwards the cause.

When the Southern army evacuated Manassas Junction, and fell back to the Rappahannock, General Jackson had to evacuate Winchester and fall back, in order to form a line or junction, if necessary. As the Federals had given up going to Richmond by way of Manassas Junction, and were landing troops on the peninsula, under General McClellan, to approach Richmond from the east, also a large force in the Valley to approach Richmond from the west, it was highly important for the Southern army to keep them from forming a junction.

The very day that General Jackson fought the Battle of Kernstown there were Federal troops leaving Winchester and marching towards Fredericksburg, and when the battle commenced, they were halted and ordered back, and that scheme was frustrated. So General Jackson lost the battle of Kernstown, but accomplished what he went to do with a very small force.

This was the only time he was ever defeated, and the only battle he lost during the war.

******

Major Jed Hotchkiss said: "General Jackson spent the night after the battle near where he had formed his line of battle in the afternoon. He never considered that he was defeated at Kernstown."

******

He made such an impression on the enemy that a large force was recalled in order to hold him in check, thinking he had five times the men he had. The enemy's loss was much greater than ours in killed and wounded, as they stood so thick that a bullet could hardly miss them if aimed low enough.

The day after the battle, while we were cooking rations on a hill south of Cedar Creek, the enemy came in sight on an opposite hill, placed a battery in position and commenced throwing shells at us, in order to knock over our camp kettles, I suppose, and we were ordered to load up the wagons, "fall in" and depart hence. Now, four regiments of our brigade marched to the left around the brow of the hill, and were soon out of view and out of danger; but Colonel A. J. Grigsby, commanding the 27th, who was always rather headstrong, marched his regiment to the right, in the main road and in full view, when a shell came tearing along through the ranks, killing and wounding twelve men.

We continued to fall back slowly until we reached Rude's Hill, Colonel Ashby, with his cavalry, covering our retreat and harassing the enemy. We remained there several days, skirmishing nearly every day.

While at this camp the militia force was disbanded and put into the volunteer companies, by which each company was considerably recruited. Our company was larger than ever before, numbering about eighty. But the militia did not like that way of doing business, for they considered it certain death to be put into the Stonewall Brigade, and wanted to choose their own companies. The consequence was the greater number of them ran off and went home to their respective counties, and there, formed cavalry companies, organised new regiments, and did good service during the balance of the war. About twenty remained in my company, and some of them made as good soldiers as ever shouldered a musket.

The enemy kept advancing on us in considerable force, and as Colonel Ashby was disputing the passage of the Shenandoah at Meem's bottom he had his white horse shot under him, but he rode him back to the rear, where he died in a short time. ("I saw this myself."—J. H.) My uncle, R. S. D. Heironimus, who belonged to Ashby's cavalry, was wounded in this skirmish.

We kept on falling back until we reached Harrisonburg, when we turned abruptly to the left and marched east to Swift Run Gap, in the Blue Ridge mountains. The enemy advanced no farther than Harrisonburg, with the exception of some scouting parties. We lay here for some time, the weather being very rough, it raining and snowing continuously.

While here the army was reorganised. As we had been mustered into service for one year, and the time expiring, most of the men had re-enlisted. They received $50 bounty and thirty days' furlough, but as only part of the army could be furloughed at once, those who did not get a furlough before we began to move never got one at all, and those who would not re-enlist were retained in service also, and received the bounty, but not the furlough.

All the companies elected company officers, and the company officers elected regimental officers, but that was the last time it was done, for after that they always went up by promotion.

Colonel A. C. Cummings, of my regiment, would not serve any longer, and our adjutant, A. J. Neff, was elected Colonel, which very much disappointed the lieutenant colonel and major. But he made a splendid officer, and did good service. We were then mustered into service for three years, or during the war.

A good many men who lived along the base of the Blue Ridge, who were liable to military duty, and some deserters, had taken refuge in the mountains and fortified themselves, and defied the conscript officers to arrest them. General Jackson sent some infantry and cavalry to capture them, when an old lady living near remarked that "The deserters had mortified in the Blue Ridge, but that General Jackson sent a foot company and a critter company to ramshag the Blue Ridge and capture them."

The day we arrived at Swift Run Gap our wagon train was in advance, and part of them had taken the wrong road and did not reach camp that night. Sergeant Parsons, of my company, was with them. The next day, when they arrived in camp, he said he stayed all night at a house way up in the mountains, and the people were so ignorant that they did not know that the war was going on. When he began to explain it to them and told them that he belonged to General Jackson's command, they said: "Oh! yes; we have read about General Jackson and his army!" He got them to show him the book. It was about old Andy Jackson, in the war of 1812.

Chapter 7

Up the Shenandoah

My father had left home for fear of being arrested and sent to prison, for he had been in the militia six months, and with our army until we arrived at this camp, when he concluded to go to Richmond and join the heavy artillery. He was over age, and could not stand active field service. I tried to persuade him to remain out of the army, for if both of us got killed my mother and three sisters would be left alone in the world. But he would go, and so we parted; but after he got to Richmond the company he joined was put in the infantry. He would not be mustered in, but returned to the Valley, and afterwards, when our army occupied Winchester, he went home and remained there during the war.

The 10th Virginia Regiment was organised in the Valley, but had been east of the Ridge in General Johnston's army ever since the Battle of Manassas. It had been trying for a long time to be transferred to the Valley under Jackson, and at last succeeded. So, the regiment came to us at this camp, and was put into the 3rd Brigade of our division, and we had considerable sport out of them tantalising them. We told them they had lain down there in good quarters all winter, doing nothing but eat and sleep; that they would soon get enough of Jackson; that he would soon take the starch out of them and make them earn their board. Sure enough, we soon had a battle at McDowell, and they got into it hot and heavy, and lost a good many men; among them their commander, Colonel S. B. Gibbons, a fine officer. The regiment acted nobly, and had a high reputation during the whole war.

General R. B. Garnett, commanding our brigade, was relieved of his command by General Jackson for some mismanagement at the Battle of Kernstown. I never heard exactly what it was; but General C. S. Winder took command of our brigade. He was an old United States officer, and very strict. General Garnett afterwards commanded a brigade in Pickett's Division, and was killed at Gettysburg.

We had heretofore always had a large wagon train to haul our cooking utensils, mess chest's, tents and blankets, but were here ordered to reduce the train, use fewer cooking utensils, and dispense with the mess chests and tents, and every man to carry his knapsack and blankets. If found in the wagons they were to be thrown away. So, we started on the march up the Shenandoah River under the new tactics, through the rain and mud; and, as we had a good many blankets and an overcoat apiece, it was a hard task, and a great many blankets were thrown away. I suppose the order was from headquarters, but General Winder had just taken the command of the brigade, and, as this order came at the same time, we all thought he was the cause of it.

As he was a kind of fancy general, and seemed to put on a good many airs, and was a very strict disciplinarian, the boys all took a dislike to him from the start, and never did like him afterwards. Whenever he would pass the brigade on the march we would sing out, "More baggage, more baggage," until he got tired of it. He wheeled suddenly around one day and told my captain to arrest the men for such conduct. I was one of the men, but it was like "*hunting for a needle in a haystack*" to find out who we were, so we escaped.

We marched on and crossed the Blue Ridge to the east by Brown's Gap, and continued until we reached the Virginia Central railroad, at Mechum's River, when we got on the cars and went by rail to Staunton.

Before we left Swift Run Gap General Ewell's Division, from General Joseph E. Johnston's army, had come and taken our position, and lay there ready to form a junction, either with Jackson or Johnston, as was necessary, and at the same time to watch the enemy in the lower Valley. General Ed. Johnson had a small force in Augusta County, and he was falling back on Staunton from the west, before General Milroy. So, when we got to Staunton, we marched west to Buffalo Gap, and, joining Johnson's command, turned on the enemy, who in turn fell back to McDowell, about twenty-five miles, and there made a stand on the top of Bull Pasture mountain.

Now, Johnson, being about six hours in advance of Jackson, did not wait until we came up, but pitched in and came very near being repulsed; but Jackson coming up in time, by double-quicking us several miles, we swept the field just at dark. Our loss was small, but Johnson lost severely, as also did Milroy.

Our brigade marched thirty-six miles that day. We carried our knapsacks twenty miles, when we were ordered to "pile them" and go for it double-quick.

The Federal soldiers knew General Johnson by sight, and, during the battle one time, being separated a little from his command, some of them hallooed out: "There's old Johnson; let's flank him!" Johnson heard them, and, waving his club in the air, exclaimed: "Yes, damn you, flank me if you can." He was wounded in the foot. He very seldom carried a sword, but nearly always a big hickory club, or cane. We always called him "Old Clubby Johnson," to distinguish him from the other Johnsons.

That was the only battle I was ever in or heard of during the war where there was no artillery used. The place was so rugged and steep that neither army could get a piece in position, nor could we get an ambulance to the battlefield. We had to carry the wounded down a steep, rocky hollow, and it took us nearly all night to do so.

The enemy retreated about one mile and went into camp, we thought, for they built a great many fires, but the next morning they were gone. They had been retreating all night, leaving some baggage and a good many wounded in camp. We were on the march early next morning, but did not overtake them until we got near Franklin, Pendleton County, a distance of forty miles, where they met reinforcements and made another stand.

We were drawn up in line of battle, and lay there all day, skirmishing some with them, but had no general engagement. At dark we retired from their front, went into camp, cooked rations, and the next morning started back. We marched east until near Staunton, when we turned down the Valley, marching north, passing by Stribling Springs, Mount Solon, Bridgewater and Dayton, on to Harrisonburg, where we were ordered to pile away our knapsacks in the court-house. We knew there was some game on hand then, for when General Jackson ordered knapsacks to be left behind, he meant business.

We marched on at a quick march down the Valley to Newmarket, where we turned east, crossed the Massanutten mountain, and over into the Page Valley, on down Page Valley until we arrived at Front Royal.

Now, General Banks, of commissary fame, had a considerable army at Front Royal and Strasburg, and we had been re-enforced by General Ewell's Division. Our advance surprised the enemy at both places, and got in between the two armies. We had some sharp fighting for a while, but we got them cut off, and captured a great many, besides wagons, artillery, etc., and the rout became general. The roads to Winchester, a distance of eighteen miles, showed wreckage of all kinds of baggage and commissary stores. We followed the retreating army all that night. Their rear guard would sometimes take advantage of the darkness and lay in ambush for us, but we would soon outflank them and move on. My company and Company F were in advance, and we had several men wounded.

When we got to Winchester, at daylight, they had made another stand in the fortifications around the town, and we had to form a line around them and charge. Our brigade did not get engaged in this fight, but we lay in line of battle on a hillside and were exposed to a severe shelling from the enemy, and lost several men in killed and wounded. The Louisiana Brigade in Ewell's Division charged the fort

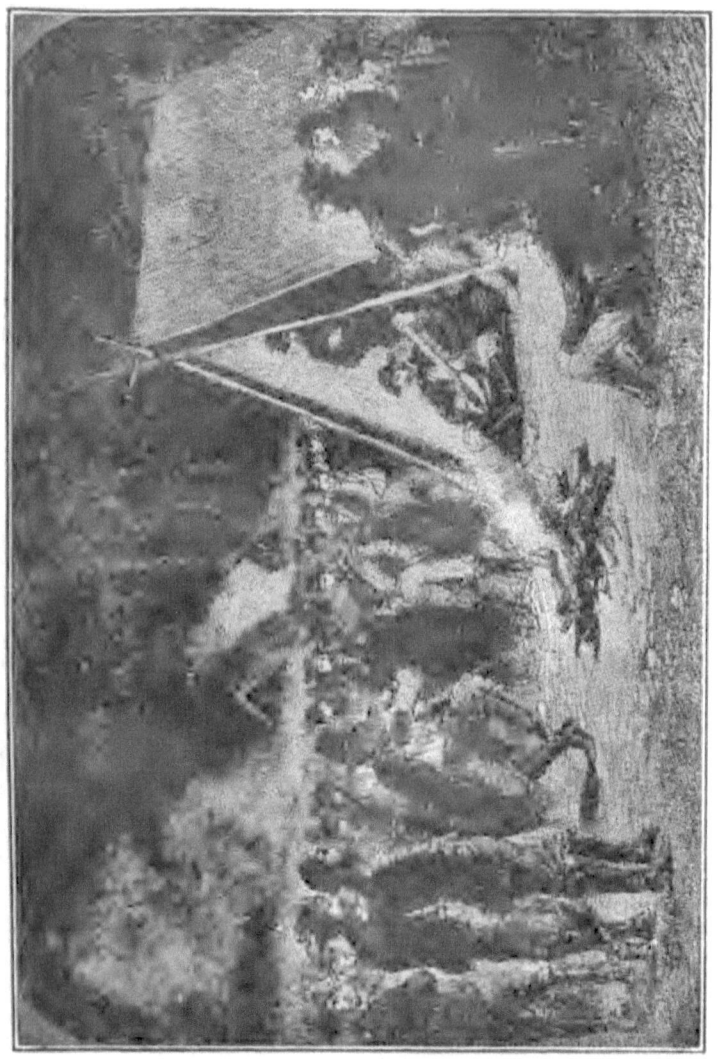

Night Amusements in the Confederate Camp.

under a galling fire. They hotly contested the place, but finally gave way at all points, and the rout became general. We followed them a few miles north of Winchester and halted; but the cavalry kept up the pursuit until dark.

We captured a great amount of commissary stores, ammunition and baggage of all kinds, also all the sutler stores in Winchester, and, I think, about 5,000 prisoners. The enemy had set fire to a part of the town in order to burn up their stores, but we were too close on them and extinguished the fire, so there were only two or three buildings burnt. In one of them I saw the corpses of two men chained to the wall; but we never knew who they were, whether Rebels, citizens, or some of their own men. A guard was put around the captured stores, which worried us considerably, for we wanted to plunder the sutlers. The main force of the enemy had taken refuge in Harper's Ferry, and there was no way of capturing them or driving them out without getting possession of the Maryland Heights, across the Potomac.

The day after the rout at Winchester our brigade, alone, marched on towards Harper's Ferry. When we got to Charleston, a few miles from the ferry, we found a small force posted there to dispute our passage. We were formed in line and my company deployed as skirmishers on the extreme left of the brigade in order to watch flankers; but we saw no enemy, and a shot or two from our artillery caused them to retreat. We then hurried on to get with the brigade.

When we got to the edge of town the brigade had passed through, and two of our cavalrymen came dashing up from another direction and wanted my captain to take his company out a short distance on the Martinsburg road and capture some of the enemy's cavalry. They were cut off from their command, but would not surrender. He told them he was ordered to join the brigade as soon as possible and could not disobey orders. The cavalrymen then said if he would only let them have ten men it would do. The captain said he would not order ten men out, but if they chose to volunteer, he would give his consent. Immediately ten men stepped out of the ranks, myself included, and went double-quick up the road, keen for a capture.

We had not proceeded far when we saw them coming down the road in a gallop. We jumped over a stone fence that ran parallel with the road, and, bringing our muskets to bear on them, commanded them to halt and surrender. No sooner was this said than a white handkerchief was seen to flutter in the breeze. All were made prisoners without firing a shot. They were composed of a squad of twelve men with a captain, and belonged to some New York regiment, and were all Germans. We took them on to town and delivered them to the guard.

In a few minutes we learned that in the morning this same squad had passed through town, riding along on each side of the street, and broke every window with their sabres, and that this brave captain had struck a lady in the face with the flat side of his sword. Had we known this when we jumped over the stone fence, we would never have called on them to surrender, but shot them down in their tracks and left their bodies there for food for buzzards. We then went into camp near Charlestown and put out pickets near the ferry—all that was left of General Banks' army was being cooped up there and at Williamsport, Md.

This fighting has been designated by some as the "Battle of Front Royal," also "Battle of Winchester;" but it was a continuous fight and skirmish from Front Royal to Harper's Ferry, a distance of fifty miles. We had no general engagement, and our loss was small; it being a kind of one-sided fight all the time. General Jackson "got the drop" on them in the start, and kept it.

The enemy's loss was great in killed, wounded, prisoners and munitions of war. In fact, it was nearly annihilated; for hundreds of them were cut off from their commands and took to the woods and mountains. This happened the 23rd and 24th of May, 1862.

Previous to this time we had fared very well in the way of rations, clothing, etc. We had the usual army rations: one pound and two ounces of flour; three-fourths of a pound of bacon, or one and one-fourth pounds of beef; coffee, rice, beans, sugar, molasses, etc.; but on account of transportation and blockade, it soon came down to meat and bread, with occasional sprinklings of the others. So, whenever we made such a haul as we did from Banks we fared sumptuously until the quartermasters got it in their clutches. That would be the last of it, especially the sutler stores. Therefore, the soldiers began to appropriate anything in the way of grub, such as hogs, chickens, apples, corn, etc., to their own use. We would not allow any man's chickens to run out into the road and bite us as we marched along. We would not steal them! No! Who ever heard of a soldier stealing? But simply take them.

Some wag in the brigade had gotten up a nickname for every regiment in the brigade. The 2nd was called "The Innocent 2nd," because they never stole anything; the 4th, "The Harmless 4th," because they had no fights in camp; the 5th, "The Fighting 5th," because it was the largest regiment and would have some rows in camp; the 27th, "The Bloody 27th," as there were several Irish companies in it, and the 33rd (my regiment), was "The Lousy 33rd," because it was the first regiment in the brigade that found any lice on them. So, this is the way it went from camp to camp: "The Innocent 2nd," "The Harmless 4th," "The Fighting 5th," "The Bloody 27th" and "The Lousy 33rd."

We lay in camp near Charlestown several days picketing and skirmishing near Harper's Ferry. I suppose Jackson could have taken Harper's Ferry, but he had to watch some armies that were threatening his rear. So, one morning my company, being then on picket, was ordered to join the regiment, and we all started on the march towards Winchester. We marched hard all day, and at dark, when within a few miles of town, our colonel came riding back along the line and told us we would have to make a forced march; that he did not know how far we would go before camping, and desired all of us to keep up if we could; if not, to keep on coming until we got up with the regiment. But when we got to Winchester I and three others of my company concluded we would stay all night with some of our friends. We could start early in the morning, refreshed, and soon overtake the command. We had a good supper, good beds and good breakfast. We started out early and found a good many soldiers in town that had done as we had.

We found out at the same time that the quartermasters had failed to take all of the sutler stores we had captured out of town, but had turned them over to the soldiers, and most of them were loaded with good things. We had missed it all, which we regretted very much. We also found out that the army had marched eight miles beyond Winchester that night and went into camp near Newtown. This made forty miles the brigade had marched that day.

We struck out in a hurry to overtake them. On reaching Newtown, now Stephens City, we met some of our cavalry that General Jackson had sent back to inform all stragglers that the enemy under General Shields was approaching from the east; also a force under General Fremont from the west; that they had formed a junction at Middletown, between us and our army, and that all stragglers should leave the road and take to the mountains on our right and follow the mountains on up the Valley until we should reach our commands.

There were about five hundred of us cut off in this way; but if we had all been together, and had a commander, we could have forced our way through the enemy's cavalry. As it was, we were scattered along the road for about eight miles in little squads of three and four.

Chapter 8

Death of Ashby

We then left the main road and went towards the mountains, keeping in the woods as much as possible. When near the mountains we came to a house, and as we were going up to it to make some inquiries about the roads, we saw a Federal soldier walking about in the yard. We did not know what that meant, but, as he appeared to be alone and unarmed, we thought there was not much danger. As he saw us coming, he went into the house. When we got to the house, we met a lady who begged us not to arrest him, as he had been put there as a guard by General Banks when his army was there. That when Banks retreated this soldier did not know it in time, and had remained under her protection. We told her we would not bother him; that we were trying to escape ourselves, and might be captured yet before night. She gave us a good dinner and we left, telling her the enemy would soon be there and she could put the soldier on guard again. We also asked him not to inform his cavalry which way we went, and he promised to do so; but whether he did or not I do not know.

A squad of cavalry was sent after us in a few hours, and we just escaped by accident. That evening there was a very hard thunder shower, and we went into a barn to keep out of the rain. While there a little negro boy came running down from the house, and said: "You soldiers had better hide, for the upper end of the medder is black wi'd Yankees." We then got up into the haymow and hid under the hay, the boy still staying outside saying: "Here they come; now they got some of your men; they'll soon be here." I had told him several times to run on to the house and not tell on us, but he still stayed, and, fearing he would draw the enemy's attention, I put my gun out of a crack and told him if he did not scamper off to the house, I would shoot him. It had the desired effect, for he left immediately. Very soon the cavalry rode by, but we were not molested. We then got out and hurried on, and would have overtaken our army sometime that night, but when we got to Cedar Creek, we found it so much swollen from the rain that it was impossible to cross it. We could not remain there, so there was nothing left for us to do but to follow up the bank of the creek to the mountains.

When we got there, we remained on the top of North mountain one whole day, traveling without road or path, keeping the mountain as our guide. At night we came down to stay at some house. After that day we kept the byroads between the mountains. Charley French, Mart Miller, John Kelley and myself remained together. We would often meet up with other soldiers in small squads, and there would be twenty of us together for a short time. But as we had to subsist upon the citizens living in this mountainous country, we were obliged to travel in small parties in order to get provisions. We would inquire every day from someone as to the whereabouts of our army. We learned it was falling back every day, closely pursued by the enemy.

We could never get ahead far enough to leave the mountains. One day we heard heavy cannonading and then we knew that Jackson had made a stand. The next day we could still hear the artillery belching forth, but it appeared to be in a different place, and as we were getting tired of the mountains, we passed through Hopkins' Gap and came out in the Valley. We stayed all night about eight miles from Harrisonburg. The next morning, we were feeling our way slowly, and trying to find out how the battle went, when we came to Mr. Thompson's farmhouse, and he told us that he was not certain, but thought General Jackson had defeated the enemy, and he thought they were retreating down the Valley.

"If such is the case," he said, "I advise you to remain here until night, and we will know for certain, and then you can soon reach your command."

We took his advice and halted, and got every soldier who came along to do likewise, until we had collected about thirty.

"Now," says Thompson, "whenever the enemy retreat down the Valley they always send out their cavalry, far and near, on each side of the main road and take all the horses they can find. I and my neighbours have some good farming horses that we don't want to lose; and if you men will go with me, we will go out on the hill in the woods beyond my house, and if they come into this neighbourhood after horses, we will give them a warm reception.

"I have a good rifle," he remarked, "that is true to its aim, and I can aim it as well as anyone, and I assure you I will bring down as many of the enemy as any of you old soldiers."

We all agreed to his proposal, for it was sport for us to have a brush with the cavalry, especially when we had the drop on them. So, we all took a position on the hill and put out a picket, who could see the road for some distance, and remained there all day. But no enemy came; and at dark we all went to Thompson's house and got a good supper, and slept in the barn. The next morning, we heard that Jackson had defeated the enemy in two different battles and they were retreating in a hurry and did not have time to plunder the country for horses.

We then went on and soon arrived in Harrisonburg, where we found some of our cavalry, who informed us that our brigade was camped near Port Republic at Weyer's Cave. We then went on towards camp, having marched about eighty miles through the mountains, and arrived there that evening. Our captain had reported us captured.

I must now go back and bring up the brigade, and give an account of its transactions from the time I left it at Winchester until I joined it again at Weyer's Cave, as was told me by members of my company.

They camped south of Newtown, now Stephens City, the first night after leaving Charlestown, and the next morning hurried on and just got through Strasburg before the enemy made their appearance. They had not yet formed a junction; but some portion of our army had a little skirmish with the enemy in order to save the wagon train. Jackson kept falling back slowly, Ashby with his cavalry covering the retreat and holding them in check.

When Jackson reached Harrisonburg, he turned to the left, taking the Port Republic road, and marched east towards the Blue Ridge. When a few miles from Harrisonburg Colonel, now General, Ashby, thinking the enemy were pressing too close to be healthy, charged them at the head of the 1st Maryland and 58th Virginia Infantry and was killed (June 6, 1862); but the enemy was repulsed.

We there lost a brave and gallant cavalry officer, who, had he lived, would have been one of the greatest cavalry generals of the war.

The death of his brother, Richard Ashby, about a year before, near Cumberland, Md., while a member of his (then Captain) company, had greatly affected him. He had sent his brother Dick with a small detachment to reconnoitre the enemy on Kelley's Island. He was ambuscaded by a detachment of an Indiana Zouave Regiment in charge of Corporal Hays, at the mouth of a ravine near the railroad. His horse made a misstep and threw him into a cattle-guard, where he was set upon by the enemy and severely beaten and left for dead. He was rescued by his brother. Turner Ashby, but was so severely wounded that he lived but a few days. He was buried in the beautiful Indian Mound cemetery at Romney, Va., July 4, 1861. General (then Captain) Ashby's behaviour at his brother's funeral, as described in *Pollard's Southern History of the War*, was touching and pathetic, and doubtless had a marked effect upon his subsequent acts.

"He stood over the grave, took his brother's sword, broke it and threw it into the opening; clasped his hands and looked upward as if in resignation; and then, pressing his lips as if in the bitterness of grief, while a tear rolled down his cheek, he turned without a word, mounted his horse and rode away. Thenceforth his name was a terror to the enemy."

Both bodies have since been removed, and now lie buried in the Stonewall Cemetery at Winchester, Va.

Now General Shields and General Fremont each had an army superior in *numbers* to General Jackson; therefore, to render Jackson's capture certain, they had divided down the Valley near Strasburg. General Fremont with his army followed General Jackson up the Main Valley, while General Shields went up the Page Valley in order to cut him off near Harrisonburg, where the two valleys intersected. They had the bag tied, but could not hold the game.

When General Jackson found they were about to form a junction he wheeled suddenly on Fremont at Cross Keys, and, after a severe fight, defeated him and put his army to flight. He could not follow him far as he had to turn and cross the Shenandoah River in order to get ahead of General Shields. The next day he attacked Shields under a great disadvantage; but after hard fighting he defeated him and the cavalry pursued them for fifteen miles.

A portion of General Jackson's command lost severely, especially Ewell's Division. Our brigade did not lose many men in either engagement. The 33rd, the regiment to which I belonged, was not engaged in this last fight, as they were out on picket watching for a flank movement.

It was said by those who knew that before General Jackson and staff had crossed the river the enemy were placing a battery in position between him and the river, and were about to fire on some of our troops; that Jackson rode up to them and ordered them not to fire; and they, mistaking him for one of their officers, did not fire, and he and his staff rode on and escaped being captured. Those two battles were called the Battles of "Cross Keys" and "Port Republic," and occurred on the 8th and 9th of June, 1862.

We lay in camp at Weyer's Cave three days, the army washing in the river and cleaning up generally, and also exploring the wonders of the cave. We were soon ordered to cook rations and be ready for another march. The day before we started, we were reinforced by General Whiting's division from Richmond. Whether they came to help Jackson to fight the enemy in the Valley or to give him a larger force in order to turn General McClellan's flank, I never knew. Be that as it may, I know they came one day and we all started down the Virginia Central railroad the next day towards Richmond.

Some of the troops were embarked on the cars, but as there were not trains enough for all, our old brigade had to march, as we had gained the name by this time of "Jackson's Foot Cavalry." We could break down any cavalry brigade on a long march. As the cars reached their destination they would return and meet us, and take another load; but we still had to march. We passed through Charlottesville and Gordonsville on to Louisa Court House, where we got on the cars and rode twenty miles to Beaverdam Station. Here we got off the cars and marched all night, the rain at intervals pouring down in torrents.

A short time before this the army around Richmond, commanded by Joseph E. Johnston, had fought the Battle of "Seven Pines." General Johnston was wounded and General Robert E. Lee was placed in command. General McClellan was concentrating his troops near Richmond and his lines were, at one place, within three miles of the city. We all knew by this time that there was some fighting on hand, and that General Jackson was hunting their rear, or flank. And, sure enough, at daylight we heard our skirmishers in front firing, and soon learned that they had attacked the enemy's flank at Mechanicsville and the enemy had fallen back on the main line.

We, therefore, marched slowly all day, and in the morning, which was the 27th of June, the firing commenced again.

A big battle was imminent; for the two armies were drawing closer and closer together. Our division was marching in the rear, acting as the reserve, and consequently moved along very slowly; but firing in front kept getting heavier and heavier, the artillery belching forth in volleys, and we all knew they were at it then. We kept moving on slowly until 3 o'clock in the afternoon, when we heard terrific firing and were ordered to load our arms and start for the scene of action double-quick. We all threw down our knapsacks in a pile, leaving one man to guard them, and kept on at double-quick through woods, fields and swamps until we arrived at a little hill, where the shells commenced bursting over us. We were formed in line of battle, where we remained a few minutes, the shells and bullets flying thick and fast. While in this position a spent ball struck my cartridge box, but did no damage. We soon advanced in line of battle through a deep swamp and up a little rise, when we heard cheer after cheer rend the air. We knew it came from Southern soldiers and that the day was ours.

When we reached the place whence the cheering came there was little left for our brigade to do; which little was to give the enemy a few volleys to inform him that we had arrived. Our brigade lost but few men, but the field was covered with dead. Colonel J. W. Allen, of our 2nd Regiment, was killed; and also, Johnnie Washington and Tom Brooks, of the 13th Virginia, old schoolmates of mine. Some of our troops lost severely—the enemy terribly. It was a hardly contested fight, but the enemy had to yield. At dark we had possession of the entire battle-field, and the enemy were in full retreat, darkness saving them from a rout.

As we were going into the fight a bullet struck in my shoe heel, and a shell burst just after passing me, and so near that it fairly lifted me off the ground, and made me see more stars than I ever saw before.

After the firing ceased our brigade marched by the flank, left in front, through a piece of woods. It then being dark, and my regiment being in the rear, about one-half of it became separated from the balance of the brigade, when Major Holliday, who was riding in the rear of the regiment, ordered us to halt until he got in front to find the brigade.

A few minutes afterwards we heard great cheering on our right, and Major Holliday, thinking it was our brigade, turned our course in that direction. Some of the men said it was not our men cheering; it was the Yankees.

"Oh! no," says Holliday, "they have nothing to cheer about," and kept on marching. We then passed down a little slope, at the bottom of which was a ravine, some four or five feet deep, with some water in it.

As we were all very thirsty, we got down in it to get water; and just as some few of the men, who had satisfied themselves with drinking, got out on the opposite bank, we were challenged by someone a short distance in our front.

"What regiment is that?" came the voice.

"The 33rd Virginia," they replied, thinking, of course, that it came from some of our troops.

Instantly a volley of musketry was poured into us at close quarters; but as nearly all of us were in the ravine we escaped with the loss of one man killed and two wounded. We returned the volley, but they had fired and fled.

It was a regiment of the enemy placed there on picket, as we learned the next day from prisoners, and we asked them what they were cheering about. They said they heard that the left wing of their army had captured Richmond. We told them they were woefully mistaken; that the left of their army was retreating as fast as the right.

We soon found our brigade; but my company was sent to the front on picket duty. Of course, I went with them; but I knew what many of the boys were up to. Shall I tell you? They were robbing the dead. That is, they were searching the dead bodies.

Now, I am not a moralist, nor capable of moralising, except in a crude way; but all my moral training caused me to abhor the idea of taking anything from a dead body, except for the purpose of restoring it to the rightful owner, be he friend or foe; and I was greatly shocked when I first learned that such things were done. But why try to conceal what is well known by all the soldiers of both armies.

Of course, the orders were very strict, and after a battle details were made from each company, so far as possible, to bury their own dead, and preserve their effects.

Undoubtedly war has a demoralising effect upon the soldier. He becomes familiar with scenes of death and carnage, and what at first shocks him greatly he afterwards comes to look upon as a matter of course. It was difficult for a soldier to figure out why a gold watch or money in the pocket of a dead soldier, who had been trying to kill him all day, did not belong to the man who found it as much as it did to anyone else.

This was among the first of the hard-fought battles of the war. There were a great many killed and wounded on both sides, and we could hear the shrieks, cries and groans of the wounded and dying all night long. The ambulances and the ambulance corps were working all night; but there were so many that all could not be attended to for several days. Thus, ended the 27th of June, 1862, and the first battle of Cold Harbor and Gaines' Mill.

Chapter 9

Battle of Malvern Hill

In the morning at daybreak, as we were still on picket, we gathered up several prisoners who had got lost from their command the night before; and while conversing with them about the battle one of them remarked that we got the best of them in that fight; but that General Shields and General Fremont had General Jackson surrounded in the Valley and would sure capture him and his command. I then told him that we belonged to Jackson's command; but could hardly make him believe it. He asked me how we got here so quick. I informed him that General Jackson and his little army had cleared the Valley of both Shields and Fremont, and was now here to help clean out McClellan, and that in less than a week we would have him in the James River.

In a few moments another Federal soldier came to me from the brush and wanted to know where our hospital was. He had his hand on his breast, and I asked him where he was wounded. He said he was shot in the breast and the ball had gone through his lungs, and that he had to keep his hand over the bullet hole so that he could get his breath. When he removed his hand, I could hear the breath puffing through the wound. I directed him to the field hospital, but never knew whether he got well or not.

Soon after, as some of us were advancing to pick up more stragglers, or whatever came in our way, I was passing by a small ravine where some bushes had grown up quite thick, and saw a man come crawling out of the ravine in his shirt sleeves with blue pants on. I halted to see what he wanted, as he did not look like a soldier. As he came up, he said, "I want to surrender to you; I have been watching for some of your infantry to come along for some time. I saw some of your cavalry in sight, but was afraid to come out to them for fear they were "guerrillas" and would kill me; and I wanted to surrender to the infantry, knowing they would treat me right."

I then told him we did not keep such animals as guerrillas in our army; that they were General Stuart's cavalry he had seen, and if he had come out to them they would have treated him as a prisoner of war, and I could do no more.

I then asked him where his coat and gun were. He said that he had pulled off his blouse and hid it in his haversack, as he thought we would shoot at anything blue we saw, whether in battle or not, and that his gun was hid in the ravine. I told him to go back and get it and bring it to me, which he did, when I stuck it up in the ground, and told him to put on his blouse and go back to the rear; that he would there find the guard with other prisoners, and to report to the officer in command.

He insisted that I should go with him, but I told him I had not time as I was on the skirmish line and could not leave; but that I would insure him that he would not be hurt.

He started, and after going a few steps he halted, and, turning towards me, said: "Look here, what troops were those who fought us

Prayer in "Stonewall" Jackson's Camp.

here yesterday?"

I told him it was "Stonewall" Jackson and his command.

"Well," he says, "by G———! I thought something was wrong all day, and that accounts for it. How did you get here so quick?"

I answered that we walked here to by the "light of the moon." He then went his way and I went mine. I think that was the first fight he was ever in, for he was terribly demoralised. I then went a short distance and picked up a long string of Catholic beads with a cross attached. I suppose some fellow was counting them over, and, in his haste, dropped them. I kept them a long time, but finally lost them.

We then saw some of the enemy near a house on a small hill wandering around as if lost, and, making our way towards them, we called them to come to us, which they started to do; but just then some of their cavalry came dashing around the brow of the hill between us and saved them from capture. But they received a volley from us when they disappeared. That was the last of the enemy we saw that day.

Chickahominy River was nearby, and the enemy had destroyed the bridge in their retreat the night before and we had to repair it before we could advance; therefore, our portion of the army remained on the battlefield all day and repaired the bridge. While six of us were carrying a log on the bridge with hand-sticks General Jackson was standing on the bridge, with his back toward us, directly in our way. As we were turning to one side to pass around him he noticed us and, quickly stepping to one side, said: "Oh! come on, never mind me," as if he were somebody of small importance.

Those few words and the farewell address that I have mentioned were the only words I ever heard him speak during the whole of his military career. I have often been close to him, just before, during and after a battle, and have seen couriers bring dispatches to him which he would read, write out something, hand it back to them and not open his mouth to speak during the time. I have seen some of his aids and staff officers ride up to him when he was sitting on the "little sorrel'" viewing the country and tell him something about the lines, or about something of importance, and he would calmly sit there for a few moments, then turn his horse and ride slowly away, his staff following, without his uttering a single word.

Such was Stonewall Jackson; a man of few words. He was not a man of moods, but always the same. He kept his own counsel. Jim, his cook and camp servant, knew as much of his intentions as anybody. He said whenever Jackson got up at night and commenced to pray, he immediately packed his haversack. "Cos den I knowed dere wuz a move on hand," he would say.

But the soldiers loved him. Every time he would pass our brigade, we would all commence cheering him, to see him raise his cap, show his high, bold forehead, and go dashing by in a gallop. No matter whether it was raining or snowing, the cap would be raised and kept off until he had passed the whole line.

It got to be a common saying in the army, when any cheering was heard in camp or on the march, that it was either "Jackson or a rabbit."

While we were repairing the bridge, we heard heavy firing on our right; but that did not disturb us, as some portion of our army was engaged every day. We did not move, however, until the 29th.

McClellan would fall back every night, and we would overtake his rear every evening when there would be some fighting done by some portion of the army. We had a considerable battle at Savage Station, where McClellan destroyed an immense amount of commissary stores, etc. I have seen molasses knee deep in the railroad ditch, and great piles of burnt coffee. Some of it was burnt too much for use, but some was scorched just enough to be good, and we went for it "heavy."

We, that is our brigade, had no general engagement until the 1st of July, when both armies met on Malvern Hill, where a desperate battle was fought. Our troops charged and recharged, and finally gained the field at dark; that was all. We could not rout them and it was with heavy loss that we gained a victory. The enemy had a good position, bristling with bayonets and plenty of artillery. They threw some shells over from their gun-boats about the size of camp-kettles, but as they were as likely to light among their own troops as ours, they soon ceased. Dark put an end to the fight, when the enemy fell back under cover of their gun-boats, and we could advance no farther.

Colonel Grigsby, of the 27th Virginia, was wounded in the shoulder, and while some of us were at a spring that evening getting some water he came along and wanted some water poured on his wound.

One of the boys says: "Colonel, does it hurt?"

"Yes, damn it," says he, "it was put in there to hurt."

The 3rd day of July we marched down to Harrison's Landing, on the James River, and while on the march I had a chill. I had not had a chill for nearly two years; but being down in the Chickahominy swamps caused it, I suppose. I lay down in a fence corner and rolled my blanket around me and was making the best of it I could.

The whole army had passed, and I had lain there several hours in a kind of stupor. Now the wagon train was passing. Hundreds of wagons, ambulances and artillery had passed and I never looked up. All at once I thought I had better draw my feet up, as I was working down in the road too far. Just as I did so, from some cause, the wagon wheels went right along where my feet had been. If I had not drawn them up as quick as I did both legs, just above my ankles, would have been crushed off by a heavy ordnance wagon. It was one of the most providential things I ever heard of, for hundreds of wagons had passed and I had never even given them a thought. If this one had kept in the track it would not have hurt me if I had let my feet remain; but the mules shied at something and ran the wagon upon my side and I had not moved one minute too soon. After the fever passed off some I got up and toddled on to my regiment. They had not gone many miles and were in camp.

The next day, the 4th of July, we lay in line of battle all day, my regiment being on picket; but not a shot was fired. The post I was on was in the woods, and in front of us was an open field; beyond the field were woods, and the enemy was on picket there. This field was full of blackberries; so, our boys and the "Yanks" made a bargain not to fire at each other, and went out in the field, leaving one man on each post with the arms, and gathered berries together and talked over the fight, traded tobacco and coffee and exchanged newspapers as peacefully and kindly as if they had not been engaged for the last seven days in butchering one another.

I was not well, and felt badly and did not go out with them, but remained on post. At the battle of Cold Harbor, as we charged across a swamp, the mud was about one foot deep, and my shoes got full of mud and gravel, and, being new and stiff, as all army shoes are, they rubbed all the skin off of my heels. My feet hurt me so much that night that I pulled my shoes off, and my feet were so sore the next morning that I could not get them on, so I had to go barefooted during that campaign. It was not for the want of shoes, however, for I could have picked up a good pair every day, as the whole country was full of knapsacks, blankets, etc.

As we had left our knapsacks behind at the commencement of the fight, we would gather up some blankets, sleep on them at night and leave them there in the morning. One morning, as it was a little rainy, I put on a blue blouse, and that evening was on the skirmish line. As we were going through a piece of woods, I thought I had better pull off my blue blouse, as I might be taken for the enemy by some "Johnnie Reb" and popped over. So, I took it off and hung it on a bush, never thinking of a fine *meerschaum* pipe I had left in the pocket until too late to go back for it; but I suppose someone got it that knew how to appreciate it.

While on this skirmish I saw a man in a kneeling position, as if in the act of firing; but upon closer examination he did not appear to have any gun. As no one was firing just then I thought strange of his position; but as I went up to him, I found him dead. He had been killed the day before, and so suddenly that he remained in the same position as when living—one knee and one foot on the ground, his arms in position of taking aim, but the gun had fallen and his head was thrown a little back.

The night after the Battle of Malvern Hill I was on a detail to guard some ordnance wagons that we had captured and which were packed together. There was a guard put around them simply to keep any one from going amongst them with fire. It was late at night when I went on post, and, being very tired, I quit walking my beat and sat down.

Directly the sentinel on the next post came to me and says: "Soldier, you must not sit down on your post, it is against orders."

I told him I knew the orders. I got up and walked a few rounds and again sat down on a stump.

He soon came to me again and says: "Soldier, indeed, you must not sit down on your post; if the officer of the guard finds you, he will punish you, and if you go to sleep you will be shot."

"Look here," says I, "what regiment do you belong to?"

"The 47th Alabama," he replied.

"How long have you been in service?"

"But a short time," said he. "Our regiment and the 48th Alabama came to Richmond a few days ago and drew arms that you fellows had captured at Cold Harbor and we were put in General Jackson's division. We have been in 'nary fight yet."

"Well," I remarked, "I thought you were some new recruit and did not know how to play off when you were on camp guard. We old soldiers sit down on our posts on camp guard every time we have a chance and signal to one another, by whistling, when the officer or relief is coming. I never go to sleep on my post; but camp guard is different from a picket post next to the enemy. So, you just go along and walk your beat as much as you want to and I will attend to mine as I please."

With that he left me and did not bother me anymore; but every few turns he would walk up close enough to see if I was asleep.

The 5th of July we left Harrison's Landing and marched back towards Richmond and went into camp three miles from the city; drew new clothing, washed up, and cleaned our arms. Thus, ended the seven days' fight at Richmond; and instead of General McClellan capturing the city, he was compelled to seek shelter under cover of his gunboats with the remnant of a demoralised army, and the loss of thousands in killed, wounded and prisoners, besides a great amount of army stores.

CHAPTER 10

General Winder

Stonewall Jackson's Corps, including his old brigade, at the close of the seven days' fight, returned from Harrison's Landing to within three miles of Richmond and went into camp. On the evening of the second day after our arrival Charley French, my dog-tent messmate, and myself got passes to spend the next day in Richmond. Neither of us had ever been in Richmond and we intended to make a day of it. But when morning came, we had orders to march to Richmond sure enough; but it was for the whole corps. We marched there and took the cars for Louisa Court House. That was the only time I was in Richmond during the war.

When we arrived at Louisa Court House we went into camp near town. The next day Tom Powell and myself got a pass from our captain to go out in the country and "forage" for something good to eat. So, we travelled around the country, stopping at farmhouses, and, finally, got a good dinner, and there heard that at the next station, a short distance off, there was a store where they kept whiskey for sale. We then sallied forth, thinking we would get our canteens full to take to camp. When we arrived at the place, the merchant told us he had some whiskey to sell, but that General Jones was making his headquarters at his house, and had forbidden him to sell any to soldiers without an order from him. I asked him what Jones it was, when he replied, "General J. R. Jones, of the 2nd Brigade." Now we were personally acquainted with General Jones, for he had been Captain and afterwards Lieutenant-Colonel of our regiment. I then studied up a plan to get the whiskey. I told him to conduct me to General Jones' room, which he did.

Upon entering his presence, I saluted him, and he recognised me and enquired my business. I then said, "General, I have a pass here from my captain for this day in order to procure some extra rations, and he told me if I found any whiskey in my rounds to bring him a canteen full to camp. The gentleman here says he has some, but cannot let me have any without your orders, and I would like to have your consent."

He looked at me a few moments, and, knowing my captain was quite fond of a dram, he said: "Now, you are not telling me a lie, are you, in order to get it for yourself? You are certain your captain will get it?"

"O, no, I am not lying, General; I will deliver it safely," I replied.

Then, addressing the merchant, he told him to let me have a canteen full. I asked him if he could not let us have two canteens full.

"No," says he, "that is enough, and I will ask Captain Grace the next time I see him if you delivered it safely."

We then got the whiskey and tried to get the merchant to fill the other canteen, but it was "no go." We each got an extra dram from him, and that was all; but Captain Grace nor anyone else ever saw or heard anything of that canteen of whiskey.

I was afraid for a long time that General Jones would ask my captain about it, but he never did. Sometime afterwards I told my captain how I had run the blockade for a canteen of whiskey on his responsibility, but he just laughed at the trick.

After leaving Jones's headquarters we started for camp. On the way we met with a very clever farmer, who sold us a nice ham, some lard and butter, and invited us to stay all night, which we concluded to do, and were treated very kindly. After breakfast the next morning we went to camp and found the brigade had marched towards Gordonsville about one-half hour before we arrived. Some of the boys had put our guns in the wagon, but our knapsacks, full of nice things that we had gotten at the Richmond fight, were carried off by some stragglers, which we regretted very much.

We soon followed the brigade up the railroad towards Gordonsville, and before overtaking it a train of cars passed us loaded with wounded from Richmond which were being taken to Staunton. As it was running very slowly, we jumped aboard and rode to Gordonsville and got there ahead of the brigade. While we were in a house getting our dinner, the brigade marched through town and went into camp about one mile beyond.

General Winder, commanding our brigade, had issued orders that morning that when the regiments halted to camp, and stacked arms, the roll should be called, and all who were absent should be bucked the next day from sunrise to sunset; that he was determined to break up straggling in the brigade. As I and my friend Powell were not there in time to answer to rollcall, we were included in the number to be bucked.

Now, bucking a soldier is tying his hands together at the wrists and slipping them down over his knees and then running a stick through under the knees and over the arms. Gagging is placing a bayonet in the mouth and tying it with a string behind his neck.

Some of the officers complained to General Winder about the severity of the order and tried to get him to revoke it; but it was no use—it had to be done. Accordingly, about thirty belonging to the brigade were taken out in the woods the next morning, placed under guard, and bucked from sunrise to sunset. It was a tiresome and painful situation, as we had to sit cramped up all day in one position, and if a fellow happened to fall over one of the guards would have to sit him up.

We were all as mad as fury about it, for it was a punishment that had never been inflicted in our brigade before. That night, after we were released, about one-half of the number deserted.

We marched the next day a short distance, but I would not "fall in ranks." I told my captain I did not intend to answer to roll call that evening, and if I was bucked again for straggling it would be the last time; that I would never shoulder my musket again for a cause that would treat soldiers in that manner.

Some of the officers then went to General Jackson and made complaint about Winder's order. He sent Winder word that he did not want to hear of any more bucking in that brigade for straggling. That was the last of it, and the only time it was ever done. General Winder would often have some of the men tied up by the thumbs at his headquarters all day for some small offense.

He was a good general and a brave man, and knew how to handle troops in battle; but was very severe, and very tyrannical, so much so that he was "spotted" by some of the brigade; and we could hear it remarked by someone near every day that the next fight we got into would be the last for Winder. So, it proved; for in a short time we fought the Battle of Cedar Run, or Slaughter Mountain, and General Winder was killed. But he was killed by a shell from the enemy before the brigade was engaged.

We lay in camp near Gordonsville about three weeks, nothing of interest transpiring, but all taking a good rest after our severe campaigns. From the time we left Swift Run Gap, about the first of May, we had marched hundreds of miles and fought seven general battles, *viz*.: McDowell, Front Royal, Winchester, Cross Keys, Port Republic, Cold Harbor and Malvern Hill, besides some smaller engagements and skirmishes, and had defeated and demoralised four separate armies, *viz*.: Milroy's, Banks', Fremont's and Shield's; had cleared the whole Valley of the enemy and assisted General Lee to defeat McClellan and banish the foe from before Richmond. We had remained in no camp over three days at one time until we reached Gordonsville; but had marched and fought the enemy, often marching all night and often through rain and mud, and never, during that time, did General Jackson have over twenty thousand men, and often not that. History does not record more brilliant campaigns within the short period of a little over two months than those of "Stonewall" Jackson.

We had in the Army of Northern Virginia General "Stonewall" Jackson, Generals A. P. Hill and D. H. Hill, General Early, General Pickett and General Longstreet. So, we would tell the enemy, or send them word, that before they could capture Richmond they would have to wake up "Early," charge the "Pickett," have two big "Hills" to climb, a "Longstreet" to pass through and a "Stonewall" to batter down, and that they would find it a hard road to travel.

While in camp near Gordonsville we heard that General Pope, from the West, had taken command of the Federal Army, and that he was going to Richmond sure. He was going to show us how to fight; that he had never seen anything but the back of a Rebel yet, and would head his dispatches, "Headquarters in the Saddle." I heard that General Jackson sent him word that it was "strange that a general would have his headquarters where his hindquarters ought to be."

We had been victorious in so many battles that the boys were rather anxious to meet General Pope; and we could hear it remarked in camp, "Just wait Hill Old Jack gets a chance at him; he'll take some of the starch out of him."

We did not have long to wait, for we soon heard that he was advancing on us and had crossed the Rappahannock River, and was in Culpeper county. On the 8th of August we left camp, marched toward the enemy, passed through Orange Court House, crossed the Rapidan river and went into camp about one mile beyond. The day was hot and several men dropped dead in ranks from sunstroke.

The next morning, we were on the march and soon heard some skirmishing. We still advanced until about 12 o'clock, when we filed out of the road to the left and were formed in line of battle in a piece of woods and halted. We had not been there long before the artillery opened out on both sides and shells rattled through the woods over our heads very lively. We advanced in line slowly for some distance and could hear the infantry at it on our right as if heavily engaged. In a few moments we reached an open field with woods on each side. As we entered it the right and left of our brigade extended into the woods. My regiment being on the right was partly in the woods. When we were about half way across the field, we met the enemy's line lying down behind a small slope. We commenced firing and advancing—the enemy returning the fire—but as our line on the left was about one regiment longer than theirs the brigade kept on advancing and coming around on a wheel.

The first line of the enemy fell back on the second; and as our regiment reached the edge of the woods, we came to a wheat field that was cut and shocked. There the firing was very heavy. We halted at the fence, when Major Holliday, commanding the regiment, ordered us several times to advance, and, as we were slow getting over the fence, he says: "Get over the fence with the colours and I know the men will follow." The colour bearer sprang over, and the whole regiment at the same time. The colour bearer was shot down; but the colours did not more than touch the ground before they were up again.

Major Holliday lost his arm and was taken to the rear. We had severe fighting for a short time, when the enemy broke. An officer came dashing down between the lines to rally them and was riddled with bullets. He was a lieutenant-colonel, I know, for I took particular notice of his shoulder straps a few minutes afterwards; they were such beautiful ones, with silver leaf.

★★★★★★

Lieutenant Colonel Louis H. D. Crane, 3rd Regiment Wisconsin Infantry, was killed August 9, 1862, at the Battle of Cedar Mountain, Va., falling from his dark claybank horse inside the fence in the wheat field. The extreme right of Union Army that day was 27th Indiana Infantry; next, 3rd Wisconsin Infantry, then the 2nd Massachusetts Infantry.

Most respectfully yours,

W. N. Thomas,
Formerly Company H, 3rd Regiment Wisconsin Infantry.

✶✶✶✶✶✶

We pursued the enemy two miles, until dark, and lay in line all night. At one time we received a shower of shells from the enemy, but we did not reply.

So ended the 9th of August, 1862, and the Battle of Cedar Run, and Mr. Pope had a chance to see the faces of the "Johnnie Rebs," but would rather have seen their backs.

Our Brigadier General, C. S. Winder, heretofore referred to, was commanding our division in this battle, and in the commencement of the fight was riding forward, giving some instructions to a battery, when he was mortally wounded by a shell from the enemy and died in a short time. I saw him as he was carried back by the brigade on a stretcher. His death was not much lamented by the brigade, for it probably saved some of them the trouble of carrying out their threats to kill him. I would not have done it had I the chance; but I firmly believe it would have been done by someone in that battle.

The next day the army was marched back to the rear a short distance and went into camp. Everything was quiet, our cavalry being deployed in front. A detail was made to bury the dead and gather up the guns, etc. I was on the gun detail. We gathered them up, loaded them in wagons and started them to the rear.

Just as we were starting for camp some soldiers, who were straggling over the battle field, commenced running and saying the Yankee cavalry was charging. We looked and saw them coming, and for a few moments it caused quite a stampede; but it turned out to be a flag of truce come to bury the dead and get the wounded. But as we went to camp, we found the stampede had gained strength as it went; we found wagons hitched up and pulling for the rear, and the troops out in line of battle; but it was soon settled down.

General Jackson fought this battle with his corps, and he gave General Pope a foretaste of what was to follow if he remained in Virginia long. We remained here two days and then marched back to our old camp near Gordonsville, and General Pope fell back across the Rappahannock.

Chapter 11

On the Rappahannock

The enemy, being heavily reinforced, commenced advancing their cavalry again, and had got as far as Orange Court House when General Lee came on from Richmond with the whole army.

On the 20th of August we again took up the line of march and crossed the Rapidan River and went on to the Rappahannock. We lay along the south bank, while the enemy occupied the north bank of the river. A continual firing, by both infantry and artillery, was kept up, each army trying to cross, or making believe they were trying to, and each army failed in every attempt, until one morning General Jackson started to the rear with his corps.

As we passed through a small village, we were ordered to leave our knapsacks in some vacant building with men to guard them. We then knew what was up the same as if "Stonewall" had told us. It simply meant a "forced march and a flank movement." We then turned our course westward up the Rappahannock, and, after marching some distance, crossed the river and turned east towards Alexandria. After marching two days and nights, with very little rest, we struck the Orange and Alexandria railroad, at Bristoe Station; captured several trains of cars, and, leaving General Ewell's Division there, went a few miles to Manassas Junction, where we captured several more trains, a large amount of commissary stores and several sutlers. We also dispersed and captured a brigade of the enemy that was guarding that point.

We were now completely in General Pope's rear, and between his army and Washington City. General Lee, with the greater portion of our army, was in his front at the river. We had no wagon train with us except ordnance wagons, medical wagons and ambulances.

We had started with but three days' rations, and if we had failed to make those captures, we would have been in a barren country without rations. We remained there all day loading ourselves with provisions. The soldiers were at liberty to take all they wanted except the sutler stores, which were kept under guard for the officers. But we would form in a solid mass around the tents and commence pushing one another towards the centre until the guard, who was not very particular about it, would give way, and then we would make the good things fly for a short time, until some officer would ride up with more guards and disperse us. We kept this up until we had gobbled up nearly everything, when we would look around for fresh supplies.

I went to the commissary building, which was full of army rations up to the roof. I soon found, in one corner of the second storey, a room filled with officers' rations and several soldiers supplying themselves with coffee, sugar, molasses, etc. When we had appropriated all we could carry, we found a barrel of whiskey, which we soon tapped; but as we had our canteens full of molasses, and our tin cups full of

"Stonewall" Brigade at Malvern Hill, July 1st, 1862.

sugar, we had nothing to drink out of. We soon found an old funnel, however, and while one would hold his hand over the bottom of it another would draw it full. In this way it was passed around. But the officers soon found us out and broke up that game.

We then sallied forth in quest of more plunder, and went to the captured trains of cars. They were loaded with everything belonging to an army—such as ammunition for infantry and artillery, harness, tents, blankets, clothing, hospital stores, and several loads of coffins for officers to be sent home in (we didn't want them), and one car was loaded with medical stores in boxes. Here we found something we did want, for each box had stored away in it from four to eight bottles of fine brandy and whiskey. We soon commenced tearing them to pieces, throwing the medicine around in every direction in search of bottles. I squeezed into the car among a number of others and got a box opened and found eight bottles of brandy in it. I then told a comrade at the car door that as I got them, I would pass the bottles to him and he should hide them away and we would divide.

Our surgeons, seeing that it was a medical car, came up and begged us to save the morphine and chloroform, as they were scarce articles in our army and they would greatly need them in the coming battle. But we paid no heed to their entreaties, telling them that we had no use for medicine. They then rode off and informed General Jackson how affairs stood. He then ordered the guard to disperse us and save the medicines. I had just passed my chum four bottles when some officer came with a guard to rout us out. I slipped the other four under my jacket. As I was passing out of the car door someone jammed me against the side of the car and broke one of my bottles; but I escaped with three. I met my partner outside, but the guard had relieved him of his four. We then went to the regiment, where I divided two of them with my captain and the company, keeping one for myself.

We now heard firing up the railroad, where we had left General Ewell, and soon learned that General Pope was coming down on us with his army like an avalanche. We remained there until dark, when we had orders to burn up everything that was left, which was soon done. When the ammunition cars got on fire they made as great a racket as if a big battle was going on. General Jackson then started on the march to the old battle ground of Bull Run.

We had had a great day of plundering and eating, and I was somewhat tired. So, after marching some distance, I lay down in a fence corner and went to sleep; but was soon roused up by the rear guard, who told me if I did not want to be captured that I had better go on, as the enemy would soon be there. I then marched on and soon came to where the roads forked. Some troops had taken one road and some the other, and I could not find out which one my brigade had taken; but I took one of the roads and reached Centerville a little after daylight. I found that my brigade had taken the other road and was a few miles west of Centerville, near Sudley church. I then started for my command, and had gone about one mile when one of our cavalrymen came dashing by leading a mule and said to me: "The Yankee cavalry are in Centerville and if you don't want to be captured jump on this mule," which I was glad to do, and we went up the road as fast as the mules could carry us.

I had a big load of provisions and five or six pounds of coffee, roasted and ground, tied up in a piece of old coffee sack, tied to my gun. In my ride it came loose and I lost it all.

I also had a fine silver watch, and, on looking for it, found it was gone. As the enemy did not appear to be following, I told the cavalryman to halt and I would dismount; that by riding in that style I would lose all my "commissary," which I could not afford to do in so critical a time, as we knew not where the next was to come from. But upon looking around I found my watch down next to my belt between my fatigue shirt and undershirt. It had got loose from the chain and slipped through the pocket in my fatigue shirt and my cartridge belt being tight had saved it.

I write thus particularly now that it may be seen to what straits we were put to in emergencies and what means were resorted to by the soldier in the field upon occasions. Such an appearance as I presented would be ludicrous enough could it be witnessed in these "piping times of peace."

I arrived at the brigade safely, with no loss but my coffee, which I had treasured very highly, as genuine coffee was a rarity for a Johnnie Reb. I found my division in line of battle in an old field, and some skirmishing going on in front. General Jackson had taken his position and was waiting for the enemy. They came up in fine style about 3 o'clock p. m., when we opened fire on them. We had a terrible fight, which lasted until 9 o'clock at night, neither party giving back, but remaining as we had commenced, and being guided in our firing by the flash of the other's guns. But the firing gradually ceased, each army retaining the same position as before. My brigade was behind an old fence, and would lie down, load and fire, and it seemed that everyone who would raise up was shot.

We lost severely. My company had but seventeen men in the fight, and we lost five killed and mortally wounded, five severely wounded and one missing, who was supposed to be killed, for he never turned up afterward nor was he ever heard of after the war. The whole brigade lost in the same proportion. Colonel Neff, of my regiment, was killed, and Lieutenant Joseph Earsome, of my company, was mortally wounded. He had just been transferred from the 2nd Regiment to ours. General Ewell lost a leg, and our loss in officers was great.

We carried the wounded back that night a short distance to a piece of woods. Major F. W. M. Holliday had been wounded at Cedar Run; Lieutenant Colonel Edwin G. Lee was absent sick, and Colonel Neff being killed, it left us without a field officer. Captain Grace of my company being the oldest officer, took command of the regiment. We had our old wheel horse, "Stonewall" left, and knew he could manage affairs.

The next morning the enemy was gone from our front, but had only changed position, and skirmishing soon commenced. My captain told me to get Lieutenant Earsome, who was shot through the bowels, into an ambulance and take him to the hospital at Sudley church, which I did. After going a short distance, he said he could not stand the jolting of the ambulance and wanted us to take him out. We did so, and, making a stretcher out of two rails and a blanket, four of us started to carry him on our shoulders, but soon met the ambulances and wounded coming back in a hurry, saying the enemy was at Sudley and we would have to go in another direction.

After going to the rear, as we thought, some distance, the enemy suddenly ran a battery up on a hill in front of us and commenced shelling. I told the other boys that we would stop and rest until we found where the rear was, if there was any rear, as the enemy appeared to be on three sides of us, and, perhaps, would soon be on the fourth; but we soon saw a yellow flag hoisted to denote a hospital, and we went to it. I then got a surgeon to examine the lieutenant's wound. When he had done so, he said that he was shot through and through and his entrails were cut; that he could not live and he could do nothing for him.

As I was a particular friend of his, he asked me to remain with him and take care of him until he died, as he knew he could not live.

I told him I would like to do so, but could not do it without permission from the captain. He begged me to go and see the captain, as he knew his dying request would be granted.

I immediately did so, when my captain said: "Certainly, remain with him; and when he dies bury him and join the company."

I went back to him and did all I could for him, but he suffered terribly; he could not lie still, but was up and down continually, and I worried with him all day and all night. The next morning, he died, when I buried him as decently as I could and then joined my regiment.

There had been some fighting the day previous, but no general engagement, as General Jackson wanted to hold his position and keep off a general battle until General Lee should arrive with the balance of the army. As Lee was following General Pope's army, and had to pass through Thoroughfare Gap, a gorge in the mountain, and his passage was disputed by the enemy, he was kept back some time. Our condition appeared critical, indeed, for we had lost severely and were being hemmed in on all three sides by nearly the whole army of the enemy; our retreat cut off, and no assistance possible until Lee and Longstreet could arrive. But the way was forced, and we could see clouds of dust rising up between us and the mountain and we knew assistance was at hand if we could hold out a little longer. Soon cheer after cheer rent the air as General Longstreet arrived and straightened out the line on our right.

The night was spent in forming troops. Our division was formed along the line of the Alexandria, Loudoun and Hampshire railroad, which had been graded before the war, but never finished, and served as a breastwork. At daylight on the third day skirmishing commenced and was kept up, but the firing increased as brigade after brigade became engaged, until about 3 o'clock p. m., when the whole line on both sides became heavily engaged. It was one continuous roar from right to left. My brigade was in a small cut, with a field in front sloping down about four hundred yards to a piece of wood.

The enemy would form in the woods and come up the slope in three lines as regular as if on drill, and we would pour volley after volley into them as they came; but they would still advance until within a few yards of us, when they would break and fall back to the woods, where they would rally and come again. They charged in this manner three times, and the third time, as they broke, we were ordered to charge, and as Longstreet's corps had turned their left, our whole line charged and the rout became general.

But the stone bridge over Bull Run became blocked up with artillery and caissons, and we could not cross with our artillery; and as it

General R. E. Lee

was getting dark, this put an end to the conflict. If we could have had a few hours more of daylight they would never have been able to rally until they reached Alexandria. It was a terrible battle, and both sides lost severely. The slope in front of us was covered with dead, dying and wounded; but my brigade lost but few, as we were protected by the railroad. Thus, ended the Second Battle of Manassas, the 28th, 29th and 30th days of August, 1862.

General W. S. H. Baylor, commanding the brigade, formerly Colonel of the 5th Virginia, was killed the evening of the third days' fight, in the railroad cut. He had just grabbed the colours of the 33rd Virginia from the dead colour-bearer and was rushing to the front. Colonel C. A. Ronald, of the 4th Virginia, took command of the brigade, and Captain P. T. Grace took command of the 33rd Regiment.

Charles Arnall, of Staunton, Va., and who was General W. S. H. Baylor's Adjutant and Chief of Staff, but now (1906) living in Atlanta, Ga., tore the flag of the 33rd Virginia from the staff that General Baylor was holding when killed, replaced it with a new one, and still has that flag, and has it on exhibition at the Confederate Reunions.

CHAPTER 12

Lee Crosses into Maryland

The next day after the battle the enemy came up with a flag of truce and a long train of ambulances to get their wounded. A few hours were granted them; and they gathered up all they could take and left. We gathered up the dead by wagon loads and threw them into a cut in the railroad—hundreds together.

I must here relate an incident that happened during this campaign, which, probably, has never before been recorded. Before we left Gordonsville, we had a general court-martial, and among the prisoners to be punished for desertion there were four to be shot from our division, three belonging to the 10th Virginia, in the 3rd Brigade, and one to the 5th Virginia, in my brigade. They were the first that had been sentenced to be shot for desertion in our division. While on the march, as we went into camp for the night near "Pisgah Church," in Orange County, their sentences were read to them. They were to be executed the next day; but in the night one of the doomed men, belonging to the 10th Virginia, by the name of Rothgeb, broke through the guard and ran for dear life and made his escape to the enemy, who were close by. The others were taken out the next day and executed;

The Barrel Shirt.

Is this soldier doing this for fun? Not much, he ain't. He was absent from camp without leave and came back drunk. The Colonel thinks this will sober him.

Tied Up By the Thumbs.

The way of the transgressor is hard.

Carrying the Rail.

Been absent without leave, and sentenced to carry the rail eight hours under guard.

Bucked and Gagged.

after which we resumed our march. In the battle of Manassas, which soon came off, all three of the officers who composed the court-martial were killed or mortally wounded (my colonel, A. J. Neff, being one of the number), and most of the soldiers looked upon it as a judgment.

But no one cast any reflections upon our colonel, for he was a splendid officer, a gallant man and always treated us with respect and kindness. He was greatly beloved by the whole regiment, and his death was much lamented.

The next year General Lee issued a general order, reciting, I think, a proclamation, pardoning all absentees and deserters who would return to their commands in thirty days. Then this man Rothgeb returned and was pardoned; but in a short time, he deserted again. He was afterwards arrested, but as the guards were taking him to Richmond to be placed in Castle Thunder he jumped from the cars while they were running at full speed and made his escape the second time, and remained North until the war closed, when he came home.

After this severe campaign and the Battles of Manassas I found myself completely used up. I had slept but little for six days and nights, and was suffering with sore feet and haemorrhoids. I had been worrying night and day with my lieutenant, who died, and could go no further. I, therefore, reported to our surgeon, as the army started on the march again, and he sent me to the field hospital near the battle ground. When I got there, I found a great many tents filled with sick and wounded—more than the surgeons and nurses could attend to. I thought it was a poor place to recruit; but upon looking around I found a great many farmers there with their wagons, who brought in supplies for the wounded, such as butter, milk, chickens, vegetables, etc. As one of them, a fatherly-looking old man, was about starting home I went to him and told him my condition and asked him if he would not take me home with him and take care of me until I got well. He was much pleased to do so, and would willingly have taken a wagon load if the doctors would consent to it; but the wounded had to remain in their charge until properly cared for.

I proceeded home with my farmer, whose name was Lee. He lived about ten miles from the hospital in Loudoun County. He and his family treated me very kindly and gave me every attention. In about a week I felt like a new man. General Lee's army had crossed the Potomac into Maryland, and as none of our troops except a few cavalry were in this part of Virginia it was open to the enemy from Alexandria, and the sick and wounded were being removed to Winchester.

After remaining at my friend Lee's ten days, I went to the hospital at Aldie, and was sent from there to Winchester, but was as well as ever. When we were within a few miles of Winchester I left the main road, "flanked" around Winchester and went home. I remained at home until General Lee's army came back from Maryland into Virginia, and camped a few miles north of Winchester at a small place called Bunker's Hill, when I left home and reported to my regiment.

A few days after the Manassas battle part of our army had a short, but hard, engagement with the enemy at Ox Hill, or Chantilly, on the Little River turnpike.

It was in this battle, and inside our lines, that General Philip Kearney, a Federal general, spoken of in both armies as "Brave Phil Kearney," was killed. The Southern soldiers had so much respect for him that his body was wrapped in a captured United States flag and sent to their lines after the battle.

The army then crossed the Potomac into Maryland, went to Frederick City and marched up the left bank of the Potomac; the enemy, under General McClellan, following. They had a considerable battle on the South Mountains and at Crampton's Gap, and afterwards a general engagement at Antietam, or Sharpsburg, on the 17th of September. General Starks, Brigadier General of the Louisiana Brigade, was commanding the division and was killed. In the meantime, General Jackson surrounded the enemy at Harper's Ferry and compelled them to surrender, capturing a large quantity of artillery, wagons, army stores and eleven thousand prisoners, who were paroled on the ground for want of men to guard them to the rear. Jackson had to hurry back to Antietam to support Lee.

The Battle of Antietam was one of the severest battles of the war. The loss was very heavy on both sides; but neither army was defeated. General Lee did not fall back until the next night, when he fell back across the Potomac into Virginia. The Federal Army was too much crippled to follow. They claimed, however, a great victory; but General Lee would have been compelled to fall back into Virginia if he had defeated the enemy. His supplies were in Virginia, and he had but a small force in Maryland, as the greater portion of his army had been killed, wounded, or had straggled before crossing into Maryland. The country was covered with stragglers from Richmond to the Potomac on account of hard marching and hard fighting, and a few days after the battle in Maryland his army was larger than it was during the fight. If the enemy had followed him into Virginia he would have been repulsed. A considerable force of the enemy did attempt to cross the Potomac at Shepherdstown, and several brigades actually crossed, but were repulsed by General A. P. Hill with great slaughter.

We remained in the lower Valley of Virginia for some time, recruiting the army and making raids on the Baltimore and Ohio railroad, from above Martinsburg down to Harper's Ferry, destroying the road, burning the ties and bridges and that company's works at Martinsburg. After destroying the road, we would fall back to Bunker Hill, when the enemy would rebuild the road and get the cars to running. We would then make another raid and destroy it again; but no general engagement followed.

One time our brigade went down to the railroad to Kearneysville, a few miles south of Shepherdstown, and while we were destroying the track a division of the enemy came out from Shepherdstown and attacked us and we had to give up the job and fall back; but before we fell back we were formed in line of battle, and my company and Company "F" were put in a small redoubt near the station in advance of the line. When the line fell back, we had no orders to leave, and remained there until the enemy had crossed the railroad above and below us and were closing in on us in front, when we left without orders, and joined the brigade at double-quick. If we had stayed a few moments longer we would have been captured.

We then fell back about one mile, in a piece of woods, and took a stand and remained until dark, but the enemy did not attack us. We had several killed and wounded. Colonel Ronald, commanding the brigade, was wounded, when Colonel Grigsby, of the 27th Virginia, took command. We started back to camp at dark and went several miles. It rained in torrents and was so dark we could hardly get along. We finally camped in an old mill that accommodated the whole brigade; and the next morning went on to our old camp at Bunker Hill.

We remained in the lower valley for some time, moving about from place to place, nothing of interest transpiring. Colonel E. F. Paxton, of the 27th Regiment, was promoted to Brigadier General of the brigade; Lieutenant Colonel Lee was promoted to Colonel of my regiment; Major F. W. M. Holliday (afterwards Governor of Virginia) was promoted to Lieutenant Colonel, and Captain Grace (my captain) was promoted to Major; consequently, we had to have a new captain, and First Lieutenant William Powell was promoted to that rank.

About the 1st of December the whole army started on the march to Fredericksburg, as the enemy were moving in that direction from

Washington under the command of General Burnside, with another "On to Richmond." Major Grace's family being all sick or dying, he resigned and went home. The first day the army passed through Winchester and camped near Newtown, and, as usual, I stopped in Winchester and remained for the night.

The next morning as I was on my way to join the command, I met Sergeant M. Miller and Private W. A. Daily of my company. They informed me that eight men of our company had deserted that night and gone home to Hampshire, with the intention of mounting themselves and joining the cavalry, as they were determined not to go east of the Blue Ridge again, being tired of the *foot cavalry*. Consequently they (Miller and Daily) were detailed and supplied with written instructions to go to Hampshire County and try to persuade them and other absentees to return to their company, and to tell them if they would do so they would not be punished; but if they refused, they would be punished to the full extent of martial law.

Sergeant Miller wanted me to go along with them and be included in the detail. I was very anxious to do so, but was fearful I would get into trouble, but he assured me he would be responsible for my absence, when I readily consented to go. Now it was rather a critical undertaking for a small squad of Southern soldiers to go into Hampshire armed with rifles, in those days, as the county was in possession of the enemy, who were camped at Springfield and Romney, and who were scouting all over the country. Our absentees lived in and around Springfield; therefore, when we reached the borders of the county, we had to move cautiously, keeping to the byroads and woods as much as possible. But we succeeded very well, as we were raised there and knew every hog-path and knew who were Union men and who were Rebels.

We remained in that neighbourhood about two weeks, stopping at houses where we would be safe in the daytime and visiting the members of the company at night. In that manner we saw nearly all of them, but got but one man (Thomas McGraw) to consent to go back with us.

The Federals had told these absentees if they would remain at home peaceably and not go to bushwhacking, they would not molest them, for they knew if they arrested them and sent them to prison, they would be exchanged and put in ranks again; but if they did not molest them the probabilities were that they would remain at home.

Those absentees were all good soldiers, but they were tired of the infantry, and said they would do service in the cavalry; they knew as soon as General Jackson found out they had joined the cavalry he would send for them and have them brought back to the infantry, and they were determined never to do service in the infantry any more. If he would give them a transfer to cavalry they would go in service again; if not, they would remain at home or go across the lines. Therefore, we could do nothing with them, as we had no orders to arrest them, and could not have gotten out with them if we had.

So, we concluded to return to our company and report. But before we started back, I told the boys I must go into Springfield and see some of my old friends. We were stopping within two miles of town, and there was a company of Federal cavalry quartered in town (Captain Greenfield's company, 100 strong). They said I would be captured; but I told them I would risk it. I was wearing a blue overcoat and Mrs. Conley gave me a pair of blue pants, so I thought if I was seen by anyone I would be taken for a Yankee.

The weather was very cold, and about one hour before dark I slipped through the woods and posted myself on a high hill about one-half mile from town, and watched where they posted their pickets for the night.

There were two roads which led through the town, and they crossed in the centre at right angles. There was a picket post on each of the four roads a few hundred yards out of town. As it grew dark, I went down the hill, through an open field in the angle formed by the roads, until I came to the rear lot of Mr. John W. Shouse's house, got over the fence, went through the back yard and onto the porch, and there waited for developments.

I had heard that the officers and some of the privates were boarding with the citizens, and that I had better be careful how I entered a house. I listened for a few moments and then looked in at the window, and, seeing no one but the family, I cautiously opened the door and went in. Mrs. Shouse raised her hands in astonishment and was as much surprised as if one had arisen from the dead. Everyone in the town, both black and white, had known me from my childhood up. There were but one or two Union men in the place, and I was not afraid of them reporting me; neither was I afraid of the blacks; but still I did not want them to know I was there.

After I got in the first house, I felt safe. I could then lay my plans for seeing my friends, as I intended to stay all night and run the blockade before daylight. I conversed with the family a short time and then got

Miss Gennie Shouse to run across the street to the house of Mr. John Hawes, who lived in my old home, to see if the coast was clear. I then went over, for I wanted to see the house that I had spent most of my boyhood days in, not knowing whether I would ever see it again. I did not stay there long, however, for Mrs Hawes appeared so frightened for fear I would be captured; besides it made me feel sad, as the old house brought back to memory scenes of other days when all was joy and peace. To think that I had to sneak back like an outlaw, in the night, to look once more upon the scenes of my childhood, and then depart to the distant battlefield, and, perhaps, leave my bones bleaching in the sun, was too much. I had to leave.

I then went up the street a short distance to the residence of Mrs. Daily, whose son, William, was in the country waiting my return. They were glad to see me and hear from their son and brother. I will state that a Rebel soldier from "Lee's Army" was quite a curiosity in that place, for the enemy had possession of the country from the time the war commenced until it ended, except during some occasional raids made by our cavalry.

The next place I wanted to visit was the house of Mr. Uriah Blue, who had lost a son in our company; but he lived near the centre of the village, and I was told there was a sentinel a few yards from his house on the store porch. But I struck out down the street whistling "Yankee Doodle," and soon met the relief picket going out to the post in the west end of town. I passed on down, walking on the sidewalk, while they kept in the middle of the street.

As soon as I arrived at Mr. Blue's house I reconnoitred a short time and then went in. Mr. Blue told me that a Federal officer had just left his house a few moments before I came. I was perfectly lionised by the family. I had intended to go to Mr. James Kuykendall's house, but learned there were five or six Yankees in there spending the evening, so I concluded it might not be agreeable to all concerned, and remained where I was. But Mr. K's family all came to see me, one at a time, as it was only a few doors away, and so were able to entertain their company at the same time.

It was now getting late, and I concluded to go to Mr. Jacob Grace's (my captain's father) house and spend the remainder of the night. His residence was the last house in the lower end of the town; so, when I left Blue's I went through the back lots and down the back street, then up through the garden to the house. There was a back porch to the house, and I knew the family stayed in the dining room in the wing building. I boldly stepped onto the porch and was about to enter when I thought I had better be careful, as there might be someone in there whom I did not care to see. So, I took off my shoes, slipped up to the window, sat down on a bench and listened. The window was down and I could not see in; but after listening for some time I found out that Mr. Yankee was in there. As it was very cold, I went into the hall of the main building and sat down about halfway up the stairs in order to retreat further up if necessary.

After sitting there some time I heard someone come into the yard and go to the well and draw some water; at the same time, I heard the dining-room door open and shut; but as no one passed through the hall I thought they were all in there still. After waiting some time and getting very cold, I heard the door open and someone come out on the porch and into the hall. I then went further up the stairs. He passed through the hall, opened the front door, and shut it. I now thought my Yankee was gone and I would go down and entertain the family; but as soon as I started down the steps someone started up, so I wheeled and ran up the first flight of stairs and then on up the second flight to the garret. When at the turn of the stairs I fell over something and came down with considerable racket. Someone exclaimed, "Who's that?" I thought all the time that, perhaps, this Yankee boarded there and was coming upstairs to go to bed; but as soon as I was challenged, I knew the voice and felt safe. It was my captain's brother, Stephen W. Grace, about my own age and one of my old playmates.

I never answered him, but started downstairs, and he kept on hallooing to me making threats, so I made myself known. After a hearty handshaking I was conducted to the sitting room, where there was a nice warm fire in the fireplace, and his three sisters. Misses Amelia, Flora and Katie, and his father, who was an invalid, confined to his bed. Well! I then and there spent several hours, I think, as pleasantly as any I ever spent in my life, for the whole family were near and dear friends to our family. They then explained to me the mistake I had made in thinking the Yankee was leaving. He had been gone for some time; had left when the one came to the well for water, and had gone with him through the back yard while I was expecting him to go through the front door.

I intended leaving there that night and going back to where I left Miller and Daily; but they insisted on me staying all night and the next day and then go out the next night, as I could stay upstairs by a good fire and no one would know it. I concluded to do so, and Stephen and I went upstairs and retired for the night—but not to sleep. I believe we talked until daybreak. The next day I enjoyed myself hugely. I stayed upstairs all day. They brought my meals up to me, and informed friends where I was, so I was thronged with company all day.

But only one came at a time, in order to avoid suspicion. Several Yankees were in the house during the day. Some ate dinner there at the same time I was eating my dinner upstairs. About one hour after dark I bade farewell to my friends, and ran the blockade between the pickets, but by a different route from that by which I had come in. I arrived safely where the boys were, who had conjectured that I was captured, as I did not return the first night.

I ran a greater risk than I thought I was running at the time by having on the blue uniform of the enemy. If I had been captured by them in their camp I would have been hung as a spy, and there could have been no reprieve for it.

Chapter 13

Start Back to Lee's Army

The next day we started to go to our command, which we heard had fought the Battle of Fredericksburg, and was then in winter quarters below Fredericksburg, near Guinea Station, on the Richmond and Potomac railroad. As we were passing through the woods and came in sight of a road that led out from Springfield, about three miles from there, I told the boys to halt and I would go down to the road and see if the way was clear before we crossed. I passed on to the road. There was a high bank on one side, but as I did not see anyone, I jumped down the bank and came face to face with Double-Thumbed John Kerns, who was walking along close to the bank and coming from the Yankee camp. I knew in a moment I was caught, for I knew him to be one of those meddlesome Union men who took the trouble to report to the enemy everything he knew about the Rebels. I knew he would have every one of us arrested if he could, and I knew if I let him pass, he would have a squad of the enemy after us in two hours.

His life had been threatened several times for having the boys arrested and reporting the citizens, and I made sure he knew me, for he had known me from boyhood up. I was just revolving in my mind whether to kill him right there or call the other boys and take him in the woods and kill him, when a few words he uttered saved his life.

"Have you been out hunting?" he asked.

It struck me in a moment, from my having a blue overcoat on, he

Field Hospital at Bull Run, August 28, 1862.

had mistaken me for a Yankee from the camp out hunting, and I concluded to keep up the deception until I got rid of him.

"Yes," I replied, "But I find game scarce."

I asked him if he had been to camp. He said he had; he had taken some butter and eggs to sell, and got a good price from the boys.

I asked him what the boys were doing, and if any of them were out on the scout.

"No," he said, "they are all lying around doing nothing."

I then asked him if there were any Rebels about that he knew of.

"Oh, no," said he, "they are afraid to come in here now, except some who have run off from the army and are at home, and I can tell you where they all live if you want to arrest them."

"No, we do not want to bother them," I replied, "if they will stay at home and not bushwhack us."

I then asked him the time of day, and told him I must hurry on to camp, and be there in time for roll call, and left him.

As soon as he got out of sight I whistled for the boys and they came; they had heard me talking to someone, and when I told them who it was and what had transpired, they said we ought to have killed him anyhow; but I did not want to hurt him if it could be avoided in any way.

But he was a very meddlesome fellow and did a great deal of mischief in the neighbourhood without doing any good for himself. He had two thumbs on one hand, and was called "Double-Thumbed John Kerns." He was killed before the war was over by some Rebel for reporting.

We then proceeded on our way and when we reached Lost River, about one day's march from Springfield, we met Lieutenant Monroe Blue, belonging to General Imboden's Cavalry Brigade, with a small squad of soldiers. Lieutenant Blue formerly belonged to my company, but had left it and joined the cavalry and was elected lieutenant.

He said business was dull in their camp and he thought he would come down into Hampshire with a squad and gather up some more soldiers, and make a raid on the Yankees and stir them up and see what they were doing. He wanted us to go along with them, as they were going to leave their horses and go in on foot. He simply wanted to get near their camp and watch the road for some scouting parties from their camp, and capture them in order to get their horses; and all we captured would be divided equally among the men. We were just keen for a raid of that kind, but Sergeant Miller would not consent to go;

he would, however, give us liberty to go if we wished.

So, we arranged the plan, and were to meet at Mr. Ewer's, on top of South Branch mountain, about six miles east of Springfield, and be ready to start at daylight the next morning. Lieutenant Blue then left us, and said he would hunt up some more men. T. McGraw, W. Daily and myself then started for the place of rendezvous, leaving Miller behind to await our return or hear of our capture, as the case might be.

The next morning Lieutenant Blue made his appearance with a guide and scout (Ed. Montgomery) and we numbered in all fifteen, each one armed with a rifle and six-shooter. We then marched down the mountain in single file until we reached the river (the south branch of the Potomac), where we found a canoe and crossed. We then kept down the mountain, going north, aiming to get in rear of their camp. It was seven miles from Springfield to the Baltimore and Ohio railroad.

We knew the troops at Springfield and Romney got their supplies at the railroad, and we would aim to post ourselves about half way between the railroad and camp and capture all that passed.

We arrived at our point of destination about the middle of the day. There was a rail fence on each side of the road, and on the west side there was a small ravine with some scrubby pines. We divided our force, placing one-half at a point near the road, and the other half at a point also near the road, but about three hundred yards farther down. If a scouting party came along, going either north or south, the first party was to let them pass until halted by the other party and then run out behind them and cut off their retreat. In this manner we would bag our game; but if the enemy should be too strong for us to attack, we were to keep concealed and let them pass.

We had not been long in position when the lookout reported a wagon and team coming from the railroad, driven by one man. So, when he got in our trap two men stepped out and ordered him to halt, and opened the fence for him to drive in and ordered him to drive up the ravine out of sight, which he did. We then got around him in order to hear the news. The poor fellow was nearly scared to death; thought he had fallen into the hands of guerillas, and that his day had come; so he commenced praying and begging; but we soon assured him that he should not be hurt; that we were regular soldiers, out on a raid of our own get up; that all we wanted of him was all the information we could get, but if he did not tell us the truth he should surely die.

He then told us that he had been sent that morning to the railroad for a load of beef for the company, but as it did not come on the cars he had to return empty; that there were no scouting parties out that he knew of; that they did not scout much, as it was too cold; that he had left two cavalrymen at the depot and each one had a large sack of mail for the troops at Romney and they would be along in a short time; that the next day there would be five wagons leave camp and go up to Patterson's Creek, about eight miles west of camp, for hay; that there would be one man besides the driver in each wagon, and four or five cavalrymen as a guard, all armed with six-shooters, and they would leave camp about sun-up. He would not have to go, as he had gone that day to the depot.

In a few moments we saw the cavalrymen coming with the mail, and when they got into our trap, we told them to ride in, and we had a fine time plundering the mail and reading love letters to the boys in the army. We now had four horses and three prisoners. We would have paroled the prisoners, but had more work to do and were afraid to turn them loose. We did not want to be bothered with them and the horses on our next day's raid, so we concluded to send them back to the rear that night. Lieutenant Blue then detailed three men to take them back to Lost River and there wait until we came.

As soon as it was dark three men started with the three prisoners, four horses and the mail, and we started for the Frankfort road to be ready for the hay wagons the next day. We stayed all night with John Martin, who lived in a secluded place, put out a picket and passed the night comfortably.

Directly after daylight we were on the road, about four miles west of Springfield and two miles east of Frankfort. We divided in two squads, as on the day before. We held a little council of war as to the best method of procedure.

Ed. Montgomery said we should lay our trap and capture the whole outfit as they came from camp, and would have daylight to make our escape in, and they would not know anything of it in camp until evening, and we would be too far ahead for pursuit. I replied that that was all very good if we succeeded in capturing all, but if any escaped they would only have four miles to go, while we would have to make a circuit of about ten before we could cross the road leading from Springfield to Romney, and they could cut us off and capture us; that I thought we had better wait until they had got their hay and capture them on their return. We could then burn the wagons and have the night to go out in, and they could not trail us after dark. But we finally concluded to adopt Ed.'s plan, as our escapade of the day before would be found out before night and our plans foiled.

It was a cold, icy morning, with a light snow on the ground. We did not have long to wait. We soon heard the wagons coming, rattling over the frozen ground, and prepared for them. There were pine bushes on each side of the road. I was in the front squad and was to halt the train. Our object was to capture; we did not want to kill anyone or fire a gun if we could help it. Our plan was a good one and would have succeeded well if the wagons had been closed up; but they were scattered along the road for a quarter of a mile. There were three cavalrymen in advance, and when they got up to our post we ran out and halted them. One surrendered on the spot, but the other two wheeled and dashed into the pines and made their escape. Some of the boys fired at them, but did no harm. I grabbed the reins of the horse belonging to the one who had surrendered, dismounted and disarmed him, and was about to mount when Ed. Montgomery came running up and wanted to ride back to the rear to see what was going on.

As soon as we halted the advance the rear squad ran out and captured one cavalryman; but there were three wagons that did not get into the trap.

The wagoners, and all who were with them, jumped out and ran at the first fire and let the horses go; so, we had to run to the wagons in order to keep the horses from running off.

There were five wagons and four guards. We got two of the guards and twelve horses; the balance escaped. As one man was running across the road Lieutenant Blue shot at him and hit him in the arm. He then ran to where he was, tracking him by the blood, and found him in the pines; took his pistol and let him go.

We were now in a critical condition. We were in rear of their camp and had to make a considerable circuit to get out. We had to cross the river, and the main road leading from Springfield to Romney, a distance of nine miles, and then open country for two miles before we reached the mountains; and we knew they would soon have the news and be in hot pursuit. So, we mounted at once. There were twelve of us, and twelve horses; but only two saddles. The two prisoners we took on behind us.

We laid on the whip and went as hard as we could go over hill and hollow, through woods and fields, and never slackened up until we had crossed the river and the road leading to Romney. When we reached the foot of the mountain, we halted to fix the saddle-blankets and arrange the harness, which were still on the horses. I told the boys we had better get up the mountain side before we halted for fear of being surprised; but they thought we were safe from pursuit. We were sadly disappointed, however, for in a few moments the head of the pursuing column came dashing over the hill not one hundred yards off.

Part of our men were dismounted, but we soon galloped off as fast as we could go, the enemy yelling and firing at us as rapidly as possible. We soon came to a fence running along at the foot of the mountain, and nine of us rode up to it, when Daily threw off a few rails and we passed through and up the steep mountain side.

Lieutenant Blue, Montgomery and McGraw went to another place to get through, but just as they had succeeded in getting over the fence, and as Montgomery attempted to mount, his saddle turned. By this time the Yankees were upon them. They captured the three horses and McGraw. Lieutenant Blue and Montgomery ran and hid in the laurels and escaped.

At the first onset we had released the prisoners and told them to take care of themselves. The nine of us who were together went up the mountain through the brush as fast as we could go, the bullets rattling around us, and the Yankees in hot pursuit. We nearly all lost our hats, and Will Daily had his eye put out by a brush.

We had made no calculation for a fight after we captured the wagons. We knew our only chance was in flight; but if we had posted ourselves at the foot of the mountain we could have ambushed and repulsed them. We did not want to hurt anyone, nor get hurt ourselves, if we could avoid it. We had made a good capture and wanted to get away with our booty. As we got near the top of the mountain our pursuers fell behind, and we made sure the other three had been captured at the foot of the mountain.

The horse I was riding happened to be the oldest in the outfit, and gave out before we reached the top. I had to dismount and lead him. The other boys wanted to wait for me, but I told them to save themselves, and I would try to take care of myself the best I could. So, they went on as fast as possible. After reaching the top I came to an open field, and, seeing a thicket of pines off to my right, I thought I would hide my horse there and then hide myself until the storm had passed.

I went to the thicket and concealed the horse the best I could and then passed out. After going a short distance, I saw the trail where my companions had just passed along. I thought I was leaving the trail

Federal Soldiers Plundering Virginia Homes.

and had come back on it again; but it was too late then to go back and move the horse. Seeing a small house not far off I went to it, not knowing whether they were friends or foes. I went into the house and enquired how long since our boys had passed along.

"About half an hour," the man said dubiously.

I sat there a few minutes when the dog commenced barking. On looking out of the window I saw the blue coats coming over the hill. I jumped up instantly.

"Where will I hide?" I asked him.

"There is no place to hide here," he replied.

I knew then I was in the hands of a Union man. Seeing a door leading to another room I started for it, but recollecting I had left my gun outside I stepped to the door and got it and then ran into the other room and crawled under the bed that was there and got behind some wool that was under the bed. By this time some of the Yankees were in the house, and I heard them inquiring about our fellows. They never suspicioned I was in there and soon went out on the porch; the man of the house following them. While they were talking out there, I heard a little girl crying in the next room.

"Oh! mother, don't tell," she pleaded.

"Hush up! I am going to tell the truth if they ask me. This is no way of stealing horses from one another."

"Well," I thought, "I am gone up for ninety days, no Providence preventing."

But the Yanks never came in the house any more, and what few stopped for information soon mounted and went on. As soon as they were gone the man came to the door and said: "You had better get out of here as quick as possible; they have gone now, but will soon return."

I felt considerably relieved, for my heart was in my mouth all the time I was under that bed. As I came out, I looked at the woman as savage as I could, and said: "You would have told on me, would you?" She never looked up and I passed on out and went back and looked for my horse, but he was gone. He must have nickered as they passed by, and they probably took him.

Now, I knew Lieutenant Blue had left his horse at Mr. Jack Thompson's, about two miles from where I then was. Therefore, I concluded, as he had been captured at the foot of the mountain, I would go to Thompson's and get his horse and wait in the bushes until dark and then escape. I went on, and when I got there, I found the family had all gone to church, except the blacks, it being Sunday. I told the black woman all about our adventure, and that I came for the horse, but that I wanted something to eat, as I was hungry as a dog. She hurried around and soon had a dinner prepared, and just as I was commencing to eat who should step in but Lieutenant Blue himself.

"Why, Lieutenant!" I exclaimed, "I thought you were captured!"

"I thought so, too," says he, "but they happened to ride over me while I was hid in the laurels and did not see me."

He then told me that Montgomery had escaped in the same manner, but that McGraw was captured, and we had lost the finest horse of the bunch.

He said he came for his horse, but that we had better eat some and then hide in the woods until night. So, we sat down and ate a hearty meal, leaving the black woman on picket at the door.

As soon as we were done, we started out, when Blue remarked that he was "so tired."

Just then the black woman threw up her hands and exclaimed, "Lord God! men, here dey is!"

We were just passing out the door onto the porch, and sure enough there they were close to the yard fence. They commenced firing at us and commanding us to halt, but we ran down the steps and around the end of the house. As we passed through the yard the little negroes there set up such a yelling and squalling as I never heard before in all my life. I thought they were all shot by the racket they made.

As we passed around the end of the house I said, to Blue: "Oh! Let's give up; they will be sure to kill us if we run."

"They will kill us anyhow if they get us, and we may as well run for it," he replied. He kept on running and I after him. They had to ride around the house to get a view of us, and by that time we were running along by a fence. We had to get over the fence and run across a large field to the woods. I can never tell how I got over that fence; whether I jumped over, rolled over, or crawled over, anyway I got over, and then we had to run the gauntlet, for by this time there were forty Yankees ranged along that fence. Each one emptied his carbine and six-shooter at us as we ran across the field. They were so sure of killing us that they never attempted to pull down the fence and ride us down, which they could have done before we reached the woods.

Now, I will explain how I know all this to be true. They had McGraw prisoner at the time, and he was sitting on a horse and witnessed it and heard what they said. McGraw was sent to "Camp Chase," Ohio, to prison; and I saw him after he was exchanged, when he told me all about it. He knew how many there were, and that they emptied their arms firing at us. He said he expected to see us drop every minute.

I expected it, too, for the bullets rattled around us on every side, and when we reached the woods, they were spatting the trees. As we ran across the field Lieutenant Blue threw down his carbine, but I held on to my rifle.

The woods were very open, and we kept on running as long as we had breath to run. After we had stopped running and were walking along, all at once—*bang! bang! bang!* came from the rear. They were still after us. We started off again on the run, and as quick as if we had not run any that day. I then undertook to throw down my Enfield rifle behind a log; but as I threw it the hook in the gun strap caught in my overcoat, and it dragged along. Said I: "Old fellow, if you don't want to leave me, I will hold on to you and we will both die together." So, I picked it up and went on.

At last we reached some thick underbrush and lay down perfectly exhausted. We heard no more of the enemy then, but concluded they were surrounding the piece of woods we were in and would have us anyhow. So, we concluded we had better try and get across the road, and then we would be in woods they could not surround.

We were sneaking along as cautiously as we could, and had nearly got to the road when we heard horses' feet. We dropped to the ground, when the command rode by, not one hundred yards from us. They appeared to have given us up and were on their way to camp. There were eighty of them when they first came on us, but had afterwards divided.

We lay there until after dark, two of the worst demoralised lads that ever shouldered a gun. I came very near being captured three times that day, and I don't know how many times I came near being killed. I was afraid of my own shadow. To hear a brush crack would frighten me. Oh! I was terribly used up. If I had seen another Yankee, I would have run all night, I think.

After it had been dark a while, we concluded we would slip back to Thompson's and see if the horse was still there, but we were afraid the Yankees had left part of their force on the lookout for us. Finally, however, we started, and, after going some distance, we heard someone talking. We jumped over the fence and lay down in the grass, but it was only some people going to church. We then ventured on, and when we arrived at Thompson's we found the horse was still there, and that the blacks had seen Lieutenant Blue throw down his carbine and had gone out in the field and found it. We saddled the horse and left. We concluded to go to a Union man's house near there and stay all night. If they searched for us, they would hardly search his house; and then we knew he was an honest Union man—a Union man from principle, not a Union man for devilment, as some were. He said we could stay all night, but if they came to search for us, he would have to tell them we were there; but said he would manage that we should have a chance to escape first. We knew we could trust him, and we slept—"Oh! how sweetly!"

It was one of the most eventful days of my life, and I always call it "Running the Gauntlet." The next morning, we started on to Lost River to meet the balance of our party at the place we had appointed; but when we got there we found none but Will Daily, who was suffering from the loss of his eye. They had all escaped safely, but had concluded that we were captured, and so went on to General Imboden's camp in Augusta County. It was, therefore, arranged that I should go to camp with Lieutenant Blue, and he would make sale of our captures and divide the proceeds equally. I was then to return with my share and Daily's, when Miller, Daily and myself were to go to our own command in Eastern Virginia.

CHAPTER 14

At Imboden's Camp

We parted there, I going with Lieutenant Blue, and Miller and Daily remaining. I have never seen them from that day to this, for reasons I shall relate hereafter. In a few days we reached General Imboden's camp, when our captures were put up at public sale and sold to the highest bidder, and the money divided, which amounted to four hundred dollars apiece in Confederate money.

There was a soldier in camp who had a broken-down horse, and he wanted to send him home to Hampshire to recruit, so he got me to ride him back. Two of the Pownell boys, who had just returned from prison, were going home to recruit, so the three of us started back for Hampshire together. After two days' march we stopped for the night at Mr. Thompson's, in Rockingham County. After dark there were three other soldiers came to stay all night. While conversing around the fire that evening, they inquired what command we belonged to. The Pownell boys told them they belonged to Imboden's command, and I told them I belonged to the 33rd Virginia, Lee's Army.

When we went to bed that night Mr. Thompson told us that those soldiers were conscript officers and were gathering up all absentees from Lee's Army, and if I did not have a pass, he was afraid they would arrest me in the morning; that I had better told them I belonged to Imboden's Cavalry. I told him I would not deny my command.

Sure enough, the next morning they told me as I had no pass, they would have to arrest me and send me back to my command under guard. I explained matters to them; that Sergeant Miller had the pass and I was on my way to report to him; but it all did no good. I had to leave the horse there and go with them to Harrisonburg, a distance of eight miles, and was put in the guard-house. I hated it very much; not because I had to go back to the army, but because I had to go back under arrest. I knew my officers knew nothing of the circumstances of my long absence, and that I would be court-martialled without Miller should appear and relieve me.

I was sent off from Harrisonburg in a few days with about thirty other absentees from our division. We marched to Staunton and then took the cars for Guinea Station. After arriving there we were conducted about six miles to General J. R. Trimble's headquarters, who was commanding the division, when we were ordered to our respective brigade guard-houses. I found two or three hundred in the guard-house, and the court-martial in full blast. Punishments of all kinds were being inflicted on the prisoners, such as shot to death, whipped, heads shaved and drummed out of service, riding wooden horses, wearing barrel shirts, and all other punishments in the catalogue of military courts-martial.

I soon sent word to Captain Wm. Powell, commanding my company, of my situation, when he came to see me in the guard-house. I explained to him how matters stood, and he said he would have me out in a few days; that I should not be punished much, but that I had been reported "absent without leave" and would have to be court-martialled; but it should be done in the regiment and should not go to a brigade court.

During this time Colonel Edwin G. Lee, Colonel of our regiment, had been assigned to other duty at Lexington, Va.; Lieutenant Colonel Holliday, who lost his arm, was elected to the Confederate congress, and Major Grace had resigned, therefore, Captain A. Spangler, of Company F ("Hardy Grey's"), was Lieutenant Colonel of the regiment. So, Colonel Spangler, Captain Herrell and Captain Eastman composed the court-martial and they all knew me personally. When I appeared before them for trial and explained to them where I had been and what I had done, and that I had never been home during the time that I was absent (for my parents lived then in Frederick County), they said they would make the punishment as light as possible. It resulted in my being put on extra duty for ten days, when I was released.

At this time the roads had become so muddy and bad between our camp and Guinea Station, a distance of eight miles, that it was almost impossible to haul rations for the army; so there was a detail of one hundred men made from our division to make pole or corduroy roads from camp to the railroad station. Some were taken out of each regiment and there were twenty-two regiments in our division. It fell to my lot to go and work the road.

We were put in command of Lieutenant David Cockrill, of the 2nd Regiment, and camped about half way between our camp and the station. We would cut down pine poles (there were thickets of them close by) and lay them crosswise, put some brush on top and then throw some dirt on that and make a splendid road.

At the time I left the brigade at Winchester the army was on the march to Fredericksburg, on the Rappahannock River. They arrived there and fought the battle of Fredericksburg the 12th and 13th of December, 1862, and defeated General Burnside, commanding the Federal Army. He fell back across the river and was relieved of his command, and another "On to Richmond" was upset by the superior generalship of Lee, Jackson and Longstreet.

During our raid in Hampshire County we remained on Jersey mountain, at different places, for some time. While there a Methodist revival was going on. We frequently attended church at night; and through the influence and earnest working of Miss Sallie Cain, afterwards Mrs. Sallie Harper (an old schoolmate of mine), who was teaching school there. Lieutenant Blue, Mart Miller and myself became seekers of religion and made a profession and joined the church. We soon afterwards separated, never to see each other again in this world. How Miller held out I never heard, but have heard that he died sometime after the war.

As for myself, I have not lived up to the doctrines of Christianity as I should. At times I have been wild and reckless, and, continuing in the army as I did, amongst wild companions, naturally retrograded considerably; but I never forgot the teachings of pious parents nor the good offices of Miss Sallie, nor the pleasure I experienced in trying to be good.

Lieutenant Monroe Blue, as I afterwards learned, for I never saw him after parting with him in General Imboden's camp, was, shortly afterward, captured by the enemy and taken to "Johnson's Island," an officers' prison near Sandusky, Ohio. As they were removing him and some other officers to Ft. Delaware he jumped from the train in the dead of night while it was running at full speed, after having knocked down the sentinel, who was guarding the door, and, by traveling at night and hiding in the daytime, finally reached Virginia. He went to his command, but was afterwards killed at the Battle of New Hope in Augusta County. He lived faithful to his professions to the end; and a better soldier never stood in ranks. Peace to his ashes.

General Lee's army remained in winter quarters near Guinea Station all winter, picketing along the Rappahannock. The enemy were on the opposite side. Our detail continued to work the road until about the first of April, when we were taken down to the river at Skinker's Neck and commenced fortifying along the hills near the river between Fredericksburg and Port Royal. We drew plenty of rations and more sugar than we had use for, and would trade sugar to the negroes for corn meal. We drew plenty of flour, but little corn meal; One day Bill Grady was sick, and we told him, to take our sugar (about ten pounds) and trade it off. When we came in at night and I saw the small quantity of meal that he had, I asked him how he had traded. He said "Pound for pound, of course." He thought that was the way to trade, he said. He never heard the last of "pound for pound." One pound of sugar was worth ten pounds of corn meal. The devices resorted to by the soldiers to procure extra rations may be interesting to those who never dream of want of "grub" in these times of peace. I will relate an instance.

Our rations were drawn from the commissary at Guinea Station. One day when the wagon went after flour two of my mess went along to help. They were to get eight barrels of flour. Sewell Merchant, one of the detail, was in the wagon, and when the first barrel was rolled in left it lying on its side, and the other eight he sat up on end. So, when the commissary sergeant looked in the wagon from the rear, he could see but eight. "All right," said he, and they drove off to the camp, but before reaching camp they halted and rolled the extra barrel out and hid it in the pines. That night several of our mess took sacks and went to where the barrel was hid and carried the flour to camp, and we had extra rations for some time.

We were expecting the spring campaign to open most any time, and the army was making preparations to move or fight, as the case might be. Lieutenant Cockrill had orders to organise a regular pioneer corps of 100 men, and to select the best workmen out of the force that he had; principally mechanics, who could build bridges, pontoons, etc., and was furnished a wagon load of tools. He had one man, who was a shoemaker, to cobble up the shoes as they wore out. One day as we were cutting down some trees that would be in the way of our artillery a limb, as it fell, hit the axe of the shoemaker and drove it into his leg, making a fearful wound. He was sent to the hospital and soon died.

The lieutenant said he must have another shoemaker in his corps, and some of them told him that I was a shoemaker, when he had me regularly detailed in the pioneer corps.

I did not want to belong, to it, for, on the march, we had to go in front of the division and carry our shovels, picks and axes, and repair the roads and bridges when necessary; and when a fight came off we had to go into the fight with a battery of artillery to cut out roads for them in the woods, or cut down timber in front that obstructed their view of the enemy, and remove blockades, etc. When lying in camp we had to repair roads and make breastworks, so it was all work and danger, and no play; although it was not as dangerous as being in the line of battle with a musket, for we had a chance to protect ourselves when at work. Sometimes also we had nothing to do during the fight; but we had to be there in readiness, should we be needed. We never let an opportunity slip to protect ourselves the best we could by digging holes to get into in case of emergency, or finding some gully that would protect us. As soon as a battle was over, we had to bury the dead. Each division in Lee's Army had a pioneer corps from that time until the end of the war.

CHAPTER 15

Battle of Chancellorsville

On the 29th of April, 1863, we left our winter quarters and marched up the river to Hamilton's Crossing, near Fredericksburg, about twelve miles from Chancellorsville.

******

Fredericksburg is on the Rappahannock River. Chancellorsville, a mere hamlet, is about twelve miles above, and to the northwest, and some two miles from the Rappahannock at its nearest point, where there is a shallow place called the United

States Ford.

Hamilton's Crossing, a station on the Richmond and Potomac railroad, is also about two miles from the river, below Fredericksburg.

A country road runs between Hamilton's Crossing and Chancellorsville, keeping at some distance from the river.

The country around Chancellorsville is high and rolling, and covered with timber interspersed with dense undergrowth, with an occasional farm; and on the south and west forming what was called the "Wilderness."

******

We found the whole army on the move, and formed in line of battle. General Joe Hooker (Fighting Joe), commanding the Federal army, was threatening to cross the river and some artillery and skirmish fighting was going on.

We now had six divisions of infantry; Early's, A. P. Hill's, D. H. Hill's (commanded by General R. E. Rodes) and Trimble's, commanded by General R. E. Colston, all belonging to Jackson's Corps; and Anderson's and McLaw's Divisions, belonging to Longstreet's Corps. General Longstreet was down in South-eastern Virginia, near Suffold, with his other three divisions, and did not come to us until after the Battle of Chancellorsville.

We manoeuvred around near Fredericksburg until the 1st of May, when we all marched twelve miles up the river to near Chancellorsville (excepting General Early's Division), as General Hooker had crossed the main part of his army and fortified at Chancellorsville. Hooker had left Sedgwick's 6th Corps at Fredericksburg to attract Lee's and Jackson's attention, while he massed his forces at another place. Stuart's Cavalry, however, soon informed them of the movement up the river. If all Lee's army had marched against Hooker the Federals could have crossed at Fredericksburg and come in on our rear. So General Early was left there to watch their movements. In the morning, on the 2nd of May, our army was lying in line of battle in front of General Hooker, near Chancellorsville, facing westward.

Three divisions of our corps under Jackson started on the march and moved south for a while, and we could hear skirmishing on our right. We could not imagine where we were going. We continued marching through fields and woods until about three o'clock in the afternoon. The day was hot, and we marched fast—the men throwing away their overcoats and blankets.

The other two divisions were in front of ours and we began to think Jackson was on one of his flank movements, when one of his couriers came back and told our general to hurry up his command, as General Jackson was waiting for it to form in line. We knew then there was business on hand. Our pioneer corps always marched in front of the division near the general and staff, and was under directions from the engineers; consequently we heard and knew more of the movements of the army than generally falls to the lot of a private.

In a short time, about three miles southwest of Chancellorsville, we came to a road leading from Orange Court House through Chancellorsville to Fredericksburg. We were halted and the three divisions formed in three lines of battle across the road to the right and left—one division in rear of the other. General Rodes' formed the first line, our division the second and General A. P. Hill's the third, but marching in column facing to the east, directly opposite to our position in the morning.

Jackson's Last Dispatch.

Near 3 p. m., May 2, 1863: General—The enemy has made a stand at Chancellor's, which is about two miles from Chancellorsville. I hope as soon as practicable to attack.

I trust that an ever kind Providence will bless us with great success.

Respectfully,   T. J. Jackson, Lieutenant General.

Later—3:15 p. m. General—The leading division is up, and the next two appear to be well closed.   T. J. J.

As yet not a gun had been fired; everything was still and quiet; the troops were tired and moved about noiselessly; there were thick woods and underbrush on each side of the road, with an occasional field or farm. While resting in this position a courier came to us, who was acquainted with some of our boys, and said we were in rear of the Yankees, and that he could not tell how it was, but we would soon see the greatest move of the war.

In a few moments Lieutenant Oscar Hinrichs, one of the engineers, came and said he wanted ten pioneers to go with him to remove a blockade in the road. I was one of the ten. We moved down the road in front and commenced clearing the road of trees that had been felled across it. There were four pieces of artillery there waiting to move forward. They unlimbered one piece, and we helped them to get it over the blockade before we had it cleared. They then fired a shot down the road, and moved on. At the same time the three lines of infantry moved forward at double-quick with a yell. I learned afterwards that the firing of the gun was a signal for all to move; and move they did with a vengeance, and moved everything in front of them.

We soon got the blockade open and all the artillery through. We then came to another blockade and soon opened that. I heard two or three shells come tearing up the road from the enemy, but heard nothing else from them until we got to Chancellorsville after dark.

It was a running fight for three miles. We took them completely by surprise, and our three divisions got merged into one line of battle, all going forward at full speed. Our artillery did not have time to unlimber and fire; they had to keep in a trot to keep up with the infantry. We ran through the enemy's camps where they were cooking supper. Tents were standing, and camp-kettles were on the fire full of meat. I saw a big Newfoundland dog lying in one tent as quietly as if nothing had happened. We had a nice chance to plunder their camps and search the dead; but the men were afraid to stop, as they had to keep with the artillery and were near a good many officers, who might whack them over the head with their swords if they saw them plundering; but the temptation was too great, and sometimes, they would run their hands in some dead men's pockets as they hurried along, but seldom procured anything of value.

I saw a wounded man lying beside the road and had got past him; but, noticing he was an officer, I ran back to him to get his sword and pistol. I asked him if he was wounded badly. He said he was not. He was shot through the foot, but thought he would lie there until the fight was over; that he was a captain of some Ohio regiment. I took off his belt and sword, which was a very fine one, but I found no pistol in the scabbard. I asked him where the pistol was, and he said he supposed he must have lost it in the fight; that he did not know it was gone; but I thought he had it in his bosom, so I unbuttoned his coat and searched him for it, but could not find it. He declared he did not have it, but he had a fine gold watch and chain. I was looking at it when he told me to take it along; but I would not do it. I told him that as he was wounded and a prisoner, I would let him keep it.

It was the 11th United States Army Corps that we first attacked and demoralised. Another corps, the 5th, was sent to their assistance, but were likewise repulsed. Our army did not halt until dark, when we came to the enemy's fortified position in and around Chancellorsville.

Our officers then commenced forming the men in line, and. getting them in some kind of order, but the men kept up a terrible noise and confusion, hallooing for this regiment and that regiment, until it seemed that there were not more than three or four of any regiment together. They were all mixed up in one confused mass. The enemy could hear us distinctly by the noise we made. They located us precisely, and immediately opened on us with twenty pieces of artillery, at short range, and swept the woods and road with the most terrific and destructive shelling that we were subjected to during the war.

Charlie Cross, Sam Nunnelly, Jake Fogle and myself were together when the shelling commenced. We stepped to one side and happened to find a sink, or low place, where a tree had blown down some time in the past, and laid down in it. We filled it up even with the ground, and it seemed as if the shells did not miss us more than six inches. Some would strike in front of us, scattering the dirt all over us. I believe if I had stuck my head up a few inches I would have been killed.

We could hear someone scream out every second in the agonies of death. Jake Fogle kept praying all the time. Every time a shell would pass directly over us Jake would say: "Lord, save us this time!" "Lord, save us this time!" Sam Nunnelly, a wild, reckless fellow, would laugh at him and say: "Pray on Jake! Pray on Jake!" and the two kept that up as long as the shelling lasted. Cross and I tried to get Sam to hush, but it was no use.

Our infantry and artillery did not reply, as we did not have a piece in position. It stood in the road just where they left it when they drove up, and every man of them was lying as close to the ground as he could get. They dug "nose holes" to get closer. The Yankees soon ceased firing, however, and the men commenced calling their commands again, making as much noise as ever. Immediately we were treated to another dose of shells as terrific as before, and with fearful effect, but for some reason it was not long continued.

If the enemy had known our situation, and the good range they had on us, and had kept it up, they would literally have torn us to pieces and nearly annihilated our corps that night. It was fortunate for us that they kept it up no longer; but it was fearful while it lasted. It was some time during the shelling that General Jackson was wounded, which resulted in his death one week afterwards.

I happened to hear of it that night, but it was not known to many of the soldiers. I was standing near some officers, who were on horseback, and heard them say something about General Jackson being wounded, and it surprised me so much that I stepped up to them and asked them if he was wounded badly. One of them replied that he was slightly wounded, and told me to go on to my command.

The next morning that road was covered for some distance with dead men torn to pieces; dead horses, cannon wheels, cannot broken off at the trunnions, caissons overturned, and desolation generally.

That night, it seems. General Jackson and his staff had gone in front of our line of skirmishers to reconnoitre, in order to throw his corps between the enemy and the river, when he met their line of skirmishers advancing. He wheeled at once and came back rapidly. Our line mistaking him and his staff for the enemy, fired a volley into them with fatal effect, killing several of them and wounding others.

******

Major Jed Hotchkiss says: "Jackson halted his men at the enemy's abattis near Chancellorsville, and, having ordered a new-line of battle from his reserves, he rode forward with his staff to reconnoitre, which, done, turned and rode back, when, in the dark, he was fired on by the men of his new line of battle, who mistook his staff and escort for the enemy's cavalry,"

******

General Jackson was shot through the right hand and received two balls through the left arm. He had to lie there during the shelling, and nearly bled to death before his wounds were staunched.

They finally got him on a stretcher and started to the rear, when some of the bearers were cut down and he fell heavily to the ground, opening the wounds afresh. They finally got him to the ambulance, and he was taken to the field hospital, where Dr. Hunter McGuire amputated his left arm near the shoulder.

The battle that day was only a prelude to what was to follow on the next two days. General Hooker had massed his troops that night and strengthened his works and constructed new ones. The next morning, the 3rd of May, General J. E. B. Stuart took command of the corps and attacked the enemy on the flank, while Lee attacked in front.

Before General Stuart took command of the corps, he saw Jackson and attempted to ascertain from him what his plans were.

"Form your own plans, General," said Jackson.

What Jackson's plans were at the time he was wounded was the subject of speculation at the time, and has been ever since. It was discussed among the soldiers in the field who generally believed that if Jackson had succeeded in getting in the rear of the enemy, between

Chancellorsville and the river (and it has been claimed this was his object), he would have been powerless to prevent Hooker's retreat across the Rappahannock at United States Ford; and that an attempt to hold the ford would have been disastrous

But I am not writing a history of the war, only of my experiences in the army. I will leave that to those wise men who are presumed to know all about it. But I am satisfied no one but Jackson himself ever knew exactly what his plans were at that time.

It would be well also to remember that couriers are soldiers taken from the ranks; that couriers have opportunities to learn more military secrets than even staff officers; that they have comrades in the army, and that intelligent soldiers composed the rank and file of both armies. The reader can form his own conclusions.

It was charge after charge, through thick underbrush, as the cry of "Remember Stonewall Jackson!" rang along the lines, until the works were gained; the enemy driven off the field and our troops in possession of his strongest position. But at what cost? The loss of life was fearful, some of our regiments being decimated.

A large brick house was fired by our shells, and it was said that General Hooker was standing by one of the columns of the porch when a shell struck it and exploded. A Federal battery of six or eight guns, near the house, was entirely disabled, not a live horse or whole cannon being left. Many of the cannoneers were found dead.

We fortified that night in order to hold our position, as we did not know how General Early would succeed in driving the enemy back at Fredericksburg. Several brigades had been sent to his assistance, and we soon learned that the enemy, under General Sedgewick, had been compelled to retreat across the river.

Meanwhile General Lee was not idle, but kept hammering away all day at Chancellorsville, driving the enemy back at some points, and holding his own. everywhere. That night General Hooker, finding all his plans frustrated and his army defeated at both points, hastily retreated across the Rappahannock, leaving a good many prisoners, arms, artillery, etc., in our hands.

Our pioneer corps then went to work burying the dead, when I witnessed the most horrible sight my eyes ever beheld. On the left of our line, where the Louisiana Brigade had fought the last evening of the battle, and where they drove the enemy about one mile through the woods, and then in turn fell back to their own position, the scene beggars description. The dead and badly wounded from both sides were lying where they fell. The woods, taking fire that night from the shells, burnt rapidly and roasted the wounded men alive. As we went to bury them, we could see where they had tried to keep the fire from them by scratching the leaves away as far as they could reach. But it availed not; they were burnt to a crisp. The only way we could tell to which army they belonged was by turning them over and examining their clothing where they lay close to the ground. There we would usually find some of their clothing that was not burned, so we could see whether they wore the blue or gray. We buried them all alike by covering them up with dirt where they lay. It was the most sickening sight I saw during the war and I wondered whether the American people were civilized or not, to butcher one another in that manner; and I came to the conclusion that we were barbarians. North and South alike.

Three of our pioneers were badly wounded by shells during the battle, and Lieutenant Pownell, who had lately been elected Lieutenant of my company, was mortally wounded, and died at the field hospital. I had given him the handsome sword I got at the first day's fight.

The day after the battle I wandered back to the field hospital to see if I could find Lieutenant Pownell, to learn how badly he was wounded, and find my sword. I found out that he was dead and buried, and no one knew anything about the sword. But as I was passing through the wounded a Federal officer hailed me and called me to his side. I found him to be the captain that I had found wounded the first day, and from whom I had gotten the sword. He had recognised me and said that I had better taken his gold watch that day; that I had not been gone ten minutes until some soldier came along and took his watch. I then regretted that I had not done so; but it was too late.

After everything was quiet, we moved down in the neighbourhood of Hamilton's Crossing and went into camp, and the doctors were busy for some time, embalming dead bodies and sending them to their friends south by rail.

Our loss was estimated at ten thousand five hundred; the enemy's at eighteen thousand; but we lost Jackson, who was a whole corps in himself. General Lee's force was fifty thousand men, General Hooker's Army was estimated at one hundred and twenty-five thousand. The Federal Army was better prepared to continue the fight than we were, for the difference in numbers was greater after the battles than before. General Hooker's Army lay on the north side of the river, with pickets along the bank, while ours was on the south bank. The picket guard of each army would go in swimming together, and trade coffee and tobacco, and be as friendly as if nothing had happened. Such is war.

General Jackson was taken to a private house near Guinea Station, the best physicians attending him, and his wife and daughter (Miss Julia, then seven months old,) came to see him. Our old brigade would inquire after him every day, and the news was that he was doing well, and we thought that he would soon be with us. But alas! vain hope! death is no respecter of persons, and we were doomed never to see him again. He suddenly got worse, and died on the 10th of May, 1863. We were terribly shocked, for we thought from what we had heard that he would surely recover.

A great many of our boys said then our star of destiny would fade, and that our cause would be lost without Jackson, as there was no general who could execute a flank movement with so much secrecy and surprise as he could. So, it proved to be; but the war might have ended the same as it did had he lived. Though the destiny of a nation may appear to be in one man's hands sometimes, yet there is One above all who controls both men and nations.

But I believed at the time, and believe now, and always shall believe, that if we had had Jackson with us at the Battle of Gettysburg, he would have flanked the enemy off those heights with his corps, if he had to take one day's rations and go around by Washington City to get there. He would have found his rear if he had any.

General Jackson would order some other general to hold some position at all hazards, and the general would reply that he was afraid he could not hold it if the enemy should press him. Jackson would say, "You must hold it; my men sometimes fail to drive the enemy, but the enemy always fail to drive my men."

General Stuart had reported to him that a considerable force had crossed the river above Chancellorsville, and threatened his left. He then sent one brigade up there after dark with orders to form a line when they came in view of the Federals, to fire three volleys and then return and take their places in line of battle. They did so, and the consequence was the force of Federals at that ford remained there during the next two days' fight, fortifying their position for fear of an attack. Such was the strategy of "Stonewall." Shortly after he was wounded, and when the enemy were rushing up fresh troops. General Pender told him that his men were in such confusion that he feared he would not be able to hold his ground.

"General Pender," said Jackson, "you must keep your men together

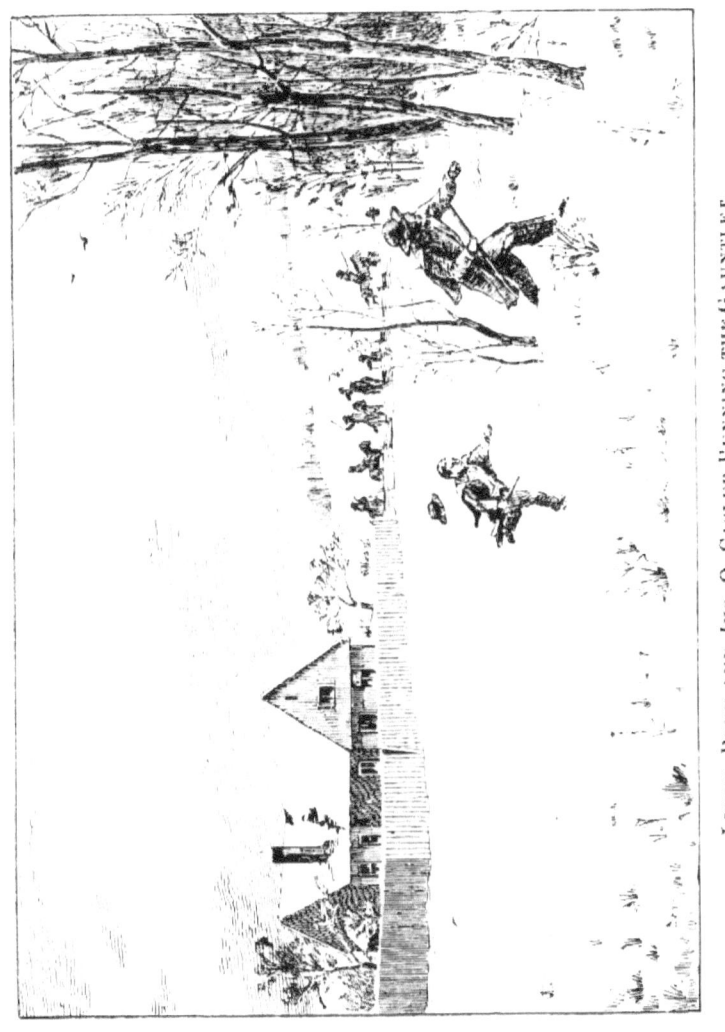

Lieut. Blue and Jno. O. Casler Running the Gauntlet.

and hold your ground."

This was the last military order ever given by Jackson. The last sentence he ever uttered was, "Let us pass over the river and rest under the shade of the trees."

Before his death he sent General Lee word that he had lost his left arm. General Lee replied that he (Lee) had lost his right arm in losing him.

He inquired minutely about the battle and the different troops engaged, and his face would light up with enthusiasm when told how his old brigade acted, and he uttered "Good, good," with unwonted energy when the gallant behaviour of the "Stonewall Brigade" was alluded to. He said:

> The men of the brigade will be, someday, proud to say to their children, 'I was one of the Stonewall Brigade.' They are a noble body of men.

Just before he died, he seemed to be caring for his soldiers, and giving such directions as these:

> Tell Major Hawks to send forward provisions to the men; order A. P. Hill to prepare for action. Pass the infantry to the front.

After his death orders came to the "Stonewall Brigade" to be in readiness to march to the house where Jackson lay a corpse and escort the remains to the railroad depot, to be sent to Richmond. The brigade rigged up in the best they had, cleaned their arms and were anxious to go, and kept waiting impatiently until, finally, the order was countermanded and we did not get to see him.

We all thought very hard of it, for we wished to show our respect for our beloved commander, and gaze on his face once more; but that small privilege was denied us. His only escort were some doctors and officials who never had followed him in battle, while the men who had followed him from Harper's Ferry to Chancellorsville had to lie idle in camp.

The news of the wounding of General Jackson filled the army with the most profound and undisguised grief. His men loved him devotedly, and he was the idol of the whole army.

Many stout-hearted veterans, who had, under his guidance, borne hardships and privations innumerable, and dangers the most appalling, without a murmur, wept like children when told that their idolized General was no more. The death of General Jackson was communicated to the army by General Lee in the following order:

> Headquarters Army Northern Virginia, May 11, 1863.
> General Order No. 61.
>
> With deep grief the commanding general announces to the army the death of Lieutenant General T. J. Jackson, who expired on the 10th instant, at quarter past 3 p. m. The daring, skill and energy of this great and good soldier, by the decree of an All-wise Providence, are now lost to us.
>
> But while we mourn his death, we feel that his spirit still lives, and will inspire the whole army with his indomitable courage and unshaken confidence in God as our hope and strength.
>
> Let his name be a watchword to his corps, who have followed him to victory on so many fields.
>
> Let his officers and soldiers emulate his invincible determination to do everything in the defence of our beloved country.
>
> R. E. Lee, General.

On Monday morning, the 11th of May, it was announced that the remains of General Jackson would reach Richmond during the day, and the mayor of that city at once requested all persons to suspend business after 10 o'clock, in token of their respect for the departed hero. All stores, workshops, the government departments, and all places in which labour was performed, were closed. Flags were hung at half-mast and a deep silence reigned over the Capital of Virginia. Large crowds filled the streets, and, in spite of the intense heat, waited patiently for the arrival of the cars from Fredericksburg.

Shortly after 4 o'clock in the afternoon the special train containing the precious burden, moved slowly into the city. Only the solemn peal of the bells as they tolled their mournful knell broke the deep silence that reigned over everything.

At the depot the coffin was removed from the cars, and placed in a hearse to be carried to the mansion of the Governor. The escort which received it consisted of Major General Elzey and staff, the State Guard of Virginia, with colours shrouded in mourning, the 44th North Carolina and the 1st Virginia Regiments (after which came the hearse and General Jackson's staff), the city authorities and citizens on foot.

The remains were escorted to the mansion of the governor and placed in the reception parlour. The lid of the coffin was removed, the new flag of the Confederacy, which had never before been used for any purpose, was thrown over it, and a single wreath of laurel laid upon the lifeless breast.

During the evening his friends were allowed to visit the body. The only change that was perceptible was that the features seemed somewhat smaller than they were in life. But there was still the firm, grave expression which had always dwelt there, and, above all, there rested upon the lifeless countenance an expression of happiness and peace so perfect and so intense that the gazer was awed and thrilled by it.

During the night the body was embalmed and a plaster cast of his features taken in order that they might be preserved in marble.

The next day all the honours that his native state could lavish upon her noble son were heaped upon him. At 11 o'clock his body was removed from the Executive Mansion, and conveyed, with appropriate ceremonies, to the Capitol of Virginia.

The procession was formed in the following order, the troops marching with reversed arms:

A brass band; the 19th Regiment of Virginia Infantry; the 56th Regiment of Virginia Infantry; the State Guard of Virginia; Major General Picket and Staff, mounted; a battery (six pieces) of artillery; a squadron of cavalry; the hearse, containing the coffin, with Major General Ewell, Brigadier Generals Winder, Churchill, Corse, Stuart (G. H.), Kemper and Garnett, and Admiral Forrest of the Navy, as pallbearers; the favourite horse of General Jackson fully caparisoned and led by his servant; the members of the old "Stonewall Brigade" who were present in the city; a band of music; General Elzey and Staff; the officials of the military department of Henrico; a carriage containing the President of the Confederate States; the Members of the Cabinet on foot; the heads of bureaux and their clerks on foot; the Governor of Virginia and his Aids; the State officers and clerks; the Mayor and city authorities; the judges of the State and Confederate Courts, and the citizens on foot.

The procession moved from the Executive Mansion down Governor street into Main, up Main to Second, through Second to Grace, and down Grace to Capitol Square. The streets were filled with large crowds. The mournful cortege moved on in silence, which was only broken by the solemn strains of music and the discharge of artillery at intervals of half an hour. Tears rolled down many cheeks, and hundreds who had known General Jackson only by his great deeds wept as though mourning for a brother. Such an outburst of grief had never been witnessed in Virginia since the death of Washington.

Upon the arrival of the procession at the square the column was halted, the body removed and borne into the capitol, where it was laid in state, in the hall of the House of Representatives of the Confederate States. At least twenty thousand persons visited the hall to behold the remains of the hero of that day.

The next morning the remains were placed on a special train and conveyed to Lynchburg.

It was hoped that General Jackson would be buried in Hollywood Cemetery, near Richmond. There Virginia has prepared a last resting place for her honoured children. There rest the ashes of Monroe and Tyler and many of the good and brave of this revolution, and it was hoped that there, too, would rest the dust of General Jackson; but it was his wish to sleep in his dearly loved home in the Valley, and thither all that remained of him was carried. On Wednesday morning the remains passed through Lynchburg. Minute guns were fired, bells were tolled, and a large procession of citizens followed the body through the city. On Thursday afternoon they reached Lexington. They were met at the canal by the corps of cadets, the professors of the Institute, and a large number of citizens, and escorted to the Institute barracks. The body of General Jackson was placed in the old lecture room, which once had been his. Two years before he had left it an humble and almost unknown man; now he returned to it with the hero's laurel wreath encircling his brow and enshrined forever in the hearts of his countrymen.

With the exception of the heavy mourning drapery with which it was hung, the room was just as he had left it. It had not been occupied during his absence. The body was deposited just in front of the chair in which he used to sit. It was a beautiful and touching scene, and brought tears to every eye that witnessed it. Guns were fired every half hour during the day, and the deepest grief exhibited by everyone.

The next day, the 15th of May, General Jackson was buried in the cemetery at Lexington, Virginia, where rest the remains of his first wife and child.

> There in the beautiful Valley of Virginia, with which his name is so imperishably connected, the hero lies sleeping. Around him 'the everlasting hills' keep eternal guard, and the deep and unswerving love of his stricken, but still glorious, mother, watches with tender devotion over his sacred dust.
> Ages shall roll away, empires crumble into dust, nations pass away, but the memory of Jackson will still shine out in all its clear and radiant splendour. And when the last great trump shall

sound, and the dim light of the resurrection morn shall break away the gloom which overshadows the world, Virginia, whose pure heart beats but for God and duty, shall there be found still watching by the tomb of Jackson. And yet he is not Virginia's alone; God gave him to the world.

After the death of General Jackson, the officers and men of the old "Stonewall Brigade" met and passed a series of resolutions, which were but a feeble expression of their feelings.

The following is an account of their proceedings:

Camp Paxton, near Fredericksburg, Va.,
May 16, 1863.

At the appointed hour there was a full attendance of officers and men of the brigade.

The meeting was organised by the selection of Colonel Charles A. Ronald, of the 4th Virginia, as President, and Adjutant Robert W. Hunter as Secretary. On motion of Captain H. Kidd Douglas, a committee of three, consisting of Colonel J. Q. A. Nadenbouch, 2nd Virginia, Major William Terry, 4th Virginia, and Adjutant E. W. Hunter, 2nd Virginia, was appointed to prepare appropriate resolutions. The committee retired, and, after consultation, reported, through Adjutant Hunter, the following preamble and resolutions, which were unanimously adopted:

'Whereas, It has pleased Almighty God, in the exercise of supreme, but unsearchable wisdom, to strike down, in the midst of his career of honour and usefulness, our glorious hero. Lieutenant General T. J. Jackson, the officers and men of this brigade, which he formerly commanded, who have followed him through the trying scenes of this great struggle, and who, by the blessings of Providence, under his guidance, have been enabled to do some good in our country's cause; who loved and cherished him as a friend, honoured him as a great and good man labouring with hand and heart and mind for our present and future welfare; who obeyed and confided in him as a leader of consummate skill and unyielding fortitude, and who now mourn his loss, unite in the following tribute of respect to his memory:

'Resolved, 1st, That in the death of Lieutenant General Jackson the world has lost one of its best and purest men, our country and the church of God, 'a bright and shining light,' the army one of its boldest and most daring leaders, and this brigade a firm and unwavering friend.

'Resolved, 2nd, That General Jackson has closed his noble career by a death worthy of his life, and that while we mourn for him, and feel that no other leader can be to us all that he has been, yet we are not cast down or dispirited, but even more determined to do our whole duty, and, if need be, to give our lives for a cause made more sacred by the blood of our martyrs.

'Resolved, 3rd, That in accordance with General Jackson's wish, and the desire of this brigade to honour its first great commander, the Secretary of War be requested to order that it be known and designated as the 'Stonewall Brigade' and that, in thus formally adopting a title which is inseparably connected with his name and fame, we will strive to render ourselves more worthy of it, by emulating his virtues, and, like him, devote all our energies to the great work before us of securing to our beloved country the blessings of peace and independence. (The Secretary of War and Confederate congress confirmed the name of "Stonewall" for the brigade and made it the official and historical name of the brigade.)

'Resolved, 4th, That a copy of these proceedings be forwarded to the widow of the deceased, and published in the newspapers of the City of Richmond, Va., with a request that they be copied by the papers throughout the state.'

Captain H. Kidd Douglass addressed the meeting in a feeling manner; among other things, stating that it was the general's wish that his old brigade should be known as the Stonewall Brigade, and moved in this connection that a committee of five be appointed to correspond with the Secretary of War in order to carry out the third resolution of the meeting. The Chair named the following committee: Colonel Funk, 5th Virginia; Lieutenant Colonel Colston, 2nd Virginia; Major Terry, 4th Virginia; Captain Frazier, 27th Virginia, and Captain Bedinger, 33rd Virginia.

Major Terry submitted the following resolutions:

'Resolved, 1st, That it is the desire of this brigade to erect over the grave of Lieutenant General Jackson a suitable monument.

★★★★★★

A fine monument and statue were erected over the grave of General Jackson and unveiled the 21st of July, 1891, just thirty years after the Battle of Bull Run. There were a good many survivors of the old brigade present.

★★★★★★

'Resolved, 2nd, That a committee of five be appointed to carry into effect the above resolution; and that for the purpose the committee be clothed with full power to appoint a treasurer and sub-committees in each regiment to collect funds, adopt design, inscriptions, etc.'

The resolutions were passed unanimously, and the following committee appointed: Colonel J. Q. A. Nadenbouch, 2nd Virginia; Captain Strickler, 4th Virginia; Lieutenant Colonel Williams, 5th Virginia; Lieutenant Colonel Shriver, 27th Virginia, and Lieutenant Colonel A. Spengler, 33rd Virginia. On motion, meeting adjourned.

C. A. Ronald, President.

R. W. Hunter, Secretary.

Chapter 16
Reorganisation

General Paxton, commanding the Stonewall Brigade, was killed at Chancellorsville, and General James A. Walker, who was Colonel of the 13th Virginia, was put in command. General Trimble, division commander, being unfit for service by reason of sickness. General Ed. Johnson took command of the division. General R. E. Colston commanded the division at Chancellorsville. Johnson always carried a big hickory club or cane, and when he got mad could work his ears like a mule, so that he had the name in the army of "Clubby Johnson" and "Allegheny Johnson."

Our army lay in camp near Hamilton's Crossing; nothing of interest transpiring, except a thorough reorganisation of the troops.

There were nine divisions in the 1st and 2nd Corps, five in Longstreet's, and four in Jackson's, up to the time of the reorganisation. After Jackson's death, about the 20th of May, 1863, the army was formed into three infantry corps of three divisions each. The 1st Corps was composed of Hood's, Pickett's and McLaw's Divisions, and commanded by General Longstreet; the 2nd of Johnson's, Early's and Rodes', commanded by General Ewell, and the 3rd of Anderson's, Pender's and Heth's Divisions, commanded by General A. P. Hill.

The cavalry was formed into one corps, commanded by General J.

E. B. Stuart; the artillery corps by General W. N. Pendleton (formerly Captain of the Rockbridge artillery), and the whole army by General Robert E. Lee.

The different divisions, brigades and regiments, previous to this time, had been scattered over different portions of Virginia, and had been called at different times the "Army of the Potomac," the "Army of the Shenandoah," but was now consolidated and called the "Army of Northern Virginia," although there were detachments often sent away to operate at different points.

Our division, commanded by General Edward Johnson, consisted of four brigades, nearly all Virginians. The 1st and 3rd North Carolina Regiments were in the 3rd Brigade, and part of the time the "Maryland Line" was attached to that brigade. The 4th Brigade was composed of the 1st, 2nd, 10th, 14th and 15th Louisiana Regiments.

The 2nd Division was composed of Virginians, North Carolinians and Louisianans, and commanded by General Jubal A. Early.

The 3rd Division was composed of Georgians, Alabamans and North Carolinians, and commanded by General R. E. Rodes.

The infantry and cavalry were always casting jokes at one another as they passed. The infantry would ask them how long it took "them things to grow out of a man's heels" (referring to their spurs), and "who ever saw a dead man with spurs on?" They would reply: "If it wasn't for them things, you'd lose your wagon trains," intimating they would have to protect them while we retreated. We would ask the North Carolinians if they had any "tar," and call them "Tar Heels." They would reply that they were just out, as they had let us Virginians have all they had to make us stick in the last fight, and call us "sorebacks," as they had knocked all the skin off our backs running over us to get into battle.

And so, it would go, but all in the best of humour, knowing that all did their duty.

About the 1st of June we got orders to cook three days' rations and be ready to move at a moment's warning. Our pioneer troops were in camp a short distance from the station, and did not get orders for rations until near night, as they had neglected us. So, when the orders did come, we had to be in a hurry. We had to draw our rations from the commissary at the "Crossing" and cook them that night. Therefore, in order to lose no time, our sergeant detailed about twenty of us to go with him to the commissary and carry them to camp. When we got there all hands were busy weighing and packing up, and we had

Last meeting of Robert E. Lee and "Stonewall" Jackson at Chancellorsville

to wait some time.

While waiting Sam Nunnelly, of the 21st Virginia, and myself noticed a large pile of hams lying there, with no one guarding them. We soon stole a ham apiece and hid them, and told some of the other boys about it. When we drew our rations and got back to camp, we found we had nine extra hams for our trouble, which was a fine treat, and kept us in extra rations for some time. The bacon the soldiers drew was side meat, the hams being reserved for the officers. We never let an opportunity pass to get extra rations, no matter if we had to steal them—never forgetting the motto that *"everything is fair in war."*

On the 3rd of June our army, Ewell's Corps, took up the line of march. Our corps went west through Culpeper Court House, and went into camp a few miles beyond, where we remained but a few days. We were soon ordered to fall in, and were marched in a hurry back through Culpeper. We heard the enemy's cavalry had recrossed the Rappahannock, and that there was fighting at Brandy Station, about twenty-five miles up the river from Chancellorsville. We were soon halted and remained there about an hour; then marched back to camp. We found out that it was a general cavalry fight, and one of the hardest cavalry engagements of the war.

The enemy's cavalry had crossed in force and took our cavalry by surprise. They had some advantage at the start, but we soon rallied and were reinforced by other brigades. It was a desperate hand-to-hand conflict, but our cavalry soon got the best of them and they retreated across the river.

I saw more men cut with the sabre that day than I ever saw before or have seen since. My uncle, R. S. D. Heironimus, belonging to Rosser's Brigade, was severely wounded by being cut through the scalp with a sabre, laying the skull bare, but he recovered. The enemy lost four hundred prisoners, three pieces of artillery and several stands of colours, besides killed and' wounded.

The next day we resumed our march, and, crossing the Blue Ridge, proceeded to Front Royal. We then turned towards Winchester. We then began to understand what was up. The Federal General, Milroy, occupied Winchester with a considerable force, and was well fortified. He had a strong position. As we waded the Shenandoah River that evening, I told the boys that we would get no rest that night until our line was formed around Winchester. Having been so accustomed to General Jackson's flank movements, we knew if he were in command there would be no halt, but we soon went into camp. I then remained that Milroy would hear of our move, and would either retreat to Harper's Ferry or be prepared to give us battle, as we could not surprise him.

We were on the march the next morning, the 13th of June, and soon heard our cavalry skirmishing with the enemy. We moved on to near Winchester, when our troops were disposed around in battle order, but there was no engagement of any consequence by our division.

That night our division was marched around to the east of Winchester, by Jordan's Springs, and came on to the turnpike leading from Winchester north to Martinsburg. We were now at Stephenson's depot, about four miles from Winchester. We were not quite soon enough, for as the head of our column got in sight of the road, we saw the enemy retreating. We were in their rear, and if we had been one hour sooner, we would have had our line formed across the road and captured the whole "outfit."

Some had already got through, but it was a running fight as it was. A large number were captured, and others dispersed and demoralised. My old brigade captured six regiments and got six stands of colours. The general gave one to each regiment and kept one himself.

The Louisiana Brigade was running parallel with a brigade of the enemy, trying to head them off; but they made such good time that they were about to get away, when they happened to meet about twenty stragglers from our army, who had fallen behind during the night, and who, while coming on, seeing the Yankees rushing along at such headlong speed, and knowing that we were in their rear, formed across the road and called on them to halt. The enemy, thinking it was another detachment of our infantry, halted and surrendered. But the Louisiana Brigade was nearby and took them in charge. That was one time stragglers came in good play. The enemy's column would doubtless have escaped had it not been for the stragglers in their front.

Our cavalry were on the flanks, and we had none there to follow the retreating enemy. So, the infantry gathered up the wagon horses and mules and mounted them, bareback and in every way, as best they could. They were the hardest looking cavalry regiment I ever saw, with their knapsacks and blankets around their shoulders; with their long rifles and no saddles, and blind bridles, and mounted on mules and horses promiscuously. Away they went down the pike, as hard as they could go, yelling and firing, as if it were big fun for an infantryman to be mounted in any shape. They were after the wagon train ahead of the infantry, and made a fine capture.

"Stonewall" Jackson Mortally Wounded, May 2d, 1863.

Hays' Louisiana Brigade charged the enemy in their forts around Winchester, driving them out and capturing their guns, and turning them on them. Early's Division charged and ran them out of Winchester, our division heading them off and capturing them. Rodes' Division was at Berryville, to cut off their retreat in that direction, and went from there to Martinsburg and captured a great amount of stores. We followed them on to Harper's Ferry, when they crossed the Potomac and occupied Maryland Heights.

General Milroy escaped, with about 300 cavalry. Our captures amounted to 4,000 prisoners, twenty-nine pieces of artillery, 270 wagons and ambulances, 400 horses, and a large amount of military stores. Our loss was small.

General Ewell was a good officer, and our corps preferred him to any other after we had lost General Jackson. He did well in routing Milroy from Winchester, but Jackson (in my opinion) would have marched all night the night we went into camp, and by daylight would have had his line of battle around Winchester, and captured the whole command. Our corps was rather anxious to capture Milroy, as he had tyrannised over the citizens of Winchester, insulting ladies (so it was reported), and rendering himself obnoxious in different ways—more so than any Federal general had done during the war; and if he had been captured by some of our men he would have fared badly.

All this time General Hooker's army was lying on the north bank of the Rappahannock, opposite Fredericksburg; General A. P. Hill remaining there to watch him. Longstreet had remained in Culpeper, while Ewell moved on Winchester, and as Ewell had cleared the valley of the enemy, the key to Washington City was open, consequently the Federal Army fell back to Washington to protect it.

This was General Lee's object—to draw the Army out of Virginia on Northern soil. A. P. Hill followed up and took Longstreet's place, east of the Blue Ridge, at Snicker's Gap, and came into the valley, while Ewell, with our corps, crossed the Potomac at Shepherdstown into Maryland. We then went to Williamsport, from there to Hagerstown, and on to Greencastle, Pa., through Shippensburg and many other villages and towns, on to Carlisle, Pa., about one day's march from Harrisburg, the capital, and then halted.

When we crossed the Potomac, we thought we would have a fine time plundering in the enemy's country, and live fine; but General Lee had orders read out that we were not to molest any of the citizens, or take any private property, and any soldier caught plundering would

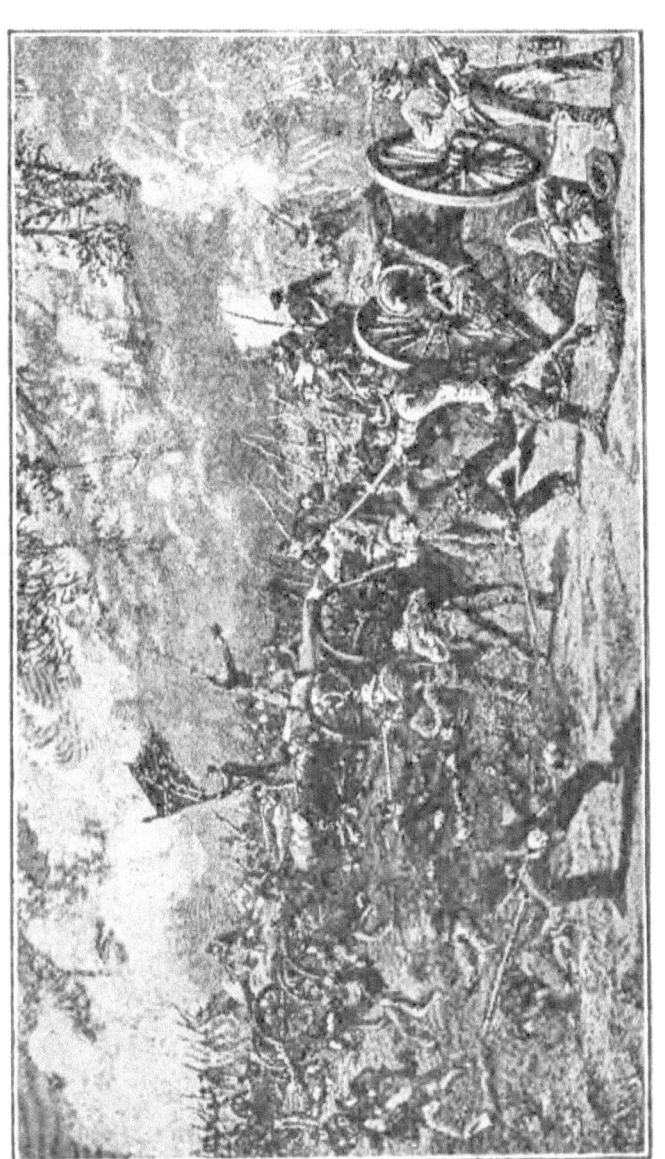

A Charge and Capture of Federal Breastworks at Chancellorsville, Va.

be shot.

The infantry did not have much chance to plunder, as we were kept close in ranks and marched slowly. We would camp every night near some town; but there would be a guard in town, and we could not get in without a pass, and after we got in were not allowed to disturb anything. Of course, we could go to the houses and get all we wanted to eat without money, for they did not want our money, and were glad to give us plenty through fear.

But our quartermasters managed to gobble up everything they came to. They would take the citizens' horses and wagons and load them up with provisions and goods from the stores; consequently, we accumulated an immense train. The cavalry were in front, and on our flanks, and they had a good chance for plundering and getting good horses. They made good use of it, too, and came out well supplied; but the infantry got nothing but what we could eat, but we got plenty of that. As soon as we would go into camp in the evening some of the soldiers would strike out into the country, before they had time to put out a guard, and would come back loaded with "grub." As we would march through the towns the ladies would usually be at the upstairs windows, waving their Union flags at us. We would laugh at them, but never disturb them. If the ladies of the South had done what I saw them do in Pennsylvania it would not have been tolerated by the Federals.

Some of them would look very sour at us, when we would ask their names so we could write them on a piece of paper, so we told them, and put the paper in water, as we knew it would turn the water to vinegar.

One day there was a very red-headed one at a window, who was very insulting, when the boys got to calling her "brick-top," and such names. She got so mad she fairly frothed at the mouth, and threatened to fire into the ranks. We then tried to persuade her to assume male attire and join the army and get satisfaction fighting us. They would make sport of our dress, when an Irishman among our troops replied: "Be jabers, we always put on our dirty clothes when we go to a hog-killing."

Cherries were ripe while we were in Pennsylvania, and there were a great many trees along the road. We stripped them both of cherries and limbs, leaving nothing but the trunks. Otherwise, we were kept close in ranks, and not allowed to plunder or destroy anything. General Lee was more strict on us than while in Virginia.

One day there was an old farmer standing by his gate talking to the boys, saying he was a "copper-head" and a Rebel sympathiser, and had quite a crowd around him. He had a fine farm and a fine house, and was well "fixed," but when any of them attempted to go in the gate he would say they had nothing to eat, as the soldiers ahead of us had already eaten him out. I listened to him awhile, but soon "tumbled to the racket," and saw he was giving us that kind of taffy to keep us out of the house. I told my chum to come on, and we would soon see what was in there. When we were about to go in at the gate the old man said there was nothing in there to eat. I told him that was too "thin;" that we would go in and see; that if he was such a good Rebel he could sacrifice a little for us; that he might never have another opportunity of feeding the Rebels, and that he ought to embrace this chance, as this was our first trip into Pennsylvania, and in all probability would be our last. We went on to the house and found plenty to eat by simply asking the ladies for it. When we went back to the road, we told the other boys that the old woman said we were to "come on," and get what we wanted, and they went. The old man saw his game was up, but I expect he raised a racket with the old woman afterwards.

As we lay in camp near Carlisle one day, and I saw we were not going to march, I told Charlie Cross, of the 10th Louisiana, a messmate of mine, that we would go out to some farmhouse and get a good dinner and some cherries. We went about one mile, when we came to a large farmhouse. A picket was posted there, and they would not let us go any farther. We then went into the house and found the family were Dutch; an old man, his wife and daughter. We asked if we could have some cherries. He said we could have all we wanted except from two trees that stood near the house; that he wanted them for their own use. When we examined the other trees, we found very few cherries, as the soldiers had stripped them. We then got up in the trees the old man had reserved and ate what we wanted and broke off several limbs, and went to the house and sat down on the porch where the old folks were, and asked them if they would not have some cherries, but they declined. We then asked them if we could get dinner. They said no, the soldiers had eaten all they had.

While sitting there, conversing with the old people, we heard a terrible racket around in the back yard, and did not know what to make of it. The old woman jumped up and ran around the house, and soon came back with both hands up. By the expression of her face we knew something terrible had happened. She kept on talking Dutch all the time. So, we all ran around to see what was the cause. We found one

"The night was lighted up by burning human bodies."

of the horses had fallen into the cistern, and there lay doubled up, all in a mass, at the bottom.

The old man then explained that he had run all his horses off to the mountains when he heard the Rebels were coming, except this one, which was an old family mare that they prized very highly for the good service she had done them, and as she was getting old, he thought the Rebels would not take her. He had turned her loose in the yard so he could watch her, but as there had been no horse in the yard for years, and the old cistern was not used any more, and had no water in it, it was only covered with some loose planks. The old mare had stepped on them, when they broke and precipitated her to the bottom.

The cistern was very wide, and about twelve feet deep. We felt sorry for the old folks, as they appeared so distressed about the fate of the old mare. They would doubtless rather have lost their best horse than to lose her. Cross, who had been an old sailor, soon climbed down the wall to see what could be done. He found her doubled up considerably, but still alive, and asked the old man if he had any stout rope. He replied that he had a block and tackle out at the barn. We told him to go and get it, and to tell two of the soldiers at the picket post to come and help. He went to the barn and got the rope. He also found some other soldiers there, stealing eggs, and got them to come along.

We then got ropes around the old mare, and fastened one end around a tree nearby, and commenced hauling away, and as we would raise her, we would dig down the bank and fill up under her, and in this way finally got her out and lifted her upon her feet. We rubbed and worked with her some time, until she stood up and commenced eating grass.

The old folks were very much rejoiced. When we all went around to the porch the old man took me to one side and told me and Cross to remain awhile and they would have something to eat. The pickets went back to their posts and the others went off, and then we were invited in to dinner. We sat down to the best meal we had had in many a day.

We parted good friends, leaving the impression that Rebels were not such a detestable set as he had been led to believe.

CHAPTER 17

Battle of Gettysburg

Rodes' Division and ours (Clubby Johnson's) had marched direct from the Potomac to Carlisle, while Early's Division had crossed the mountains east, and gone to York, where they captured some ninety-day men who were guarding the place, whom they paroled and sent home. Longstreet's and Hill's Corps had not advanced far into Pennsylvania at this time.

After lying in camp one day at Carlisle we started on the march and returned towards the Potomac, when we met the paroled prisoners that Early had captured at York. General Johnson made them pull off their shoes and give them to his men who were barefooted. Some of our men thought it was cruel, but Johnson said they were going home, and could get other shoes quicker than he could, as he had work for his men to do.

We marched on until one day we turned abruptly to the left and crossed the South Mountain to the east. We had not heard a gun fired, nor heard anything about the Yankees until we had reached the top of the mountain, when we heard some artillery firing a long way off. Some of the boys remarked that "Old Early" had found some of the Yankees some place. We had no idea that the two armies were closing together, and that the greatest battle ever fought on the American continent had virtually commenced; but, of course, our officers knew.

We marched on down the mountain and heard the battle raging louder and fiercer; and just before sundown we reached the battleground, and saw some of the wounded and a great many prisoners. We learned that Early and Hill had attacked the advance corps of the enemy and driven them (with great slaughter on both sides) from the field and through the town of Gettysburg, on to the adjoining heights of Cemetery Ridge. Our division was marched over the battlefield and around to the east of Gettysburg, and took position that night on the extreme left of our army. We soon heard that the two armies had concentrated at that point, and that the ball would open in earnest at daylight. This was the night of July 1st, 1863.

The battle raged with increasing fury for the next two days. It commenced on the 1st of July, 1863, and lasted three days—the whole of both armies being engaged on the 2nd and 3rd.

Our pioneer troops had a good time during that battle. We had to remain near our division, but were not in much danger except from a few shells that would pass over us occasionally.

Lee's Army was the attacking party, and the enemy were strongly entrenched on the ridge, and acting on the defensive. General Lee wanted to turn their left; the hardest fighting was on our right and centre. Our whole division had less to do and was in less danger than any other portion of the army, as we had in our front the rugged and steep ridge of Culp's Hill, covered with trees and huge rocks. As the men advanced, they could protect themselves. They had to fire at an angle of about forty-five degrees to reach the breastworks on top of the ridge, and it would have been foolhardiness for any troops to attempt to charge the works at that point. The main object of our division was to make a bold front and keep up a continual firing, with an occasional charge, where the ground would admit of it, in order to attract the enemy's attention, while Longstreet was to charge and turn their left.

The enemy had every advantage of position, and would repulse every charge that was made. Our troops would at different points drive them from their works, but could not hold them for want of proper support.

The charging column would be nearly annihilated, and if a position were taken, they would not have men enough left to hold it. During the evening of the third day all the artillery on both sides opened fire (about 400 pieces), and it was the most terrible cannonading I ever heard. I was in a position where I could see the smoke from both sides along the whole line, which was in crescent shape, and it was one continual roar. I could not distinguish one report from another.

Night closed the terrible havoc, with nothing accomplished, both armies resting on their arms in the same positions they occupied the day before. That night the left of our army withdrew quietly from its position in front of the enemy, fell back beyond Gettysburg, and formed a line of battle in a good position, and laid there in line all day the 4th of July, expecting to be attacked by the enemy. His position was too strong for our army to successfully attack, and General Lee did not have ammunition enough to risk another engagement, except on the defensive. But I suppose the enemy had enough of fighting, too, for they never left their works during the day, and everything was quiet.

Thus, ended the Battle of Gettysburg; and, as General Lee had failed to drive the enemy from their position, there was nothing left for him to do but to retreat into Virginia.

During the second day's fighting we were rather short of rations, and, as all the people in the neighbourhood had fled for safety, leaving everything in their houses, we found plenty to eat by going to them and helping ourselves.

There was one large farmhouse close by where we pioneers were placed, and we went to it and found a bountiful supply of provisions.

The family must have left in haste, as the table was still set, with the dishes on it, just as if they had left their meal and run for dear life. We found several barrels of flour, a smokehouse full of bacon, a springhouse full of milk and butter, the garret full of crocks of apple butter, and everything eatable that is kept in a well-to-do farmhouse of a Pennsylvania Dutchman. If we did not live well for two days, and fill our haversacks full of good things there, I don't know a good thing when I see it. We would build fires in the stoves and outside and bake bread, cook meat and chickens, milk the cows, and run the plantation generally. We told the boys in the regiment about it, and some of them came over and cooked rations and carried them back for others. But in the evening of the third day, by some carelessness, the house caught on fire in the second storey from the stovepipe.

I was on the hill watching the artillery duel, and happened to look towards the house and saw the smoke coming from the roof, and knew it must be on fire. Several of us ran to the house. The men that were cooking inside did not know it was on fire. We then ran upstairs and found it all in flames, and too far gone for us to save. We then went to work and carried everything out of the lower storey and basement, except the stoves, and put them in the garden near the barn. The house was soon reduced to ashes, but it was done accidentally, and we regretted it very much. There must have been several young ladies living there, for we found their pictures and clothing in the bureau drawers, and also letters from their sweethearts in the army.

I suppose that when they came back and found their house burned, they thought it was set on fire by the shells, as several had hit near there, and one had gone through the barn. They could see by the things we had saved that it was not burned intentionally.

That night, when the army fell back, our pioneers never received any orders to leave, and we remained there all night. The next morning, as some of our cavalry were scouting around, they came to us and asked our officer what we were doing there, and if he did not know that our whole army had fallen back beyond Gettysburg that night.

Our lieutenant replied that he did not know it, and that he had no orders to leave; but the cavalryman told us there was nothing between us and the Yankees, and that we would soon be captured if we did not get away in a hurry; that they were just on a scout to see and watch the enemy's movements.

But we had been moved around so much, and moved in the night sometimes, that we did not know where to go, nor which way to start.

One of the cavalry offered to pilot us out, when we started, and by making a considerable circuit we arrived at our division in safety. If the Yanks had pushed out from their front that morning, they would have picked up many a straggling Rebel; but they did not appear anxious to see any Rebs. They remained quiet all day.

The night of the 4th we started on the retreat towards the Potomac. We had such an immense wagon train that we travelled very slowly, keeping the wagon train in front. The next day our rear guard and the enemy had several little skirmishes, but we were not bothered much except at one place. The Federal cavalry dashed into our wagon train as it was crossing the mountain, and turned about twenty wagons over and down the mountain side. The citizens would run out of the woods in some places and cut the spokes of the wheels, until one or two of them got killed for their trouble, when they ceased.

One day we were out of rations, and our officers let us kill any stock we found to get something to eat. We had stopped near a mill and large farmhouse, and some of the men were searching through the mill for rations. Down amongst the wheels they found a large lot of store goods that had been hidden there from a store nearby, so they loaded themselves down with them and carried them off. I went to the house and found some of the soldiers carrying off the beehives, but the bees stung one fellow so bad that he had to throw the hive down. Just then General Walker rode up and reprimanded them for taking the bees, and made them leave them.

I saw a beautiful young lady and her mother on the porch of the house, the only occupants about, and they were weeping so bitterly at the losses they had sustained from the soldiers that I had no heart to take anything. Just then I saw a soldier crawling out of the window with a ham of meat, and, as the young lady saw him, she commenced crying again, and said: "There goes the last mouthful in the house; what will we do?" and gave me an imploring look, and asked me if I could not do something for them. I knew it was no use for me to interfere, but, recollecting that General Walker was nearby, I ran around the house and told him the situation of affairs, when he rode around and made the man give the ladies the ham of meat, and they thanked us so kindly on their bended knees, the tears flowing down their cheeks, that it made an impression on me that I shall never forget. I went back to my command as well satisfied as if I had eaten a hearty meal. The looks of that beautiful lady imploring me for mercy did me good all over, although I knew our own dear women in Virginia had suffered ten times more from brutality of soldiers than these ever did.

When we arrived at Hagerstown, Md., our army halted formed a line of battle and made breastworks, in order to give battle should the enemy advance. Their cavalry had got between our army and the river, in order to destroy our wagon train; but General Imboden, with his cavalry and the wagoners, had repulsed them and driven them back, and saved the train.

The pioneers of each division were then sent on to Williamsport, on the Potomac river, a distance of six miles, and put to work building a pontoon bridge. We had brought pontoons along when we first crossed the river, and left the bridge there while we were north; but the enemy's cavalry had made a raid in our absence, and had cut the bridge loose, and a great many of the pontoons had floated off; consequently, we had to build some rough ones. We went to a lumber yard and carried the lumber to the bank of the river, and in two days had built sixteen pontoon boats, or scows.

The lumberman remarked, as we were taking his lumber, that the lumber was worth five dollars per hundred in gold. I told him to charge it to Jeff Davis & Co.—that General Lee's army was worth more than his lumber in gold. The river was full and past fording when we arrived at it, and the ferryboat was kept busy taking men across and bringing ammunition back for our army. The cavalry were swimming their horses across all the time we were at work, the army lying in line of battle, waiting for us to get the bridge built. When we got the boats made, we got some tar and borrowed the wash kettles around town to boil it in. The old women wanted to raise a row when we took their kettles, but we promised to bring them back; but we didn't. We then caulked and pitched the boats, launched them in the river, loaded them with lumber and went down the river to Falling Waters, five miles below, and put in the bridge. We there gathered up ten of the original pontoons that had been cut loose by the Yanks, and that had lodged along the river for a distance of five miles. Then the good ones we had saved and the sixteen new ones made twenty-six in all. It took all of them to reach across the river. When the bridge was completed the army commenced crossing the river, but the bridge was kept full all the time with ambulances, medical wagons, ordnance wagons and artillery, and such things as had to be kept dry, consequently there was no room for the infantry to cross, except one division, that was guarding the bridge. The rest waded the river at Williamsport. The greater portion of the wagon train had to ford at the same place. The water would come up under the arms of the men, but by crossing in a body and using their guns to steady themselves, they all got over safely.

We brought out 5,000 prisoners and had paroled 2,000 on the field, who had been captured at different places before the battle commenced. We also had an immense wagon train. We lost but few wagons, and only one or two pieces of artillery, that had been broken down.

The enemy's cavalry made a charge to capture the bridge, not knowing there was infantry lying behind the brow of the hill until they came close upon them, when the infantry poured such a volley into them at close quarters that they were nearly annihilated, and horses without riders were seen running in every direction. As the last ones crossed the bridge, they cut the cable that held it on the Maryland side, and the bridge floated around to the Virginia side.

That night, when everything was quiet, with sharpshooters on each side of the river, and the rain pouring down, we pioneers slipped down to the water's edge and drew out the ten good pontoon boats, loaded them on the wagons and sent them to the rear, and at the same time scuttled and sank the ones we had made up at Williamsport; but we worked very quietly, and made no noise, for we expected a volley every minute from the other side, but there was not a shot fired.

I will now give a detailed account of General Ed Johnson's Division of the 2nd Corps (my division), from the time it crossed the Potomac River, going north, until it returned. Other divisions and corps crossed at different times, at different places, and marched different roads.

We waded the Potomac River on the 18th of July, 1863, at Shepherdstown, what is now West Virginia, camped in Maryland, and moved by easy marches to Middleburg, on the State line between Maryland and Pennsylvania, and camped there the 23rd; then on to Greencastle and Marion, and camped near Chambersburg, and remained there one day. Then through Chambersburg and Green Village, and camped near Shippensburg. On the 27th we marched through Shippensburg, Palmstown, Stowestown, Mount Rock, and camped near Carlisle.

We lay in camp at that place the 28th, about twenty miles from Harrisburg, the capital of the State. The 29th we marched back over the same road through Mount Rock, Stowestown and Palmstown, and went into camp. The 30th we passed through Shippensburg and Green Village, then turned to the east through Scotland, destroyed a railroad bridge, and camped near Fayetteville.

On the 1st of July marched through Fayetteville, Griffenburg Springs and Cashtown, arriving on the battlefield at 4 o'clock p. m. A. P. Hill's Corps and Early's Division of the 2nd Corps had been fighting all day, and were driving the enemy when we arrived. We were marched around Gettysburg and took position on the extreme left, at Culp's Hill, but were not engaged that day. General R. E. Rodes' Division crossed the South Mountain, near Carlisle, and marched to the battlefield on the east side of the mountain, and arrived in time on the 1st of July to take part in the battle, and drove the Federals through Gettysburg.

The division was engaged more or less during the next two days, with varying success, sometimes advancing and gaining temporary advantage, then falling back and taking another position; sometimes losing heavily, and sometimes lightly, some brigades losing more than others, but the aggregate loss was less than several other divisions.

We started on the retreat from our line of battle at midnight of the 4th of July, moved along very slowly, waiting for the wagon train and artillery to get strung out in advance. Then marched all day, passing through Fairfield and Fayetteville, and camped at the foot of South Mountain at 10 o'clock at night. On the 6th we marched over the mountain, through the villages of Mountain Dale, Caledonia Springs and Frogtown, and camped to the left of Waynesboro.

On the 7th, marched through Lightersburg and camped three miles from Hagerstown, Md. The 8th and 9th remained in camp. On the 10th the pioneers were marched to Williamsport, on the Potomac River, and commenced building pontoon boats, the army remaining near Hagerstown in line of battle and entrenching, receiving ammunition from the Virginia side.

On the 11th the pioneers floated the pontoon boats, loaded with lumber, down the river five miles, to Falling Waters, and made the bridge.

The army crossed the Potomac into Virginia the 13th and 14th, at Falling Waters, and we took up the bridge the night of the 14th, making twenty-seven days that the division was north of the Potomac.

So ended the Pennsylvania campaign and the battle of Gettysburg. Our loss has been estimated at 15,000—the enemy's at 18,000, besides the 5,000 prisoners on each side. Captain William Powell, of my company, was severely wounded, which was all the loss our company sustained; but there were very few in the company at that time. In one of the charges on our right a colour-bearer in one of the Louisiana regiments in our division was cut off from his command and found that he would be captured, so he tore the flag from the staff, pulled off his clothes and wrapped the flag around his body, then put his clothes on over the flag. He was captured and went to prison. When he was exchanged and arrived in Richmond, he took off his clothes and unfurled the flag. Soldiers love their colours with such devotion that they will die in defending them, and consider it a disgrace to have them captured, and especially the colour-bearers.

"Billy," or Wes Gulp, was born and raised at Gettysburg, but had been living in Virginia for some time, and was a member of the 2nd Virginia Infantry, Stonewall Brigade, and was killed on Gulp's Hill the third day of the battle.

In a few days our army moved on up the valley, and, crossing the Blue Ridge, went into camp in Orange County, with the Rapidan River as our line of defence.

Chapter 18

Interesting Adventures

My father and family were living in Frederick County, about fifteen miles west of Winchester, and as we had given up all hope of emigrating to Missouri, they had concluded to move to Rockingham County, Virginia, the first opportunity. When our army drove the enemy out of Winchester and went on to Pennsylvania, my father came on after the army to see me. He overtook us the night we camped on the line between Maryland and Pennsylvania, and stayed all night with me, when we consulted as to what had best be done. I advised him to return home at once and move as soon as possible to Rockingham, as we did not know how long our army would remain north of Winchester, and if we fell back before he got moved, the chances were that he might not be able to get through for another year, as the enemy would occupy Winchester as soon as we left. He then left me, to return home and move farther south.

When our army reached Winchester, on our way to Orange County, I had not heard a word from my father—whether he had moved or not—and was very anxious and uneasy about the family, and thinking: perhaps they did not know we were falling back, and would be caught and captured while moving, I therefore stated the circumstances to our lieutenant, and asked permission to leave the army and go to my father's, that I might assist them if they had not left, and if they had moved I would return to the army the next day.

The lieutenant said that he could not give me permission to go, as it would have to come from higher authority, and that a pass from him would not amount to anything, anyhow; that he could not take the responsibility on himself to grant me leave of absence, but, if I went, he would not report me, and if I returned as soon as possible, without being arrested, he would not have me punished; but if I was arrested for being absent the martial law would have to take its course, and I would have to take the responsibility on myself.

So, with that understanding I started for home, and by keeping the by-roads I arrived there that night. I found my mother and sisters in a great state of excitement and fear. They had heard that our army was falling back, and told me father had taken one load to Rockingham, a distance of seventy miles, and had returned and started with another, and if he went on, he would not be back for several days, and that my sister Mary had gone on horseback with my uncle, who belonged to the cavalry. But while we were pondering over this state of affairs my father drove up with the team. He heard that our army was falling back, and had unloaded the wagon at Strasburg, in Shenandoah County, and made all haste to return for the family.

So, we loaded up in a hurry, and by daylight were on the road to Winchester with the wagon and a one-horse buggy. When we got within nine miles of Winchester, we heard that our army had already passed through, and there would be no troops between us and the enemy. We were then afraid to go on for fear of being captured and losing the team, especially if I was with them, so we concluded to take a by-road and keep near the mountains until we arrived at Strasburg.

That evening the rain poured down in torrents, and when we arrived at Hog Creek, a small stream that crossed the North-western turnpike, we found it so swollen from the rain that it was impossible to cross. I did not like the idea of remaining there in that public place all night, for I wanted to travel on during the night; so, I waded into the stream to see if we could risk it, but found it impossible to do so. I waded until the water reached my armpits, and found it getting deeper and swifter. There was no alternative but to camp on the bank of the creek all night.

At daylight the waters had so receded that we could cross in safety, and we did so. As we neared Winchester, we heard that some few of our cavalry were still in the place, and that the enemy were not advancing. We then concluded to risk it by going through Winchester, as we would have a good macadamised road to travel, while if we took the by-road it would be rough and muddy. But in crossing a small washout in the road one of the hind wheels chucked down in a hole, and as the wagon was very heavily loaded it strained and cracked the axle. We passed safely through Winchester, but when we arrived at Middletown, five miles from Strasburg, we found the axle had given way so much that we could go no further.

My father then went to Major Crisman, a farmer nearby, with whom he was acquainted, and borrowed a large wagon of him, so we could get on to Strasburg. We unloaded the contents of our wagon into it and proceeded on our journey. When we arrived at Cedar Creek, we found the bridge burned, and had to cross the creek at a miserable ford. The wagon being a four-horse wagon, with a heavy load on it, our two horses could not pull it up the bank on the opposite side, so we had to camp another night on the bank of a creek and run the risk of being captured. But by good luck, with all the bad luck mixed with it, we arrived in Strasburg the next day. We felt considerably relieved, as no enemy had yet been heard of in the neighbourhood.

We then unloaded Major Crisman's wagon, and my father took it back, and returned with our wagon when he had a new axle put in. We loaded up and proceeded on our journey safely, nothing of interest transpiring until we arrived at Lacy Springs, in Rockingham County, where my father had rented a house of Mr. Barly, and where he had left his first load of goods. We found that Sister Mary had arrived there in safety. I remained a few days at home, helping them to fix things up, when I filled my haversack with good "grub," bade them farewell, and started across the mountain on a by-path to the army, in Orange County.

The first night I stayed with a farmer in Swift Run Gap, at the foot of the Blue Ridge. The next evening, I arrived at Standardsville, on the east side of the ridge, in Green County, and there found several soldiers on their way to the army—some of them musicians belonging to the 10th Virginia band. They wanted me to stay all night with them, but I went on.

After traveling about two miles, I met a man on horseback and two soldiers walking. He halted me and wanted to know where I was going. I replied that I was "on my way to my command."

"Have you a pass?" said he.

I told him I had not. He then said he would have to arrest me and take me to the army; that he had orders to arrest every soldier that had no pass or furlough, and take them to headquarters; that he had arrested the two men that were with him; and told me to turn round and go back to Standardsville with him, and he would take us to the army the next day.

It surprised me very much, for he was dressed in citizens' clothes, and did not look like a soldier that had seen any service. So, I sat down by the side of the road and wanted to know who he was, and what command he belonged to. He replied that he was a "conscript officer," and that he did not belong to the army, but that he lived in Standardsville.

I then told him that he could not arrest me; that I was an old soldier, and was on my way to the army; that my home was many miles behind me, and that I would arrive at the army the next day. I then commenced abusing him for keeping out of the army, and told him he had better take a musket and go in ranks, instead of hunting up men that were in the service; and that I did not intend to go back with him.

He then said he would make me go, and pulled out his pistol and threatened to shoot me. I just dared him to shoot, and told him that I would bet that he never shot at a Yankee or anyone else in his life; that he was coward, or he would not seek for such an office in order to keep out of the range of bullets. I then scolded the two soldiers who were with him for being arrested by such a "puke" as he was.

One of the soldiers then came to me, and, whispering, told me they were Louisianans, and for me to come and go back with them, and we would put the "fixins" on our bold conscripting officer that night. I knew then they had some plan to escape; so, after quarrelling awhile longer with him, I told him I was very tired after walking all day, and if he would dismount and let me ride back to town, I would go; but if not, I would remain where I was.

He concluded that was the best he could do, and I got on his horse and rode back; but I abused him so much he threatened, if I did not stop, to make me walk. I told him if he did, I would not go a step further, so that settled it. When we arrived in town it was dark, and he took us out to the edge of town and put us in a small brick jail (the county jail).

But before leaving us we made him promise to bring us something to eat. I then told him there were several more soldiers up there at the hotel, and to go and bring them also, and we would have a fine time. He said he would, but I knew some of them had guns, and if he went to fooling around them, they would kill him. I did not care if they did; but he never brought them down; neither did he bring us anything to eat, and we never heard of him afterwards.

As soon as he had gone, we inspected our room by the aid of matches, and found it had two windows with iron gratings across, and a fireplace in one corner. There happened to be an old musket standing in one corner. So, we soon formed our plan, which was that when he brought us something to eat, we would knock him in the head with the musket and then make our escape. But we waited in vain. After a long time, we commenced hallooing, and yelled as loud as we could; but no one came. We then concluded to try another plan. We tore out all the sash in the windows and made a fire in the fireplace. I divided my rations with the others, and as we had table knives in our haversacks, we commenced digging the mortar out between the bricks near one window. As soon as we got one brick loose, we took the stock off the gun, and, using the breech for a pry, we soon made a hole large enough to crawl through, but still prepared, if anyone came, to adhere to our first plan. But everything remained quiet.

The jail appeared to be in an isolated place, for we made as much noise as possible, to attract som one there. When the breach in the wall was large enough one of the Louisianans got out, and I passed him the gun-barrel. He surveyed the premises, and found no one about. We then handed out our baggage, and left. After going a short distance, we held a council of war. The other two soldiers said they had deserted the infantry, and were going to join Major Harry Gilmore's command. That they were tired of the infantry, but would go in the cavalry, and insisted that I should go with them, but I would not consent. I told them I was going on to the army. They said that fellow would arrest me again. I told them he would not. I then parted with them—they going one way and I another. I then walked down the road about two miles, and lay down and slept until daylight.

The next day I kept in the big road and went on to the army, unmolested. I never saw nor heard anything more of my bold "conscript officer." I arrived in camp that evening, and told everybody of my adventures, but was not punished in any way.

Our division was camped at Montpelier, President Madison's old homestead, a few miles from Orange Court House. As the weather was hot and dry, we did not have any work to do, but lay idle in camp and took a good rest, and recruited up after our severe campaigns.

There was a large cornfield between our pioneer camp and where our brigade was camped, and the corn was in roasting-ears; but there was a guard kept stationed around the field to keep the soldiers from stealing the corn. There was a road through the field, and on one side the Rapidan River. Every day some of us would go through the field to the brigade, and as we came back, we would steal a few ears of corn, and then hide them under our jackets, so the guard could not see them. On the river side there were no guards stationed. We would go above the field and go in swimming, taking sacks along, and swim down the river until we had passed the guards and gotten opposite the cornfield, when we would get out of the water and fill our sacks with corn, and then swim back, keeping the sacks under water. We managed in that way to steal about half the corn that was in the field, although it was guarded night and day as long as we remained in that camp.

Directly after we arrived at this camp there were about thirty soldiers belonging to the 1st and 3rd North Carolina Regiments in our division, who deserted in a body and took their guns with them. They started for home in North Carolina, intending to resist arrest if molested; but when they arrived at the James River, they found every ford and ferry guarded, and could not cross. They undertook to force their way, with the result that some were killed and wounded on both sides, some escaped, and ten were captured. They were sent to Richmond and court-martialled immediately, and sentenced to be shot to death. They were then sent back to their regiments to be executed in the presence of the whole division, as a warning to the balance of us. When they arrived our pioneer corps were detailed to dig the graves, make the coffins, put up the posts and bury them. We planted ten posts in the ground, about three feet high and about fifty feet apart, all in line, boring a hole in each post near the top, and putting in a crosspiece. We dug one large grave in the edge of the woods, large enough to hold the ten coffins.

When everything was completed and in readiness, the division was formed in a hollow square around the field, except the side the posts were on. The prisoners were then brought from the guard-house, conducted by a heavy guard, accompanied by the chaplain and surgeons. As the column entered the field they were headed by the fifers and drummers—the drums being muffled-splaying the dead march. They had some distance to march before arriving at the place of execution, and I noticed that they kept step and marched as precisely as if they were on drill.

On arriving at the place, they were halted, and the chaplain talked to and prayed with them. Then an officer took each man, conducted him to his post, placed him on his knees, with his back to the post and

"Stonewall" Brigade Marching into Pennsylvania.

his arms hooked over the crosspiece, and his hands tied together in front of his body, and then blindfolded him.

One hundred and fifty men composed the detail for the execution of the prisoners. They were taken from the different commands of the division. The posts before which the prisoners were placed were fifty feet apart. Ten men marched out in front of each prisoner—making one hundred in all in the front line. One-half the guns were loaded with ball cartridges—having been prepared by some officer so the soldier would not know whether his gun was loaded with ball or not. In the rear of each ten men there were five more soldiers with loaded guns, as a reserve, to finish the execution should any of the condemned men not be killed at the first fire. At the command: "Ready! Aim! Fire!" one volley was heard, all the guns in the front rank being discharged. Then a surgeon stepped forward to each prisoner and felt his pulse. They found two of them, not dead, when the reserve guard stepped out and fired again. When they were pronounced dead, the division was marched by them in two ranks, in order that all might see them.

After the troops had gone to camp the wagons drove up with the coffins, and it was our duty to untie them, place them in the coffins and load them in the wagons. The one that I helped to put away had received, four bullets in his breast, and the rope that his hands were tied with was cut apart by a bullet. We then buried them. The chaplain, being an Episcopalian, performed the services according to the ritual of his church.

It cast a gloom over the entire army, for we had never seen so many executed at one time before. But we knew it would never stop desertion in the army, for I believe the more they shot the more deserted, and when they did desert, they would go to the enemy, where they knew they would not be found. One day the whole army was formed near Orange Court House and marched in review in columns and inspected by the officers. They kept us marching around all day, and at night we returned to camp.

As we were cleaning up camp one day, we were divided into two squads, sweeping with brush brooms and doing police work generally. As we finished, we met in rear of the camp, and each squad claimed they had done the most work, until, finally, one fellow belonging to the other squad, named James Roadcap, of the 10th Virginia, got mad at some remark I had made, and struck me over the head and face with his brush broom. I flew at him, and we had a regular knockdown for a few minutes, until some of the others separated us, for fear the officers would see us and put us in the guard-house. But I mashed the knuckle of my little finger against his head, and it is in that fix today, although not the least in my way. I think every time I look at it that it is one of the relies of the war. But Jim and I were soon good friends again. I carried a crippled hand for several days, and told the officers I had a boil on it.

CHAPTER 19

Retreat across the Rapidan

In September, as the enemy had advanced their lines from the Rappahannock to the Rapidan, we were moved down the river several miles north of Orange Court House, and camped at Pisgah Church, and commenced fortifying along the south bank of the Rapidan.

The first day they took us out to work we reported to the engineers, who were laying off some gun-pits for artillery in a potato patch, near a large farmhouse, and as the pioneers had to wait until they were laid off before we could go to work, we soon commenced digging potatoes.

I had gotten some distance from my squad and was very busily occupied with the potatoes, not noticing that they had gone to work at the pits, when General George H. Stuart (Maryland Stuart), Brigadier of the 3rd Brigade, happened to notice me and saw what I was doing, and came riding up to me, and, before I knew it, was alongside of me.

"What are you doing here?" said he. He took me so by surprise that I wheeled around, not realising who had spoken.

"Digging a gunpit," I replied.

"The h—l you are," said he, "you are digging potatoes; now go back to your place and let those potatoes alone."

But I had my haversack full of potatoes, and the boys joked me for a long time about it, and by the time those pits were done there wasn't a potato left in that patch.

The Yankee pickets were quartered in some houses along the river on the opposite side from us, and our boys would make up a volunteer party and wade the river at night, surround the house and capture the whole post, just for amusement, and get some good, genuine coffee. They had to get the consent, however, of some of the officers first.

They had made several successful raids of that kind when, one day, as we were working near the river, we located a good post to capture, and as General Ewell came riding up at that time some of the boys asked him if we could not go over that night and capture the post. He remarked that it would not amount to anything, and that we would be running a risk that was not at all necessary, and that he had found that if a soldier did his duty in the ranks, he had enough to do without volunteering to do any more.

I often thought of his advice afterwards, and was pleased to think that he would not rush us into danger unless it was necessary.

As we were making trenches for the infantry, we would divide out in squads of three, one pick for two shovels, and as soon as we would finish one piece, we would move on up the line. One evening the lieutenant had gone to camp and left us in charge of Sergeant McGhee, of the 23rd Virginia, and when the time arrived to quit work the squad that I was with had not finished our space. As they were all returning to camp, I proposed that we should go, too, and leave it unfinished. The others sanctioned my proposal, and we went to camp.

On arriving there, the lieutenant inquired if the line was completed. The sergeant replied that there were several spaces unfinished. He wanted to know, then, "Who was working at them, and who proposed leaving it undone?" He was informed that I was the one. He ordered me before his august presence and commenced cursing me, and wanted to know why I did not remain and finish it. I replied that we had done as much work as the balance of the corps, and had gotten that much ahead of them, and that I did not consider that we were required to remain there longer than the others, but that if they would have remained I certainly would.

"And furthermore," said I, "you must not curse me, or I will report you to headquarters."

He then ordered the sergeant to take me out and make me pile brush for one hour. I went out with the sergeant, but told him that "I would not pile brush," that "I would go to the guard-house first." That was one advantage a private had over an officer. An officer can punish a private, but he dare not curse him.

The sergeant then went back to the lieutenant and told him what I had said. He then sent for me and talked very mildly, and said that he did not want to punish me; that he knew I was a good hand to work, and that he wanted that to be the last time I disobeyed orders. He knew that I would report him, and he wanted to smooth it over. He told me to go to my quarters, and he never cursed me afterwards.

Several days after that someone stole his watch out of his tent, and the next morning he had the long roll beat at daylight, and we were ordered to fall in and be ready to march at once. None of us knew that he had lost his watch but the one who stole it, and we were taken by surprise to think there was a move on hand. But it was a ruse of his to search the whole corps for his watch; but no watch was found. He never did get it or hear from it. The fellow who stole it was as sharp as he was, and made way with it. We always suspected Sam Nunnelly stole it, but never knew. Sam would risk his life for a watch.

On the 8th of October the greater portion of our army crossed the Rapidan, and by a circuitous route, through Madison Court House, came to the Rappahannock River, west of where General Meade's Army lay, the object being to make a flank movement and get in rear of his army and between him and Washington City.

We met a small force of the enemy, who wanted to oppose our passage across the river, but they were soon driven back by our cavalry. We had left some of our troops on the south bank of the Rapidan, and the enemy had crossed there, but were repulsed and driven back.

By this movement General Meade learned General Lee's intentions, and fell back towards Manassas Junction. Our advance troops under General A. P. Hill attacked him at Bristoe Station, but were repulsed. He failed to get in his rear, and before the whole army was up and in line General Meade had fallen back again beyond Bull Run and commenced fortifying. As Lee was too near Washington to effect a flank movement, there was nothing left for him to do but fall back across the Rappahannock. As we fell back, we destroyed the railroad and burned the bridges.

As we were tearing down the stone abutments of a bridge one day several of us were sent to the base of the "butment" to roll the rocks in the river. Some of the men above, not noticing the party working below, threw a large rock down on us, but fortunately no one was hurt except myself. One corner of the rock grazed my head and cut a gash about one inch long, and stunned me considerably; but I soon recovered and was all right except a sore head for several days. It was a narrow escape, for if it had hit me squarely it would have fairly mashed me.

The flank movement was planned all right, but failed in its execution, as the enemy found out our movements soon after we started. We did not have Jackson, with his secrecy and midnight marches, to take them by surprise. He was the only general in the army that could make a move of that kind successfully. It was the same kind of a move, and over some of the same ground, that he had made in rear of

"Stonewall" Brigade at Culp's Hill, Gettysburg, July 2, 1863.

General Pope previous to the Second Battle of Manassas. Our other generals were good defensive generals, but we never had a general that could execute a flank movement like General Jackson. During the balance of the war we had to fight the enemy when attacked, and fortify in order to hold our own.

After crossing the Rappahannock our division went into camp near Brandy Station, and as the weather was getting cold some of the soldiers commenced building winter quarters, although we had no orders to do so.

My mess hesitated in building quarters, fearing that we would have to move again, and leave them, but as regiment after regiment continued to build and the officers were having permanent quarters put up, we concluded that we would build also. Charley Cross, Sam Nunnelly, John Hawkins and myself were messing together. We went to work in earnest and put up a nice log shanty, covered it with clapboards, went to an old barn nearby and got some planks for a floor and bunks, built a stick chimney, and were prepared to live in high style.

The evening we finished it I built a fire in the fireplace to see how my chimney would draw. Hawkins cooked supper, and just after dark we were seated on the floor partaking of our evening meal, and complaining of being very tired, as we had worked hard, when the unwelcome sound of "long roll" aroused us from our reveries, and we had to fall in ranks, bag and baggage, and march off at a quick march down the river to Kelley's Ford, where Rodes' Division was quartered.

We learned that the enemy had crossed in force, taking our troops by surprise and capturing the greater portion of two regiments. We were halted in Rodes' camp, where his men had rushed out in line of battle in order to check the enemy, and had left everything belonging to them in their shanties except their arms. We remained there about one hour, and plundered their camp thoroughly, taking whatever we could make use of. We then marched back, passed our quarters, and continued all night towards Culpeper Court House. That was the last time I saw our shanty from that day to this.

That night, on the march, Sam Nunnelly came to me and gave me what he thought to be a bag of smoking tobacco, as I was a great smoker and he did not use the weed. So, I filled my pipe to take a good smoke, but, after a few puffs, I found I had something besides tobacco in my pipe, as it burned my tongue and seemed to set my mouth on fire. I then went to a light to examine the contents of the bag, and found it to be cayenne pepper. I was going to fight Sam about it, thinking he had done it intentionally, but he declared he thought it was tobacco, as it was in a tobacco sack; but we kept the pepper all the same, and used it on our meat.

General Early's Division was guarding the river above our division, and had two brigades on the north side of the river, and a pontoon bridge thrown across. They were attacked in the night, taken by surprise, and nearly all captured. There were not many killed or wounded in these engagements, but we lost about 2,000 prisoners and two strong positions, and General Lee was compelled to fall back across the Rapidan to our old position, that we had left in October. It showed a good piece of generalship on the part of General Meade, and neglect on the part of our division commanders, but as the enemy had never been known to make an advance in the night with such desperate and quiet charges, our troops were taken by surprise before they could realise the situation.

The second night of our retreat I laid down in a fence corner near Culpeper Court House, by a good fire made of rails, went to sleep with my feet to the fire, and got to dreaming of having my feet mashed as in a vise, and awakened with so much suffering that I at once grabbed my feet and found that my shoes were burned to a crisp, and held my feet like a vise sure enough. I took them off in a hurry and could never get them on again. I had to go on to camp barefooted, although the weather was severely cold.

When we arrived in camp Sam Nunnelly was missing, and we thought he was captured; but some of the boys said they would bet he was out plundering some place.

Sure enough, the next day Sam came riding into camp on a crippled cavalry horse he had picked up, bare-backed and with a rope bridle. He had such a load of plunder that he looked like a Jew peddler. The boys all commenced teasing him and wanted him to "divide up." They wanted to know if he had joined the cavalry, and where were his spurs, and stripes, as we thought he ought to be a brigadier.

Sam was as good-hearted a fellow as ever lived; a brave soldier, and, one of the best foragers in camp. If there was anything to be had for love or money or by stealing it, Sam would have it; but he was the greatest of all in plundering a battlefield. Sam said he intended to keep that horse to forage with, but he soon had to turn him over to the quartermaster.

Our division was camped near, and guarding Germanna Ford, on the Rapidan. On the 27th of November General Meade crossed the river and undertook a flank movement around our army; but our division was marched out to intercept him, and as we were marching along the road near Mine Run, we were suddenly attacked. The division was thrown into confusion for a few moments, but General Johnson soon faced them in line towards the enemy, and charged them so vigorously that they were soon repulsed, and by the time the other division arrived the battle was over. Our loss in killed and wounded was about 450; the enemy's must have been double that number, as we fought the 3rd Corps (Frenches) and one division of the 5th.

We were marching in front of the division as usual, when all at once we heard firing in our rear on the road that we had just passed along. The attack was so sudden and unlooked for that if it had not been for the presence of mind and indomitable courage of General Johnson, the other officers and the men, the whole division might have been routed and the flank of our whole army turned, our strong position taken and a repetition of the affair of Brandy Station and Kelley's Ford enacted. But as it was, General Lee formed his line that night on the south bank of Mine Run, on a commanding position, and fortified.

For several days General Meade lay in front of us with his whole army, and kept up a skirmish and artillery fight, but declined a general engagement. We heard from some prisoners that at one time he had ordered an attack, but thinking our position too strong he countermanded the order and fell back to the north bank of the Rapidan.

While we lay in line of battle on Mine Run two men belonging to the Louisiana Brigade were sentenced to be shot, and were taken out in front of the works to be executed, but they broke and ran to the enemy's line and escaped. The guards fired at them, but did not hit them, and did not try, I suppose, for we did not want to see any of the soldiers executed, and would give them every chance to escape that we could so as not to incriminate ourselves.

After everything was quiet, we marched back and went into winter quarters near Orange Court House. Our pioneer troops happened to get some good quarters, already built, that had been vacated by a battalion of artillerymen. So, we were repaid for the quarters we lost at Brandy Station.

When we were camped at Pisgah Church, early in the fall, John Hawkins, of the 23rd Virginia, was acquainted with a family named Kube, near Mine Run, and insisted that I should go on a visit with him one Sunday to see them. I readily consented as soon as he had informed me that there were two or three good-looking young ladies there. We paid them a visit and spent a pleasant time. I was considerably smitten with one of them, Miss Mollie, and, being invited to come again, we visited them at every opportunity, and I came nearer falling in love than I had during any time of the war.

When we were lying in line of battle at Mine Run we were near the house, and several shells fell in their yard, and, of course, Hawkins and myself sympathized with them and watched every opportunity to offer them protection should they need it, as the family was composed of a widowed mother and three daughters, their son and brother being in a different portion of the army, and the husband and father dead.

After going into winter quarters, we visited them several times and enjoyed their company hugely. The other boys would tease us and want to know when we were going again to "Cuba." We lay quietly in camp, with nothing to do except keep the roads in repair between our camps and Orange Court House, where we drew our supplies. Thus, ended the campaign of 1863.

CHAPTER 20

Battle of the Snowballs

General Meade displayed better generalship than any General in the Northern army that we had to contend with, except General McClellan, and came nearer baffling General Lee than any of the others by his vigorous and prompt movements and his secrecy in every movement from Gettysburg to Mine Run.

The pioneer troops were divided into messes of twelve, and one of the twelve remained in camp to cook, while the others went out to work. During the winter of 1863 and '64 I was cook for our mess.

One day as they returned from work Sam Nunnelly brought a pig along that he had caught in the road near some negro shanties, and gave it to me to raise. I told him I did not want to be bothered with it, but he insisted we should keep it, and as it was quite a pet we adopted it and called it "Susan Jane." It would run around the quarters and eat the scraps and find some corn at the stables and get plenty to eat. At night we would let it sleep in our shanty under the bunks; but when we got up every morning it would be lying in the fire-place in the ashes to keep warm. Every wash day we would wash it clean in the suds, and then make it stand up on the bed until it got dry. It was a white pig and improved rapidly, and was as tame as a dog and would follow any one who called it. I had to tie a clog to it to keep it from following some of the soldiers to their camps.

One day it got loose from the clog and I could not find it; but someone told me they had seen it following some Georgians who belonged to Rodes' Division. I hurried over to Rodes' Division, which was camped about one-half mile from us, and just got there in time to save its throat from being cut, and it being made a feast of by the Georgians. It was a great pet in camp and I had to watch it continually to keep it from being stolen from me, as it would make good pork any time. Everyone who knew it said they never saw a hog increase in weight so rapidly.

About the first of April I concluded to butcher it and have a barbecue for the whole company, as it would weigh about two hundred pounds, and we did not know how soon we would have to start on a campaign. Lieutenant Cockrill, of the 2nd Virginia, had spoken for the head for his mess; but we were all doomed to disappointment, for a few days before the slaughter was to take place "Susan Jane" turned up missing, and we never saw her again. I always thought the Louisianans stole her, as they had made the attempt several times. Anyway, I lost my pork.

Soldiers are very fond of pets, as I think all persons are who are isolated from home. Nearly every separate command had some kind of pet. The Louisiana Brigade had a medium sized dog, black and white spotted, very intelligent, called "Sawbuck." Nearly everyone in the division knew the dog. He would go into battle with the brigade, dashing up and down the line barking and making all the racket he could. One time he got wounded in the fore leg, and never would go in again. The boys said "Sawbuck" was playing "old soldier." If he would happen to get lost from the brigade when they went into camp after a day's march, he would station himself by the road and watch for the stragglers until he saw one belonging to his brigade, then follow him to camp. He knew every man who belonged to Stafford's Louisiana Brigade.

My father came from Rockingham to see me in this camp and brought me a new pair of boots and some new clothing; also a box of good things to eat, which were relished by my mess. He remained with us several days and then went home. Some of the boys would get up parties and dances in the country, and have a houseful of ladies. We would take the musicians from camp, and, altogether, spent a pleasant time that winter.

Considerable snow fell that winter, and every time it snowed the soldiers would turn out and have snowball battles. One day our division challenged Rodes' Division to battle in a large field. They came out, and the battle raged with various success until towards evening, when a great many of our division got tired of it and went to camp. When Rodes' men saw our line weakened they brought up some fresh troops and made a charge and ran us into our quarters, and then fell back, formed a new line and dared us out It looked rather bad for us to be defeated in that way, so some of the boys went to General Walker and got him to come out and take command.

It was fun for Walker, so he mounted his horse, collected his staff, and sent conscript officers all over camp and forced the men out. We had signal corps at work, took our colours out in line, had the drummers and fifers beat the long roll, had couriers carrying dispatches and everything done like in a regular engagement with the enemy.

In the meantime Rodes' men were making snow balls, and had piles of them along the crest of the ridge ready for us when we should charge. Some of their officers on horseback started on a raid to get in our rear and capture our wagon train. They did get in our rear and came across three wagons that were going to the station for rations, and rode alongside and commenced whipping the mules and started off with them at a gallop, the drivers not knowing what it all meant. But our officers got after them and recaptured the wagons and dispersed them, and they had to make a circuit of about five miles to get back to their lines. Several of them lost their hats and never did find them.

When General Walker got everything in readiness, and the line formed, he ordered us to charge up close to Rodes' men and then wheel and fall back, so as to draw them after us and away from the piles of snowballs they had made. When the drums beat, we were to wheel again and charge them and run them over the hill and capture their snowballs. We did so and the plan worked successfully. At the same time the Louisiana brigade slipped around through the woods and struck them on the left flank, by surprise, and the rout was complete. We ran them on to their camps and through them, and as some of the Louisianans were returning, they stole some cooking utensils from Rodes' men and kept them. We captured several stands of colours, but we had lost several in the earlier part of the fight. Officers would be captured and pulled off their horses and washed in the snow, but all took it in good part. After the fight was over we went out with a flag of truce and exchanged prisoners.

It was probably the greatest snowball battle ever fought, and showed that "men are but children of larger growth." The Richmond papers had several columns each giving an account of the battle. If all battles would terminate that way it would be a great improvement on the old slaughtering plan.

Directly after we went into winter quarters, near Orange Court House, the Louisiana brigade and our brigade joined together and built a large log house, covered it with clapboards, erected a stage, organised a theatrical troupe of negro minstrels and gave performances nearly every night to a crowded audience.

Admission one dollar—net proceeds to be given to widows and orphans of Confederate soldiers.

Noble T. Johnson, of the 5th Virginia, was one of the end men, handled the bones, and was one of the most comical characters I ever saw. He could keep the house in a roar of applause all the time. Miller, of the 1st Louisiana, was banjoist, and a splendid performer. They would write some of their own plays, suitable to the times and occasion.

One splendid piece was called the *Medical Board*—a burlesque on the surgeons. The characters were a number of surgeons sitting around a table playing cards, with a bottle of brandy on the table, which was passed around quite frequently, until one doctor inquired how they came to get such good brandy.

"Oh! this is some that was sent down from Augusta County for the sick soldiers, but the poor devils don't need it, so we'll drink it."

Then a courier would come in and inform them that there was a soldier outside badly wounded.

"Bring him in! bring him in!" said the chief surgeon.

When brought in an examination would take place with the result that his arm would have to be amputated. Then the poor fellow wanted to know if when that was done, he could not have a furlough.

"Oh! no," replied the surgeon.

A further examination developed that his leg would have to be amputated.

"Then can I have a furlough?" said the soldier.

"By no means," replied the surgeon, "for you can drive an ambulance when you get well."

It was finally determined by the medical board, as he was wounded in the head, that his head would have to come off.

"Then," says the soldier, "I *know* I can have a furlough."

"No, indeed," replied the surgeon, "we are so scarce of men that your body will have to be set up in the breastworks to fool the enemy."

Many such pieces as the foregoing were acted—burlesques on the officers, quartermasters and commissaries, or whatever was interesting and amusing. Taking it all together we had splendid performances. I have never seen better since the war, as we had amongst us professional actors and musicians; and the theatre became a great place of resort to while away the dull winter nights.

As I was a shoemaker and had a few tools, such as awl, claw-hammer and pocket-knife, I was prepared to half-sole the boys' shoes. I made my own pegs and a last. The next thing, and most important, was leather. Sometimes we could get government leather from the quartermaster; but in order to obviate that difficulty I formed a partnership with Sam McFadden, a messmate, of the 14th Louisiana. Sam was to steal the leather, such as cartridge-box lids, saddle-skirts, and housings from the harness, as they were very common on the Virginia harness used in the army. We would then charge five dollars in "Confed" for half-soling, and divide, which kept us in spending money.

One night as we were returning from a visit to our brigade, in passing the tent of the colonel of the 2nd Virginia, we noticed his McClellan saddle hung up on the outside. Sam said that was a good chance to lay in a stock of leather, as the firm was about out. Consequently, we clipped the skirts off and went on to our quarters; but as there were several soldiers in our shanty who did not belong there, we concluded to leave the saddle skirts on the outside until the coast was clear, knowing full well the colonel would raise a racket in the morning about his saddle being cut.

After the crowd had dispersed, we went out to bring in our stock, but it was gone. Someone had stolen it from us. We never did hear of those skirts again, and were afraid to inquire for fear the colonel would hear of it and have us punished.

Our division was not called out for any active service during the winter of 1863-4 until in March, when the Federal cavalry crossed the Rappahannock under Kilpatrick and Dalgren on their raid to capture Richmond. They were repulsed, when our corps was sent down to the old battlefield of Chancellorsville to head them off, but they did not return that way. After lying there one day our corps returned to camp. As I was cook, I was left in camp, and had charge of the camp in their absence. The boys reported that the old battle ground was full of bones bleached white by exposure, as the bodies of the slain had been covered very shallow, and the rains had washed the dirt off.

We were kept busy fortifying along the Rapidan, making roads and doing picket duty until May 4, 1864, when we heard that General Grant had taken command of the "Army of the Potomac" in person and was crossing the Rapidan at Germanna and Ely's fords with his whole army, intending to turn General Lee's right and march on to Richmond.

My old Company A was quite small at this time. It consisted of Sergeant William Montgomery and John Tharp, who had returned to the company from Imboden's cavalry; James Gaither, William Sivells; Captain William Powell, who was not well yet from his wound; Jos. Carder, who was detailed as Commissary Sergeant; Elisha Carder, the drummer nicknamed "Purty," Joe McNemar, who was sick in the hospital, and myself, detailed in the pioneer troops.

Lee's Army left camp on the morning of the 4th of May and marched all day towards the enemy, passed by Mine Run and the house where Miss Mollie Kube lived. I called in and gave her farewell and have never seen or heard of her since. So that wound up my army courtship.

The next morning, the 5th, we were on the march again and soon heard the skirmishers engaged. It was not long until the Battle of the Wilderness opened with great fury. We pioneers were halted while the battle raged the hottest, but were soon ordered up to the front and commenced fortifying.

We found our troops had repulsed and driven the enemy some distance and we were ordered to make a line of works in order to hold our position. We worked with the troops nearly all night and had a very good line by daylight.

I got a pocket diary out of a dead Yankee's pocket that evening and he had written in it that morning just after he had crossed the river. It ran thus:

> May 5th our corps has crossed the river safely and seen no Rebels yet; have not heard a gun fired.

But the poor fellow soon met the Rebels and lay cold in death. I kept the diary for a long time intending, if I ever had an opportunity, to send it home to his parents, as their address was in it. He was from Pennsylvania; but, having lost it, I have forgotten his name. On the 6th the battle raged again with fury. Grant making the attack at different points along the line, but he was everywhere repulsed with great slaughter, as our men had gathered up all the guns from the dead and wounded, and had them loaded and ready for a charge. Towards night the troops on our right charged the enemy under Generals Shaler and Seymour, capturing them and nearly all of their commands. They came near routing the whole army; but it was then dark and they did not know how successful they had been, and did not push on.

General Grant, on the 7th, seeing that he was foiled and outgeneraled, commenced moving to the right. A portion of our army, keeping on the move parallel with him, had considerable skirmishing and fighting. Our corps remained in the Wilderness on the 7th to watch their movements and bury the dead. At one place in front of the 3rd Brigade, where the enemy had made a desperate charge on the 6th, we buried five hundred of them that lay in line as they fell. Our troops at this place only lost two men, and one of them was shot accidentally.

Sergeant Bradly, nicknamed "Doggie" because he could bark like a feist, of Company F, was on the skirmish line on the fifth. He always held to the theory that if a man was born to be killed, he would be killed anyway and there was no use in trying to protect himself from the bullets. As the firing was heavy, and each man behind a tree on the skirmish line, someone hallooed to "Doggie" to get behind a tree or he would be killed. He replied that if he was "to be killed the tree wouldn't save him," and remained where he was. In a few moments he was shot dead. I never believed in such a theory and would shield myself all I could.

One evening one of our officers was telling us that he had found a wounded Yankee officer down in the pines; that he had a fine gold watch and had taken it off and wrapped it up in a piece of paper and put it in his pants' pocket; that he was mortally wounded and unconscious, and would die soon, when he would go back and get the watch, as he did not like to take anything from a wounded man. Sam Nunnelly heard him telling this. That was enough for Sam—he was soon missing. When he came back, I asked him if he had not been down there and taken that watch from the Yankee. He said he had, as the man was about dead anyhow, and that the Lieutenant would never see that watch.

As we started out to bury the dead there was one of the Federals lying beside the road, who had been killed about the first fire, and had lain there nearly three days. I had noticed him the first. I and another soldier started to bury him, when the other fellow said: "Hold on until I search him." I said that was no use, as he had been lying there so long, and thousands of troops had passed by him, and that he had probably been searched before he got cold. But he kept on searching and finally found forty dollars in greenbacks. I then wanted him to divide, but he refused to do so. After that I searched everyone I helped to bury, but found nothing but a few pocket-knives.

We got out of rations during this battle and could not get to our wagons, but the Yankees had four or five days' rations of "hard tack" and bacon in their haversacks, and we would get them from the dead. I have been so hungry that I have cut the blood off from crackers and eaten them.

On the 8th our corps moved on down the line as General Grant was concentrating his force near Spotsylvania Court House. But General Lee had headed him off, and there was considerable fighting that day. Our whole line was formed in the evening, and that night we fortified again. General Longstreet's Corps, commanded by General Anderson, fought them on the 8th, General Longstreet having been wounded on the 6th.

There was considerable skirmishing and artillery firing on the 9th, and General Sedgewick, commanding the 6th United States Corps, was bantering some of his men, so it was reported by prisoners, about dodging their heads at the whistling of the Rebel bullets, and said that we could not hit an elephant at that distance. A moment afterwards he was killed, pierced through the brain by a Rebel bullet. He was one of their best corps commanders.

On the 10th they made a desperate attempt to carry our works on the left of our corps, and succeeded in getting over the works at one point, but were repulsed and driven back to their lines. Each army would fortify at night, and through the day, when not fighting, in order to hold the ground, they had gained, and resist an attack. On the night of the 10th Sam Nunnelly came to me and said we would get over in front of our works that night and plundered the dead, as he knew there were plenty of them there that had never been searched. I told him I would not do it, as we would be in danger of being shot by our own men as well as the enemy. But he said he would go by himself and crawl around and "play off" wounded. So, he went, and was gone all night, coming back at daylight. He got three watches, some money, knives and other things. He would risk his life any time for plunder.

On the 11th there was some skirmishing and heavy artillery firing from both sides, and everyone who had to be near the front had a hole dug to get into. Our line in front of our corps was crescent shaped—

our division in the centre, Hill's and Longstreet's to the right and left. We were exposed to shells from two directions and shells from one direction would drop in behind the works from the opposite angle. Therefore, on part of the line we had to throw dirt on each side of the ditch.

While making a ditch of this kind on the 11th they opened on us with artillery. Most of the pioneers ran to another ditch, which was already completed, for protection. Several of them, myself included, remained where we were working, and among the number was one great, big cowardly fellow named Ayleshire, of the 10th Virginia, who always carried a big knapsack and wore a No. 13 shoe. He was six feet high and could take half a plug of tobacco at one chew. At the first fire he fell flat to the ground. As the shells passed over, he would attempt to rise to run to the works, but by the time he would get on his hands and knees another shell would pass over, when he would fall flat and stretch out as before. He would then attempt to rise again, but never did get on his feet to run. He kept up that motion while the shelling lasted, which was about half an hour. He had nearly pumped himself to death, and had the ground all pawed up with his feet—the balance of us laughing at him and hallooing to him to "Run Ayleshire! run Ayleshire!" If I had known I would be killed for it the next minute I could not have helped laughing at him, it was so ridiculous. I was wishing a shell would take his knapsack off without hurting him. If one had I believe he would have died right there from fright.

On the night of the 11th every preparation was made for a big battle, as both armies lay close together. The space between the two lines was thick with underbrush and little jack oaks, which stood so close that we could not see twenty steps in advance. The artillery was posted behind the works with the muzzles pointing over and the horses were all taken to the rear. The cannoneers themselves had pits dug to shield them. The ambulance corps, the bands and musicians, with the pioneers, all had pits to get into, as at times the shells would fairly rain over us.

As the army had been marching, fighting, or working, night and day ever since the morning of the 4th, with but little sleep, one-third of the men were allowed to sleep at a time, on their arms. The others had to keep on the lookout for an attack. We had a skirmish line a little in front of the works and a line of videttes on top of the works. A detail of pioneers was sent back to the rear to cook rations and bring them up before daylight.

But just at daylight on the morning of the 12th, it being so foggy that a man could not be seen ten feet away, and having massed their troops in front of our corps, and in front of the crescent, or horseshoe, the enemy made a charge, and before the men knew it, they were coming over the works in front of the second brigade of our division in solid column. They filed out to the right and left, firing at us behind our breastworks.

The result was they got possession of that part of the works held by our division, captured sixteen pieces of our artillery, and about two-thirds of our division, together with our Division Commander, General Ed. Johnson, wounded our brigadier, General Walker, and demoralised the balance of the division. All that escaped had to "run for it" some distance, but were soon rallied by General Gordon, who took command and formed into line. The troops from the right and left of our line closed in and checked the enemy until Hill's and Longstreet's corps came up, when the enemy were driven back, and part of the works regained, but the battle raged with great fury at that point from daylight until dark; bullets rained and shells shrieked, but we never did recover all our lines, nor our artillery.

The enemy had the key to our position, and if they had not been checked there by the most desperate fighting on record, the whole of Lee's army would have been routed, and General Lee knew it. He came dashing up to take the head of the troops in a charge, knowing full well that the men would follow him any place he went; but the soldiers caught him and held him back, when General Gordon rode up and made him go back, saying: "General Lee, you must go to the rear; we are Virginians and Georgians, and we will recover your lines, won't we, boys?" They answered with a yell, when Gordon took them to the front, and General Lee was forced to the rear.

As there has been some controversy in regard to what troops took General Lee to the rear, I will here explain and settle that controversy. The Texas Brigade took General Lee to the rear on the 6th of May, at the Battle of the Wilderness. Under similar circumstances the Georgians and Virginians took him to the rear on the 12th of May at the Battle of Spotsylvania Court House, or "Bloody Angle."

Sergeant Will Montgomery and John Tharp were captured, and James Gaither, after getting out some distance, as he turned around to look at the enemy, was struck by a ball in the eye and fell dead. That was three more of Company A gone, which left but two in ranks, William Sivells and myself.

I was going to the front that morning with rations, but the fight opened before we got there. The firing with small arms was kept up during the whole night, and we had to form a new line across the Angle and work all night through a thicket of pines. Some were building breastworks, cutting down trees, which fell in every direction, some carrying them and piling them up, others with picks, shovels, bayonets and tin-cups throwing up earth on top of the logs, it being at the same time so dark we could not see each other, and we so sleepy we could hardly stand up.

I was digging with a pick, and every time I would stick it in the ground it would get fast in the pine roots, which was very aggravating. The bullets whistled around us all night, and every few minutes someone was hit with a ball. Daniel Hoffman, a North Carolinian, was shovelling after me as I was digging, and I heard a bullet "*spat*," when he fell over and hallooed out that he was "hit."

"Are you hurt bad?" I asked.

"No, I think not," said he. "I am hit in the leg." His brother George was working along the line some place, and I called to him and told him Daniel had a "furlough," and to come and take him to the rear. He did so, and I never heard of him afterwards.

It got to be a common saying among the soldiers, when a man got wounded, that he had received a "furlough," and the length of his furlough was rated according to his wound. If mortally wounded he had his "final discharge." A soldier who received a moderate wound was considered in luck, as he could go to the rear and get a rest and nurse his wound, wounded soldiers being the only ones furloughed.

Generals Lee and Ewell walked up and down the line all night encouraging the men to work, and telling us that "the fate of the army depended on having that line done by daylight, and I knew by the way they acted that it was a critical time. At daylight the works were filled with troops expecting a charge; but everything was quiet. General Grant had withdrawn his troops from our front and we lay undisturbed all day.

Chapter 21

Back in Company A

That was one time I cannot help but think General Grant displayed poor generalship, for he had gained a great advantage over us. If he had made a desperate attack that morning with the superior number of troops he had, he certainly would have driven us from the

Federal and Confederate Pickets Trading Tobacco and Coffee in the Rappahannock.

field and turned our flank and captured a great portion of the army and compelled General Lee to surrender then and there, instead of a year hence. But he quietly gave up all the advantage he had gained with such immense loss, being baffled again, and started on another flank movement. He kept up those flank movements until he arrived at Petersburg on the south side of the James.

Every move he would make brought him nearer Richmond; but he was going all the time in an oblique direction, with General Lee's army moving parallel with him, and every time he attempted a direct course he was headed off and confronted by Lee. After every battle Grant would dispatch north that he was so many miles nearer Richmond, which was true, and they in the North would think he was driving us straight back, when the fact was, he was no nearer, so far as the army was concerned, when he reached the James River than he was at the Wilderness. He could have gotten that close, as respects distance in miles, on the 5th of May, without a battle; but he had lost thousands of men in the attempt, and was just wearing our army out by degrees, for what we lost could not be replaced, as we did not have the men to draw from.

No prisoners were being exchanged at this time, and General Grant knew if he lost ten thousand men every day they could be replaced by new ones, while we could not get a man. General Lee had about fifty thousand men when the Wilderness fight commenced and General Grant one hundred and twenty-five thousand.

During the battle on the 12th there were two trees cut down with bullets that stood between the lines. One was eighteen inches across the stump, the other, a pine, twelve inches across. They were cut so near off that they fell, and nothing but bullets hit them. I have heard that the stumps were taken up and taken to Washington and kept there as trophies.

It is related that as the Federals were rushing our prisoners to the rear and punching them with bayonets to hurry them up, "Clubby" Johnson, who was also a prisoner, halted in the road and, waving his "club" in the air, cursing, swore he would not move another step, but die there if they did not quit bayoneting his men; and that he worked his ears backward and forward and was in a terrible rage. They then quit punching them with the bayonets and all were marched to General Grant's headquarters. I was told this by Bob Coffman since the war. Bob belonged to the 10th Virginia Regiment and was captured at the same time.

We lay still for several days, with the exception of some skirmishing, until the 18th, when General Ewell took our corps and moved in front of our works to find out what the Yanks were doing. If they kept still for a few days it was a sure sign they were making a move of some kind. We marched several miles to the front and found the enemy had abandoned the ground in front of us.

Our skirmish line, however, suddenly came to their wagon train as it was moving along the road and captured a great many wagons; but as the balance of the troops were marching along the road some distance behind, the enemy sent some of their infantry back and drove off our skirmish line and recaptured them before our troops could be formed in line of battle. The enemy, thinking it was some cavalry, attempted to charge us, but were repulsed. They finally brought up more troops and it seemed at one time that there would be a general engagement.

Our troops lay silently in line, "and just at dark we could hear the enemy ordering a charge. The command was "Forward! Remember Fort Pillow! Charge!" But they could not tell exactly where our line was, as our men were ordered not to fire until they came close up. The enemy would charge a short distance, fire a volley and then break and run back. We could hear the officers rallying them and ordering another charge. This they did three times, the command being the same, to "Remember Fort Pillow! Charge!" Our line never fired a shot and the enemy soon retired. We lay there for some time and then fell in and marched back to camp that night.

We had just heard of General Forrest killing the negro troops at Fort Pillow, and it seemed to inspire the enemy with great bravery to have revenge.

Our troops had captured a whole company of Federals that evening who had been stationed at Washington all the time of the war as heavy artillerymen, and only a few days before had been ordered to the front and given muskets to guard the wagon train. They were captured the first engagement they were in, and without firing a shot, and were sent to Richmond. They hated it very much, but there was no help for it. There was one very clever fellow among them who took it so hard that I would have assisted him to escape, but had no opportunity.

General Lee, anticipating General Grant's move, marched out and formed a line of battle between the North Anna and South Anna Rivers before General Grant reached the North Anna. Being baf-

Building Fortifications on the Rapidan

fled again, there being no fighting except some skirmishing, General Grant swung around to the right when he found Lee confronting him at Hanover Junction.

On the 23rd, and again on the 25th, General Grant made attempts on the Confederates, but was repulsed. General Grant then left the North Anna, and on the 27th and 28th his entire army was across the Pamunkey.

General Lee formed his line so as to cover all the wagon roads and railroads leading into Richmond from a distance of about ten miles. General Ewell being now unable, from ill health and the loss of one leg, for service in the field, was assigned to duty in Richmond, and General Early took command of the corps, General J. Pegram commanding Early's Division. General Gordon commanded our division in place of "Clubby" Johnson, now a prisoner.

Colonel Wm. Terry, of the 4th Virginia, was made Brigadier of our brigade. It was recruited to some extent by putting in ranks some of the musicians, the wagoners and pioneers that belonged to the brigade, and calling in nearly all that were on different details. So, I left the pioneer corps, took a musket and went to my old company, which consisted of Captain Powell, Sivells, Will Pollard, from Rockingham (who had to go into the infantry from the cavalry because he had no horse), and myself.

The day I went to the company they were lying in the breastworks across a level field and the enemy were in the woods a short distance in front of us. Their sharpshooters would get up in the tree tops and fire at every fellow who showed himself behind the works. The sun was hot and we had to lay in the ditches all day and nearly suffocate, and when we would want water would draw straws who should go for it. The one whose lot was to go would take as many canteens as he could carry and run the gauntlet to the rear, to a small ravine. While filling them he would be safe, but he had to run back again, for the sharpshooters would open fire on him as soon as he started. Several got shot in this way.

Every move we would make we would fortify, and the enemy would do the same. The country was dug up along the whole line from the Wilderness to Richmond, and nearly every fight would come off in the open field or woods, for as soon as we were fortified the enemy, instead of attacking us, except in a few instances, would undertake to flank us.

One day, about 1 o'clock, our division was ordered to leave the works we were in and move farther to the right, some of Hill's Corps being ordered to take our place. We had our flags stuck up on the works, and the artillery pointing over; the horses being in the rear. When Hill's men came, they had sneaked down the line unperceived by the enemy, and, being very tired, they lay down to rest. When we left the works, we made a rush for a piece of woods not far off, and the enemy saw us leave and fired at us.

After we had marched down the line some distance, we heard terrific firing back at the place we had left. We were halted and formed along the works, expecting a general attack, but in a short time everything was quiet, and we soon learned the cause of the firing, as we were told by the prisoners. It seems the enemy had seen us leave the works in front of them, but had not seen Hill's men come in and take our places, and they concluded, as there was no infantry there, they would charge the works and capture the artillery. Consequently, they formed in three lines and charged across the field; but Hill's men held their fire until they were close to the works and then opened on them with a deadly volley of musketry, and grape and canister from the artillery, and nearly annihilated them.

They then came out of the works and charged them in turn, capturing nearly all that were left alive, and all without the loss of a man.

We were marched on that evening some distance, Pegram's Division being in front, feeling for the enemy. Suddenly the division ran onto a full corps and had to fight terribly to keep from being surrounded before our division could arrive. We went forward double-quick, and when we came up Pegram's men were falling back. We formed in line across an open, sandy field, and were ordered to throw up a hasty work in order to check the enemy.

There was a fence nearby, and a large pile of cordwood near a house, and every soldier took a load of rails or wood and, laying them along the line, would dig up the sand with his bayonet and throw it over with a tin cup or tin plate, or with his hands, and in a few minutes we had very good defence.

I never before saw men carry such loads of rails, or work so hard, as they did on that occasion. It undoubtedly saved our two divisions, for by the time Pegram's men got back to us they fell in behind our works, and the enemy, seeing a formidable line in front, halted.

General Terry complimented us very highly, and said that he knew if men would not flinch under those circumstances, and under a galling fire, they could be depended on for anything, and that he did not see a man shrink from duty, and that he was proud that he commanded such a body of men, although few in number.

That night we fell back about a mile to a good position and threw up a line of good works. We lay in this position several days, not much fighting being done, except on our extreme right. Our rations of corn bread and bacon would be cooked in the rear and brought up to the front, three days' rations at a time; but as we were moving about so much and changing positions all the time, we often missed our "grub."

We were allowed one pint of corn meal (not sifted) and one-fourth of a pound of bacon for one day's ration, and as there was nothing in that country to steal, we were pretty badly off. The corn bread would get so hard and mouldy that when we broke it it looked like it had cobwebs in it. Numbers of the citizens came into our lines who had been robbed of everything they had, and their houses burned besides, and we often divided our scanty rations with them to keep them from starving.

The poor in Richmond were suffering for something to eat, and when the soldiers heard of it the whole of Lee's Army voted to give them one day's rations; and that was done several times to my certain knowledge. After being up and losing sleep for three nights, one evening I thought I would have a good rest, but was soon ordered to report to General Gordon's headquarters with my gun.

When I arrived, I found about two hundred soldiers there, detailed for special duty. We were then taken up the line and deployed in a swamp in front of our lines, in shape to take the enemy by flank. As soon as we were ordered to move forward it commenced pouring down rain, but we moved on and soon came to the enemy's line, and, taking them completely by surprise, they were thrown into confusion. As soon as our guns opened our main line from the breastworks moved forward, and we drove the enemy about two miles and captured about one thousand prisoners and took position at their works, but on the opposite side. We were kept awake all night by false alarms and firing from the pickets. During this campaign if we got two hours' sleep out of twenty-four, we were doing well.

The next night I was put on picket in this swamp, and it came my turn to stand the first two hours. I was so near the enemy that I could not light my pipe and so sleepy that I could not keep my eyes open to save my life, and I knew that if I sat down, I would be fast asleep.

I pleaded with the officer of the guard for "God's sake and for the sake of humanity to not leave me on post, for it was impossible for me to keep my eyes open," but of no avail, as he replied "that all were in the same condition."

I was more frightened than I had ever been in any battle during the war, for I could conceive of no way to keep awake and was not allowed to walk my beat. I well knew what my fate would be if found asleep on the outpost, which was death by a drum-head court-martial; I would have rather died a dozen deaths on the field of battle than be disgraced by being shot to death for negligence of duty.

I, therefore, braced myself on the ground, and, resting my chin on the muzzle of my gun, would soon be fast asleep, only to be awakened by falling. In that manner I worried out the two hours—the rain continuing to pour down all the time. I thought it was the longest two hours I ever spent in my life. I never was so sleepy before or since. When finally, relief did come, I went back to the reserve and rolled up in my gum blanket and slept—oh! how sweetly—the rain pouring down all night, but an earthquake could not have awakened me. Those engagements were called the Battles of Bethesda Church.

Chapter 22
Second Battle of Cold Harbor

General Grant then moved to Cold Harbor, where he could have been the 1st of May without firing a gun; but that was McClellan's plan, and Grant did not want to follow any of his predecessors, but take a new route for Richmond by the Wilderness. But he had to adopt all of their old routes, and fail as they did.

On the 3rd of June he was determined to fight the decisive battle of the war, and massed his troops and rushed them on our works amidst a storm of shot and shell that it seemed no men could stand, but they were repulsed with great slaughter. The battle did not last more than one hour.

It was the most destructive that had been fought during the war, considering the length of time the engagement lasted. It was estimated that he lost ten thousand men in that short time, and his troops, it is said, seeing it was a useless slaughter, could not be induced to try it again. That place, the second Cold Harbor battle, was called "Grant's Slaughter Pen." The men were left there to rot, as Grant would not bury them; neither would he allow us to do so.

There were fourteen different assaults made along the line in that short time and all repulsed with the above results, and but very few Confederates lost; but the enemy were no nearer Richmond than before, and Grant had to adopted another plan.

During this time General Grant had sent an army under General Sigel up the Shenandoah Valley in order to destroy railroads in our rear and cut off our line of retreat; but General John C. Breckinridge came from Southwest Virginia with his division, and gathered up some scattering troops in the Valley, together with the cadets from the Virginia Military Institute, and met General Sigel at New Market. Sigel was defeated on the 15th of May and retreated to Winchester. General J. C. Breckinridge then left the Valley and reinforced General Lee at Hanover Junction and remained with us until after the Battle of Cold Harbor. But in the meantime, another army was sent up the Valley under General Hunter, whose march was opposed by General William Jones, a cavalry commander, with a small force of cavalry. General Jones was defeated and killed at the Battle of Piedmont, in Augusta County.

The enemy soon had possession of Staunton and our railroad communication, and continued his march on through Lexington to Lynchburg. At the same time a large Federal force was approaching Lynchburg from West Virginia under General Crook, who joined Hunter at Staunton. Should they capture Lynchburg we would be cut off from our base of supplies. Therefore, General Breckinridge was sent from Lee's Army to get between Hunter and Lynchburg and defeat him; but he failed to do so, and had to protect Lynchburg with his division, the cavalry and some militia.

It was a critical time, and as Grant, being defeated in his plans, had changed his base to the south side of the James River, our corps, under General Early, was started out on a forced march to Lynchburg, two hundred miles distant. We marched one hundred miles, to Charlottesville, in four days. The night we arrived there it was my turn to cook rations. The wagons were late coming up, and by the time I drew rations and cooked them the long roll beat to fall in. My feet were so sore that I had to crawl around the fire and cook on my hands and knees. I got no sleep the whole night. So, when we were ordered to fall in I went to Dr. Baldwin, our surgeon, and showed him my feet and told him that it was impossible for me to march any farther. He said we would not march that day, as we were going to take the cars from there to Lynchburg. I told him I could stand that very well.

We loaded up and started out, the artillery, wagon train and ambulances keeping on the wagon road. Some of the divisions also had to march all day, as there were not trains enough to transport all at once. They had to go to Lynchburg, unload, and return and load up again.

We had a fine time until our engine broke down, when we had to unload and camp all night. When the train came, we were crowded in, and just as we got on the high bridge over the James River at Lynchburg, the rear car jumped the track; but as we were going very slowly and the soldiers commenced hallooing to the engineer, he stopped. Some of the men jumped off for fear the whole train would be pulled off the bridge. One or two were killed and some fell on the bridge, and some caught in the timbers and were badly hurt. But they soon tumbled the rear car off the track and rushed on to the depot.

It was rushing times then, as the Yankee shells were falling in the edge of Lynchburg. We unloaded and went double-quick through the city and out to the fair grounds and formed a line of battle, threw out skirmishers, and went to our old trade—fortifying.

Our division and Pegram's were on the ground, but Rodes' Division was still behind and would not get up until that night. General Gordon wanted to attack the enemy that evening, but General Early would not consent to do so until Rodes arrived. General Gordon said the "Yanks" would be gone by morning. Sure enough, at daylight we found they were many miles ahead of us, and all had gone towards Liberty.

We then started on a forced march to overtake them; but I could not march, and Dr. Baldwin gave me a pass to remain in the rear and get in an ambulance when they overtook us, or else go back to Lynchburg to the hospital.

I did not want to go to the hospital just for sore feet, although they were raw and bleeding; but I thought they would be all right in a few days, and I waited for the ambulances. When they came up, I got in and arrived in Liberty, now Bedford City, a distance of twenty-five miles, the next day. There we heard that the advance of our army had overtaken the rear of the enemy at Liberty, now Bedford City, near night, and had driven them on to their main line; but they had the night to retreat in again. This was repeated every day until our army reached Salem, Roanoke County. Every evening our army would overtake them; but night would again save them. As it was, after we attacked them at Hanging Rock Pass, they were scattered to the mountains and disbanded, and made their way to the Ohio River and points in West Virginia in small squads, and had to subsist off the country.

The cavalry followed them up; but General Early, with the infantry, turned at Salem and started down the valley towards Staunton. When the ambulance I was in arrived at Liberty the doctors there had orders to put all the men in the hospital who were unable to march, and I was left at Liberty, now, Bedford City. I remained there seven days, and was nearly eaten up by the bugs at night, and did not know from which I suffered most, my feet or the bugs.

As soon as I heard the army had gone down the valley I applied for my discharge from the hospital. I could have stayed there longer; but as my parents and sisters lived in the valley at Dayton, I knew it would be a good excuse to get home for a few days. As the railroads had been destroyed, there was no transportation, and I had to "foot it" twenty-five miles to Lynchburg. I arrived there next day and took the cars, around by way of Charlottesville, to Staunton. There were a good many in the cars going on to the army from the different hospitals; also, quite a number of stragglers. We were to draw rations in Staunton, but when we arrived there Early's army was one day ahead of us, and had taken all the rations with them and we got none. The citizens had also been stripped of provisions by having both armies to feed.

We started down the turnpike, thinking we would get something to eat in the country; but after trying at every house for five miles without success I told the boys I was going to kill the first thing I came across that would do to eat. I was anxious to get home that night, but knew I could not make it unless I ate something, as I had not eaten a mouthful since leaving Lynchburg. The first house I came to I went into the yard and commenced throwing my ramrod at the chickens, but the old woman saw me and "fired" me out. We soon came across some hogs in the road. I loaded my gun, and as I was trying to slip around them to head them off, they started to run, and I fired and hit one just behind the shoulder, and he fell over in the fence corner and never squealed. I had killed him dead. As we were not near camp, we did not have to use the bayonet. We then saw some officers coming down the road, and we threw the hog over the fence and went and sat down on the opposite side until they parsed. We then "skinned" a ham and cut out as much as we wanted, when we left. Some more soldiers coming up, we told them to draw their rations of pork; and I don't think there was any of that hog left but the hair.

The next point to make was to get some bread and coffee. I went to a house and inquired for bread; but, as usual, they had none. I was not to be baffled in this way, however. I went around to the kitchen and told the old negro woman that I would give her plenty of meat if she would give me some bread. "You bet" the bread was forthcoming immediately. We then cooked our meat, had a good square meal, and

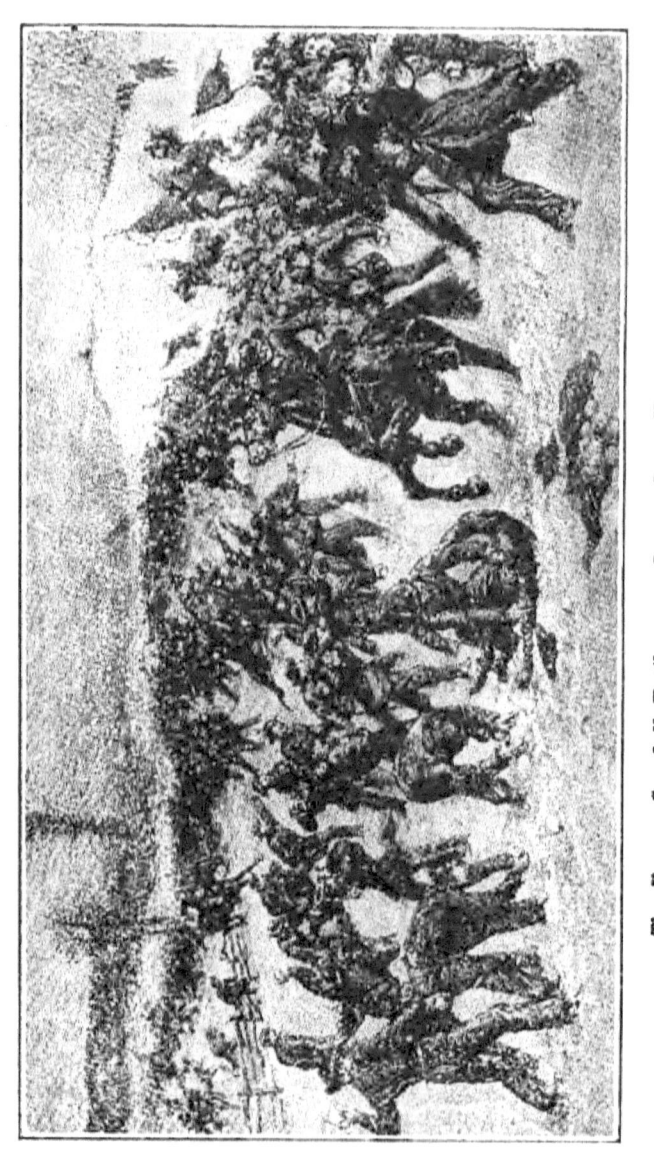

The Famous Snowball Battle, near Orange Court House, February, 1864.

proceeded on our journey. I arrived at home that night after a twenty-five-mile march and one meal.

I remained at home in Dayton a few days, hearing from the army every day. It was still marching on north down the valley toward the Potomac.

I did not like the idea of marching on after the army such a long distance, as the time had arrived in the progress of my soldiering that I was about "played out." I could not stand hard marching and was broken down other ways and completely used up by hard service and severe exposure. I had no energy or activity left and just felt like lying down and resting in one place for months; but I knew I could not stay at home, and that I must follow on after the army or be arrested by the provost guard.

My sister Sallie at that time wanted to make a visit to our friends and relatives in Frederick and Hampshire Counties; and as my father had a horse and buggy, we concluded that we would follow up the army in that style, as it was more agreeable and comfortable to me than walking. I thought also that, perhaps, I could come up with the army near Winchester. So, we started out, my discharge from the hospital and my musket being a good pass. When we arrived at Winchester, a distance of ninety miles, we heard that General Early had crossed the Potomac River into Maryland, and was advancing on Washington City. He had sent orders back to Winchester to hold all the stragglers and absentees from the army in Winchester until his return from Maryland, as it was not safe to follow on for fear of being captured by the enemy. My sister wanted to go fifteen miles west of Winchester to our uncle's. As I did not want to lie around Winchester, I wanted to go with her into the country and wait for the army; but I knew I could not get a pass to go through the pickets.

We stopped at Miss Afflick's, and I sent Sallie around to the provost marshal's office to get a pass for herself and driver; we determined to see if we could not run the blockade in that manner. When she arrived at the office, she found an old acquaintance there, Mr. Tom Wilkins, from Dayton, who belonged to the 10th Virginia, and who was temporarily detailed provost clerk. She very easily got a pass from Tom for her and myself, and when she came back, we proceeded on our journey to our uncle's unmolested.

I remained there several days, until I heard that General Early had returned from Maryland and was in camp near Winchester. My uncle then hitched up his team and we started for camp; but when we got near Winchester, we heard considerable firing, so we halted until we could hear further news. We stayed all night near Winchester and found out next morning that our army had fallen back during the night, and that the Yankees were in possession of Winchester.

I then came to the conclusion that I had better be making myself scarce in that neighbourhood. I, therefore, started on foot by the mountain road up the valley, knowing that I would soon get with them, as they would not go far. I soon fell in with two other soldiers and we travelled on until we reached the valley turnpike at Woodstock, when we found we were ahead of the army, as they were camped at Fisher's Hill and were fortifying.

I reached my command the next day. I found them in camp on Cedar Creek, a few miles north of Strasburg; but found no Company "A." Captain Powell had gone home, as he could not stand the service on account of his wound. Joseph Carder was in the hospital at Lynchburg and William Sivells had gone home to Hampshire. Elisha Carder, with his drum, and I, with my musket, were all there was left of Company A fit for duty, and I felt considerably discouraged. I was put in Company "F" under Captain A. H. Wilson (the Hardy Company), but made up my mind that I would leave the regiment and go into the cavalry, or to some partisan ranger company, the first opportunity. I hated to leave the old brigade, as I had been with it so long; but I was of no use in the infantry. I could not stand marching any longer, and had no company, and I must either go to the cavalry or leave the service.

The officers in the regiment, and Captain Martin, our commissary, gave me the name of "The Last of the Mohicans." The whole division was considerably reduced, as we had lost about two-thirds of the number captured at Spotsylvania Court House, and kept losing men all the time, with no recruits except possibly a few from the hospitals. Our whole brigade did not number over 500 men. Each of the other brigades in the division contained about the same. There were not 100 men in my regiment, all told. The three Virginia Brigades in our division were consolidated into one.

The soldiers and officers cared very little for exact discipline. We drilled very seldom, and dress parade was played out. Very little camp guarding was done, and when we did have a camp guard, they would sit on their posts unconcerned. In some ways the discipline was as good and strict as ever; but we were on the march or fighting nearly all the time.

One day a soldier was sitting on his post as camp guard, and had taken his gun to pieces and was cleaning it when the "officer of the day" happened to come along and asked him what he was doing there.

"Oh," said the soldier, "I am sort o' sentinel."

"Well," said the officer, "don't you know it is against orders to sit down on your post while on duty, much less to take your gun to pieces in that manner?"

"That used to be the law in the commencement of the war," replied the sentinel, "but it's sort o' played out now."

"Yes, but I want you to understand that I am officer of the day, going on my rounds."

"Are you?" replied the sentinel. "Well, just hold on 'till I get this old gun together and I'll give you a sort o' salute."

It showed how careless and indifferent the soldiers had become about technicalities; but in a fight, or on picket in "the front" they were as dutiful as ever.

CHAPTER 23

Skirmish at Winchester

General Early had marched into Maryland and fought a Battle at Monocacy bridge, defeated the enemy, and continued his march to within four miles of Washington City. He laid there one day and then returned to Virginia. It was said that he could have taken Washington, as there were but few troops there; but the move was made to draw a large force from General Grant's Army and relieve General Lee, which it did, as troops were sent to Washington at once.

It was during this battle that two of my former messmates and intimate friends, who have been mentioned before, passed out of existence, and will be dropped from further mention—Jacob Fogle and Sam Nunnelly. Fogle was killed in the charge, and Nunnelly turned up missing. Whether he was killed or captured or died in prison is unknown, for he was never heard of afterwards, and inquiries for him since the war failed to reveal his fate; but he is numbered with the great army of unknown.

After remaining in camp a few days, after I had reached the army at Cedar Creek, we started on the march towards Winchester. After getting below Newtown we were filed out to the left of the road and formed in line of battle and ordered to load our arms. We were not thinking of a battle and it took us rather by surprise when we heard the skirmishers firing. When I went to load my gun, I found I had no cartridges; but in place of cartridges I had a withered bouquet of flowers a young lady had given me at Dayton. I had thrown my cartridges away when I left the hospital and had forgotten about it; but I soon borrowed some from the others.

We were ordered to advance, when the enemy gave way, and we had a running fight from there to Winchester. There they made a short stand, but were soon routed and put to flight. We ran through the streets of Winchester pell-mell, at full speed—the ladies waving their handkerchiefs and cheering us on. We halted that night in the open fields below Winchester with rain pouring down upon us in torrents.

We then manoeuvred in the lower valley for some time, in and around Bunker Hill, Smithfield and Berryville, until the enemy advanced on us, when we, in turn, fell back, without a general engagement, to the south bank of Cedar Creek. That was the last battle I was in while belonging to that brigade; and I was the only man of Company A that was carrying a musket My career in the Stonewall Brigade was soon to terminate.

The next day we lay in line of battle in the hot, broiling sun of August, without a particle of shade, from daylight until dark. The enemy was lying in line on the hills on the opposite side of the creek, and considerable skirmishing was going on all day along the banks of the creek. At times it was very heavy on our right, the enemy opening on us once in a while with artillery. We could see the smoke from their guns, and occasionally a shell would come whistling by; but we seldom heard the report, although we were not more than a mile away. I suppose the reason for our not hearing the reports so near can be accounted for by the peculiar shape of the country and direction of the wind; but it appeared singular to us.

After dark our army fell back to Fisher's Hill, about two miles south of Strasburg, to our intrenched position. That night I was taken desperately sick, and I thought I would surely die. I had them get the doctor and he said I had the cholera morbus. He gave me some relief, but I was very sick the next day. It was the worst attack I ever had in my life. It was occasioned, they said, by lying in the hot sun all day.

The second day the army started on the move again, towards Winchester, as the enemy had fallen back. I was put into an ambulance and taken to Winchester and there left at the hospital. I got permission in a few days to go to my uncle, J. H. Heironimus, who lived in the country. I remained there one week, but was afraid of being captured, as the Yankees were scouting everywhere. My uncle took me to Winchester, and got permission from the surgeon of the hospital to let me stay at a private house, which I did, but had to report to the hospital every day for medicine, as I had the chronic diarrhoea. I remained there until the 19th of September, the day the big Battle of Winchester was fought.

General Sheridan attacked General Early at daybreak down on the Opequon Creek. As General Rodes' Division was down near Bunker Hill there was no chance for Early to fall back until Rodes formed a junction with him. By that time the troops were so hotly engaged that retreat in good order was impossible. General Rodes' Division was nearly cut off; and as he was bringing them into action he was killed, which was a severe loss.

I was in Winchester at the time, and it was thought there that it would be a short fight, and I went to the hospital to see what orders they had, but found they had none to move. I knew I would have to ride if I got away, and I did not like the way the battle was raging, for it appeared to me that the musketry was getting closer and that our right was being turned. Just before sundown the enemy's cavalry had flanked our cavalry, and the whole line was going back. I could see them on the hills west of Winchester.

I then started out of town on foot, but soon got into a wagon, and when we reached the south end of town, we found all our wagon train parked there, and the army routed. Our wagons, ambulances and artillery commenced dashing up the pike, three abreast, and the infantry in the fields on each side were running—every fellow for himself. Every few minutes a shell would go tearing through the wagon train and make the camp kettles and things fly; but dark soon put a stop to the rout.

If the enemy had pushed on a little longer, they would have captured nearly the whole command, for Early's Army was completely routed, and there is no use in denying the fact. It was the first time I ever saw it routed and stampeded; but the army had fought well all day.

General Early had about 8,000 infantry and 2,500 cavalry, and General Sheridan 40,000 infantry and 11,000 cavalry, and our line never gave back until both flanks were turned. General Early was to blame for the defeat. He displayed poor generalship. He ought to have fallen back to Fisher's Hill in time, and not fought a general battle with such odds, in that place, where the valley was so wide and open. The corps never had any confidence in him afterwards, and he never could do much with them. He was as brave a general as ever lived, and did well when he commanded a brigade or division under some other general; but when he had command of a corps, and was operating by himself, he displayed no strategy whatever. He would fight the enemy wherever he met them and under any circumstances, no matter if he had but one brigade and the whole northern army came against him. He would always show fight. It was a critical time with our army and it required generals that knew how to strike a blow and at the same time save their men.

This may appear unusual criticism coming from a private in the ranks; but after three years' service in the thick of the fight, under various commanders, and under every variety of circumstances, and with opportunities of observation, such as fall to the lot of pioneers and picket guards, it would seem that a man of ordinary intelligence might have opinions which are entitled to consideration.

The next day the army arrived safely at Fisher's Hill; but we had lost considerably. It was said, however, that General Sheridan lost more men than Early had in his whole command.

I was sent on with the sick and wounded to Harrisonburg to the hospital. When we got there, we were ordered on to the Staunton hospital, as the Harrisonburg hospital was overcrowded. There was a young soldier in the wagon with me who belonged to an Alabama Regiment, from Wetumpka, Ala., and who was wounded slightly in the neck. After we passed through Harrisonburg, I told him we would get out of the wagon and go to my home in Dayton and stay there until we got well; that I did not intend to go to a hospital as long as I had a home that near to go to. We then got out of the wagon and went across the fields to Dayton.

We had been there but three days when we heard that General Early had been defeated again at Fisher's Hill, and was falling back towards Staunton, and the "Yanks" would soon be in Dayton, so we took my father's horse and started to "refugee" towards the mountains. The roads were full of citizens "refugeeing" with their stock and valuables.

When we arrived at Harnsberger's farm, on Muddy Creek, we found Captain Stump, from Hampshire County, who belonged to Imboden's command, lying there very badly wounded through the head. He insisted that we should take him along with us and take care of him, as he would rather die than be captured.

He had one of his company with him and a black boy waiting on him. We told him we would do all we could for him and would defend him to the last. So, we hitched our horses to Harnsberger's carriage and took him on six miles farther to a friend's house.

After remaining there a few days we heard that Early was still falling back and that Sheridan's cavalry was scouting the whole country. We then moved him farther back to the foot of the mountain on Briery branch and stopped at a small house. I rode out in the settlements every day to get rations and find out the news.

We could still hear that the Yankees were spreading their scouting parties farther and farther into the country every day, and Captain Stump was fearful they would come across us and that we would be captured. We told him there was no danger and that we would move him if it became necessary; but one day they came within two miles of us and we concluded to move farther into the mountains. We found out from the man we were stopping with that by going up a deep hollow or gorge in the mountain about six miles we would find an old vacant house; but there was no way to get to it but by a bridle path.

So, nothing would do Captain Stump but we must go to that house. He was suffering terribly from his wound, as he was shot through and through the back part of the head, and could sit up but a short time. We had to pour cold water on the wound every few minutes out of a coffee pot to relieve the pain; but he repeated he would rather die than be captured and would try and ride the distance on horseback.

We then started on the march, but had to stop every mile and get him off the horse and let him rest while we bathed his wound. He had more fortitude and endurance than any man I ever saw before or have seen since. We finally arrived at our rendezvous and made him as comfortable as we could under the circumstances.

The second night we were there his wound pained him so severely that we were afraid he would have the lockjaw. He said he could not stand it till morning if he did not get relief of some kind, and insisted that I should go to Sangersville, a distance of ten miles, for a doctor. We tried to persuade him that it would be useless, as no doctor would come, and could do him no good if he did come, and that by pouring water on the wound continually it would give him relief. But he still insisted that I should go, and if the doctor would not come, he could send some morphine, which would give relief,

I then procured a pine torch, as it was very dark, saddled the best horse, and started down the mountain. I got along very well for two or three miles until it commenced thundering and lightning in a most terrific manner. In a short time, the rain poured down in torrents, putting out my light and leaving me in darkness as dense as in a cave. But

I still kept on, the horse following the path by instinct, until I reached the settlements and got into the wagon road. It was still raining, but not so hard, and was not quite so dark. I still had four miles to go, but with great difficulty, and losing the road several times, I finally reached Sangersville about 12 o'clock and found a doctor.

It was as I expected; he would not go. He said he knew the place very well and it would be impossible, in the rain and darkness, for us to find our way back that night, and insisted that I should stay until morning and he would go with me. I pleaded with him my best to go with me, but in vain. I then told him to give me some morphine and I would return, or make the attempt. He did so, and said he would come to see the captain in the morning.

Under these promises I started to return, but it seems the horse was bewildered and could not keep in the road where it led through the woods, and I often found myself out of my path in the woods. I would then get down and strike a match and feel my way to the road. In this manner I proceeded until near the mountain, when I came to a branch. I thought I would ride up the bed of the branch until I came to the place where the road recrossed it; that by so doing I could cut off about one mile, and that I could keep in the bed of the branch better than in the path. But I found it a difficult task, as the branch was obstructed by drifts, logs and rocks. The water was shallow, and by the aid of the streaks of lightning I could manage to get around them.

Finally, my horse came to a stand just as I had gotten out on the edge of the bank to get around some logs, and, with all the whipping and spurring I could do, I could not make him move. Just then, by the aid of the lightning, I saw that the horse was standing on the edge of a perpendicular rock, and I could not see the depth below. I quickly dismounted and turned the horse around and got him on solid ground. I then tied him to a tree, took off the saddle, rolled myself in the blanket and slept until morning. It rained, thundered and lightened the whole night.

Under most circumstances I would have felt some fear and lonesomeness; but, strange to say, nothing of the kind entered my mind. The next morning at daybreak I resumed my journey, and at the first house I came to, which was the last one I would pass, I stopped and got my breakfast, and told them of my adventure of the night.

They all remarked that they were not surprised at me not getting through that place, as that thicket of pines was haunted, and there had never anyone been able to go through there after dark, as they would invariably get lost, see ghosts, and hear unusual noises, groans, etc. There had been a man murdered there once, they said, and no sum of money could be laid down that would induce them to sleep there as I had done. I had heard nothing of the kind, however, and paid no attention to their ghost stories. I was too mad all night to think of fear, and to have met a well-disciplined ghost would have been company and amusement for me.

When I arrived where Captain Stump was, I found him considerably better. He said he got relief directly after I had left, and was sorry I had gone, and that if he lived, he would do anything in his power to help me. But, alas! like many a dear and near friend that I have had in old Hampshire County, he never lived to see the war over. Many of my old-time friends and comrades who survived the war also have passed over the river and are quietly resting under the shade of the trees, while I still live (but in a far distant state), and seldom see anyone that I ever knew in my younger days.

The doctor never came the next day, as he promised, nor did I ever see him again. In a few days we persuaded the captain to go down in the settlements, as there was no danger of being captured, for if he were to die in that lonely place, we would be unable to give him a decent burial. After placing him in kind hands we heard the enemy were falling back down the valley, when we bade him farewell and started to Dayton.

CHAPTER 24

Battle of Cedar Creek

When we arrived in Dayton, we saw a distressing sight—ruin and desolation on every hand. The enemy, in falling back, had burned all the barns and mills on their line of retreat.

The greater part of Sheridan's Army had been camped around Harrisonburg and immediate vicinity. One regiment at that time was camped at Dayton, four miles south, and several regiments were camped in the advance at different points. His cavalry had scouted the country and done picket duty near General Early's lines. Some of our cavalry would scout inside of the Yankee lines and in their rear to find out their movements, strength, etc.; principally men who were acquainted with the country and knew every by-road.

One day Frank Shaver, of the 1st Virginia Cavalry, and Campbell and Martin, of the 4th Virginia Cavalry, were passing along a by-road between Dayton and Harrisonburg, when they unexpectedly came

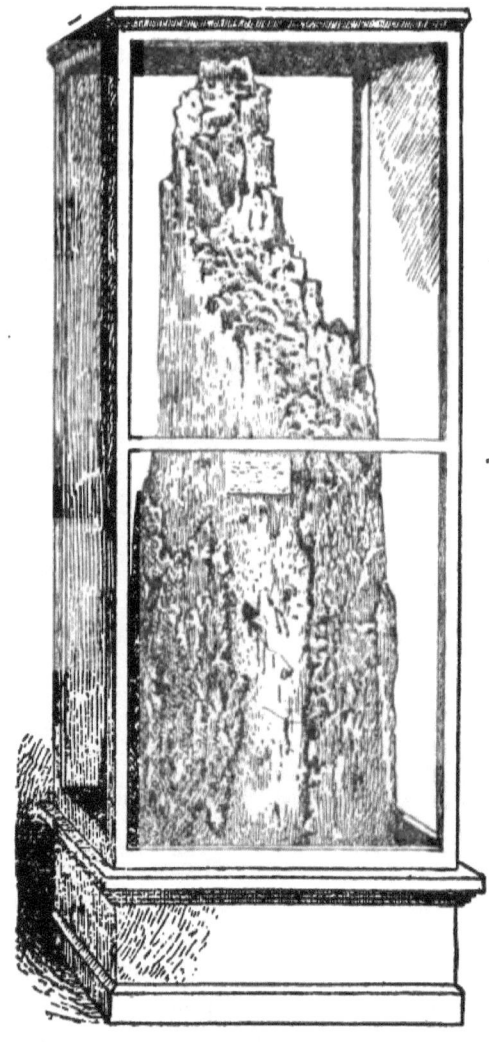

Stump of the Tree Cut Down by Bullets at Spottsylvania
Court House, May 12th, 1864.
Taken from "The Blue and Gray."

upon three Yankees. It was either fight or be captured; and as they preferred fighting the ball soon opened. In the affray one of the "Rebs" was wounded and one of the Yankees killed and one captured, while the other one made his escape and returned to camp. The "Rebs" left in a hurry, taking their wounded man with them. It so happened that the one killed was Lieutenant Meigs, a promising young officer of General Sheridan's staff, and greatly beloved by the general.

He was so enraged about his death, particularly as the one who escaped had reported to him that they were ambushed by bushwhackers, that he issued orders that Dayton should be burnt to the ground and also all the habitations for five miles around. Consequently, the torch was applied to houses and barns in the country, and the citizens of Dayton given one hour to move out of their houses into the fields. But the colonel of the Federal Regiment camped at Dayton knew they were regular soldiers who did the killing, and, thinking the order inhuman, refused to fire the town until he could prevail upon General Sheridan to countermand the order.

A petition was sent to him signed by the whole regiment to that effect. In the meantime, the citizens, who were all old men, women and children, had to remain out in the fields during that day and night. No orders came during the next day, when my mother and Mrs. Williams went to General Custer's headquarters, about one mile from the village, and begged him to relieve them of their suspense.

He informed them that he had just received a dispatch from General Sheridan countermanding the order to burn the town; then, turning to one of his staff officers, he told him to ride to the village and tell the citizens to move back into their homes, that they would not burn them. The ladies returned with the staff officer, who informed the citizens that "Through the mercy of General Custer their property was saved."

It was the 116th Ohio Regiment of infantry that was quartered in the town, and but for the gallantry of that noble Ohio regiment the town would have been in ashes and the inhabitants rendered homeless.

Lieutenant Dutton, quartermaster of that regiment, was at my father's house making out the payrolls, and did all he could to protect the family; and when the Federal Army fell back, he bade them an affectionate farewell and said: "When I return again I hope to bring an olive branch of peace."

But not so with the country, for nearly every house and barn within the circle of five miles was burned. It was a rich neighbourhood, with fine residences and outbuildings, and the barns full of grain and farm implements. They were not even allowed to save their household property. Oh! those who never saw war have no idea of the ruin, desolation, death and suffering it brings. My mother, father and sisters went through this ordeal, and related the scenes to me when I arrived at home.

In a few days after this burning took place our army began the advance on the enemy, when he in turn fell back to Winchester, burning all the mills and barns on the route. General Sheridan had orders from General Grant to reduce the Shenandoah Valley to such a state of poverty that a crow, in flying over it, would have to carry his rations to keep from starving; and it looked like such would be the case. The mills and barns were full of grain, and Grant knew the valley was a rich store-house for General Lee's Army. If he could not whip us out, he would starve us out. Such is policy in war.

Poverty stared the citizens in the face, as this was in the fall season of the year, and too late to raise any provisions. Their horses and cattle were all gone, their farm implements burnt and no prospects of producing anything the next year. Thousands of them "refugeed" with the Federal Army, as all were furnished transportation anywhere north, they chose to go.

There lived a family by the name of Baugh on the valley turnpike, two miles north of Harrisonburg, consisting of father, mother and seven children—five daughters and two sons. Four of the daughters were grown. When the Federal Army passed their house on their way back to Winchester, they told this family they had better get in their wagons and go with them and they would be given transportation to any point north they wished to go. That there were hundreds of families going, and that they were going to burn up the valley so that no one could subsist there. It had that appearance, for hundreds of barns and mills were then burning; so, the old people consented to go, as it looked like starvation to stay.

They then gathered up some clothing and bedding and got into the wagon; but the grown girls would not go and determined to remain where they were. The Federals then told them if they did not go with them, they would have to burn their house down over their heads, and they would be compelled to go. The girls told them they could burn if they wanted to, but remain they would.

Consequently, the house was fired and burnt to the ground; the girls trying to save what they could by dashing into the house and rescuing what they could carry out. Some of the Federals, seeing their determination, assisted them and saved most of the property.

After the Federals had left one of the girls went across the field to Mr. Armentrout's, a neighbour about one-half mile distant, procured a wheelbarrow and moved their goods to his house. They then lived with their relatives and friends until the war closed.

After the war I married Miss Martha E. Baugh, one of those same girls. We still have a mirror frame that was saved at that time, but the glass was broken and I had a new glass put in after marriage, and keep it as relic of other days.

But thousands preferred to remain, let the consequences be what they would. It caused hundreds to take up arms for the South, who had, up to that time, remained out of the army. Our cavalry followed close after the burners and dealt out vengeance with a vengeful hand. Whenever they caught a party burning, they would take no prisoners, but shoot them down; and often threw them in the fire alive when they caught them burning their own homes.

The main body of the enemy's infantry marched down the main road, our infantry following, while the enemy's cavalry were scattered over the country in small squads doing the burning.

Some of the Federal soldiers would burn the property with fiendish delight and not let the people save anything, not even wearing apparel, while others, more humane, would not burn them if they could possibly avoid it, and would tell the women that they would set them on fire in order to shield themselves and obey commands; but that they would fire them in such places that it would not do any harm for some time, and as soon as they got out of sight they, the women, could extinguish the fire. I saw several barns after the war that were saved in that manner, but they were very rare cases.

As to the Battle of Cedar Creek, the 19th of October, 1864, where General Early attacked General Sheridan's Army, commanded by General Wright, I will make this statement as told me by a relative of mine, Mr. Sewell Merchant, of the 2nd Virginia, who was wounded in both legs and had one amputated on the field. I took him from the hospital in Harrisonburg to my father's house, where he remained until he got well. He said that our army attacked the Federal Army at daylight, routing them, capturing their camps and a great amount of baggage. That after the Federals were driven off our army was halted and in a short time the whole army were plundering, and had nothing in line of battle but a thin skirmish line; that when the Federals returned there was nothing in shape to resist them but this skirmish line, which soon gave way, and the whole army went pell-mell back to Fisher's Hill.

Now, whoever was to blame for our army not pushing on when the enemy were routed, and for being allowed to scatter and plunder, it is not for me to say. But it was a terrible oversight, and was the cause of the disaster in the evening. It was reported that General Gordon was anxious to push on after the enemy, but that General Early objected. The enemy, finding no one in pursuit, had halted at Newtown, eight miles from Winchester.

Now, I wish to correct some erroneous statements in regard to General Sheridan's "twenty-mile ride," made in one hour, and which has been repeated in song and story until it is believed to be true by the rising generation.

I will prove by General Sheridan's own words that he only rode *eight* miles in *one hour and a half,* and only five of that at a lively gait. In *Personal Memoirs of P. H. Sheridan,* Vol. II., he says:

> Toward 6 o'clock on the morning of the 19th the officer on picket duty at Winchester came to my room, I being yet in bed, and reported artillery firing from the direction of Cedar Creek.

Then he says:

> We mounted our horses between half-past 8 and 9.

Then later he says:

> I returned to the road, which was thickly lined with unhurt men, who, having got far enough to the rear to be out of danger, had halted, without any organisation, and began cooking coffee, and I arrived not later, certainly, then half-past 10 o'clock.

He also says:

> Between half-past 3 and 4 o'clock I was ready to assail.

Cedar Creek is fifteen miles south of Winchester, where the battle commenced. The enemy fled to Newtown, seven miles from Cedar Creek and eight miles from Winchester, where General Sheridan arrived at half-past 10 o'clock; then consumed the time until 3 or 4 o'clock in forming his troops ready to advance, with no enemy nearer than five miles. Now suppose General Early had followed on instead of halting, where would General Sheridan's ride come in?

Any reasonable person would say between Winchester and Harper's Ferry, thirty-two miles north of Winchester.

I am a great admirer of the truth, especially in relation to historical facts. Let the truth be told, no matter whom it hurts, for the rising generations.

Another fictitious poem is *Barbara Frietche* of Frederick City, Md., wherein it was said that Stonewall Jackson was indifferent about the actions of the soldiers in regard to threatening to shoot the ladies for waving the "Stars and Stripes" until he saw this old lady, when he ordered them to desist. No such circumstance as related in that poem of Whittier's ever happened. It was too un-Jackson like. On the other hand, if one of his soldiers had attempted such a dastardly outrage, Jackson would have had him shot on the spot. Jackson's men were soldiers in every sense of the word, and had mothers, wives, sisters, daughters and lovers at home, and knew how to protect and defend defenceless females regardless of their politics.

This is confirmed by Dame Barbara's own nephew, Valerius Ebert, of Frederick City, who writes to a Northern paper:

> As to the waving of the Federal flag in the face of the Rebels by Dame Barbara on the occasion of Stonewall Jackson's march through Frederick City, Md., truth requires me to say that Stonewall Jackson, with his troops, did not pass Barbara Frietche's residence at all; but passed through what in this city is called 'The Mill Alley,' about three hundred yards, from her residence, then passed due west towards Antietam, and thus out of the city. But another and stronger fact with regard to this matter may be here presented, *viz.*; the poem by Whittier represents our venerable relative (then ninety-six years of age) as nimbly ascending to her attic window and waving her small Federal flag defiantly in the face of Stonewall Jackson's troops. Now, Dame Barbara was at the moment bedridden and helpless, and had lost the power of locomotion. She could at that period only move as she was moved by the help of her attendants.

These are the facts, proving that Whittier's poem upon this subject is pure fiction.

Here is another mistake which has often been told in song and story, and spoken of by prominent orators: That at the surrender of Lee's Army at Appomattox General Lee offered his sword to General Grant and that he refused to accept it.

Following is an extract from Colonel Charles Marshall's letter, who was General Lee's Chief of Staff, and who was present at the surrender:

There is one very important matter I wish settled. It is this: General Lee did not meet General Grant in the McLean house in the morning of April 9th, 1865, for the purpose of then and there effecting a surrender of his army. It was simply for the purpose of hearing General Grant's terms.

As a matter of fact, if they had not suited General Lee, he would not have accepted them; but General Grant's offer was so liberal, so magnanimous, and so chivalrous that it was accepted at once.

It is well to add that had General Grant's terms been less favourable than those he made. General Lee would not have accepted them, no matter what the circumstances might have been. We had become accustomed somewhat to deal with desperate circumstances.

I wish to have another matter understood before beginning a consecutive narrative of the surrender.

This is in regard to General Horace Porter's statement, made repeatedly, orally and in writing, that General Lee offered his sword to General Grant. General Lee never offered his sword to General Grant, and the latter never refused it.

I was with the great Southern chieftain from the time he greeted General Grant in the McLean house until he rode away, and the only time the mention of a sword was made was when Grant apologised to Lee for his dress, explaining that it was not possible for him to get access to his baggage and at the same time keep the appointment.

The terms of capitulation expressly excepted side arms, and in view of that fact it would have been a most unusual procedure for General Lee to have offered his sword to General Grant. These matters are unimportant in themselves, but it is well for the sake of history to have them cleared up.

When General Grant had written his ultimatum embodying the terms of surrender, he took it to General Lee, who remained seated.

General Lee read the letter and called General Grant's attention to the fact that he required the surrender of the cavalry horses as if they were public horses. He told General Grant that

Confederate cavalrymen owned their horses and they would need them for planting a spring crop. General Grant, at once accepted the suggestion.

CHAPTER 25

Attempts to Wade the Potomac

I remained at home in Dayton for a few days, but had to report to the hospital in Harrisonburg. The doctor in charge there would not give me permission to remain at home, although it was only four miles, but said I was not fit for duty in the field, and that I could do duty in the hospital as Ward Master.

Our army was so "hard up" for men that as soon as one was fit for duty he would be sent to the front, and a sick one, as soon as he was convalescent, would have to nurse or be Ward Master until he was fit for active service.

I remained there as Ward Master until sometime in December, 1864, when our corps, then in the Valley, was placed under command of General John B. Gordon and ordered to Petersburg. General Early was left in command of the valley, with a few regiments of infantry and some cavalry. As the army marched through Harrisonburg I bade farewell to a great many of the boys that I knew in the brigade, and in the old pioneer corps, but there was not one man of Company A there, and but few of Company F. Elisha Carder, our drummer, had been given a musket and was wounded at Fisher's Hill, and had gone home; Will Pollard having been wounded at the Battle of Winchester, September 19, 1864. Joseph McNemar had returned to the regiment from the hospital while it was in front of Petersburg in 1865, and was captured at Hatcher's Run and remained in prison, until the close of the war, and he was the last representative of Company A.

When I saw there was no Company A, and never would be, I told Captain Wilson, of Company F, that I intended to go to the 11th Virginia Cavalry, Company D, from Hampshire.

"Well," he said, "you can go as far as I am concerned, and I wish I could go myself." That if I went, he would never report me.

In a few days we had orders to move the hospital to Staunton, and as I was fit for duty, I got my discharge to report to Company A, 33rd Virginia Infantry. But, as I was familiar with the hospital office, I got some blank discharges and filled one out to suit myself, which was to report to Company D, 11th Virginia Cavalry, Rosser's Brigade. It was camped at Swope's Depot, west of Staunton.

I went home and stayed one day, and then went to Staunton and reported to the provost marshal, and he furnished me transportation to Swope's Depot. I was soon with the 11th Cavalry, and found Lieutenant Parsons in command, and several that I knew. Kennison Taylor was there under the same circumstances, as he was an old member of the 13th Virginia. John Daily, Eph Herriott and a good many that I cannot recollect now were there; also, a great many that I did not know, but they were all Hampshire boys, and I felt at home. I told Lieutenant Parsons that I came to join his company. He advised me to go and see Major McDonald. I did so, and told him my situation; that I had no company, but did not want to desert the cause, and would like to be in his command, and if I could not join it, I would go to some partisan ranger company. He replied that he would like for me to remain, and that I should do so, but if General Lee called on him for me, he would have to give me up, as it was his orders to deliver up an infantryman when caught in the cavalry.

I told him what Captain Wilson said, and that I had no fear of being called back to the infantry. But there was another difficulty in the way; I had no horse, and each soldier had to furnish his own horse; but I knew I could, get one some way or other. The third day after I arrived in this camp the brigade was disbanded for the winter, and sent to different portions of the country to get provisions for their horses.

The squadron I was with, composed of the Hampshire and Hardy Companies, were ordered to Lost River, in Hardy County. John Daily happened to have an extra broken-down horse that he wanted to send to Hampshire to recruit, and he gave it to me to ride. So, I fastened a good lot of blankets on him and mounted. We happened to go by my father's house, and I got his saddle, but it was a citizen's saddle; so, when we arrived at Brock's Gap, I exchanged his saddle with Bud Peterson for a Confederate cavalry saddle, and went on to camp. The squadron went into winter quarters near Mathias, on Lost River.

After remaining there a few days and helping to build quarters, Ken Taylor and myself started to Hampshire to capture each of us a horse. The others bade us farewell, and said we were bound for Camp Chase. We continued on until we reached Joseph Pancake's, on the "South Branch" of the Potomac, where he turned over the horse he was riding and I delivered Daily's horse to Joseph Patterson. We were now both afoot, but determined to go to the Yankee camp and capture a horse apiece.

We then went to Romney, where Taylor's parents lived. We ma-

Maynadier T. Bruce - August, 1866

Fraternally
Maynadier T. Bruce

noeuvred in that county as far down as Springfield for some time, and finally fell in with William French, of the 13th Virginia, "Manny" Bruce, of McNeil's Rangers, and Ed Montgomery, and formed a plot to watch the road for a squad of straggling Yankees, capture them, take their horses and turn the prisoners loose. But the weather was very cold, with snow on the ground, and the "Yanks" did not venture far from camp.

We finally heard that there was a cattle speculator, quartermaster or government agent, or something of the kind, by the name of McFern, who came out from Cumberland, Md., every week on Patterson's Creek. He bought all the cattle he could find, and if a Southern man would not sell him, he would take them anyhow, or if he heard of their selling them to go South, he would take them, and he generally had a good pile of greenbacks with him.

We did not care who or what he was; it would be a picnic for us to get him and take him "in out of the wet." Therefore, we marched across Middle Ridge early one morning in the cold and snow and posted ourselves in a schoolhouse that stood near the road leading from Frankfort up the creek. We would keep one man on post near the road, while the others would remain in the schoolhouse; but we were afraid to make a fire, for fear of attracting attention. We waited and watched all day, but in vain, for our man never came. At dark, being cold and hungry, we went to a house nearby and the gentleman gave us a good drink of apple brandy, a good supper and a good, warm fire to sit by, which was quite refreshing.

We then held a council of war to determine how to proceed. Montgomery, French and Taylor were in favour of going to the mouth of Patterson's Creek, on the "North Branch" of the Potomac, cross over into Maryland and get horses out of a camp of condemned cavalry horses that were there recruiting. Manny Bruce, who was raised in Cumberland, was in favour of going into Cumberland and getting good horses, as he did not want any of the old, broken-down ones.

Now, there were about 12,000 troops camped in and around Cumberland, Md., and it was quite a risky business wading that river and going into that camp; but Bruce said he knew every hog-path, and he would pilot us safely. I was indifferent about which route we took, and Bruce, seeing this, insisted that I should go with him to Cumberland. So, things were arranged in that way. Bruce and I started for Cumberland, and French, Montgomery and Taylor for the Potomac, to the condemned camp. We gave each other goodbye. We did

How the Soldiers Captured Hogs.

not know whether we would be killed or land in prison or be hung as spies. It was a critical and dangerous move, but we were hardened to such work, and did not care.

After traveling through the snow for several miles Bruce and I came to the conclusion that we could not make the trip on foot, as it was about twelve miles, and get out safely by daylight, so we concluded we would stop at some farmhouse and get horses, ride them to the river and turn them loose. At the next house we came to we stopped and wakened the old man and told him that we had a very important trip to make that night, and that we were "given out" entirely, and could not make it on foot, and that he should let us have a horse to ride, and we would return him safely. We did not tell him which army we belonged to, but pretended we were Yankees, as we had on English-grey overcoats, which appeared blue after dark. He told us that he had but one horse, and be could not think of letting it go for any consideration. We offered to pay him for it, but it was "no go." I then told him it was a case of necessity, and if no persuasion would do, we would take the horse anyhow.

So, we proceeded to the stable and got the horse, and both mounted, it, bareback, and rode to the river at the place where we expected to wade it, as Bruce said there was a "riffle" there, and we could wade very easily. The weather was very cold, but the river was not frozen over.

When we got to the ford we learned that there was a picket post on the opposite side. We could see their fire and see the men standing around. So, we were foiled, and did not know what to do, but concluded to go down the river until we could find another rift or bar, and then wade.

After going some distance, we thought we had found the desired place, and made preparations to take to the water. We each procured a long stick, and as we were armed with six-shooters, we kept our belts on. When we started into the water it was very cold, and kept getting deeper every step. When it reached our waists, we unbuckled our belts and swung them over our shoulders to keep them dry; but as we proceeded it got deeper and deeper, until nearly up to our armpits. As I was in front, I halted and told Bruce we could not make it, as I could tell by feeling with my stick that it was still deeper further on, and that we would get so chilled that we could do nothing if we got across safely, and that if we got down with our overcoats on we could not swim with them, and would be sure to drown. He said: "No, we cannot make it, and will have to give it up."

We then came out of the water and went to a house about one-fourth of a mile from there, and by that time our clothes were frozen stiff. We wakened the man of the house, not knowing whether he was Rebel or Union, and told him "for God's sake" to make a fire, as we were nearly frozen to death. He got up and made a roaring fire, which felt very comfortable to us. After drying and warming ourselves we lay down by the fire and took a short nap. When I awakened, I had burned my boots so badly that the whole front came out of one of them. I told Bruce we must get out of this before daylight, or we would be captured. We then tried to hire the man of the house to take us a few miles on his horses, but no go; he would not do it. So, we drew our pistols and informed him that we would make him go. We then marched him to the stable and got two horses and mounted them, taking him along.

We had not proceeded more than one mile when we came across the old horse we had ridden to the river and turned loose. We then discharged our man and sent him home, giving him a $5 bill on a broken bank in Michigan that I had gotten while in Maryland. We mounted our old horse and arrived at the house where we had procured him by daylight. We found them perfectly delighted at the return of their horse, as they never expected to see him again. They insisted we should remain and have a good, warm breakfast, which was very acceptable. During our travels in the night we passed by a house where a sleighing party from Springfield and Frankfort were having a dance. I knew several who were there, but we did not stop or make ourselves known, as we were engaged in more pressing business at that time than "tripping the light fantastic toe."

After partaking of breakfast, we started on until we arrived at Joshua Johnson's, who had several sons in the Confederate Army—one, William Johnson, was lieutenant in my old company, and had died at Charlottesville, Va.— and we knew we would be welcomed. We needed rest and sleep. Mr. Johnson gave us a good drink of brandy and put us upstairs to sleep, promising to keep a lookout for us if any Yanks should pass along, and to waken us about 4 o'clock, as we wanted to get out of that neighbourhood that night, for fear the boys that went to the condemned camp might have stirred up the enemy and they would make it red hot for us.

We slept sweetly until Mr. Johnson roused us up from our peaceful slumbers, gave us another good dram and a good supper, when we sallied forth for fresh adventures. We proceeded up the creek until we came to the path that led across Middle Ridge to the South Branch. There was a negro cabin there, and Bruce was acquainted with the coloured man who lived in it, as he had lived in Cumberland with the Lynn family. Bruce made him believe that he was Sprig Lynn, and that I was Johnnie Fay. He "took it all in" and believed it firmly, as Bruce could relate to him many incidents of his boyhood days.

We then inquired of him if McFern had gone up the creek that day, but he did not know, as he had been away all day himself, but we could find out by going to the next house. Bruce went on to the next house, while I stood picket in the road. We still had it in our heads to capture him if we could. So, when Bruce returned, he brought the joyful news that McFern had gone up the creek that morning, and was still up there, buying cattle. We then determined to have him, if it took us all night. There was a lady in that neighbourhood who requested us, if we captured him, to hold him as a hostage for her father, whom the Yankees had in prison as a citizen, and it was my full determination to do so.

As we proceeded up the creek we were overtaken by a man in a wagon, and we got in and rode a short distance. We soon found that he was a Rebel, and we divulged our plans to him. He told us that we would find McFern at one of two houses that he located. We then got out of the wagon and waited some time, in order to keep suspicion from our friend, and then cautiously proceeded to the first house and inquired for our man, but they said he was not there; that we would find him at the next house, Mr. Davis Rees'.

We then knew how to lay our plans. I was to arrest him while Bruce was to watch that no one else interfered. We belted our pistols, already cocked, under our overcoats, walked up to the front door of the house, and knocked, passing ourselves off as Yankees. A young lady came to the door and we asked her if we could stay all night. She said she supposed we could, and asked us to come in. We then walked into the front room. She sat some chairs up to the fireplace and requested us to be seated there. There was no one else in the room.

We had no sooner taken our seats than the young lady left us and went into the dining room. As she opened the door, I saw several men seated there. I tapped Bruce on the shoulder and told him to come on. We went into the other room and found some seven or eight men, mostly citizens. We bid "Good evening" to them and took our seats side by side. They seemed a little surprised at our abruptness, but said nothing, and soon resumed their conversation. In a few minutes we knew which one was our man, and Bruce touched my foot as a sign to proceed. I then opened the conversation.

"Your name is McFern, is it not?"

"Yes, sir."

"You are buying cattle for the United States Government, are you not?"

"Well, not exactly. I am butchering them."

"Well, Mr. McFern, you can consider yourself our prisoner," I said, at the same time rising and walking up to him with pistol drawn, Bruce at the same time standing up with his pistol ready. McFern, thinking we were Yankees, wanted to know, very insolently, what he had done to be arrested for in this manner, and what authority we had to arrest him.

"Simply," says I, "because we are Rebels, and you are a Yankee, or working for the government, and we want those cattle you have to take to the Southern Army, and you along with them."

If a cyclone had struck the house it would not have more surprised him, and all that were there, as they did not think there was a Rebel under arms within forty miles of that place.

He commenced begging at once, and as I was standing by him holding my pistol in hand, with the muzzle pointed to the floor, my finger on the trigger, and searching him for arms with my other hand, my pistol, I suppose from the numbness of my hand, accidentally went off and bored a hole through the floor. He then pleaded "for God's sake" not to kill him, and the women commenced screaming and begging me not to shoot him, I explaining all the time that it was an accident, and that he would not be hurt. One of the men in the room spoke up and said he knew it was accidental. We finally got quiet restored.

He declared he had no arms but a pocketknife, and gave that to me, but as I was searching him, I felt a big, fat pocketbook, but did not take it just then. We then made preparations to go. He said he had twenty-four head of cattle in the yard, but had let the young ladies of the house have his horse to go sleighing that evening. We gave him his overcoat, and, as we stepped out of the door, I told him he had better let me carry that pocketbook, for fear of an accident, and that I would trade gloves with him, also, as he had a nice pair of lamb's wool gloves, and mine were quite worn.

CHAPTER 26

On the Road to Prison

I guarded him while Bruce, after pressing two or three of the young men who were there into service, drove the cattle out of the yard and counted them. There were twenty-four big, fat cattle. My old school teacher, Ziler Chadwick, was in the room at the time, but I did not let it be known that I knew him, and he avoided recognising me. A young Mr. Herriott was there also. Chadwick was teaching school in the neighbourhood.

After starting the cattle I told Bruce to take charge of the prisoner and I would take charge of the cattle, as it would be difficult to drive them. It was my full determination to bring the cattle and prisoner out South, for we had made arrangements with the coloured man to help us drive them across the Ridge from his house. But after we had proceeded about one mile Bruce came running to me and told me that the prisoner had gotten away from him, and we had better "skip out," as he would give the alarm and have the Yankees after us. I was vexed considerably, and upbraided him for being so careless, when he said it made no difference, as there was plenty of money in that pocketbook to get us all the horses we wanted. I asked him how he knew what was in it. He said McFern told him there was nearly $900 in it, and he knew he had told him the truth, and if we had captured him in the morning, we would have gotten $2,500. So, there was no other course to pursue, and we left the cattle in the road and departed.

We hurried on down the road to the old coloured man's, and gave him $5 to take us across the ridge on his horses, which he did. For fear of getting separated we went to a cabin in the woods and aroused them. By the light from a pine torch on the hearth we divided the money and found it as McFern had said, nearly $900 in greenbacks. Bruce then told me he let him go on purpose, as he did not want to be bothered with him.

We then went on the "South Branch" to Vause Herriott's plantation, and roused him up and asked him to let us stay the remainder of the night. It was arranged before we got there that I was to buy Vause's fine bay horse, and Bruce was to buy a fine black mare from Frank Murphy.

So, after we had, gone to bed, I asked Vause what he would take for the horse. He said $225 in greenbacks, but as I wanted him for service, and he was afraid the Yankees would take him, I might have him for $200. We had not told him of our capture, and he did not think we had any money, but I told him I would take him. He then wanted to know where we had made a raise. Bruce told him we had been to Cumberland and made a capture. But in the morning, when I handed him $200 and took the horse, he was very much surprised. We then told him how we got it, and he became very uneasy, and wanted us to leave immediately, as he said the Yankees would be sure to be after us, and if they found us there, they would burn him out. We told him we were as anxious to leave as he was to have us, and to help us across the river, as it was quite high. I swam the horse across, and Vause took Bruce across in the canoe, when we both mounted and started for Romney. We did not stay at Romney long, but went on to Mr. Pancake's. I left nearly all my money with Mrs. Sallie Pancake and went to Patterson's and got the saddle I had left there, and, mounting, I began to feel like a cavalryman. Bruce went on to Frank Murphy's and bought the black mare, when he, too, was well mounted.

I intended to go right on to the company, but meeting William French and George Arnold at Pancake's, they persuaded me to go back with them to Jersey Mountain, as some more of Company D were coming in, and we would make a raid on the railroad and capture a train of cars. I concluded to do so.

We first went to their stronghold up in the mountains, called "Fort Defiance," and from there on down the mountain to Frank Ewer's place, and then down on the "Levels" to Swisher's, where I got Mrs. Swisher to go to Paw Paw Depot, on the Baltimore and Ohio railroad, for me, and run the blockade with some grey goods to make me a new suit; also a pair of boots and a lot of calico. I wanted to take the calico out South, as it was a great object at that time. A young lady who could sport a calico dress those times felt rich, as all the wear was homespun. As Bid Leopard used to say, we could board a week in the Valley for a yard of calico or a Hagerstown almanac. He and Bill Herbert, both cavalrymen, once took a load of almanacs to the Page Valley and made a fortune in "Confed." But I am digressing, and will return.

I had left some money with Mrs. Scanlon to run the blockade for me and get some clothes also, thinking if one failed the other would not, and if they both succeeded, I could very easily dispose of all I could carry at a handsome profit when I got South. I wanted the clothing mainly for myself and father's family. William French and I were together for some time, scouting around to see what we could pick up.

At Swisher's I met my old friend and comrade in arms, Mr. Charles French, but he was only with us a short time. We went from there up the South Branch one night and learned that a sleighing party was having a dance at Mrs. Brooks', across the river. So, we left our horses at Forman Taylor's and crossed the river on the ice, and engaged in the dance until nearly daylight. We had to do our traveling at night and lay by in the daytime, for fear some scouting party of the enemy would capture us. At those dances I would meet girls and young ladies that I had been raised with and had gone to school with, and enjoyed myself hugely.

One night I was in Springfield and sat up at a wake with a dead child of John Seeders, and before daylight James Parsons and myself left and stopped at George Johnson's, a tavern stand, where we remained a short time. Just as we were leaving, at daybreak, and going through a little passageway between the main building and kitchen. Parsons, who was ahead, just as he got to the gate, wheeled around to me and said: "Run, for God's sake, the Yankees are right here." So, I wheeled and ran and went up the steps and into the icehouse. By that time the Yanks were in the house, but did not see me. They proved to be a squad of infantry from Green Spring Station, and did not stay long, but I thought I would freeze to death while they did stay, as I had to remain in that cold icehouse.

Every time Johnson came out of the house, he would shake his hand at me, as he knew I was looking out of the latticed window. They would not trouble Parsons, as he was staying at home. Finally, they left and I came down, and they were not out of sight of town before I was down on the square.

William French and myself went to several dances, and had a fine time with the girls, and I never enjoyed myself better in my life. But those happy days were soon to be over, and days and months of misery to follow.

There was no chance to capture a train, and I had made all my arrangements to go on to the company. I had gotten my money from Mrs. Sallie Pancake, had bought a good cavalry saddle from W. J. Long, had bought a pistol (as the one I was using was borrowed) and had gotten my clothes from the tailor. I had to make a trip to Mrs. Scanlon's to get the things she had bought for me, and had intended to go out by the Grassy Lick road, but as there were several of the company going in another direction, they insisted that I should come back and go that way, which I did. I was induced to do so, however, more from the fact that some young ladies, the Misses Murphy and some others, wanted to send some valentines by me to the boys.

The day I started out I met John Lynn, Manny Bruce, M. Lovett, of Company D, and Captain Stump at Frank Murphy's. Lynn and Bruce were going to McNeil's Company, Lovett was going to stay at Murphy's, and Captain Stump would have me go home with him and stay all night, as I had been so attentive to him when wounded. I spent the night with Captain Stump. Lovett was to meet me at Stump's at 9 o'clock the next morning. We were to go together, and, after we got up the road a few miles, take a bridle path across the mountain. I spent a pleasant night with Captain Stump at his sister's, Mrs. French, and it was the last night for him on this earth. The next day he was murdered in cold blood.

The next morning, after breakfast, we saddled up our horses and waited awhile for Lovett. When the hour had passed that he was to meet me, and as Captain Stump wanted to go down the river, near Romney, to his father's, I concluded I would ride on slowly, and I told him to tell Lovett to hurry up and overtake me, and thus we parted. When I reached the place at the road where the path led across the mountain I left, word at a house there for them to tell Lovett that I had gone on up the road, as I was not acquainted with the bridle path.

After going some distance, I came to where the roads forked, one road leading to Moorefield, the other through the Bean settlement to Lost River. I took the latter road, but they ran nearly parallel with each other for some distance, gradually widening out. There had been a little thaw the day before, but it had frozen that night, and the roads were one sheet of ice, and my horse being smooth shod it was difficult to get along. I had the goods that I had bought under the saddle, and the boots tied behind, and was carrying the saddle that I had borrowed from Bud Peterson at Brock's Gap.

As I was riding along, thinking I was safe from the enemy, my horse pricked up his ears and threw up his head, and I knew he saw something. Looking ahead I saw a man riding across from the road I was in towards the other road, with the cape of his overcoat thrown back, and I could see the red lining. I halted for a few seconds, but thinking it was some of Major Harry Gilmore's command, or Captain McNeil's men, as I knew they were camped near Moorefield (and our men wore such coats), I rode on, but had not gone far until I saw several men riding about in the woods in a suspicious manner, and concluded, whether they were Rebels or not, that I would get out of there. So, I wheeled my horse around, threw down the extra saddle I was carrying, and put spurs to my horse and went down the road as fast as I could go. I could see no other way of escape. But as soon as I had wheeled and started, they commenced firing at me, and the bullets whistled by, but I kept on. I knew my horse was fast, my greatest fear being that he might fall on the ice; but when I got to the forks of the road, I saw ten or twelve men just ahead of me. I dashed in amongst them, as I could not check my horse.

One fellow grabbed the reins of my horse, while another had his pistol levelled at my head, when some of the others pulled me off the horse and commenced taking my things. I was quarrelling with them all the time, thinking they were Rebels, as they were dressed like Rebels and talked like them. I kept asking them what they were. They said they were Rebels and belonged to Gilmore's command, and that I was a d—d Yankee spy.

I told them I was a Rebel and had papers in my pocket to show them where I belonged. They replied that if I was all right, I would get all my things back again; that Harry Gilmore was on behind. They wanted to know if there were any more soldiers down the road. I told them there was one coming behind me (meaning Lovett). They said if I told them a lie, they would kill me.

One took my hat and gave me an old one about three sizes too large; one took my overcoat and vizer, and gave me a citizen's coat; another took my haversack and pocketbook, with $125 in it; another pulled at my boots, but I held my foot so it would not come off, when he called on a companion to take hold of the other boot, which he did, throwing me flat on my back and straddle of a small tree. Each man continued pulling at a boot until they pulled them off. One of them put on my boots and gave me his old ones, which were a size too small. I could not get my heel any further into them than the top of the counters. They took my fine horse and gave me a young horse they had picked up along the road, and a citizen's saddle. In a few minutes all that change was made, and as it was a bitter cold morning, I felt the change very perceptibly. They then left one man to guard me, and the balance rode on.

They were the "Jessie Scouts," or Captain Blaser's Scouts, and numbered about thirty men, under the command of Major Young—as desperate a set of guerrillas as ever graced a saddle. They dressed like Rebels, and would go in advance of the command, which was some distance behind.

After they had all left, I asked the one who was guarding me to tell me the truth, what they were, whether they were Yanks or Rebs.

"Oh, we are all Rebs," he said, "and belong to Gilmore, and you will get all your things back."

I then began to think they were Rebels; but in a short time, the main column came in sight, and as soon as I saw them, all dressed in blue, my guard punched me and asked me what I thought of those fellows. I told him he need not tell me any more lies, that I knew where I was now. So, when they came up, about 400 of them, he turned me over to the guard, and, sure enough, Major Harry Gilmore was there, but he was a prisoner, and his cousin, Hoffman Gilmore, also. They had thirteen prisoners, and among them John Lynn and Manny Bruce. They made the prisoners ride single file, with a guard on each side of each prisoner.

They had come out of Winchester by the Moorefield road, piloted by a deserter from Gilmore's command, for the express purpose of capturing Harry Gilmore. They captured him at a house where he had his headquarters. As soon as that was accomplished, they started back to Winchester by way of Romney, picking up all soldiers they met. We had not gone far until they brought Lovett in. He blamed me for his capture, because I did not take the path across the mountain, and I blamed him for our capture for not being on time, as he had promised. If I had been fifteen minutes sooner, I would have been beyond the turn of the road and would have escaped; or if I had been fifteen minutes later, I would have been with Lovett, and we would have gone the bridle path, and both escaped capture. So, my fate at that time hung on fifteen minutes of time either way. What a trivial circumstance often changes the tide of a man's life!

I was uneasy all the time after I was captured about Captain Stump, as I knew that he had gone down the road and would be deceived by them; and I had often heard him say that he would rather die on the field of battle than fall into their hands. But as we went on and they did not bring him back I began to hope that he had given them the slip, and especially after passing his father's house. But we had not passed the house far when I saw him lying dead in the road, with nothing on but his pants and shirt, and his face all black. But I knew him by his home-made pants, and remarked that there lies Captain Stump. John Lynn said it was not Stump, but I was sure of it, and it proved too true.

The scouts said they had killed the chief of all the guerrillas, as he was heavily armed, having two or three six-shooters, besides a carbine.

One of them told me that when they rode up to the house Stump came out and attempted to get on his horse, and they shot him through the leg; and after they had captured him he said he could whip all of them if they would give him a chance, and that when they got out in the road they gave him a chance, and commenced firing on him until they killed him. Another one told me that after they left the house and got in the road, their commander said that he was an old guerrilla chief, and told them to kill him, which they did, and I believe that part is true.

That was the last of Captain George Stump, a good and brave soldier. He always carried several pistols, and his command called him "Stump's Battery." One of the scouts told me that when they captured me, as I dashed up into them, he had his pistol cocked and pointed right at my head, with his finger on the trigger, and was in the act of firing, when he saw I could not check the horse, and did not fire. I was just that near death that time.

Chapter 27

Prisoners on the March

It was a very cold day when we were captured—the 5th of February, 1865—and they kept on the march all day, and until about 9 o'clock at night, when they halted on the road leading from Romney to Winchester, to feed their horses. I had suffered terribly from the cold, having been warmly dressed when captured, but now nearly stripped. The change was as sudden as taking a cold bath.

When they stopped to feed, I was in hopes they would stay all night. While our guards were building a fire, I whispered to Bruce that now was our time to escape. He said "Hush." I was more anxious for Bruce to escape than myself, for they had captured him once and condemned him as a "spy," but he made his escape, and afterwards went into service, and I knew if they found that out it would go very hard with him. When they took Bruce's coat away from him, they gave him a Yankee blue overcoat, and gave me a black one. As some of the guards were busy making fires, others kept us huddled up together, and kept counting us; but Bruce and I kept stirring around to confuse them. Directly afterwards I saw Bruce walk out of the ring and mix up with the men that were feeding the horses. As soon as the fellow commenced counting us again, I began stirring around to confuse him and to make two men out of myself if I could, to give Bruce as much time as possible, but he soon found there was one missing and gave the alarm.

Some two or three of them ran down in the woods and fired several shots, but they did not get Bruce, and I have never seen him since, but heard that he went a short distance in the woods and laid down behind a log until the command moved on. I would like to see my old partner once more on earth and talk over our adventures, but I do not expect ever to have the opportunity.

After the horses had been fed and had rested a short time, we resumed the march. As we were crossing one of the mountains, we were suffering so intensely with the cold that I asked the officer in command if we could not walk awhile, as our feet were nearly frozen. He said we could if the guards would walk with us, which they were glad to do, as they were nearly as cold as we were. So, we all dismounted, but I happened to be in advance and could see no chance of escape. We had not been walking long, however, until the rear man in the line broke ranks and jumped down the side of the mountain and made his escape. The guard fired several shots after him, but without effect.

They then made us mount, and were more strict than ever, for they made one of the guards take the rein of each prisoner's horse and lead him, and they had orders to carry their pistols cocked and to fire on us if we made an attempt to escape. One reason why they travelled in the night was they were afraid that the different commands camped around Moorefield would rally and head them off between Romney and Winchester and release the prisoners.

Finally, about 3 o'clock in the morning, we arrived at Capon Bridge and went into camp. They put the prisoners in a house, where we had a fire and we got thawed out. I stole a pair of gloves out of the pocket of one of the guards who slept in the room with us that night, and wore them the next day. Directly after daylight they saddled up, and during that day we arrived in Winchester. We were taken to General Sheridan's headquarters and brought into his august presence. When we were arraigned, he pronounced sentence on us to the effect that we were "guerrillas of notorious character, and should be kept in close confinement at Fort McHenry, Baltimore, Md., during the war, and not be exchanged."

He had issued orders a short time before that all Rebel soldiers captured inside of his lines should be treated as guerrillas. He claimed his lines extended up to our picket posts, when sometimes the pickets of both armies would be twenty miles apart. He claimed the intervening space. We were then assigned to the guard-house at Winchester.

I was very uneasy for fear they would find out about us capturing McFern; but they never, as long as I was a prisoner, said a word about it. They knew such things were customary in both armies at that time. I never expected anything else, if I got captured, but to be stripped and robbed, and *vice versa*.

I was uneasy about another thing, which was that I had two discharges in my pocket from the hospital. One ordered me to report to Company A, 33rd Virginia Infantry, and the other to Company D, 11th Virginia Cavalry. As I was a cavalryman when captured, I told them I belonged to the cavalry, and it went on record that way in the prison. When I got my discharge, I was put down as a private in Company D, 11th Virginia Cavalry, and they never knew I belonged to the infantry. So, when I landed in the guardhouse at Winchester, I had an old hat, old boots, pants, and an army jacket. That was all the good I ever got out of over $400 that I had captured from McFern, except two canteens of apple brandy. The officers at the guard-house at Winchester called us out, one at a time, made us strip, and searched us all over and searched our clothing. I told them they could find nothing on me after those "Jessie Scouts went through me." They laughed and said "they guessed not, for they were worse than a dose of salts."

The next day after landing in Winchester we were taken out of the guard-house and marched through a blinding snowstorm to Stephenson's depot, five miles below Winchester, and put in a cattle car and taken to Harper's Ferry. There we had to stand in the snow for four hours waiting for a train to take us to Baltimore. I had no blanket nor overcoat, and I got so cold that I borrowed a blanket from one of the guards and laid down in the snow and rolled up in it. At last the train came and we were put in a good warm car that had a stove in it, and some time that night we arrived in Baltimore, and were taken to the slave-pen prison. The next day, which was the 8th of February, we were mustered in line and marched out to Fort McHenry. They made us march in two ranks in the middle of the street, while the guards marched on the sidewalks. There being a thaw that day, the water was running considerably, but we had to wade every place where the water ran across the road, and were wet above our knees.

When we arrived at Fort McHenry, we were taken to the provost marshal's office and our names, company and regiment taken down, and also had to undergo another strict search. There we met the crossest, most tyrannical man, for a provost marshal, that we had encountered yet. He cursed us black and blue, and wanted to know where we got those blue clothes we had on. I told him that their soldiers had taken ours from us and given us those in return. He said: "That's a d—d lie; you stole them off our dead soldiers on the battlefield."

We were then conducted into the prison, a large brick building that had been used as a stable before the war, and put in a room where there were about 250 prisoners. There was one large stove in the room, and two rows of bunks on each side, with a hallway through the centre. The bunks were not divided, but all in one, the second tier being just one floor above the other, at a distance of about five feet. It was about ten feet to the ceiling. We were put in there about dark, cold, wet and hungry, and could draw no rations until 12 o'clock the next day.

We began to look for some place to lie down, but found every foot of space occupied except the hallway, and that was about two inches deep in mud and slush. There was a small yard to each prison, and the prisoners could go out and in when they chose until 8 o'clock at night. We then tried to get to the stove, but could not even get near enough to see any of it except the pipe. It was terribly cold, the thermometer registering below zero. There were a great many crippled soldiers in there who had been captured on the battle-field at Winchester, some of them one-legged and one-armed, and they had the preference at the stove.

We were wondering what we would do, as we were "fresh fish" and did not know the ropes yet, and were thinking our only chance was to lie down in the mud, when the door opened and a sergeant called for "that last batch of prisoners that came in." We eagerly went forward and wanted to know his wishes. He said we were too thick in there, and he would take us to another room, where we would be more comfortable.

We were pleased with that idea, but alas! vain hope! many of us went to our doom.

As each one's name was called, he was ordered to step outside. When my turn came, and I stepped out, I was escorted between two guards through that yard into another, and into a building that was full of cells, with a narrow passage-way against each wall, and was handed over to a sergeant who had a big bunch of keys hung to his arm. He opened one of the cell doors and told me to walk in.

"What is the meaning of all this?" I inquired.

"You will find out before you get out," he replied.

I had no blanket and there was no fire in the whole building, and it shocked me so to think that I would freeze to death in that terrible hole that I nearly sank to the floor. Presently they opened the door to put another one in with me. He had a blanket, but seeing that I had none he started back and asked the sergeant to put him in with a man that had a blanket; but I grabbed him and pulled him in my cell and said "For God's sake come in here." At the same time the sergeant shut the door and locked it.

He proved to be Hoffman Gilmore, cousin to Major Harry Gilmore, and was courier for his cousin. His home was in Baltimore and he had not been in service long; neither had he seen any hardships, so when he was placed in the cell he gave up, and broke down entirely, and said we might as well conclude to die, that we never would get out alive.

Presently there was another prisoner put in our cell by the name of John Rafter. He belonged to McNeil's Company of rangers and had not seen much service. They were both younger than I was, and as I was rather hardened to privations and dangers, I thought it would not do for us all to give up, so I commenced trying to cheer them up, and put on a lively air and told them we were worth a hundred dead men yet. By that means I inspired some vigour and confidence in them and myself, too.

The prisoners were all distributed in the cells in that way, three in a cell. The cells were five feet wide and eight feet long, made of two-inch oak plank doubled, with a hole in each door ten inches square with iron bars across, and ventilator holes just opposite in the brick wall. The cold wind blew right in on us, and it was the coldest spell of weather during the winter of 1864 and 1865.

We finally lay down on the floor close together, and, covering ourselves over head and heels, tried to sleep, but we just lay there and shivered. We were afraid to go to sleep for fear we would freeze to death.

I said to the boys: "This will never do," and I jumped up and commenced dancing and singing and running around for exercise. I made them get up, and we walked around the cell for hours in single file, holding to one another's coats, for it was dark as a dungeon, and we took that precaution to keep from running against each other. Then, when we got tired, we would lie down awhile and rub our feet and limbs, for we were very scantily clothed. We kept that up until 12 o'clock the next day, when we drew some rations, which consisted of a piece of bread and a piece of meat; and small at that. And that was our rations while we stayed there.

Every day at 12 o'clock we would get a slice of bread and piece of salt pork; and every third day we would draw a quart of bean soup, with about three beans to the quart; but if we had no cups to put the soup in, they would pass on and not give us any at all. None of us had any cups at first, and, as I saw I was about to lose my soup, I grabbed up my old hat and, by sinking in the crown from the outside, I made a depression large enough to hold my soup, and, soaking my bread in it, ate it that way. The other boys said they could not do that; but I took notice they "tumbled" to it the next time soup came round, and continued to do so until we procured cups.

We had no money, no tobacco nor pipes and no writing material. I had some acquaintances in Baltimore before the war, but did not know whether they were there now or not. Hoffman Gilmore had scores of wealthy relatives in Baltimore, but to get word to them was the question.

The second day I was there I got one of the guards to give me a paper and he brought me the *Baltimore Gazette*. I scanned it over in a hurry to find by the advertisements someone that I knew, and soon found the firm of H. K. Hoffman & Co., wholesale grocers, No. 45 South Howard street. It was like a beacon light to me. If someone had entered the prison at that time to release me it would not have filled me with more joy than to see that well-known name of H. K. Hoffman. He was once a merchant in Springfield, had boarded at my father's house when single; had married there and had always been a fast friend of our family. I did not know his politics, but that made no difference; I knew he would help me in distress. I then begged the guards for paper, envelope and stamp, and wrote to him to please send me a little money.

The next day I received a letter from him with five dollars in it. It was a Godsend to us; and I don't think five dollars ever did so much good to anyone in this world as that did to us. I divided with my comrades. I did not get the money, but the amount was sent into me by the provost marshal in sutler's checks, and we had to spend it with him. The provost would not let us buy anything to eat, but would let us buy tobacco, etc. The first thing I invested in was pipe, tobacco, matches, paper, envelopes, stamps, candles and quart cups. It was quite dark in our cell in the day time, and the candle made it more cheerful and we even imagined it made the cell warmer.

Hoffman Gilmore then wrote to his friends and soon received a check for twenty dollars, and we were then we fixed with respect to funds. As I had cheered him up in his first distress, and relieved his wants with money, he became one of the best friends I ever had and remained so during our sojourn in prison. He often said that if it had not been for me, he believed he would have died in that cell.

Our prisons were located outside of the main fort near the water. There were three large, long, brick buildings, each one divided into four rooms, two below and two above. One room was full of cells on the ground; the other room on the ground floor of the same building was used as a guardhouse for their own men. One room above had Confederate officers confined in it, while the other was full of bounty jumpers. Each room had a small yard attached to it. The next building in the row, which was the one we were put into, had "Rebel" prisoners in one room; the other room, on the ground floor, was full of "bounty jumpers," while the one above them was full of Rebel citizen prisoners. The room above the Rebel prisoners was full of negroes they had picked up wherever they could find them, and they kept them there until they got two or three hundred, when they would ship them to the front, and fill up again. I never knew what was in the other brick building. I give this description in order that the reader may fully understand what transpired afterwards.

Around each prison and yard there was a high plank fence with a parapet on top with sentinels walking day and night. At night they were placed in the yards also. A sentinel walked in front of our cells all the time and one stood in the door of the building. If a prisoner wanted to go out into the yard, he would inform the guard, when he would sing out, "Sergeant of the guard, cell No. 10," or whatever number was called for. The sergeant would then come if it suited his convenience (if not he would not come for one or two hours), unlock the door and take the men out—but one man at a time—then have two guards conduct him out and back.

The regiment that was doing guard duty there was the 91st New York, and they had never been to the front and did not know what war was, and, consequently, did not know how to treat prisoners, although there were a few who treated us kindly. There was one sentinel, who, whenever he got on our post, would slip us some coffee, or do any favour he could, unperceived; but he was the only one and I have forgotten his name. The provost marshal's name was Captain McDermott, a perfect tyrant, even to his own men. They had given him the name of "Black Jack" and he went by that name among prisoners and soldiers alike.

I would sing songs, hymns, and dance; anything to make it lively and pass off the time. One night I was in a big way singing some religious hymns, when all at once old "Black Jack" stuck his nose in the door and said: "I don't want so much d——d piety in there." The sentinel remarked that he had told me to hush and I wouldn't do it (which was a lie). "Black Jack" then said: "If they make any more noise fire in among them and that will settle them." He would come sneaking around to see what he could hear at night, and would always give us a cursing. I sent word to him the second night we were there to send us some blankets. He sent word back that "his government did not furnish Rebel prisoners with blankets, and that we should stay in there until we froze or rot, he didn't care a d——d which."

I sent word back—for spite—that I would not die there unless he took me out to that gallows and hung me. There was a gallows erected out near the fort, where they had hung Leopold as a spy a short time before we went there, and they all called us "gorillas" and "cell-rats." Every few days some of them would come in and say: "Three of you 'gorillas' are to be hung tomorrow." Sometimes they would say five or ten, just as it suited them.

After we had been there about one week the weather moderated some, and they would let us out in the yard to walk around for one, two or three hours, and we would have an opportunity to talk with the other prisoners, as they would put us in their yard. One day we saw them fixing the trapdoor to the gallows, and at the same time they told us there would be ten "gorillas" hung the next day. It made us feel rather bad that night, and we began to think there was some truth in it. I believe old "Black Jack" would have hung us, but was afraid our government would retaliate. In a few days after we were put in the cells the men commenced getting sick, and there were fresh prisoners put in every few days until there were seven in each cell. They happened to put Ned Bonham in our cell. He belonged to the 12th Virginia Cavalry, and was an acquaintance of Gilmore's and myself, and we three messed together during the remainder of our stay in prison.

When we lay seven in a cell, we laid crosswise, and the seven of us would fill the cell from one end to the other, and we had to all lie spoon fashion at that. There were two of the seven that were six feet, and as our cell was only five feet we had to "spoon" considerably to get the six-footers in. When one turned over, we would all have to turn. There was not room enough for one man to lie on his back.

Sometimes some of them would want to turn and the others would not turn, and then we would have a row and punching of ribs, until we all got in one notion.

But we did not remain crowded long, for they began to sicken and die, and our cell was soon reduced to four. They would take the pneumonia and die in a few days. One man in a cell next to me died in twenty-four hours after he was taken sick. The sergeant would come along in front of the cells in the mornings and want to know if there were any sick. If there were any that were able to walk, he would take them up to the hospital to the doctor, who would prescribe for them, give them some medicine and send them back. If they were not able to walk, they would lie there until they died, or were nearly dead, and then be carried to the hospital on a stretcher. By that time the disease would have such a hold on them that they were almost sure to die. But few got well. Out of eighty prisoners that were in the cells, forty died or were sick in the hospital in thirty days.

I told the sergeant one morning that I was sick and wanted to go to the doctor. There was nothing the matter with me, but I wanted to go out of curiosity, and to have a walk and some exercise. He took me along with a number of others, and we had to stand on a long porch in the cold until the doctor got through with his breakfast, which, I thought, was about one hour. Finally, when he came and examined us, and asked me what was the matter with me I told him I had the itch, as a great many had that complaint, and it was the best excuse that I could offer. He gave me some medicine for it, which I threw away on my way back to my cell. That was the last time I volunteered to go to the hospital.

One night, about midnight, they opened the door of our cell and put a fellow in who was yelling and screaming and crying like he was scared to death. He laid down on the floor and kept crying and moaning at a terrible rate. We began to make sport of him, and wanted to know what regiment he belonged to. He said his name was James Glenn Gatelow, and that he did not belong to the army at all, and he "never done nothing," and he did not know what they put him in there for.

Finally, we found out all about him. He was an idiot they had picked up near Winchester because he had some soldier's clothes on. He was a more fit subject for a lunatic asylum than a prison like that. But we had a great deal of sport out of him while he remained in prison.

CHAPTER 28
Released from Prison

One day when we were out in the yard with the other prisoners, we heard there were some sick and wounded who were going to be exchanged, and the other prisoners had thought it terrible that we were kept in the cells. One man, a Louisiana sergeant, who was going to be exchanged, took down all our names, the company and regiment to which we belonged, and put them in his boots. When he got to Richmond, he reported our treatment to President Davis and Commissioner Ould and had our names published in the Richmond papers. My parents happened to get one of the papers, which I saw after I got home. Our authorities at Richmond sent word to the United States authorities that we were no guerrillas, but regular soldiers, and if we were not released from the cells, and treated as other prisoners of war, they would put a like number of Federal prisoners in close confinement during the war.

So, one day, as they were returning us to our cells from the yard, the sergeant told us we could get the things that we had in the cells, as we were not to go back there anymore, but should remain in the barracks with the others and be treated better. Then such a shout of joy as went up—it made the very walls shake. We knew nothing then of this order from Richmond, but heard about it afterwards through some guards.

About this time the 91st New York was ordered to the front, as it was a large regiment and had done no service except guard duty. Then Captain McDermott, alias "Black Jack," received a furlough to go home to New York. While there, on a big spree, one night, he fell down a considerable flight of steps and broke his neck, as reported to us by the guards. That ended his career.

The 91st New York was replaced by the 5th Ohio, a regiment that had been in service during the war and was considerably reduced in numbers. It was sent to Fort McHenry to do guard duty and recruit. Captain McEwan was made provost marshal. He was a perfect gentleman and treated us like human beings. He soon came into our prison and said: "Well, boys, how are you getting along?" I saw that he would do to talk to, so I stepped out and told him that we were doing very well except that we were not allowed to buy anything to eat, and that some of us had money, or could get it from our friends, and as our rations were short, we would like to buy some. It seemed to surprise him that such was the case, and he said we could buy whatever we wanted. I then told him the sutler had no bread and the baker wanted money. He said he would have some bread checks issued, and when we received any money, we could take part in sutler checks and part in bread checks.

After that we fared and were treated as well as a prisoner of war could expect. The change was great, indeed. The room was not crowded, we had a good place to sleep, a stove to sit by, and could buy some extra rations, and had plenty of blankets. We were in the cells thirty days, and during that time saw no fire and had but one blanket, and were allowed but one scanty meal every twenty-four hours. They can talk about the Libby prison and Andersonville, but I will guarantee that there never was greater suffering or a greater death rate in any prison than in the cells of Fort McHenry during the war. I look back upon my experience there with horror to this day, and wonder how I came out alive.

When we were in the regular prison, they would take forty of us out every day to work and clean up about the fort, which was light work and good exercise and they could always get plenty of volunteers to go out to work. I often went out—would rather do so than lie around the prison. Sometimes they would take ten or twelve out in the edge of the city to a rolling mill to load wagons with cinders and haul them back to the fort to make roads and walks. We would meet Rebel sympathizers at the mill and they would give us money and the guard would go with us to the grocery and we would buy corn meal and molasses, and such things, for about one-half what the sutler would charge us.

Sometimes some of the boys would give the wagon drivers some money and a canteen and they would go and get some whiskey, but did not let the guard see them. I got some once that way and took it into the prison and gave my chums a dram. One of our fellows got too bold about it and brought some in prison several times that way and would sell it to the bounty jumpers at a fabulous price, and was making a speculation of it. In one corner of our prison we had a hole cut in the partition between us and the bounty jumpers, and would carry on trade with them—a chew of tobacco for a "hardtack" two chews for a quart of coffee, and so on. They never had any money, and the most of our prisoners had some and could buy tobacco.

Those who had no friends to send them money were always making rings, breastpins, fans, watch-chains, etc., out of gutta-percha, and put silver and gold sets in them. It was like a manufactory every day;

and we could sell them to the guards and they would sell them again down in the city for double what they gave for them. There was a continual trade going on all the time. We never drew any coffee and the jumpers could get all they wanted.

One day one of our fellows traded them some whiskey and two of them got a little tight and beat one of their comrades, whom they had a grudge against, nearly to death. About midnight the guards rushed in, but could not find the men; but they got them at daylight and took them to the provost marshal, and he kept them tied up by the thumbs for three days to make them tell where they got their whiskey. They refused to tell, but he suspicioned that it came through our prison. After that when we were brought in from work our canteens were searched, and that broke up the liquor traffic.

I had written to several of my friends who were inside the lines; but the provost marshal had to read all letters that were sent, and all that were received, and if they did not suit him, he would destroy them.

I had an uncle, S. M. Heironimus, who was a merchant in Webster, Taylor County, W. Va., and a strong Union man. I wrote him for some money and clothes. I had, also, another uncle there at the time, but I did not know it, H. W. Heironimus, and he sent me a suit of clothes in a box, with some apples and chestnuts, and two dollars in money. I received all but the apples and chestnuts. They were confiscated, as our friends were not allowed to send us anything to eat. My uncle also wrote that he would be in Baltimore in a few days to do some business for H. K. Hoffman, and he would attend to my wants, which he did as long as I was in prison.

Every week or so he would send me two dollars. One time he came out to the fort and brought me a new hat, but they would not let him see me. I happened to be out at work that day, and saw him going from the provost marshal's office up to the general's headquarters, and hallooed at him, but he did not stop and did not speak, being afraid they might arrest him.

There was a commission of ladies in Baltimore that furnished Rebel prisoners with clothing. They would get our names from the papers as we were captured, and write to us as old acquaintances. One day I received a letter telling me I should be supplied with clothing if I needed it. It was signed Miss Dora Hoffman. She also wrote to a number of others. I think she was president of the society. I did not need any clothing, as my uncle had supplied me with all I was allowed.

When we wanted clothing, we had to go before the provost and be examined, and whatever he gave us permission to have we could get; if anything was sent not in the permission the whole was confiscated. So, we had an old ragged suit that we kept on purpose to put on when we went out to be examined by the provost. I suppose forty different men have worn that suit out to be inspected. The prisoners were well supplied by that commission of ladies, and they received thousands of blessings from the poor prisoners—thanks to their kind and generous souls!

We would have laws and regulations of our own in the prison. We had a court-martial to punish any one for stealing, and we made each one keep as clean as possible. There was a high post in the middle of the yard with a cross-piece on top, and every day when it was not too cold there would be someone sitting upon that post, as we could have a fine view of the steam tugs plying their trade up and down. On the west side of the fort was the Patapsco River, and way down the river as far as the eye could reach was Fort Carroll.

One day the "Red Sergeant" came into the prison yard and called for forty men to go to work around the fort. We called him the "Red Sergeant" because he belonged to the artillery and wore red chevrons on his coat and was a great, big, red-faced Irishman. He soon got nearly enough, but lacked one or two men, and as they were slower than usual in volunteering, he got out of patience. Looking around he observed a fellow by the name of Royston sitting upon the post.

"Here, come down from there and go to work," he cried out to Royston.

"I ain't going out today," replied Royston. "I was out yesterday, and I'm sick, anyhow."

The sergeant called a file of men and told them to cock their guns, and then pulled out his watch.

"I'll give you just five minutes to get down. If you don't do it in that time, I'll have you shot," he said.

"All right, I'm not coming down," said Royston, coolly.

Everything was as still as death for about three minutes; all of us standing around and expecting them to fire on Royston, who continued sitting there as calmly and unconcerned as if nothing unusual was transpiring. When the sergeant wheeled around and walked off, we fully expected to see him shot. Royston said he had made up his mind to die right there, and I believe he would have done it.

There was an ant bed in the lower end of the yard, and every day there would be from five to ten prisoners around that bed, picking off lice and having them and the ants fighting. They would have a regular pitched battle, and would get up bets on them. Sometimes the aunts would drag the louse off, but often times a big louse would stand them off. It was great sport for the prisoners.

We had a violin in prison and a fifer with his fife, and would have dances at night, and often had dress parade with the fife and an old camp kettle for a drum, and read out a long string of orders for the next day, and all such amusements to keep up our spirits and relieve the monotony of prison life. Rats were ready sale. The prisoners would cook and eat them.

Lovett wanted to raise some money one day and adopted a novel plan to do so. He had an old watch key, and walked up and down with the sentinel with the key in his hand until he attracted the sentinel's attention to it, and then remarked that there was a key that once belonged to "Stonewall Jackson." The sentinel wanted to buy it at once; but, of course, Lovett would not part with it for any consideration. Finally, after a great amount of begging, Lovett was induced to take five dollars for it. I suppose that key is held as a trophy to this day, but Jackson never saw the key.

When we were first put in the cells and heard our sentence, we made application to take the oath of allegiance, but they were too sharp for us and would not let us do so. They knew it was a scheme to get out; but as time rolled on, we all knew that the Confederacy was bound to fall when the spring campaign opened; and when we heard of the surrender of General Lee, the 9th of April, it did not surprise us. There were lively times about the fort, firing guns, etc., but a sad look among the prisoners, for we did not know our fate—whether we would be transported or what would become of us.

In a few days, however, their joy was turned to sadness by the assassination of President Lincoln, the 14th of April, 1866. We were sorry, too, because we knew they would think that the South had something to do with it, and then we knew that it would have been better for the South if he had lived. When we first heard it at night, we did not believe it, but next morning the flag in the fort was at half-mast and the minute guns were firing, and during the day the fort and city were draped in mourning.

About one week after that Captain McEwan came into our prison and told the prisoners who had been sentenced there during the war that we had served our term out, as the war was over, and that he

Manny Bruce and John O. Casler Capturing McFern, a Federal Quarter-master.

would go to work and have us released, which he did on the 1st of May, 1865.

We all marched up to the general's headquarters and took the oath of alliance to the United States Government and signed our names. The next morning, we were marched outside the walls of our prison, in two ranks, ordered to halt, and then, "Break ranks, march!" That was the last military command ever given me. Here is a copy of my oath, which I still have in my possession:

United States of America.

I, John O. Casler, Private 11th Virginia Cavalry, of the County of Rockingham, State of Virginia, do solemnly swear, in presence of Almighty God, that I will henceforth faithfully support, protect and defend the Constitution of the United States, and the Union of the States thereunder; and that I will in like manner abide by and faithfully support all acts of Congress passed during the existing rebellion with reference to slaves, so long and so far as not repealed, modified or held void by Congress, or by decision of the Supreme Court; and that I will in like manner abide by and faithfully support all proclamations of the President made during the existing rebellion, having reference to slaves, so long and so far as not modified or declared void by decision of the Supreme Court; so help me God.

John O. Casler.

Subscribed and sworn to before me at Ft. McHenry, Md., this first day of May, A. D. 1865.

John Z. Mount,
Major and Commissary of Prisoners.

The above-named has light complexion, black hair and grey eyes, and is 5 feet 6 inches high."

The following is my discharge from prison:

Office Commissary of Prisons,
Ft. McHenry, Md., May 1, 1865.

In pursuance of instructions from Commissary General of Prisoners, dated Washington, D. C, April 29, 1865, the Provost Marshal is hereby directed to release from confinement John O. Casler, 11th Virginia Cavalry, he having taken the oath as prescribed in the President's proclamation of December 8, 1863.

By command of Colonel Daniel Macauly.

John Z. Mount,

United States of America.

I, **John Castler Pvt 11th Va Cav¹y** of the County of **Rockingham** State of **Va** do solemnly swear, in presence of Almighty God, that I will henceforth faithfully support, protect, and defend the Constitution of the United States, and the Union of the States thereunder; and that I will, in like manner, abide by and faithfully support all acts of Congress passed during the existing rebellion with reference to slaves, so long and so far as not repealed, modified, or held void by Congress, or by decision of the Supreme Court; and that I will, in like manner, abide by and faithfully support all proclamations of the President made during the existing rebellion having reference to slaves, so long and so far as not modified or declared void by decision of the Supreme Court: So help me God.

John O Casler

Subscribed and sworn to before me, at **Fort McHenry Md,** this **First** day of **May**, A. D. 186**5**.

John F Mount
Maj & Com'y of Pris

The above-named has **Light** complexion, **Black** hair and **Grey** eyes, and is **5** feet **6** inches high.

FAC-SIMILE OF OATH.

Office Commissary of Prisoners,
Fort McHenry, Md. **May 1st 1865**.

Special Orders,
No.

In pursuance of Instructions from Comy Genl of Pris dated Washington DC April 29th 1865 the Provost Marshal is hereby directed to release from Confinement John Casler 11" Va Cav He having taken the Oath as prescribed in the Presidents Proclamation of Dec 8th 1863

By Command of
Col Danl Macauley
John F Mount
Maj and Comy of Pris

FAC SIMILE
OF
RELEASE FROM PRISON

Major and Commissary of Prisoners.

Last Order of R. E. Lee.

Headquarters Army of Northern Virginia, April 10, 1865.—General Order No. 9.—After four years of arduous service, marked by unsurpassed courage and fortitude, the Army of Northern Virginia has been compelled to yield to overwhelming numbers and resources. I need not tell the survivors of so many hard-fought battles, who have remained steadfast to the last, that I have consented to this result from no distrust of them. But feeling that valour and devotion could accomplish nothing that could compensate for the loss that would have attended the continuance of the contest, I determined to avoid the sacrifice of those whose past services have endeared them to their countrymen.

By the terms of the agreement officers and men can return to their homes and remain until discharged. You will take with you the satisfaction that proceeds from the consciousness of duty faithfully performed, and I earnestly pray that a merciful God will extend you his blessing and protection. With an unceasing admiration of your constancy and devotion to your country, and a grateful remembrance of your kind and general consideration for myself, I bid you an affectionate farewell.

R. E. Lee, General.

CHAPTER 29

Arrives at Home

During my three months of prison life but one prisoner escaped, and he escaped as we were unloading the wagons that hauled cinders from the rolling mill. He was in one of the wagons cleaning it out. When he had finished, he fastened up the tail-gate from the inside and, seeing the guards were not looking, he laid down in the wagon-bed, which was very deep, and the wagoner drove on out the gates; and that was the last we ever saw of him. But the driver must have known he was in there, for if he had looked back, he would have seen him, or when he got out of the wagon, he must have seen him. But the wagoners were citizens, and frequently favoured the soldiers.

The young fellow had an uncle living in Baltimore, where he probably went. He was not missed from our squad until we went in at night, when the guards counted us. Instead of forty men there were only thirty-nine. Then there was a commotion raised. They hunted all through the barracks, and inquired what squad he was working with, and who was guarding him. They finally found out who it was that had gotten away.

The provost marshal came in the prison and offered any of us our liberty if we would go with them to the city and help find and recognise him; but none of us would go. The guards went, however, and hunted for him all night, and for several days, but never found him.

After we "broke ranks" at the prison gates we scattered out in squads of two and three together, and went to the city. There were about one hundred and fifty released that morning; and about one hundred left in prison, as there were none released but the sentenced prisoners. We were the first batch of prisoners that were released from any Northern prison after surrender. It was before prisoners were furnished transportation. Prisoners were being released in small squads all summer, but some did not get home till late in the fall.

I went directly to my uncle, H. W. Heironimus, who was salesman for the wholesale grocery of H. K. Hoffman & Company, 45 South Howard street, to thank him and Hoffman for their kindness. I told them I would pay them some day; but they would not listen to it. I stayed all night with my uncle, at his boarding house, and the next day he bought me a ticket for Winchester, gave me a carpet-sack full of clothes, and some money, and I boarded the train. I looked like a full-fledged Yankee carpet-bagger going South for an office, instead of a released Rebel prisoner.

I met several of our prisoners on the train. Some of them stayed in Baltimore several days, and some started home on foot, and I have never seen but three or four of them since. The citizens of Baltimore were very kind to prisoners. It made no difference whether they had acquaintances and relatives there or not, they were furnished new suits of clothes, money to go home on, and plenty to eat and drink.

A party of them, so I afterwards learned, who had started to walk home, had not gone more than five miles when they met a gentleman on horseback, who, seeing they were from prison, asked them if they had any money. When they told him, they had none and expected to walk home, he opened his purse and gave them a twenty-dollar gold piece and told them to go to the nearest station and get on the cars, which they did.

When I arrived in Winchester, Va., I went out to my nucleus, some fifteen miles, and remained several days. I had plenty of relatives in the adjoining counties of Morgan and Hampshire. I paid them a visit, also, and had a fine time; but was considerably broken down in health and spirits.

While in Morgan County I met my cousin, Smith Casler, who had belonged to Sturdivant's Battery of Artillery, and was at Lee's surrender. On his way home he had come by my father's, in Rockingham County, and spent some time there. He told me all about the siege of Petersburg and the surrender of Lee's Army. His brother, Charles Casler, was a member of the 11th Virginia Cavalry, and had died in prison at Point Lookout, Md. Therefore, there, was one missing, and one vacant chair in that household.

I then went to Winchester, but found no conveyance up the Valley. I determined, however, not to walk, and would sit by the roadside waiting for someone to come along in a buggy or wagon, so I could ride with them as far as they went. I kept this up, catching a ride occasionally, until I arrived at Harrisonburg, Va., a distance of sixty-eight miles from Winchester. I found my father and family living on a farm, only two miles from Harrisonburg. I arrived there shortly after dark. Then there was joy in that household. The prodigal son had returned and the fat hen was killed! I found my father, mother and three sisters all well, but having hard times, as they had lost nearly everything they had by the war.

I never saw the Stonewall Brigade after I parted with it in Harrisonburg in December, 1864, when on their way to Petersburg, but it was in all the campaigns in and around Petersburg, and surrendered with the army at Appomattox Court House with very few members and officers. I was not quite four years in it, but it was just four years from the time I left home to join the army until I arrived at home from, prison.

It was a very trying time to most of the Southern soldiers the last two years of the war, especially those who had families, for oftentimes their families were living inside the Federal lines, poorly provided for, enduring untold hardships, while the soldiers had no means to supply their wants, and could not even hear from them.

It took nerve and patriotism to remain in ranks under those circumstances, being poorly clad and fed, the pay, when it did come, being nearly useless for any purpose, and with very little prospects of our cause succeeding. But they still held on with indomitable courage and heroism that is unparalleled in the history of any nation.

On the other hand, the army of the North were well fed and

clothed, paid in good money, given large bounties, and had the prospect of a life pension, with their families far distant from the seat of war well provided for.

The difference was immense, for the Southern soldier had nothing but love of country and patriotism in view; but he remained to the bitter end.

I do not consider myself a hero by any means, and do not wish to be understood as one; neither do I consider myself a coward, for I have been in positions that tested me thoroughly, and such as a coward could not stand. But I always went where duty called me and did the best I could, and let fate do the rest—going no further than I was obliged to go. No man dreaded going into battle more than I did, or was more anxious for one to be over; but the die was cast, and I was reconciled to take what came, be it good or bad. A soldier in the ranks is like a piece of machinery—he moves and acts as commanded.

Chapter 30

Justice to Absentees

In giving a roster of Company "A" my old company, hereto appended, I wish to say, in justice to its members, that I have marked on the muster rolls, as leaving the army or going home and remaining, as good soldiers as ever bore a musket.

Many had become tired of the infantry and wanted a transfer to the cavalry. They had been brought up in a mountainous country and were used to horseback riding and unaccustomed to walking long distances, and in other ways were less fitted for the infantry than for cavalry service. But as it was impossible to get a transfer, and as no furloughs were granted to men whose homes were inside the Federal lines, they would go home whenever the opportunity presented itself; but still did service in some shape, either in the partisan ranger companies, or as independent scouts.

Those men lived along the northern border of Virginia, adjacent to the Baltimore and Ohio railroad, and would form little parties of from eight to twelve and make raids on said railroad; sometimes capture a train or tear up the track or burn a bridge. The consequence was that the Federal Army had to keep about ten or twelve thousand troops—cavalry, infantry and artillery—posted along the railroad from Cumberland, Md., to Martinsburg, Va., in order to protect the railroad and keep communications open.

Therefore, about fifty absentees from my company and other companies from the border kept that many Union soldiers employed and kept them from doing duty at the front. Although it was irregular and against the orders of the Confederate Government and the commanding officer, General R. E. Lee, it was done on their own hook, and, being rather between the lines and in a mountainous country, the Federal soldiers seldom captured any of them, and the Confederates could not get them to bring them back to their lawful commands; therefore, they operated in a territory of their own, and did the South considerable good, though not sanctioned by the proper authorities.

The Federals had possession of Hampshire County, W. Va., during the entire war, except at short intervals; but there were only ten of my company captured at any time, *viz*.: Edward Allen, Mike Bright, Sergeant James P. Daily, Robert C. Grace, Thomas McGraw, Sergeant William Montgomery, David Pence, John Tharp, Joseph McNemar and myself; the particulars of which are more fully set forth in the following:

Muster Roll of Company A, 33rd Virginia Infantry (Stonewall Brigade).
Captain, Philip T. Grace; promoted to Major September, 1863; resigned November, 1862.
First Lieutenant, Simeon D. Long; left the command in September, 1861, and never returned.
Second Lieutenant, Jacob N. Buzzard; died of pneumonia in Winchester, Va., February, 1862.
Third Lieutenant, William Johnson; died in Charlottesville, Va., August, 1862.
First Sergeant, James G. Parsons; promoted to Third lieutenant April, 1862; resigned September, 1862.
Second Sergeant, William Montgomery; severely wounded at First Battle of Bull Run, July 21, 1861; served in the 18th Virginia Cavalry two years; came back to Company A January, 1864; captured at Spotsylvania Court House May 12, 1864; remained in prison until close of the war.
Third Sergeant, James P. Daily; wounded March 23, 1862, at the Battle of Kernstown; captured and died.
First Corporal, Monroe Blue; promoted to Second Lieutenant in 18th Virginia Cavalry; captured in 1863; taken to Johnson's Island; while being transferred to Fort Delaware made his escape in Pennsylvania; came on to Virginia and shortly after-

John O. Casler's Capture by the "Jessie Scouts," February 5, 1865.

wards was killed in the battle of New Hope, June, 1864.

Third Corporal, James Connelly; left the company in September, 1862, and went home.

Second Corporal, A. A. Young; slightly wounded July 21, 1861; left the company in September, 1862, and went home.

Allen, Edward; slightly wounded July 21, 1861; captured March 23, 1862, at the Battle of Kernstown; exchanged and went home.

Allen, Herman; went home in September, 1862.

Adams, James; killed Battle Bull Run, July 21, 1861.

Adams, Jacob; went home September, 1862.

Arnold, George; went home November, 1863.

Baker, Andrew; killed in skirmish, August, 1863.

Baker, John K.; went home November, 1862.

Blue, William I.; killed First Battle of Bull Run, July 21, 1861.

Blue, Michael; hired a substitute July, 1861.

Bright, Michael; captured at Battle of Kernstown March 23, 1862; exchanged; wounded at Antietam.

Berry, Joseph; went home in September, 1862.

Cadwallader, Joseph; severely wounded July 21, 1861.

Casler, John O.; transferred to 11th Virginia Cavalry, January, 1865; captured February 5, 1865; was in prison till close of war.

Carder, Elisha; drummer until September, 1864, then took a musket; wounded at Fisher's Hill.

Carder, Joseph; sick in Lynchburg when war closed.

Dagnon, Michael: Marylander; discharged in one year.

Daily, William A.; joined partisan rangers in 1863.

Doran, Daniel; discharged in 1862.

Earsome, Joseph; transferred from 2nd Virginia Regiment; elected 2nd Lieutenant July, 1862; killed at Second Battle Bull Run, August 30, 1862.

Furlough, Thomas; killed July 21, 1861, First Battle Bull Run.

French, Charles M.; joined partisan rangers in November, 1863.

Grayson, John; went home November, 1862.

Gross, Thomas; killed March 23, 1862, Battle of Kernstown.

Gaither, George; died in hospital, July, 1868.

Gaither, James; killed May 12, 1864, Spotsylvania Court House.

Grace, Robert; wounded March 23, 1862, battle of Kernstown; captured and died.

Halderman, John; conscripted August, 1862; killed at Second

Battle Bull Run, August 30, 1862.
Hass, James; died in hospital at Lynchburg, April, 1863.
Hartly, Elijah; killed March 23, 1863, Battle of Kernstown.
Hartley, Andrew; went home November, 1863.
Hollenback, Amos; killed July 21, 1861, First Battle Bull Run.
Harris, John; went home September, 1862.
Kelley, John; went home November, 1862.
Linthicum, James; went home December, 1861.
Long, J. W.; went home November, 1862.
Miller, Emanuel; went home November, 1862.
Miller, Martin; wounded severely March 23, 1862, Battle of Kernstown.
Marker, Polk; killed July 21, 1861, First Battle Bull Run.
McNemar, Joseph; captured at Farmersville, Va., 1865; in prison when war closed.
Montgomery, Edward; joined partisan rangers 1863.
McGraw, Thomas; died in prison, Rock Island, Ill.
Gates, George; killed August 30, 1862, Second Battle Bull Bun.
Parker, Joseph; went home November, 1862.
Pence, Hugh; transferred to 18th Virginia Cavalry September, 1863.
Pence, Samuel; killed August 30, 1862, Second Battle Bull Run.
Pence, David; in prison when war closed and died on road home.
Perrin, Charles; died in hospital at Charlottesville, Va., August, 1862.
Perrin, Ralph; killed August 30, 1862, at the Second Battle of Bull Run, aged 16 years.
Pollard, William; wounded at Battle of Winchester September 19, 1864.
Powell, Thomas; went home November, 1862.
Powell, H. William; elected 1st Lieutenant April, 1862; promoted to Captain October, 1862; severely wounded at Gettysburg July 3, 1863, and never after fit for duty.
Pownell, Newton L.; made 1st Sergeant January, 1862; promoted to 2nd Lieutenant April, 1863; killed May 3, 1863, at Chancellorsville.
Pownell, Albert; transferred to 18th Virginia Cavalry November, 1862.
Rhinehart, John; severely wounded at First Battle of Bull Run

when well joined cavalry.
Rizer, John; had a case of measles and was discharged.
Shelly, David; went home November, 1862.
Sivills, William; sick at close of war.
Short, George; went home September, 1862.
Simmons, David; went home January, 1863.
Stockslager, Cul; went home November, 1862.
Swisher, Frank; went home sick December, 1861.
Tharp, John; captured May 12, 1864, at Spotsylvania Court House; in prison when war closed.

The foregoing embraces only the officers and soldiers of Company "A." A further reference to the organisation and roster of officers of our regiment, brigade, division and corps might be interesting to the students of the history of the war.

The field officers of the 33rd Regiment the first year were: Colonel, A. C. Cummings; Lieutenant Colonel, J. R. Jones; Major, Edwin G. Lee, and A. J. Neff, a cadet from the Virginia Military Institute, Adjutant; Randolph Barton, a Virginia Military Institute cadet. Sergeant Major. Our first Lieutenant Colonel, William Lee, was killed at Bull Run July 21, 1861.

At the reorganisation and re-enlistment in April, 1862, the company officers elected the regimental officers. Colonel A. C. Cummings went to Southwest Virginia in some other branch of service, and was elected to the Virginia Legislature; and Adjutant A. J. Neff was elected Colonel. He was killed at the Second Battle of Bull Run, August 27, 1862. Major Edwin G. Lee was elected Lieutenant Colonel; afterwards promoted to Colonel, and assigned to other duty in Lexington, Va. Captain F. W. M. Holliday, of Company "D" was elected Major, and lost an arm at Cedar Mountain August 9, 1862. He was afterwards promoted to Colonel, and elected to Confederate Congress; afterwards Governor of Virginia. Captain David Walton, of Company "K," was made Adjutant, and served as such until the surrender. Captain Randolph Barton was made a staff officer. Captain P. T. Grace, of my company, was promoted to Major, and not long afterwards resigned on account of sickness in his family, some of whom died. Captain George Houston was promoted to Major, then Lieutenant Colonel, then Colonel; was killed March, 1865, in front of Petersburg, Va. Captain Eastman, of Company "I" was promoted to Major, and was killed at Gettysburg July 2, 1863. Captain A. Spangler, of Company "F," was promoted to Major, then Lieutenant Colonel, then Colonel, and was in command of the regiment at the surrender, and Captain Golliday, of Company "D," was promoted to Major. Lieutenant Colonel J. E. Jones was promoted to Brigadier General of the Second Brigade.

General T. J. Jackson (Stonewall) was the first Brigadier General of the Stonewall Brigade, then Major General of a division, then Lieutenant General of the Second Corps. He was wounded at Chancellorsville, Va., May 2, 1863, and died the 10th of May, 1863.

General Richard B. Garnett was the second Brigadier General. He was put under arrest after the Battle of Kernstown for ordering the brigade to fall back (when about to be flanked, as he supposed) without orders from General Jackson; but was never court-martialled. He afterwards commanded a brigade in Picket's Division, and was killed in the charge at Gettysburg July 3, 1863.

General C. S. Winder was the third Brigadier, and was killed at the Battle of Cedar Mountain, Va., August 9, 1862.

Colonel W. S. H, Baylor, of the 5th Virginia Regiment, was promoted to Brigadier General of the brigade (being the fourth one), and was killed at the Second Battle of Bull Run August 30, 1862.

Colonel C. A. Ronald, of the 4th Virginia Regiment, took command of the brigade through the Maryland campaign,, and was wounded in a skirmish on the Baltimore and Ohio railroad at Kearneysville, Va., in September, 1862; but was not promoted to General.

Colonel J. W. Grigsby, of the 27th Virginia Infantry, then commanded the brigade until November, 1862, when Colonel E. F. Paxton, of the 27th Virginia Infantry, was promoted to Brigadier General as the fifth one. He was killed at the Battle of Chancellorsville May 3, 1863.

Colonel James A. Walker, of the 13th Virginia Infantry, Ewell's Division, was the sixth Brigadier General, and was wounded at the Battle of Spotsylvania Court House the 12th of May, 1864, when Colonel William Terry, of the 4th Virginia Infantry, was promoted to Brigadier General for the seventh one. He was in command of the brigade at the surrender, April 9, 1865, and a few years afterwards was drowned in a river in Southwest Virginia.

The division was commanded by General Jackson, General Talliaferro, General Trimble, General Stark (who was killed at Antietam), General R. E. Colston, General Edward Johnson, "Clubby" (who was captured May 12, 1864, at Spotsylvania), General John B. Gordon, who afterwards commanded the corps, and General Clement A. Evans.

The 2nd Corps was commanded by General Jackson, General Ewell (who lost a leg at the Second Battle of Bull Run), General Jubal A. Early, and, lastly, by General John B. Gordon, who was in command at the surrender of the army, and was loved and christened by the corps as "Our Second Jackson."

Major Jed Hotchkiss was Topographical Engineer on General Jackson's staff from the commencement of the war up to Jackson's death, and was then Chief Engineer of the Second Corps to the close of the war, and was considered one of the best officers of the kind in the Army of Northern Virginia.

CHAPTER 31

Devotion of the Soldiers

About one-third of the Stonewall Brigade was from what is now West Virginia, although the South never had any West Virginia Regiments designated as such, for it was all Virginia clear to the Ohio River when the war commenced and for some time afterwards.

A greater part of the 2nd and 27th Virginia Infantry and two companies of the 33rd Virginia, with scattering ones in other companies and regiments, were from West Virginia. General Stonewall Jackson was from West Virginia.

A few politicians, the Federal Government and the Baltimore and Ohio Railroad company seceded and divided the State and the citizens of neither State had any say in it. What was wrong in the Southern States for seceding from the Union was right in part of Virginia seceding from the State. It shows conclusively that "might makes right." Then, again, the citizens of neither State had any voice in making the dividing line. The Baltimore and Ohio Railroad company made that line suit their own financial interest.

When the said railroad company procured their charter for their road through Virginia the stipulations were that they were to pay a yearly tax for said charter, and in dividing the States they crooked the line from the mountains and run across the Valley, taking in Berkeley and Jefferson Counties, that rightfully belonged to the Valley district and to old Virginia; but as their road crossed the Potomac River from Maryland at Harper's Ferry, in Jefferson County, and ran through that county and Berkeley County, they needed those two counties in their business; hence the crook. Let the student of history look on the map and see the line dividing the two States and he will perceive the zigzag course it pursues and bear me out in my statements.

The only thing right about secession is whether the party who secedes are able numerically and financially to carry out their designs; if they are it is all *right*, in the eyes of the world; if not, it is all *wrong*; it is all owing to "whose bull is gored."

The New England States threatened to secede several times from the Union, never dreaming that it was wrong, but did not consider themselves quite able to succeed; and it is a great pity that the Southern States had not deliberated before seceding and arrived at the same conclusion. It would have saved thousands of lives and millions of property and money.

But, thank God! the secession movement and the slavery agitation is settled forever, and our country is once more united. If it ever has any more ruptures or disunions it will not be on either of those lines; and let us hope that never again while time lasts will our fair country be involved in another, what they call a civil war.

Now, as to the cause of the war, I have nothing to say but this: The war seemed to be inevitable; but as to who were right and who were wrong, it is not for me to say, for both sections had their grievances, and two wrongs never made one right. They simply "had it in" for one another and fought it out, settling the dispute forever. It might have been patched up and postponed a few years, like it had been before by the "Missouri Compromise," and other remedies, but the bubble had to burst, and burst it did.

No man living knows more about the ill-feeling that existed between the two sections than I do, for I was born and raised on the border of Virginia, near the Potomac River, and had heard this contention from my earliest recollections; knew of and witnessed the division in the Methodist Church; and heard every day the agitation of the slavery question all through the "fifties," and was right in the neighbourhood when the torch was applied to the combustibles when John Brown seized Harper's Ferry and attempted to arm the slaves to butcher the whites indiscriminately. Then the South was fired by indignation and was determined from that time to separate from the United States Government.

I was no secessionist, and hoped the trouble would be settled without recourse to arms; but when the war came, I shouldered my musket in behalf of my native State and defended her to the last; and, although the Stars and Bars went down and are furled forever, they never went down in disgrace, but they will be remembered by a people who gave their best blood and treasure tb sustain them. But I hope it will be a warning to future generations to guard against dissensions of all kinds, and not involve our fair land in another civil war.

There are no truer people to the Stars and Stripes today than the people of the South; none who would sacrifice more in their defence against an invading foe.

To illustrate more fully this devotion to our flag, I will relate an incident that happened in London, England, since the war. It has already been published, but is worthy of being preserved:

> Sometime after the war Colonel P. R. Winthrop, a Southern soldier from Louisiana, was traveling in Europe, and while in London, England, attended the Alhambra theatre with some friends to witness a ballet dance called 'All Nations.' A corps of ballet dancers, dressed in the uniform worn by the soldiers of each nation, and bearing the flag of the nation whose uniform they wore, would appear and dance—one corps after the other. As all the countries were being represented, some would be applauded and some were hissed. When the United States and the 'Stars and Stripes' were represented the audience began to hiss. Colonel Winthrop, who was seated in the back part of a box, looking on, in a not very interested way, at the first hiss sprang to his feet and to the front of the box, and, leaning far out over the rail, waving his hat over his head, his face lividly white, his eyes fairly blazing defiance at the crowd beneath and around him, he opened his mouth and there rang through the theatre the most blood-chilling yell, a kind of cross between the savage cry of the infuriated Zulu warriors and the screech of a wounded tigress.
>
> For an instant the very music ceased; every one turned to gaze at the author of the unearthly sound; even the musicians forgot the presence of the dancers for whom they were playing. Suddenly, in the lower part of the house, a long, lank figure, with

In the Cells at Ft. McHenry, Maryland.

white hair and beard, arose, and, standing in the aisle, took up and gave back an answering yell to Winthrop's cry, and in the same peculiar, half-fiendish manner. Then all around from different quarters of the theatre men arose and began to cheer in the hearty, vigorous, English fashion.

The house was full of Americans on their way home from the Paris exposition.

An august personage who happened to be in the back part of one of the boxes, seeing that a terrible row was imminent, with that ready tact for which he was famous, came to the front of his box and began applauding; of course, in a moment the storm was stilled, and the whole audience was cheering the American flag. Some of them expressed astonishment at the feeling exhibited by the American, Winthrop, inasmuch as he had spoken of being in the Confederate Army and fighting against the Union flag. He snapped out in reply: 'That was a fight of our own family, between Americans, and is settled, forgiven and forgotten, and the flag that was hissed tonight is now my flag as thoroughly as it is the flag of the men who fought under it in our civil war, and—

'I would right some wrongs where they are given if it were in the Courts of Heaven.'

All were anxious to know where he acquired that peculiar wild yell he gave when the audience hissed the flag. He said that was the 'Rebel yell' with which the Southerners charged in battle, and that he was sure the man who had first joined in his protest was some old Southern soldier, because of the answering of the 'Rebel yell.'

The other cheering at first, he told us, came from old Northern veterans from America. He had heard their cheers at Fredericksburg and Gettysburg, and that it meant fight; that they had been witnesses to a splendid illustration of the only difference in the character of the people North and South in the United States; that the Southern people were more impulsive and quicker to resent an insult, while the Northern people were more calm, cool and slow, but would none the less surely and positively fight when necessary, and when once aroused, just as the Northern men in the audience, they were the most determined and courageous of men.

The soldiers in each army got such an acquaintanceship with each other during the war as they never would have gotten in any other way, and those who were in the army and saw service at the front always respected each other. Each knew he met foemen worthy of his steel, for they had been tested on the field of battle.

On the other hand, the men who were never in the army, and who wanted to do their fighting after the war was over, are those who have kept up most of the dissensions and ill feeling since. True soldiers will protect one another when necessary, regardless of the army they were in, for we are all Americans and are proud that we were American soldiers.

To illustrate this, I will relate an incident that came under my personal observation:

When I reported to the provost marshal in Baltimore, after being released from prison, I told him that I wished to remain in the city for a few days and would like him to give me protection from the mobs and bummers. He replied that he had no authority to give anything, but to go about my business quietly, seek no quarrel, and if anyone imposed on me to call on some of the Federal soldiers scattered over the city and they would protect me. The next day, when some of us were invited into a saloon to drink, one of our crowd happened to have his military buttons still on his coat. One of those non-combatants stepped up to him and commenced cutting them off, saying he could not wear those buttons around there. There happened to be two Federal soldiers present who immediately sprang to their feet, and one of them knocked the fellow down, remarking that he could not insult a Rebel soldier in their presence, and made him leave the house.

War, with all its terrors, is a great civilizer, if civilization means respect for other people's opinions.

CHAPTER 32

Conclusion

I cannot close these reminiscences of the war without paying to the noble women of the South the highest tribute that can be paid them, which is to record their sublime, self-sacrificing devotion to the soldier and the cause in which he was enlisted.

At an early period of the war, and in the darkest days that followed—during the entire struggle, in defeat as in victory—they encouraged and sustained us with cheering words and noble actions.

I have often remarked that there were two classes of people in the

South that upheld the cause from beginning to end. They were the soldiers in the field and the women at home. How devotedly they would work to supply the army with food and clothing. They would always send such clothing to us as they knew we needed, such as underclothes, knit socks, etc. They would make hats out of cloth, spin, weave and make outer garments entirely of homespun; cut up their fine carpets to make blankets, and make hundreds of other sacrifices to render us comfortable.

How often, when in camp, would we anxiously look over the hill to catch a glimpse of the wagon coming from home, knowing full well there would be a box for this one and that one, filled with such delicacies as they could procure from their scanty means; and what joy there would be in camp to eat something that mothers, wives, sisters, daughters or lovers had prepared; and how anxiously the mails were watched to receive some sweet missive from the loved ones.

They suffered equally as much as the soldiers in the field, though not by wounds and death; but the suspense and grief was agony itself. My dear old mother, who is now in heaven, spent many an hour on her bended knees praying for her dear and only boy, and not only her boy, but others as well, for she had relatives who wore the blue. She could often hear the raging of the battles, as several were fought near my home. But as dearly as she loved me, she would not let me stay at home long when I happened to get there, but advised me to return to my command and be a faithful soldier. She would rather hear of my death on the field of battle, although it would nearly break her heart, than to hear of my being branded as a deserter; for all our ancestors had been engaged in the wars of our country, and had acted honourably—the Indian wars, the Revolutionary war, the war of 1812 and the Mexican war—and there had been no blot or stain of desertion attached to any of them, and she did not want to hear of it in any of her race.

After a battle it would often be days and weeks before our people at home would receive any tidings of the dead and wounded. Oh! the suspense! It was terrible. That is why I say they suffered equally as much as we did; for every old soldier knows the suspense preceding a battle is worse than the battle itself.

No doubt the women of the North were just as devoted to their loved ones as the Southern women; but they had no such difficulties to contend with, as their government kept the army well supplied. No doubt they, too, sometimes, when cut off from their base of supplies, and in the enemy's country, suffered terribly; but the South was cut off from all foreign supplies from the first, except what little ran the blockade; besides, we had no manufactors to speak of.

General Lee's Army was mainly supplied with clothing by the women of the South. The only thing we were well supplied with was ammunition, and that was mainly procured, at one time, through the aid of the women, whom I have known to dig the earth from under old houses, boil it, and get the saltpetre. Sometimes details were made, from those subject to conscription, to dig saltpetre, which privilege many stay-at-homes were anxious to avail themselves of to keep out of the army; but the ladies shamed them and called them the "saltpetre boys," and told them to go and get a musket and go into the army, that they would dig the saltpetre.

No one can tell, and no pen describe, the sacrifices and sufferings of those dear ones; and they never gave up as long as there was a soldier in the field. But I am sorry to say that a great many of the male citizens were whipped the second year of the war, and, as our star of destiny began to wane, they seemed to gather in everything they could before the wreck was complete.

The world knows what the women of the South have done since the war in organising memorial associations, caring for the dead, building monuments and Confederate Homes, and yearly strewing their graves with flowers.

But I must close. I could write pages about those noble women and never exhaust the subject.

Had the country been as resolute as *the army and the women* the red battle flag with the Southern cross would be floating still, instead of drooping and furled with no hand to give it to the winds—furled and dragged in the dust of defeat, but glorious forever.

Observe how my memory leads me back to those old days and makes me linger in the haunted domain of the past—reviewing the gallant figures, and heroic struggles, listening again to the brave voices and living once more in the bright hours that are dead.

But what is left to us poor "paroled prisoners" except memory? Leave us that at least, for, as I awake at morning or rest my weary head at night, after the lapse of more than a quarter of a century, the murmur of the river breeze is the low roll of drums from the forest yonder, where the camp of infantry are aroused by the reveille.

In the moonlight night, when all is still, a sound comes borne upon the air from some dim land. I seem to hear the sound of bugles for the cavalry to mount. In the thunder of some storm I hear the roar of artillery and the bursting of shells.

All these things are so burnt in my brain and memory, and the scenes of many desperate struggles are so interwoven with my past life, that if life is spared me for many long years yet they never can be erased. No, never! never! never!

The following appeal from the ladies of the South, which was printed in Columbus, Ga., in 1862, and circulated throughout the Southern Army (a copy of which I have in my possession) may be read with interest at this time:

Letter from the Women of the South.
To the Soldiers of the Confederate Army.

Soldiers: The President, Congress, the public press and your Generals have told you their high estimate of your noble devotion in re-enlisting for the war. We, also, as your mothers, wives, daughters, sisters and friends, claim the right to thank you. It is the grandest act of the revolution, and secures immortality to all concerned in it. It awakens anew the enthusiasm with which we began this struggle for liberty, and removes all doubt of its eventual success. Such men, in such a cause, cannot be overcome. In the dreariness of camp life, you may sometimes have imagined yourselves forgotten or little cared for. Counting up your privations and danger, you may have doubted their full appreciation, and fancied that those who stay at home and risk nothing, while you suffer and bleed, are more esteemed than yourselves.

We beseech you harbour no such thought. You are constantly present to our minds. The women of the South bestow all their respect and affection on the heroes who defend them against a barbarous and cruel foe. In their resolution they are as firm and determined as you in yours not to lay down your arms 'till independence be won. When that sacred vow shall have been accomplished your reception by us will more than attest our sincerity. It shall also be shown, while the contest goes on, by our efforts to increase your comforts in the field and to lighten the burdens of the ones left at home. For your stricken country's sake and ours, be true to yourselves and our glorious cause. Never turn your backs on the flag, nor desert the ranks of honour or the post of danger. Men guilty of such infamy would sell your blood and our honour, and give up the Confederacy to its wicked invaders.

In after years, from generation to generation, the black title of tory and deserter will cling to them, disgracing their children's children. But no stigma like this will stain you and yours. Brave, patriotic and self-sacrificing in time of war, you will be honoured in peace as the saviours of your country, and the pride and glory of your country-women. We beg you to keep near your hearts these memorials of affection and respect, and to remember them especially in battle, and we invoke for you always the protection of a kind and merciful Providence.

Mrs. L. Illgos, Mrs. T. M. Nelson, Mrs. A. Shepherd, Mrs. Dexter, Mrs. C. Walker, Mrs. H. L, Benning, Mrs. M. Chambers, Mrs. S. C. Tarpley, Mrs. Anne Dawson, Mrs. J. Dawson, Mrs. M. E. Shorter, Miss L. Rutherford, Miss E. Munnerlyn, Miss S. Threewitts, Miss Anna Bennett, Miss Rogers, Miss Lou Hurt, Miss Tarpley, Miss M. T. Shorter, Mss Lila Howard, Miss Torrance, Miss Buckley, Miss Anna Leonard, Misses Ellington, Misses Shepherd, Misses Benning, Misses Malone, Misses Abercrombie, Misses Hardaway, Mrs. I. M. Gale, Mrs. R. Patton, Mrs. Geo. Woodruff, Mrs. R. Ware, Mrs. S. C. Law, Mrs. L. E. Cairns, Mrs. Julia Brice, Mrs. B. Gordon, Mrs. Rosa Aubrey, Mrs. M. A. Flournoy, Mrs. Robert Hardaway, Mrs. Virginia Sneed, Mrs. Patton, Mrs. C. Shorter, Mrs. E. R. Hodges, Mrs. James Warren, Mrs. Seaborn Jones, Mrs. T. Threewitts, Mrs. P. H. Colquitt, Mrs. Jas. A. Shorter, Mrs. Shaaf, Mrs. Wm. Woolfolk, Mrs. Fergusson, Mrs. Buckley, Mrs. E. Shepherd, Mrs. A. O. Flewellen, Mrs. Rogers, Mrs. A.B. Longstreet, Mrs. H. Meigs, Mrs. John Banks, Mrs. D. Moffett, Mrs. J. E. Hurt, Mrs. Augusta Erskine, Mrs. Goetchius, Mrs. J. A. Strother, Mrs. C. J. Williams, Mrs. Z. H. Gordon, Mrs. C. T. Abercrombie, Mrs. L. Q. C. Lamar, Mrs. A. G. Redd, Mrs. R. P. Malone, Miss C. F. Hargraves, Miss C. Ragland. Miss Sue Banks. Miss E. Moffett, Miss Anna Forsythe, Miss M. E. Dawson, Mrs. John Carter, Mrs. Robert Carter, Mrs. D. Hudson, Mrs. S. E. Wilkins, Mrs. M. D. Flournoy, Mrs. L. G. Bowers, Mrs. J. B. Hill, Mrs. H. Branham, Mrs. Abercrombie, Mrs. A. Lowther, Mrs. Dr. Tickner, Miss Mary Rutherford, Miss Mary Hodges, Miss Bessie Hardwick, Miss M. M. Gordon, Miss Anna Tyler, Miss V. Mason.

I also append a letter from Miss Nannie J. Reevs (and I see no impropriety in doing so, as, on its face, it shows the writer to be a true Southern lady) to Lieutenant J. W. Johnston, of the 24th Tennessee Infantry. The letter is still in the possession of Mr. Johnston, who has allowed me the use of it for this purpose. As the young lady says: "It is quite romantic"—this writing to soldiers. It is interesting as showing what true soldiers the ladies can be.

The circumstances are as follows: When General O. F. Strahl's Brigade, of General Frank Cheatham's Division (Lieutenant Johnston being attached to that brigade), were passing on the cars, through Loachapoka, Ala., on their way from Dalton, Ga., to Demopolis, Ala., the ladies collected there threw bouquets to the soldiers, as was their custom. The one Lieutenant Johnston received contained a slip of paper with this written on it: "A soldier is the lad I adore." Signed, "Nannie J. Reevs." When the brigade arrived in camp Lieutenant Johnston wrote a letter and mailed it to her address, although he did not know her, never had seen her and never did see her. The original is written in a beautiful hand, and the composition shows a true lady in every respect. It was a common occurrence for soldiers to correspond with ladies they never saw. Lieutenant Johnston would not part with it for any consideration, but keeps it as a relic of other days:

Loachapoka, Ala., March 10, 1864.

Mr. J. W. Johnston:

I have the honour to acknowledge the receipt of your very unexpected missive, which was handed me a few days since. It proved very interesting to me and merits in itself a reply that I am not equal to. Notwithstanding, I shall not hesitate to send you one, though I feel, very sensibly, my utter inability to interest you in the least.

It is overleaping the rules of etiquette to write to a total stranger, but etiquette to a great degree has been discarded, as these are war times, and I love romance exceedingly; therefore, I shall be pleased to receive and answer a letter from you at any time, if by so doing it will serve to while away many lonely hours incident to a soldier's life, who is cut off from the hallowed influence of relatives and friends. I do not send you this letter to make sport of, but to inform you that yours was highly appreciated.

'Yes, the soldier is the lad I adore;' because he loves his country and freedom and nobly battles for them. I sincerely hope that each brave and gallant soldier of the South may soon reap the glorious reward of his labour."

I have but little use for croakers and speculators, who skulk at home and gain every cent of Confederate money they possibly can. While substitution was the theme their money was their might, but by dint of speculation they've made their money back. But now Congress has served them right; they have to shoulder box and gun and walk the soldier's track. I see so many who say: 'We are now whipped; just as well give up,' but I'll assure you that I have never claimed that we are whipped or a ruined people, nor will I own such until our patient soldiers admit that they are conquered.

I felt very confident that there would be a regular engagement up at the front when you all came rolling back from Demopolis, but I was agreeably disappointed. Guess you were somewhat surprised when the order was countermanded and you had to return; but the soldier's life, like the will-o'-th-wisp, is one continual succession of brightening and darkening changes; flitting like a blaze of glory to one point and *anon* returning dark and gloomy, as his country's prospects vary from one extreme to the other. Oh! how delighted I would be if the glad welkin sound of peace could be heard throughout our land again—

'When peace shall hold easy sway,
'And man forget his fellowman to slay.'

But there will ever be something to mar my happiness, even when this cruel war is over, which is this: I have lost my only brother, who was good and affectionate, indeed, and no less brave and patriotic. He gallantly fought and nobly braved every hardship and fiery trial that seemed peculiar to the ill-fated defenders of the once proud and glorious Vicksburg. Yes, he breathed his last on the banks of the Mississippi River a few moments before he was to take passage on the boat for home, after he was paroled. He had acute rheumatism which he had contracted in the trenches. The pain struck his heart, which caused him to die immediately, with nothing but the cold earth for his bed and the canopy of heaven for his covering. His remains were interred at Vicksburg. He now rests with God in heaven, no doubt, for he was a zealous Christian.

Mr. Johnston, I have worried your patience, I fear, with this desultory communication. If so, excuse me, if you please. I shall expect to hear from you at your earliest convenience.

With best wishes for your happiness and safety, I subscribe myself.

Very respectfully,

Nannie J. Reevs.

Oh, South! there's no national shepherd to keep
Your flock from the pinchings of hunger and cold;
Hark! hear you the wail of your suffering sheep.
As they wander dejected away from the fold.

Appendix

A Daring and Famous Raid.

In February, 1905, I had some business to transact in Dallas, Texas, and while strolling along Elm street I noticed a sign reading "Bruce Liquor Company." The name Bruce attracted my attention and reminded me that I once had a friend and fellow-soldier in the army whom we called "Manny" Bruce (I mention him in a preceding chapter in this work as a companion in one of my adventures). I concluded to step in and inquire if they knew anything of "Manny" Bruce.

I saw an elderly gentleman and spoke to him, when the following conversation ensued:

"Is your name Bruce?"

"Yes, sir."

"Are you from Cumberland, Maryland?"

"I was born and raised there, but have been in Texas for twenty-five years."

"Are you the Bruce we in the army called 'Manny' Bruce?"

"I am, sir, but my right name is Maynadier."

"I once knew you, Mr. Bruce. I was raised in Hampshire County, West Virginia, just across the Potomac from Cumberland. I was in company with you on a little adventure during the war in January, 1865, in Hampshire County, and finally you and I were captured by General Sheridan's 'Jessie Scouts,' commanded by Captain Blazer."

He exclaimed at once: "Why, who are you?"

I then told him that he made his escape that same night on our road to prison, but that I was taken on to Fort McHenry and remained there until the war was over.

He again said: "Who are you?"

Col. Chas. Marshall.   General Lee.   General Grant.   Sheridan.
Last Days of the Confederacy—Arranging the Terms of Surrender.

I told him that my name was Casler, that I belonged to Company A, 33rd Virginia Infantry, but at the time of our acquaintance was transferred to the 11th Virginia Cavalry.

He replied: "This is not my old friend, John Casler, is it?"

I assured him it was the same John.

"Where have you been since the war?"

"I emigrated to Sherman, Texas, twenty-eight years ago, and have been in Dallas many times, but did not know you were here."

"Well, John, I would rather see you than a brother."

Without going into the particulars, there was a genuine love-feast right there and then, the old bottle of applejack was uncorked and we took a drink in remembrance of the hills and valleys of old Hampshire County.

This was on the 5th of February, 1905, and I reminded him that it was forty years to a day since we had met; that it was February 5, 1865, when we were captured—a curious coincidence, as the sequel will show.

I found him prospering and at the head of a flourishing wholesale business, *viz*.: "The Bruce Liquor Company," 398 Elm street. We talked over old times, and I called on him often while there and went with him to Sterling Price Camp, United Confederate Veterans, when he became a member of the camp.

I gave him one of my books (the first edition) to read. He was much interested in it, and told me that he had taken very little interest in war matters since the war; that he was young at the time, only 16 years old, and that my work was a revelation to him. He insisted that I should have another edition published, and asked me to write up the incidents of the following raid and adventure and have the story in the book as an "Appendix," as I was not in this raid, but Bruce was. I, therefore, give the story, gathering the relation of the incidents of the raid from the most reliable authority I could get. And it was *one* of the most daring and adventurous raids by a small body of men ever accomplished during the war, and should go down in history as such, and every participant in it should be immortalised as a hero.

It is impossible, at this date, to get the names of all of the men who participated in this raid, but I give those of whom I can learn.

A short time after the war commenced Captain John H. McNeil organised a company of scouts to operate along the Potomac river and the Baltimore and Ohio railroad, in what is now Hampshire County, West Virginia. They were daring young men, and accustomed to riding horses from their youth up. They were principally from Hampshire, Hardy and Rockingham Counties, in Virginia, and Cumberland, Maryland. But some were from other states and counties. One, Richie C. Hallar, was from Missouri, a younger brother of Lieutenant William Hallar, of Quantrell's command. They were attached to the regular Confederate Army and under the supervision of the different generals who operated in the Shenandoah Valley, but were on detached service all the time, and were called "McNeil's Partisan Rangers." They were something like "Roosevelt's Rough Riders," except that the "Rangers" saw a great amount of hard service in four years, whilst the "Rough Riders" did very little but got a great deal of glory.

They would harass the enemy wherever found—capture their pickets and scouting parties, destroy their wagon trains, destroy the railroads and bridges, capture trains, and gather information about the movements of the enemy. They and a few others kept an army of Federals estimated at fifteen or twenty thousand employed and on guard along the Baltimore and Ohio Railroad from New Creek Station to Martinsburg, a distance of about one hundred miles. They made many daring raids, captured thousands of prisoners, destroyed millions of property, etc. But their most daring, adventurous and thrilling raid is the one of which I am about to relate, and which I shall give in the words of Sergeants John B. Fay, J. L. Vandiver, John Dailey and M. T. Bruce, who were participants in it, and among the principal actors.

Captain J. H. McNeil was mortally wounded while guarding a bridge in the Shenandoah Valley in the fall of 1864 and died in Harrisonburg, Va. His son, Lieutenant Jesse C. McNeil, then took command of the "Rangers," which generally numbered from sixty to eighty men for duty. But on this "Cumberland raid," as it is called, there were sixty-five picked men, who were acquainted with the country, and some from other commands—Lieutenant Isaac Parsons, Robert Moorehead, Sergeant John Dailey, Edward Washington, Joseph Pancake, John W. Poland, John S. Arnold, Sergeant Joseph Kuykendall, Eph Herriot, Joe Shearad, John Cunningham and Jacob Gassman, belonging to the 7th and 11th Virginia Cavalry, Rosser's Brigade, all under command of Lieutenant Jesse McNeil.

Here is an account of the raid, written by Sergeant John B. Fay, who was one of the principal movers in planning the details. This band of adventurous spirits rode fifty miles into the enemy's country, over hills and mountains, forded rivers and creeks, on the 21st of February, 1865, in bitter cold weather and with the snow about two feet deep,

Capture of Generals Crook and Kelley.

captured the pickets, got the countersign, then rode along the main street of Cumberland, Md., a city of 8,000 inhabitants, mostly Union people, where an army of 8,000 Federals were quartered, to two of the principal hotels, the "Revere House" and "Barnum's Hotel," about two squares apart, on Baltimore street, and captured General George Crook, in bed at the Revere House, and General B. F. Kelley, in bed at Barnum's Hotel, and took them safely out south, having ridden ninety miles in twenty-four hours. They were then sent to Richmond, Va., and soon exchanged for two Confederate Generals of the same rank. That was the main reason for this daring raid. They also captured Colonel Thayer Melvin, General Kelley's Adjutant General and Chief of Staff. They did not intend to bother with him, but he got in their way and they had to take him along.

Generals Kelley and Crook were Major Generals. There were also quartered at those hotels Brigadier Generals R. B. Hayes (afterwards President of the United States), Lightburn and Duvall, and Major William McKinley (afterwards President of the United States), but, as Fay says, they were after "bigger fish," and did not want to be incumbered with too many prisoners, as it would have been detrimental to their escape.

They did not know at the time that such "big fish" as two future presidents were left behind.

Sergeant Joseph L. Vandiver, of McNeil's Rangers, says:

> From where we started, near Moorefield, on our perilous journey the snow was about two feet deep in the mountains and gorges. At times we were compelled to dismount and lead our horses, until we reached the residence of Mr. R. B. Seymour, a Southern sympathizer. When I told Seymour our plans, Seymour said, 'For your sake, for God's sake, and for your mother's sake, turn back. There are over 8,000 troops in and around Cumberland; you have only a handful; you will never return alive.' The old man, seeing we were determined, turned loose upon us a whole barrel of apple brandy. We filled our canteens and proceeded on our journey.
>
> After fording the Potomac, which was running with ice and slush, and wetting every man up to the knees, we passed on down the main road from New Creek to Cumberland, which was travelled by scouts and others, passing ourselves off as Ringgold's Cavalry from New Creek.

Moorefield is southeast of Cumberland. We were now six miles west of Cumberland, on the Maryland side. Our main object now was to capture the picket post and get their countersign; then we would be safe. We knew where their pickets were posted and where the reserve post was. When we advanced on the first post—

'Halt! Who comes dere?' rang out on the air.

'Forward, boys,' said I, 'it's a Dutch sentinel.'

We soon captured the sentinel, with two others, and asked for the countersign.

'Me no geef it.'

'Bring me my bridle rein,' said I. After placing the bridle rein around his neck, he said: 'Bool's Kaap.'

Not understanding that they asked the other two sentinels what the countersign was. They, being Americans, replied: 'Bull's Gap.' Half the prize was now won. Taking one of the pickets along with us, we proceeded to the reserve post, one-half mile distant, with the threat that if we had been given the wrong countersign death would be his portion.

Arriving at the reserve post we were halted, when we informed the guards that we were 'Ringgold's Cavalry, from New Creek, with important dispatches for General Kelley.'

While parleying over the countersign we surrounded the picket post of ten or twelve men, and called on them to surrender. They did so. We then broke up their guns, threw them into the fire, paroled the pickets and told them to remain there until they returned, knowing full well that we would succeed in our adventure or be captured before the alarm could be given.

Our way was now clear, and, riding into Cumberland at the foot of Baltimore street, we rode up the street whistling and singing 'Yankee Doodle.' Arriving at the hotels we divided, a squad of men dismounting at each hotel whilst the others remained on their horses. The details entered the hotels and ordered those two generals to dress and follow them. John Dailey was one of the party that entered General Crook's room, and he secured some important papers, together with several stands of colours.

Maynadier T. Bruce was born and raised in Cumberland, Md. When General Imboden's Cavalry passed through Cumberland on their way to the Pennsylvania and Gettysburg campaign, Bruce, then a boy of 16 years, ran away from his father, taking a horse, and joined Imboden's command. He was orderly for General Imboden for some time, finally joining McNeil's Rangers. He was in this Cumberland raid, and his recollections are about the same as John B. Fay has related. Bruce, with several others, stopped at Romney to talk to the "girls" and get something to eat. While there the Federal cavalry dashed into them, and wounded J. W. Poland and captured Sergeant Joe Shearad.

This squad fell back on the rear guard. When the Federals came up, they were repulsed and driven back, but captured Lieutenant Griffith, of the Ringgold Cavalry. McNeil's men then paroled the Lieutenant with the understanding that he was to be exchanged for Sergeant Joe Shearad.

He agreed to that arrangement and Bruce gave him a horse. He went to Cumberland and stated the case of his parole, but the authorities there would not agree to it, and Lieutenant Griffith considered his parole sacred and remained out of service during the war.

As the command passed down Baltimore street to the canal, they broke the glass in some of the stores and supplied themselves with a quantity of "store clothes." They then passed the government stables where the officers' horses were kept. Part of the company stopped there and, overpowering the guard, took several horses from the stables. The horses all had blankets on them. Bruce got two fine horses and John S. Arnold got "Philippi," General Kelley's horse. In the early part of the war General Kelley was wounded in a small engagement at Philippi, in West Virginia. He was the first General wounded in the war, and the citizens of Philippi raised some money and purchased the finest horse they could find and made a present of it to General Kelley. He called the horse "Philippi," and it was considered the finest horse in that command. General Kelley had ridden the animal from 1861 until his capture in 1865.

Some two weeks before this raid Bruce, Sprigg Lynn and Hallar went into Cumberland in disguise and remained there three days and nights, stopping at the home of Lynn's mother. Bruce saw his father and walked around "Rose Hill" and other important points. Their object was to wreck a train on the Baltimore and Ohio Railroad that was conveying troops from the west to General Grant's Army in front of Petersburg, Va. They failed in their undertaking and returned safely to Moorefield, Va.

Charles James Dailey, one of McNeil's rangers, was the son of the proprietor of the Revere House, and his sister was the *fiancée* of Gen-

The Confederate Soldier's Return Home.
"What does he find?"

eral Crook at the time of this capture. General Crook, after the war, married Miss Dailey and General Kelley married Miss Clara Bruce, cousin of Mr. Manny Bruce, who was in this raid. Strange things will happen in this world, but we are all proud, both North and South, that we are Americans.

Capture of Generals Crook and Kelley.
By the McNeil Rangers.
By John B. Fay.

Toward the close of the late war, about an hour before daybreak on the cold, frosty morning of February 21, 1865, a troop of Confederate cavalry, sixty-five in number, under Lieutenant Jesse C. McNeil, having forded the Potomac, surprised and captured the pickets, rode into the heart of the city of Cumberland, Md., captured Major Generals Crook and Kelley, together with the latter's Adjutant General, Major Melvin, and, without the loss of a single man, carried their distinguished prisoners back into the Confederate lines. Six or eight thousand troops were encamped in and around the city, which had long been the headquarters of General Kelley, commander of the military district of West Virginia, and in consequence this exploit created a great local sensation, but for obvious reasons made no marked impression upon the public mind.

To enable the reader to form a correct idea of the military situation at the time, a slight retrospect at the outset will be necessary. The debatable ground which lay between the opposing armies in Northern Virginia, both east and west of the Blue Ridge, covered an extensive territory, running parallel to the Potomac, and embraced sometimes the length of two or more counties southward. During the latter part of the war this region was dominated by three famous Confederate partisan leaders, Mosby, Gilmore and McNeil. Their forces sometimes intermingled, but ordinarily the operations of Mosby were confined to the country east of the Shenandoah River; those of Gilmore to the Valley of Virginia; while McNeil's special field of action lay to the westward, along the upper Potomac, and the line of the great South Branch. McNeil's command was composed principally of volunteers from Virginia and Maryland, though nearly every Southern and not a few of the Northern States had representatives in the ranks.

Nearly every station, avocation and profession in life furnished its quota to this famous band of partisan rangers. Aristocrats of the bluest blood and their rough, unpedigreed comrades; lawyers, preachers, doctors and merchants, in fact and embryo; clerks and hardy mountaineers, college graduates, mechanics and sturdy farmer lads; the man of mature age and the inexperienced youth all mingled in harmony, and one would have been hard to please who could not find in this organisation an agreeable social circle or congenial mess. Moorefield, in the rich and fertile valley of the South Branch, was the principal headquarters of this command, and Harrisonburg, in the Shenandoah Valley, its reserved base of operations. In a daybreak attack on a company of Pennsylvania cavalry, who were guarding a bridge over the Shenandoah, near Mt. Jackson, in the fall of 1864, Captain McNeil received a mortal wound. His son, Lieutenant Jesse C. McNeil, an officer of great courage and gallantry, though somewhat excitable and indiscreet, was next in command, but General Early hesitated to give him full control and made several efforts to get someone who, in his opinion, would be more competent to wear the mantle of our valiant and astute old captain.

Matters remained in this condition when, some time in February, 1865, Lieutenant McNeil consulted with me about the feasibility of getting into Cumberland and capturing Generals Kelley and Crook. He referred to a suggestion that I had made his father, in his lifetime, to capture General Kelley, and informed me of his desire to secure both generals, if, on examination, it was found to be practicable. Cumberland was my native place. I had on several previous occasions entered it with ease—once remaining a week—and on my giving McNeil every assurance that his design could be successfully carried out, it was determined to make the attempt. I was commissioned to proceed at once to Cumberland, or its vicinity, and prepare the way for our entry, by learning the number and position of the picket posts, the exact location of the sleeping apartments of the generals and any other information deemed necessary. Selecting a comrade, Ritchie C. Hallar, a lad from Missouri, not yet out of his 'teens, but of well-tested courage and prudence, I started forthwith, and a few nights after our departure from Moorefield found us upon the north bank of the Potomac, a few miles west of Cumberland. At this point the required information was procured, and, retracing our steps, by daylight we were twenty miles away, enjoying a welcome breakfast with a bachelor friend, Vanse Herriott, near Romney.

From here Hallar was despatched to intercept Lieutenant McNeil, who, in our absence, was to have twenty-five well-mounted men prepared and move leisurely in the direction of Cumberland, ready to act on my report. Cumberland, which had then a population of 8,000, is situated on the north bank of the upper Potomac, at the confluence of that river and Will's creek, and on the site of old "Fort Cumberland," the frontier post in colonial times, from which General Braddock, in 1755, set out on his expedition across the Alleghanies to Fort Duquesne. It is just opposite a peninsular neck of land in Virginia, the elongation of the Knobly mountain range, which here presses so far north as to cause an abrupt bend in the river and nearly to cut this portion of Maryland in two, the distance across to the Pennsylvania line being only six miles. At the time of which I write 6,000 or 8,000 troops occupied the city, and on the night of our entry, in addition to the resident commander, Major Generals Kelley and Crook, and Brigadier Generals Hayes (since President of the United States), Lightburn and Duvall were temporarily in the city.

A greater harvest of generals might have been reaped had we been aware of this latter fact. Sheridan's Army lay at Winchester and a considerable force of Federal troops were strongly entrenched at New Creek (now Keyser), an important station on the Baltimore and Ohio Railroad. The first-named point is southeast of Cumberland and the second southwest, and both are nearer Moorefield than Cumberland or New Creek by eighteen miles. These facts will show the hazard of a trip from our headquarters to Cumberland, and the liability of being cut off, to which any small force of Confederates discovered in the vicinity of the latter place would Be exposed.

When McNeil and party arrived at the rendezvous, in addition to those of our own command, there were a number, probably a dozen, belonging to Company F of the 7th and D of the 11th Virginia Cavalry, of Rosser's Brigade. The men and horses were fed and rested here and the shades of that evening saw us upon our ride. Our route lay ever Middle Ridge and across the valley of Patterson's Creek, through the ridges beyond to the base of Knobly mountain, where, taking a north-easterly course, we came to a narrow gap, leading up to open fields on the mountain top. Passing up this gap, over an icy read, we found the fields above covered with snow drifts of uncertain depths, which forced us to dismount and lead our struggling horses. Having reached the road, through a lower gap to the Seymour farm, we quickly descended the mountain into the valley and crossed the Potomac into Maryland.

At this juncture Lieutenant McNeil led the troop into a neighbouring field, and, calling a number of us together, rode to the residence of a prominent citizen close by, where he held a little council of war. In this participated Sergeants Vandiver, Dailey and Cunningham, Privates R. G. Lobb, Charles Nichols, Lieutenant Isaac Parsons and J. W. Kuykendall, the two latter of Rosser's Brigade, myself and probably some others whom I cannot now recall. After saying that there was not then sufficient time to enable us to reach Cumberland before daylight by the route laid down by me, the lieutenant proposed that that part of the expedition be abandoned, but to prevent the trip from being an entire failure, he suggested that we should surprise and capture the pickets at the railroad station nearby, at Brady's Mill.

The prizes for which we had come so far were estimated by quality, not quantity, and a company of infantry was not esteemed a fair exchange for two major generals, so his proposition met with emphatic and almost unanimous dissent. It is proper here to say that my route contemplated flanking the neighbouring village of Cresaptown, moving on to the well-known national road, and taking that thoroughfare, which was not picketed, to enter Cumberland from the northwest, by way of the "Narrows," a famous pass through Will's mountain. This would have doubled the distance to be travelled from the point at which we passed the river, but it was the only prudent and reasonably safe route, and but for several unnecessary delays already made, for which Lieutenant McNeil himself was responsible, ample time had been left to pursue it.

The fact remained, however, as McNeill had declared, that we could not then get to Cumberland by that route in the required time, and if we were to proceed further on our expedition we must at once take the shorter route, the New Creek road, and try our chances, by surprising and capturing the pickets on that road, to get into the city without raising an alarm.

The attempt to pass quietly through two lines of pickets promised but doubtful results, but this being the only satisfactory alternative, we determined to try it. Lieutenant McNeil and Sergeant Vandiver, followed by Kuykendall and myself, rode ahead as an advance guard, the rest of the troop, under Lieutenant I. S. Welton, keeping close behind. A layer of thin, crusty snow was on the ground, and, although it was an hour and a half before dawn, we could see very well for a short distance. The New Creek road skirts the base of Will's mountain, running almost parallel with the railroad and river, and all three come close together at the mouth of a deep ravine. About two miles from Cumberland, where the road deflects to the left and winds up through the ravine and over the hill to the city, a cavalry picket was stationed at the mouth of the ravine, and as we neared this point a solitary vedette was observed standing on the roadside, who, upon noticing our approach, gave the challenge, "Halt! Who comes there?"

"Friends from New Creek," was the response.

He then said: "Dismount one, come forward and give the countersign," when, without a word Lieutenant McNeil, putting spurs to his horse, dashed towards the picket, and as he passed, unable to check his speed, fired his pistol in the man's face. We followed rapidly and secured the picket, whom we found terribly startled at the peculiar conduct of his alleged "friends." Two comrades, acting as a reserve, had been making themselves cosy before a few embers, under a temporary shelter in a fence corner about a hundred yards in the rear, and these, hearing the commotion in front, hastily decamped towards the river. They got no farther than the railroad, however, for we were close upon them, and in response to our threats of shooting they halted and surrendered. They belonged to Company B, 3rd Ohio, and from one of them, the desired countersign for the night, "Bull's Gap," was extorted under menace of instant annihilation at the end of a halter. Mounting these men upon their horses, which we found hitched near the roadside, we took them into Cumberland and out again, when one was turned loose by his weary guard minus horse and equipments, but plus a very remarkable experience.

The imprudent action of Lieutenant McNeil in firing, as he did, a shot which might have caused a general alarm and forced us to abandon our design, created some displeasure among the men, and, sharing in this feeling, I insisted that Kuykendall and myself should take the advance in the approach to the next inner post. This was assented to and we moved on with the determination that no more unnecessary firing should be indulged in on our part. The second post was fully a mile away, over the high intervening hill and located at the junction of the road we were on with the old Frostburg pike. This post consisted of five men belonging to the 1st West Virginia Infantry, who were comfortably ensconced in a shed-like structure, behind a blazing log fire and all busily engaged at cards.

As we drew near the circle of light one of the number was observed to get up, reach for a musket, and advance in front of the fire to halt us. To his formal challenge Kuykendall answered: "Friends, with the countersign." We kept moving up in the meantime and when the demand was made for one of us to dismount and give the countersign, noticing an impatient movement among our men in the rear, to mislead the picket and enable us to get as near as possible before our intended dash was made, I shouted back in a loud voice: "Don't crowd up, men! Wait until we give the countersign." We did not find it necessary to give it, however; there was an open space around the picket post, which allowed no chance of escape, and we were close upon them. The next instant a swift forward dash was made, and, without a single shot, they were surrounded and captured. Their guns and ammunition were taken and destroyed, and they were left unguarded at their post, with strict instructions to remain until our return.

On its face this would appear to have been a very unwise thing, but it was the best we could do. We had no intention of returning that way, but we rightly trusted that before the men would realise the situation and get to where an alarm could be given our work in the city would have been done. We were now inside the picket lines, and before us lay the slumbering city. The troop was halted here for a short time while Lieutenant McNeil hastily detailed two squads of six men each, who were directly charged with the capture of the generals. Sergeant Joseph W. Kuykendall, of Company F, 7th Virginia Cavalry, a special scout for General Early and a soldier of great courage, coolness and daring, who had once been a prisoner in Kelley's hands and had a personal acquaintance with him, was placed in command of the men detailed to secure that General. To Sergeant Joseph L. Vandiver, a man of imposing figure and style, was given charge of the capture of General Crook.

An interesting fact in connection with this latter is that among the number were Jacob Gassman, a former clerk in the hotel which General Crook occupied, and whose uncle then owned the building; and Sergeant Charles James Dailey, whose father was landlord at the time, and whose sister, Mary, is now Mrs. General Crook, and was probably then his *fiancée*. The duty of destroying the telegraph lines was imposed on me, and Hallar and others detailed as my assistants. These preliminaries being arranged, we moved on down the pike, rode into Green street and around the Court House hill; then over the Chain bridge across Will's Creek, and up Baltimore street, the principal thoroughfare of the city. Taking in the situation as they rode along, the men occupied themselves in whistling such Yankee tunes as they knew, and bandying words with isolated patrols and guards occasionally passed. Some of our men were disguised in Federal overcoats, but in the dim light no difference could be noticed in the shades of light blue and gray. Part of the men halted in front of the Bamum House, now the Windsor hotel, where General Kelley slept, and the others rode on to the Revere House, where General Crook reposed in fancied security. A sentry paced up and down in front of the respective headquarters, but took little notice of our movements, evidently taking us for a scouting party coming in to report.

Sprigg Lynn, of Kuykendall's squad, was about the first to reach the pavement, where he captured and disarmed the sentry, who directed the party to the sleeping apartment of General Kelley. Entering the hotel, the party first invaded a room on the second floor, which proved to be that of the adjutant general. Arousing him they asked where General Kelley was and was told that he was in the adjoining apartment, a communicating room, the door of which was open and which they entered at once. When General Kelley was awakened, he was informed that he was a prisoner, and was requested to make his toilet as speedily as possible. With some degree of nervousness, the old general complied, inquiring as he did so to whom he was surrendering. Kuykendall replied: "To Captain McNeil, by order of General Rosser." He had little more to say after this, and in a very short space of time both he and Melvin were taken down into the street and mounted upon horses, the owners of which courteously gave the prisoners the saddle, and rode behind. In this manner they were taken out of Cumberland, but as soon after as separate horses could be procured, they were given them.

At the Revere House an almost identical scene took place. The sentry having been taken and disarmed, the capturing party ascended the stone steps of the hotel and found the outside door locked. The door was opened by a small coloured boy and the party entered. The boy was greatly alarmed at the brusque manner of the unexpected guests, whom he evidently suspected of improper intentions. When asked if General Crook was in the hotel, he said: "Yes, sah, but don't tell 'em I told you," and he afterward made the inquiry: "What kind 'o men is you all, anyhow?" While Vandiver and Dailey were getting a light in the office below, Gassman went to No. 46, General Crook's apartment, and, thinking the door was locked, knocked at it several times.

A voice within asked: "Who's there?"

Gassman replied: "A friend," and was then told to "come in."

Vandiver, Dailey and Tucker arrived by this time and all entered the room. Approaching the bed where the general lay, Vandiver said in a pompous manner: "General Crook, you are my prisoner."

"What authority have you for this?" inquired Crook.

"The authority of General Rosser, of Fitzhugh Lee's Division of cavalry," said Vandiver, in response.

Crook then rose up in bed and said: "Is General Rosser here?"

"Yes," replied Vandiver, "I am General Rosser; I have twenty-five men with me, and we have surprised and captured the town."

That settled the matter as far as the *bona fide* general was concerned; he was immensely surprised at the bold announcement, but knowing nothing to the contrary, accepted Vandiver's assertion as the truth, and submitted to his fate with as much grace and cheerfulness as he could muster.

Speaking to me afterwards of his sensations at the time, the general said: "Vandiver was just such a looking person as I supposed General Rosser to be, and I had no reason to doubt the truth of his statement. I was very much relieved, however, when I found out the real situation, and that the city and garrison had not been taken."

General Kelley and his adjutant were taken some time before Crook was brought out and mounted, but when this was finally done and the headquarters and other flags were secured, in a quiet and orderly manner, the entire party rode down Baltimore street to the Chain bridge. A large stable was located here, and from this several fine horses were taken, among them "Philippi," General Kelley's charger. The taking of these horses caused some delay, which greatly excited Lieutenant McNeil, who, calling for me, ordered that I should lead them out of the city at once. Turning the column to the left, I led it down Canal street and on to the canal bank, where, a few hundred yards below, at the locks, we came unexpectedly upon a dozen or more guards, whom we surrounded and captured.

We destroyed their guns and ammunition, but did not encumber ourselves with more prisoners. From this point the column went at a gallop down the towpath, until halted by the picket, posted at the canal bridge, a mile below town, on the road to Wiley's ford. The column not halting, as ordered, one of the pickets was heard to say: "Sergeant, shall I fire?" when Vandiver, who was in front, shouted: "If you do, I'll place you under arrest. This is General Crook's bodyguard, and we have no time to waste. The Rebels are coming and we are going out to meet them."

This explanation seemed satisfactory. We passed under the bridge, beyond the picket post—the enemy's outmost guard—and across the

Potomac.

We were four or five miles away before the boom of a cannon was heard giving the alarm. Sixty rough and rugged miles intervened between us and safety, but I doubt if there was a man in the troop but now felt at his ease. Elated, proud and happy, all rode back that cold winter morning over the snow-clad Virginia hills. Our expedition had been a grand success and our every wish was realised. A mounted force from Cumberland in pursuit came in sight on Patterson's Creek, but kept at a respectful distance in the rear until after we had passed Romney, when they pressed upon our guard, but, on the exchange of a few shots, retired. On reaching the Moorefield Valley, a battalion of the Ringgold Cavalry, sent from New Creek to intercept us, came in sight. We were on opposite sides of the river, in full view of each other, and soon our tired horses were being urged to their utmost speed; the Federals endeavouring to reach Moorefield and cut off our retreat; while our great desire was to pass through the town with our prisoners and captured flags and exhibit to our friends and sweethearts there the fruits of our expedition and the trophies of our success.

It soon became evident, however, that the fresher horses of the other side would win the race, and, convinced that the town could not be reached and safely passed, McNeil suddenly led his men into the woods skirting the road, and, taking a well-known trail, passed through the ridge east of Moorefield to a point of security seven miles above, where we encamped for the night. In the previous twenty-four hours we had ridden ninety miles, over hill and mountain, valley and stream, with very little rest or food for men or horses, and, as may be readily imagined, heartily enjoyed the night's repose. Our prisoners received the best possible care and attention, and early next morning pursued their enforced march "on to Richmond" by way of General Early's headquarters at Staunton.

The following are *verbatim* copies of the only official reports of the affair on record in the War Department at Washington, and have probably never before been published:

Headquarters
Army Northern Virginia
February 24, 1865.

Honourable John C. Breckinridge, Secretary of War:
General Early reports that Lieutenant McNeil, with thirty men, on the morning of the 21st, entered Cumberland, captured and

brought out Generals Crook and Kelly, the Adjutant General of the department, two privates and the headquarters' flags, without firing a gun, though a considerable force is stationed in vicinity. Lieutenant McNeil and party deserve much credit for this bold exploit. Their prisoners will reach Staunton today,

R. E. Lee.

Cumberland, Md., February 21, 1865.
Major General Sheridan, Winchester, Va.:
This morning about 3 o'clock a party of Rebel horsemen came up on the New Creek road, about sixty in number. They captured the picket and quietly rode into town, went directly to the headquarters of Generals Crook and Kelly, sending a couple of men to each place to overpower the headquarters' guard, when they went directly to the room of General Crook and, without disturbing anybody else in the house, ordered him to dress and took him downstairs and placed him upon a horse ready saddled and waiting. The same was done to General Kelly. Captain Melvin, Assistant Adjutant General to General Kelly, was also taken. While this was being done a few of them, without creating any disturbance, opened one or two stores, but they left without waiting to take anything.

It was done so quietly that others of us who were sleeping in adjoining rooms to General Crook were not disturbed. The alarm was given within ten minutes by a darkey watchman at the hotel, who escaped from them, and within an hour we had a party of fifty cavalry after them. They tore up the telegraph lines and it required almost an hour to get them in working order. As soon as New Creek could be called, I ordered a force to be sent to Romney, and it started without any unnecessary delay. A second force has gone from New Creek to Moorefield, and a regiment of infantry has gone to New Creek to supply the place of the cavalry. They rode good horses and left at a very rapid rate, evidently fearful of being overtaken. They did not remain in Cumberland over ten minutes. Prom all information I am inclined to believe that instead of Rosser it is McNeil's Company. Most of the men of that company are from this place. I will telegraph you fully any further information.

Robert P. Kennedy
Major and A. A. C.

But little remains to be added. Lieutenant McNeil secured at last his long-deferred Captain's commission, but did not enjoy it, the war ending soon after—sometime in May, 1865—and, in accordance with the stipulations of Lee at Appomattox, McNeil surrendered his command for parole. Since the war he has married and returned to the West, and for many years has been a citizen of Illinois. Many of his troops have since passed from time into eternity, and the survivors are scattered far and wide.

Although a Major General of volunteers and also by brevet. General Crook's lineal rank in the regular army at the end of the war was Captain in the 4th Infantry. Since then he had risen to the grade of Major General and was but three removes from full command of the Army of the United States when he died at Chicago in 1890, in command of the military department of Missouri.

General Kelley, after long enjoying a sinecure post in the civil service and a modest pension, died on his farm in the Alleghanies in 1891.

Major Melvin is a distinguished member of the bar of West Virginia, who, since his creditable career in the army closed, has had the honour of presiding on the bench over one of the most important circuit courts in that young and prosperous state. J. B. Fay.

HISTORY OF THE STONEWALL JACKSON BRIGADE MEDAL.

In the winter of 1862 and 1863 the Marquis de Lafayette, of Paris, France, a descendant of Lafayette of Revolutionary fame, visited the armies of the North and South, then engaged in a bloody war. After visiting the Federal "Army of the Potomac" he visited the Confederate "Army of Northern Virginia." He became a great admirer of Stonewall Jackson and his Corps, and especially of the "Stonewall Brigade." After returning to France he had 5,000 bronze medals made at his own expense, intending one for each member of the "Stonewall Brigade." The latter part of 1864 he succeeded in shipping them in a blockade-runner commanded by Captain Lamar, of Savannah, Ga. He landed them at Wilmington, N. C, then shipped them by rail to Savannah and hid them in the basement of a warehouse that stood on the wharf to keep them from falling into the hands of the Federals. They remained there until the war closed. Lamar died and they were forgotten. In 1893, when tearing down that old warehouse, they were found covered with rubbish and very much corroded. Mrs. Lamar was still living, and they were turned over to her and distributed to the

Lieut.-Gen. John B. Gordon, of Georgia.
(From a war-time photograph.)

survivors of the "Stonewall Brigade" wherever found.

An Interesting Incident.

In 1894 General Edward L. Thomas, a Georgian, and who commanded a brigade of Georgians in General Lee's Army, came to Oklahoma Territory and was appointed Indian agent for the Sac and Fox Indians, and was elected Commander of Oklahoma Division, United Confederate Veterans. General Thomas died, in 1897, at South McAlester, I.T., when I was elected Commander of the United Confederate Veterans to fill his place, and while holding that position I received a letter from Mrs. Louis N. Walton, of Beverly, New Jersey, inquiring about General Thomas. She had seen notice of his death in the papers. I answered her letter, telling her who General Edward L. Thomas was, and the following letter, which is quite interesting and historical, I received in answer to mine:

Beverly, N. J., April 13, 1898.
Mr. John O. Casler, Com. Ok. Div. U. C.V., Oklahoma City, O T.:

Dear Sir—General Edward L. Thomas is not the man I mean. The General Thomas that I desire information of died either in the summer of 1895 or 1896. I tried to find this little sketch of his war record in Philadelphia, because I saw it in the *Philadelphia Evening Telegraph*. I put the paper away carefully, but it was accidentally destroyed by one of my servants before I clipped the piece out.

They do not remember it at the *Telegraph* office; have searched files of paper for it without success.

"They tell me that 'Henry George Thomas' was a Confederate General, and that 'George Henry Thomas' was a Union General, and that the one in Oklahoma must be the one. He is not, for he (the one I mean) died earlier than 1897.

I met him in Philadelphia in 1863. He fainted on the pavement in front of my aunt's house one summer morning; her servants carried him into the house, and we used the proper restoratives and sent him in a carriage to the Baltimore and Ohio depot when he was able to continue his journey. He was in company with a younger man, whom I never saw again until I saw his face in the papers as the murderer of President Lincoln (John Wilkes Booth). Their faces are indelibly stamped on my memory; also, the conversation. Though we urged them to tell us their names they refused, though they assured us they were very grateful. I think they feared we would betray them because we were Union women.

No true woman would be guilty of such an act, for suffering always appeals to her heart, sometimes against her better judgment. My aunt daily left her luxurious home to nurse the sick and wounded soldiers at the Filbert Street Hospital (near Broad Street Station of Pennsylvania railroad). There were a dozen Confederates there at that time, and they were just as carefully cared for as the Union soldiers. She lost her life from too great devotion to the work.

Booth told us that 'his friend had been ill, and in his anxiety to reach home had over-estimated his strength.' Taking my aunt's hand in his and looking her full in the face, he said: 'Would you befriend us if you knew us to be enemies?' Her reply was: 'If thine enemy hunger, feed him; if he thirst, give him drink,' etc. 'You are a noble woman, and have ministered to a man whose life can illy be spared. May God bless you for your kindness,' was Booth's reply.

My aunt entered into life eternal December 31, 1864, and never knew the name of either man, or of the tragic death of Booth. Not did I, until Lincoln's death, know who Booth was; nor, for over thirty years, did I know the name of the sick man, until I read his death notice in 1895 or 1896.

I was a very young girl at the time of this meeting. I am the only one living of the quartet. I shall never forget those two hours, nor the shock I received at seeing Booth's face as the face of an *assassin*. I had woven a romance around him, and expected to see his beautiful brow crowned with laurel. Alas! for my dream.

Both men were in citizen's dress. General Thomas was a medium-sized man, dark moustache, closely cropped hair swarthy complexion, and had a white silk kerchief knotted around his neck. The piece I refer to spoke of his illness, in 1863, in Philadelphia, from a wound on the back of his neck (that accounts for the kerchief); that when on his way to join his command he was recognised in Baltimore as an escaped prisoner of war, and was taken to Fortress Monroe. So, he must have been captured the day after we saw him. I cannot remember the initials of his name, and he must have been in the *thirties* when I saw him, for he was much older than Booth. Since reading that sketch, I remember that 'Booth's' sister, 'Mrs. Clark,' lived only three squares from my aunt's, and I suppose she was caring for him in his illness.

I think that General Thomas must have belonged to a Virginia family. Was there not more than *one* General Thomas in the Confederate service?

I thank you very much for your answer to my letter. If I have put you to any expense, I am willing to compensate you. I wanted to keep this little clipping, if I could get it.

Very truly yours, Mrs. Louis N. Walton.
P. O. Box 21, Beverly, N. J,

Note—Booth was a Southern sympathizer and would assist prisoners to escape whenever he could. He had assisted this General Thomas to escape from Fort Delaware.

Their Game of Poker was Spoiled.

L. T. Dickinson, Commander N. B. Forrest Camp, Chattanooga, Tenn:

This sketch represents a true incident. Jones' brigade of cavalry was raiding in West Virginia; we were halted near Moore field while our advance was reconnoitring. There were gamblers in the army who never missed a chance of plying their trade. While halting as above stated, several card fiends climbed the fence of a cornfield, where they could procure 'chips' in grains of corn. Spreading an oil cloth on the ground, the game of poker proceeded, when, suddenly, there came a *b-o-o-m* from a neighbouring hill, followed with a 'Where-is-ye-where-is-ye—bang!' A shell which struck the ground and burst, scattering a cart load of dirt over them. The players fell over one another in a heap, save Charlie Hutton of the Maryland battalion. He held three aces and a pair of tens, 'chips' enough to feed his horse, and wouldn't throw up his hand. As he lay back on his elbow with one foot in the air, he yelled out in the direction of the Yankees, 'Say, you fellows over there! Don't be careless with them things!' But the only 'call' he got was from the bugler, who quickly sounded 'Mount.' Gen. Jones had a little game of bluff of his own, and our battalion was sent off to drag brush on a dusty road to make the Yankees believe another brigade was coming up.

Conquered Banners.

John S. Arnold.
Sergeant Co. F. 4th Virginia Cavalry.

John Dailey.
Sergeant Co. D. 11th Virginia Cavalry.

Gen. George Crook.

Gen. B. F. Kelley.

Capt. J. C. McNeil.   Lieut. J. S. Welton.

John B. Fay.

Jos. Kuykendall. (Captured Kelley.)

J. L. Van Diver. (Captured Crook.)

Sketches of the Life of Captain Hugh A. White, of the Stonewall Brigade
By His Father

ENTERS THE ARMY
Correspondence from April, 1861, to August, 1862

He remained at the Seminary until his second session closed. He stood his examinations, attended the marriage of a friend, and reached home about the middle of May, 1861. He was then twenty years and eight months of age. His appearance, though not indicative of serious disease, was such as to awaken some uneasiness in the minds of his friends. The professors said he had confined himself too closely to his room and his books during the winter. His father feared that the privations and exposure of the camp might be fatal to his health, and held a full interview with him, in which he sought to convince him, that Considering his age, his acquisitions, his tastes and habits, he could more effectually serve both God and his country, by spending the summer as a colporteur, than by entering the army at that time.

He also urged, that after spending the summer in that way, he might then, in eight months more, complete his course in the Seminary, obtain license to preach, and enter the army as a chaplain. A commission had already been sent to him from the Board of Publication, at Philadelphia, inviting and empowering him to labour in their service for such time, and in such a field as he might prefer. But the war had already begun, and this commission, of course, could not be accepted. There was a good supply of books, however, in the depository at Lexington, and he was urged to use these in the service of the Committee of Lexington Presbytery. But, having listened to his father as he always did, with the most deferential attention, he replied substantially as follows:

> Father, what you say has much force. But this is to be no ordinary war, and for young men like me to hold back will have a very bad moral effect. The superior numbers and resources of the North will make it necessary for every man in the South, not disabled by age or infirmity, to take part in the work of resistance. I have thought and prayed much over this question for the last two months. To be entirely candid, I observed a day of fasting and prayer at the Seminary, with a view to learn what the will of the Lord is, and the result is as firm a conviction that I ought at once to take part in the defence of my native State, and especially of you and mother, as I ever felt that I ought to preach the Gospel.

His appearance, manner and thoughts, impressed the memory and heart of his father in a way never to be forgotten, and under the impression thus made, he said: "Go, my son, and the blessing of God go with you." And although he fell, the blessing of God did go with him.

The students of Washington College had formed themselves into a volunteer company, with the title of the Liberty Hall Volunteers, and chosen their Professor of Greek, James J. White, their captain. Hugh at once enrolled himself as a private in the ranks of this company, under the command of his eldest brother, whom he had always loved and reverenced, almost as he did his father. This company was composed almost exclusively of those then connected with the College, or who were recent graduates of the College. It consisted of seventy-two in the aggregate, more than half of whom were professors of religion, and about one-fourth of whom were candidates for the ministry It embraced an amount of intellectual and moral worth rarely equalled in any military company.

On the morning of the 8th of June, 1861, they were formed in front of the Court House in Lexington. The Court House square, the main street, the windows of the houses, were crowded with the citizens of the town and of the surrounding country. They were well drilled, handsomely equipped, and made a very imposing appearance. A beautiful Confederate flag, wrought by the hands of the ladies of Falling Spring congregation, was presented in very appropriate terms by the Rev John Miller, and received in a few pertinent words by Capt. White. A brief address was then made to them, and prayer offered for them and their invaded State, by the father of the captain; after which, the command was given, and with solemn step, they marched away amidst the sighs and tears of the whole community. A large number in carriages, on horseback, and on foot, followed in their rear to the river, a mile below the town, then returning entered the Presbyterian Church, where prayer and praise were offered to the God of grace, who is also the God of battles.

In the First Battle of Manassas, such was the gallantry displayed by this company, that they won from Gen. Jackson the designation of "more than brave young men." Twelve of them have fallen in battle. Seven have died of disease contracted in camp. Fourteen have been wounded in action. They have been in thirteen pitched battles, and many combats, in a period of eighteen months; and on no occasion have they failed to evince a high order of courage. From the casualties of battle and disease they are now commanded by their fourth captain.

As they awaited orders at Staunton, Hugh wrote to his father:

You will be glad to hear that our destination is Harper's Ferry. We leave tomorrow morning, and are all in good spirits. The people here have been very kind, and made our condition really pleasant. Many of our men have enjoyed their hospitality at their houses, and the others have enjoyed it at their camp. Some hearts, it may be, are now swelling with the desire for military distinction, and some heads becoming dizzy with anticipations of earthly glory. But I confess I am either too cowardly or too stupid to belong to either class. They may win the laurels, provided only that our cause triumphs. And of our final success you would not doubt, had you seen the men who left town this morning to repel the enemy from our north-western border. They appeared to be good soldiers and in good spirits.

But they will have hard work amid great difficulties. Several other regiments are expected tonight. Among them we expect to see the Hampden Sidney boys. The attention of the authorities seems to be directed to the north-west. If the enemy persist in seeking to advance, or to hold the nearer points already taken, there will be bloody work. But it is of no use to prophesy evil. They have come, more are coming, and they must be met. I am sure it will relieve your minds of much anxiety to know that we are going to Harpers Ferry, to meet open enemies, and not the traitors of the north-west. I write at night, amidst all sorts of noises. The boys are packing their knapsacks, laughing, talking, whistling, and singing. We are all well and in good spirits. With best love to all at home,

>Your devoted son,
>
>>Hugh.

A few days before leaving home, he wrote to his sister in Montgomery, thus:

> I expect to leave this week in brother James company. Though the time for us to leave home, perhaps never to return, is so near, yet we are quite cheerful. When mother first heard of our orders to leave, she was very sad, but she is now in good spirits, making preparation for our departure. She, with all of us, feels that it is a duty calling for great self-denial, yet one we must meet with cheerful courage. How wonderfully have we thus far been preserved from great effusion of blood. At Sumter and Acquia Creek we have gained bloodless victories. May God continue thus to shield us. Of course, I hope to escape death, and live to preach the gospel: But if not, living or dying, I am the Lord's. If we are conquered, farewell forever to the bright visions of philanthropists and Christians as to the civil and religious freedom America was to maintain at home and scatter abroad. But if we conquer, as I think we shall eventually, these visions and hopes may again be cherished.

>>Camp Stephens, June 24, 1861.
>
> Your letter was the first received since I left home. The affection expressed in it, and now, I know, following me from day to day, is a source of joy. Deprived of the pleasures of home, the love of those we have left behind is like sweet incense to the heart. The farther apart we are scattered, the stronger and tenderer are the bonds which bind our hearts together.
>
> I am now four miles from Martinsburg, and about six from the Potomac. We have not the comforts of home, but what we have we enjoy greatly. Last night we slept on the ground without unrolling our knapsacks, expecting to meet the enemy before morning. I spread my blanket over two large rocks firmly embedded in the earth, and fitted myself in the hollow between them. As it threatened to rain, I took my musket for a bedfellow and held my cartridge box in my arms. Soon the rain began to fall, but with perfect indifference to this I fell asleep. I have

already learned to prefer the canopy of heaven for my roof, and the stars as my lights by night. In Winchester I contracted a severe cold while sleeping in a house. Four nights in the open air have nearly cured me.

I have found much pleasure in meeting with old friends. At Winchester nine of my fellow-graduates met. It was the largest and happiest reunion we have enjoyed since parting. Almost every day brings some new enjoyment of this sort, awaking memories of the past, and recalling joys which seemed to be gone forever. Do not suppose therefore that mine is a sad condition, calling for sympathy. We have our sources of sadness, like other people. But we also have our own peculiar joys. Indeed, one thought of the cause in which we are engaged, is enough to scatter all gloom, and fill us with gladness.

Yesterday we heard two sermons and attended a prayer meeting. This gave the appearance, at least, of holiness to the day, but still if you had looked into our camp yon would have thought it the busiest day of the week. Some were cooking, others cutting wood, and others pitching their tents. It is painful but necessary to spend the Sabbath in this way. Our religious privations are what we feel most keenly We seek to remedy this by a brief prayer meeting held every night after roll call. Nearly all the members of our company attend with becoming seriousness. May the trials of our country work in it a great moral reformation. If so, we may hope for true and lasting prosperity when peace shall again come. If not, God will overturn in the future as he is doing now. May he speedily redeem our world from sin and ruin.

Give all your household my warmest love. My mind and heart are full of you.

The first great battle in which he participated was that of Manassas, July 21, 1861. In this he was much exposed, fought bravely, but escaped unhurt. Two days after this memorable conflict he wrote to his father thus:

Manassas, July 23, 1861.

My Dear Father: I wrote to you yesterday that you might know of our safety You will hear more of the particulars of the battle of the 21st than I have time now to give. Our company has suffered sadly. Five are dead and seven wounded. Oh! how sad a blow is this. Who thought that our ranks would thus be thinned and so many be hurried into eternity? Where are their souls? This thought often perplexes and saddens me. I pray that I may hereafter be fair more zealous in seeking to bring sinners to Christ, that if they die, they may only sleep in him. I wish that I was with you; to join in ascribing praise and glory to the good Providence which preserved me in such danger. Everyone in the fight was in imminent peril. Balls flew fast around and over us, and many of our brave comrades fell at our side. But brother James and I, though separated for a while during the first charge, soon met again, and side by side we passed through the remaining scenes of the day. We are unhurt. Though our loss has been great, the field is ours.

The enemy were put to flight and chased for miles. The killed on either side are not known as yet. They will number hundreds, however. The loss of baggage, wagons, artillery, and prisoners on the part of the enemy is immense. At least fifty pieces of cannon, some of them turned against their former owners, before they were out of reach, would be in itself a glorious success. But when we remember that in their attack on us, they were prepared in every way for advancing to Richmond, with haversacks filled with provisions, preparations for rebuilding bridges, confidently expecting to march over us here, and pass on in triumph to our capital—when we remember this, we may hope that their defeat will so dishearten them as materially to check their progress. It was a full trial of their strength.

They fought bravely—for their regulars and best soldiers were engaged. But they could not stand the charge of bayonets. Every time we advanced, they fell back. Who would not praise God for thus overthrowing those, who, on his holy day, sought to execute their wicked purpose to crush those who sought to defend their liberties and their homes? It was an awful Sabbath. How often I longed to be with you, enjoying the privileges of the Sabbath. Even one hour would have been delightful. But God ordered otherwise. We are all in his hands. He casts down and he keeps alive. May he speedily crown our cause with complete success! If it please him, may I again see my father and mother in peace, and spend my life in preaching his gospel. The scenes in which I am now engaged are very sad; yet the taste of victory, though bought by precious blood, is sweet. But to preach would be far better.

I have not time to give you a full description of this battle; and perhaps it would only give you the greater pain to learn what danger we were in. But surely, if God has spared us in this most protracted and bloody battle, as he has, he can spare us in the future. There was an incessant roar of cannon and musketry for over eight hours. The hardest fighting was from eleven to four o'clock. We were in this.

Our town has again been called to mourn. Wm. Page and Fr. Davidson have been taken. Our immediate relatives are safe. H—— M—— stood his ground bravely, and came out untouched. Give full love to all at home—especially to mother's anxious heart. But my love for all increases daily. Send word of my safety to sister, brothers George and Henry, and to my aunts Georgie and Martha. Warmest congratulations and love to sister Mary Lou., and greetings to my new nieces, my dear parents, and all at home. I hope to see you again in peace. But if we do not meet here again, we have a home in Heaven.

On the 5th of August he wrote to his brother George, giving him a full and admirable description of the battle. But as many such descriptions have been written by others, and as we do not wish to tax the patience of our readers, we only give a sentence or two with which he closes the letter.

> Brother James and I heartily unite with you in praising the grace which has spared our lives in this bloody battle. He and I joined in the pursuit beyond the Stone Bridge. We saw the enemy as they passed through the woods a mile ahead of us, and we returned to attend to our wounded and dead. Night soon closed the scene. The next day we buried our dead. It rained the whole day, and that night we sat up around our fires. Bro. J. had religious service over their graves.
>
> It is a great victory; but may I never pass through such a scene again. Death and hell may rejoice on the battlefield, but let man be silent. May God, who has won this victory for us, now give us peace. My best love to sister Willie and the children.
>
> Your aff. brother,
>
> Hugh.

The hardships endured in the service seriously impaired the health of his brother, Capt. James J. White, but though urged by his general, surgeon, and many others, to leave the army, he persisted in remaining until September. By this time his sufferings became so great, and his symptoms so threatening, that he was constrained to tender his resignation of the command of his much-loved company—the Liberty Hall Volunteers. His resignation was accepted with deep regret by those whom he had led through so many dangers and sufferings. But no one felt or could feel so sadly, on this occasion, as his younger brother, whom he had taught in college and guided in battle, and who had ever looked up to him with feelings of the tenderest fraternal affection.

Soon after he left the army, he wrote to this brother the following letter, in which it is obvious to all who knew him, he exerts himself to repress his feelings.

Near Centreville, Sept. 12, 1861.
My Dear Brother: I received your letter from Manassas. I regret the difficulties which delayed you on your way, but am glad to think that this afternoon you are in Rockbridge and perhaps now at home. I am on picket at the house to the right of our encampment, and though the breeze is pleasant and the sun bright, I cannot restrain the desire to be with you. I feel your absence much. I have not the pleasure now of sitting in your tent and enjoying your company. I feel lonesome. But this will wear off in a few days, I hope.

I fear you had a very uncomfortable ride last night. The rain poured down here from ten till after one o'clock. I bore it patiently for an hour, hoping to endure it to the end. But the rain wore out my courage, and I went into the house. I only bettered my condition in keeping dry. The room was close, and the company I was in rendered my night very uncomfortable.

I fear a stage ride at night, in such a rain, caused you much Buffering. But this is forgotten if you are now at home. I see the sun going down behind the Blue Ridge. How much more beautiful it would appear if the North Mountain and the Brushy Hills formed the horizon. You must attribute this talk to your absence from me and your presence at home. Though I feel thus, my joy at your getting out of the service is great. My health is perfectly good. I am young and without any incumbrance. No one therefore is better fitted for enduring hardships. As to the danger to which my life shall be exposed in the future, I seek to commit this to Him who orders all things for His own glory. If cut down now, how much in vain has my life been. How little has been done.

This thought gives me more trouble than any other. But even this may be quieted by a calm trust in One who supplies all my deficiencies by His abundant grace, and can as easily accomplish His purposes without as with me. And when the path of duty is so plain, when we stand in the breach to defend all we hold dear, when those who seek our ruin make themselves more and more hateful, by a want of every noble feeling and purpose, and by the practice of outrages which increase daily, how can we restrain the desire to inflict on them the punishment they so well deserve. This desire is in proportion to my love for those at home, and as the war has strengthened the latter, so has it also the former.

There was a considerable show of battle near Falls Church yesterday. The enemy, it is said, advanced with a brigade of infantry, six pieces of artillery, and three hundred cavalry, coming in by a flank movement to the left and this side of Munson's Hill. They were met by six hundred of our infantry, with two pieces of artillery and some cavalry. The enemy were driven back five miles, with the loss of three killed and seven taken prisoners. We lost nothing in any way This you know was only a skirmish of almost daily occurrence. We are perfectly quiet here, and have no evidence that an advance is intended.

A committee was appointed this afternoon to draft some resolutions with reference to your resignation. They will report tomorrow. Rest assured that the affection they may express is really felt. Many of them regret your absence almost as much as I do.

Your affectionate brother,

Hugh.

To his sister, who hoped to meet him on her visit to Lexington he says:

I suppose you are now in Lexington. My presence might add something to the pleasure of your visit, and would, if proper, fill me with joy. But do not let my absence, as you hint in your last letter, detract in the least from your pleasure. I am very comfortable and happy here, and as to any peculiar danger, attending my position, I am as safe here beneath the shield of God's protection, as if at home sitting beneath my own father's roof. There is a great buzzing among editors and rumour-circulators in general. I have learned not to allow myself to be disturbed by them. I wait quietly for the order to march, and then go ahead.

Near Centreville, August 30, 1861.

My dear Father: I wrote you a long letter a day or two since, which I hope has been received. I write now before breakfast, just as the morning sun is looking into my tent, not knowing where I shall be when that sun sets. We are expecting every day, almost every minute, an order to march. Our advanced guard has taken from the enemy some hills within six miles of Alexandria, from which our men can look into that city, and can see the dome of the Capitol at Washington. A place so near the tyrant's throne, and of such commanding importance, must be a source of contention between the two armies. It cost a struggle to gain it. Five or six of our cavalry who took the position were killed, but more than this of the enemy perished, and eight were taken prisoners.

I have almost abandoned the hope of returning to the Seminary next session. This is a great disappointment to me yet one from which, if my life is spared, I may yet derive great benefit. Service in the army may give me a hardihood and experience which will help me even in the ministry You may smile at this, and say it is easy to extract sweet from bitter when a misfortune is inevitable. So, it is—and that is just what I am trying to do. It is of no use to fret and destroy both my own peace and that of others, and do no one any good. So, if the winter *is* before me, and I must contend with frost, and snow, and ice, instead of grappling with Hebrew roots and knotty points in theology, I have not a word of complaint to utter.

Nor do I anticipate much suffering. With a blazing fire to warm us by day, and a sufficiency of blankets to cover us at night, we can get along comfortably. It may only fit me the better, if need be, for being a missionary in the Arctic, regions. Thus, you see, under any circumstances, I shall derive sweet from bitter—and heat from cold. Tell mother that I have ample clothing and covering for some time to come. When brother J. returns, he can direct as to the preparation of my winter equipments. We are much pained to lose him, but his resignation is not more painful to us than it is necessary to himself. We can only repay his kindness by a life-long affection, and this the whole company will repay.

    Your devoted son,

                Hugh.

    Near Fairfax Station, September 16, 1861. My dear Father: We moved from our camp near Centreville this morning, and came five miles to the east. We have a very pleasant encampment here; but the camp we left—on account of the length of time spent there, and the many comforts surrounding us—had become like home. We regretted to leave it. However, since brother J left, the place had become lonesome to me. Every point was associated with him, and his absence made the association unpleasant. On this account I was very willing to leave it. The new scenes which now surround me, will make me more happy.

Do not think from this that I am unhappy. I am not. Absence from you all, of course, deprives me of many joys. But I am certain that we in camp are more cheerful than you are at home. We soon become accustomed to this manner of life, and enjoy it. I can truly say that, as a general thing, I am as contented as I ever was in my life.

I have had some expectation of a visit from you. I heard that during your absence from home, attending Presbytery, you might run clown on a visit to Manassas. How refreshing to us would such a visit be. Your friends here, including General and Mrs. Jackson, expressed the strongest desire that you should come. But our hopes are not realised, for I hear that you are again at home. But if you could come, I am certain that you would be gratified and we benefited. For our company's sake I wish you would come; many of them, though not members of the church, are faithful in reading their Bibles, and serious in their attendance at our nightly prayer-meetings conducted by the professing Christians of the company in alphabetical order. For their sakes, as well as my own, I do wish you would come. You might be better able to comfort their parents and friends at home by coming and spending a short time with them in camp. In our brigade (the Stonewall) are four Rockbridge companies—the Greys, Rifles, Artillery, and our own.

I suppose brother J. has received the resolutions adopted by our company on the occasion of his lamented resignation. They do honour to him, to the company, and to ——, who wrote them.

        Your devoted son,

                           Hugh.

They soon returned to their old encampment at Centreville. To his sister, Mrs. Wade, he writes:

It gives me both pleasure and pain to hear from loved ones at home and elsewhere. Their expressions of love, so warm and deep, are very grateful. But the anxiety they feel, by day and night for us is the chief cause of sadness to me. They think of us as homeless, houseless, and friendless—pinched with cold and hunger—cast forth as food for the invading enemy I confess there is some truth in all this. That we are deprived of many comforts, everybody knows and feels. We are also often subject to many hardships. But with our sorrows, we have our joys. And even if our condition were tenfold worse than it is. we would be glad to endure it for our homes. If, there be one in the army who does not find it more pleasant to endure the hardships of the camp, than to be at ease at home, he ought to be, if he is not, a Yankee.

No amount of exposure injures my health. I have often awoke from my bed of earth and pillow of rocks, more refreshed than if I had slept on feathers. I hope, therefore, that you will ease your heart of the burden of anxiety you feel for your two brothers. We hope we give in return equal love for yours. We are fighting in defence of those at home, and the greater the struggle, the greater our love for them. It is far more painful to think of our hardships amid the comforts of home than to endure them—especially with those, who, if the silver cord which binds them to this world were broken, would ascend at once to Heaven. Our bodies, what are they? Our souls, we hope, are safe. Let light from heaven then fall upon us, and it is simply impossible for this world to look dark.

Rest assured that the tender love of a sister meets the warm love of her two soldier brothers. Let all of our anxieties cease, for God is our hope. Give our best love to Dr. Wade and all the children.

Write to father and mother as often as possible. They did enjoy peace, but the recent fighting has excited their fears and made them very sad again.

What a happy home your group of children must make. How happy they must be not to know what is going on around them.

    Your devoted brother,

                   Hugh.

To the same, he writes, October 1, 1861.

On Saturday night a violent rain destroyed at once our fire and our supper. We bought some pies, however, which afforded us a good supper. In the morning I was lying in bed wondering where breakfast would come from, when a servant came to my tent and said, there was a box for one of our company at the colonel's tent. I went up and found the one you sent me. There was breakfast just at hand. The old ham was most timely. It supplied us for some days. On that and the eggs we lived high. Nothing too could have been more agreeable than the dried peaches. Our cook makes good pastry, and the fruit is sweet enough without sugar, which is scarce. Indeed, all you sent was most suitable. Both you and they at home, have been most attentive to my wants.

I should be delighted to see your children. A frolic with them would do much to supple my joints and raise my spirits. Belle would be large enough to follow me through the fields. Liberty thus to ramble would make me feel like a bird released from its cage. But I must forego these pleasures for the present, hoping that the time will yet come again for me to enjoy them.

To his father he wrote, September 6, 1861:

Amid the present excitement, matters of small moment are apt to be forgotten. I write therefore to remind you all, if you have forgotten the fact, that this is my twenty-first birthday. According to law, I am today a *freeman*. But really, I am far less of a freeman than formerly. Indeed, what a contradiction it is to say, that I am now free, and that one year ago I was under authority. Now I am bound by military rule—kept within a field around which armed sentinels stand whom I cannot pass without a written permission from my commander. This is only one of the ways in which my once free limbs are held closely fettered.

Formerly, when you alone were my ruler, the woods and the fields were mine, and nothing kept me from a full enjoyment of all I needed. But this morning, since the sun of my freedom has risen, how few of, my former blessings do I enjoy If that was servitude and this is freedom, let me always live a slave.

Were I at home this morning, I should not feel like one released from control, but rather like one cast for the first time in deep water, and who shudders to make the plunge, distrustful of the treacherous deep.

Instead of freedom from your control, I feel more disposed than ever to do your bidding—to keep closely in the path you may mark out for me. I know that you have sought to teach us independence, by making us choose for ourselves in many things. But we have all, I think, sought to know, and preferred to abide by your judgment. So, I shall always do. Indeed, I am not vet cut of mv instructor's hands, and when I am, the difficulties which will beset my path, will call more loudly than ever, for parental instruction and advice. You see therefore, that I still look forward to years of discipline and control, before I can trust myself to my own government. Indeed, I never wish to be free either from your advice or control.

When General Jackson was ordered to an independent command in the valley, his old brigade—"the Stonewall"—was not permitted to accompany him. He went alone, attended only by a portion of his staff. It was a great affliction to his old troops to be left. The following extract refers to this occasion:

Centreville, October, 1861.

My dear Father: I do not think that any man can take General Jackson's place in the confidence and love of his troops. I wish I could go with him, though my hardships should be more than doubled. I have learned to look up to him with implicit confidence, and to approach him with perfect freedom, being always assured of a kind and attentive hearing.

He addressed his brigade, as they were formed near their encampment, just before he left. Among other things he spoke substantially thus: 'You were first in the Army of the Shenandoah, you are first in the Army of the Potomac. You turned the tide of battle on the 21st of July. You are first in the affections of your people, and first in the heart of your general.' He closed amid the applauding shouts of his devoted soldiers; sat for an instant looking his men steadily in the face, and listening to their cheers, then turned, put spurs to his horse, and dashed off to his new and hard field of labour.

After a fearful battle, he writes:

> Our company has been more than decimated, yet we are all willing, I trust, to fall in the same way. The necessity is on us, and let God determine what our sufferings shall be."

Writing from Centreville to his mother, he says:

How much I would give to be permitted to spend this Sabbath day in Lexington. We have no house of worship here, and are thus deprived of the delights of the Sanctuary. One day of sacred rest like hundreds which have passed away, uncared for, and unimproved, would be at this time a feast of fat things to my soul. We are almost entirely cut off here from the reviving influences of social worship. A prayer-meeting every night, is in part a substitute. Mother, in your anxiety for my bodily comfort and welfare, I hope you will not forget my soul. The atmosphere surrounding that, is as cold as that which surrounds my body. How much I wish that the power of divine grace was more at work' within me. But though cast down I will not despair, but still trust in God.

Of the death of a fellow-soldier, another of the "more than brave" Liberty Hall Volunteers—a native and resident of Rockbridge, he says:

> You have doubtless heard before this of the death of another of our company; I refer to W J. Thompson. His body, I suppose, passed through Lexington this morning, to reach his widowed mother today. He was cut down almost in a day. No one here was aware of his danger until the night before he was taken to the Junction. The next news from him told us of his death. He died of typhoid fever, rendered more incurable by some disease of the stomach. He was a professing Christian, honouring the name by a character which was above reproach, and by a conduct which evinced the sincerity of his profession.
>
> He was delirious much of the time after he became ill, but was permitted to enjoy an hour or two of consciousness a short time before he died. These hours he spent in making some necessary arrangements of a secular nature, and in reading his Bible, ac-

companied by audible prayer. We have therefore good grounds to hope that he has entered his home in heaven, though his remains may now cast sorrow over his home on earth. He is the tenth of our company who has fallen.

Surely the hand of the Lord is heavy upon us. But how little apparent good results. I greatly fear that as His chastisements have not softened our hearts and thus been made a savour of life unto life, they will prove a savour of death unto death, in hardening them, and thus rendering us vessels of wrath fitted for destruction. How shall we remedy this? How shall we avert God's anger, which seems daily to gather strength? O that all hearts would turn unto the Lord, and by penitence and faith seek the only refuge from His wrath. 'Turn thou us, O Lord, and we shall be turned.' This must be our prayer, for God alone can help us. Father, you urge me to seek to be useful. Would it be proper for me to conduct religious services whenever an opportunity offers? And should I connect the other parts of the service with a short address? If you approve of this, I will seek such opportunities.

He wrote, first playfully and then seriously to his youngest brother—a mere boy—as follows:

Centreville, Nov. 1, 1861.
My Dear Brother: Don't I owe you a letter? My only reason for not answering you sooner is, that my letters, no matter to whom directed, are intended for all at home. But as I wish to get another letter from you, I will direct this one to you. H. M.'s going home makes me feel like going too. Just think, after all my traveling, marching, fighting, since I left home, only one day's travel will carry me back. I can leave here in the morning, and that night, I may sleep with you in our old bed at home. Why can't I take this trip? Because I am not sick. I have done nearly everything the other boys have done, but they have gotten scratched in battle, or are sick in some way, and gone home, while I am neither wounded nor sick, and must stay here.

However, I will not complain of this. It is much better to stay here well, than to go home sick or wounded. Father spent several days with us, and no doubt has told you all about his visit. Did he tell you that I would not invite him to dine with me? I did advise him, for his own good, to dine with Gen. Jackson.

It so happened that day we had no bread for dinner, all we had was beef? without bread or anything else. How could I ask him to dine with me, when there was no dinner? I fear he thinks our living is very scarce and very poor. But with now and then nothing to eat—generally a plenty, and always enjoying what we have, we get along very happily.

Yesterday afternoon, all the Virginia troops in this army were assembled around the main fortification, where Gov. Letcher, standing on the embankment, spoke to them as they stood around it, and presented to the colonel of each regiment a Virginia flag. It was an exciting scene. The soldiers looked well in their new winter suits, and their faces showed that they had brave and cheerful hearts within them.

You closed your last letter by quoting from scripture a prayer for me. You do not know how much gratified I was at this. To know that those at home pray for me is a source of great comfort and joy at all times. How glad I am when *you* join in that prayer. May this disposition to pray for me, lead to earnest prayer for yourself, and to an implicit trust of yourself to the Saviour of us all. Join with me, morning and evening, and with all at home around the family altar, in committing ourselves to Him who can alone protect and save us.

To his father.

I have received your letter of the 30th *ult.* Your spirits seem depressed. I wish I could lighten the burden which seems to oppress you. I hope it does not arise from my absence and the circumstances around me. Could you hear the merry laugh of our boys, and see their gambols, often as joyous as ever the college campus exhibited, you would not think of us as in so sad a condition. We are now used to and contented with our position—especially since success begins to crown our arms.

I have done a little of late in the ministerial work. Mr. Miller, the chaplain in our regiment, has called on me twice to conduct prayer-meetings. I felt some reluctance to do so, but still found pleasure in complying with his request. I made a short address at the second meeting. I am much afraid that my life will be cut off, and that I shall fall as the barren fig tree. Little has yet been done, and when shall I do more? Now is the time, but where are the fruits?

How much I long to sit once more within the house of God at home. But the true temple of the Lord is the humble and the contrite heart.

He adds:

I am glad, father, that you always say something in your letters for my spiritual good. My wants are far greater in this respect than you imagine. May the prayers of parents so wonderfully blessed heretofore, and the privileges we now enjoy, through the grace of God, conspire to supply my spiritual necessities.

Speaking of the conversion of a member of his company, he says:

How happy it makes me to hear of even one sinner returning to God.

Referring to his youngest brother, the only member of the family not a professor of religion, he says:

I tremble and join with you all in prayer for T. I have a sweet and strong confidence that the covenant will embrace all, and at length gather us to one home in Heaven.

He frequently concludes his letters to his parents thus:

Hoping that God will yet restore me to you and the work of the ministry, your devoted son.

To his mother he says:

I am much happier than you, I expect. Indeed, I could not be more comfortable in camp. Be cheerful, mother, for God is with us both.

It has been stated that when Gen. Jackson left Centreville to take command in the valley, the Stonewall Brigade was not permitted to go with him. On his arrival at Winchester, Col. Preston was despatched to Richmond for the purpose of representing to the authorities there, the importance of reinforcing Gen. Jackson. This was accordingly done, and with others, this much-loved brigade was ordered to follow him. This was joyful news to those who had parted, as we have seen, so reluctantly with their honoured and much-loved leader. They were soon on their way, and the following letter describes their march from Centreville to the neighbourhood of Winchester, in November, 1861.

My Dear Father: According to the orders received at Centreville, and mentioned to you in my last letter, we marched from that place to the Junction on last Saturday morning. We reached the latter place about midday, expecting to take the train for Strasburg in a short time. But we were disappointed. The train did not come for us until late in the night, and we could not leave until Sunday morning. This delay was made more distressing by the rain which fell fast all Saturday afternoon, and continued for some time into the night. We had to take it without any shelter, keeping one side dry by the fire while the other was drenched with rain. All that we got to eat was such scraps as we happened to bring with us, or could pick up by the wayside.

But these things were forgotten when the clear sun arose on Sunday morning. We rode all day, and at sunset reached Strasburg. After exercising much patience, which, you know, is seldom found in hungry men, we got some supper, then spread our blankets in the freight cars, and were soon lost in sleep. You may know that few were able so to remember that Sabbath day as to keep it holy. Many forgot the day altogether, and were surprised when reminded of it. I sought to keep my thoughts on sacred subjects, thinking often of the delightful services enjoyed at home, and longing for the privilege of joining in them once more: The first sound too that reached my ear on entering Strasburg, just after sunset, was that of the churchgoing bell. I greatly desired to obey its summons, but could not. So, committing myself in secret to Him who watches over me so constantly, I fell asleep.

Monday morning, we left Strasburg at 11 o'clock, and marched to this place, a distance of fifteen miles, by sundown. It was the first long march we had taken for many weeks; but the boys stood it remarkably well. My feet were blistered, but by the use of a prescription mother gave me on leaving home, they are already almost well. Our camp is on the borders of a beautiful forest, which furnishes us at once with wood for our fires and leaves for our beds. The lands around us are very rich; almost every hill is covered with flocks of sheep or herds of cattle—serving to reimpress me with the conviction that I have a glorious country to fight for."

Winchester, December 24, 1861.

My Dear Father: I wrote you a note as we were on our way to

the Potomac. Our work is done, and last Sunday night found us encamped on the spot we left on the preceding Monday morning. Yesterday we received an order from Gen. Jackson to report at once to him on special duty. We came joyfully at once, and our company is now acting as body guard at his headquarters. We are encamped in a pretty lot on the borders of the town, and hope soon to be very well situated.

You may wish to hear of our expedition to the Potomac. Its object was to destroy a dam in the river, which feeds the Chesapeake and Ohio Canal. We reached the river Tuesday night, marching fifteen miles the first day and thirteen the second. We had no tents with us, and slept on the ground in the woods every night. Only two or three companies were engaged on the work at one time. The rest were reserved in case an attack from the enemy, at any point, might require a large force to repel it. Four regiments lay back about a quarter of a mile from the river. One lay just over the brow of a hill above the dam. A company of riflemen was stationed in a stone mill, on the bank of the river to fire on the enemy across the river. That the men might destroy the dam without being fired upon by the enemy, a breastwork was thrown up in the night below the dam and obliquing down the river. This much was done before the enemy were aware of our presence.

But protected by the breastwork on one side and the dam on the other, they were out of danger. To get to and from their work they went and returned by night. After thus working for some days, the enemy, on Thursday, opened their cannon upon the mill in which were the riflemen. One ball went through one wall and lodged in the other, and a shell burst within the mill. Our men were therefore forced to fly, but in doing so had to run a terrible gauntlet. One narrow pathway up the hill for near 250 yards was the only way of escape for them, and all along that path they were exposed to the fire of several regiments from the opposite side of the river. Our regiment, at the time, lay on the brow of the hill above—heard the incessant fire and welcomed the boys, as one by one they escaped unhurt from this shower of balls. We too were unable to give them any help, because the enemy were so hidden behind the banks of the canal as to be concealed from our view, and so far off as to be out of the range of our guns.

The firing at length ceased, and only one of our men, our townsman, Joshua Parks, had fallen. But all were not yet safe. Ten sought shelter behind the trees and were unable to move, lest their positions should be made known and thus escape become impossible. All therefore remained behind two or three trees with their dead comrade at their side, from morning till evening, afraid to move a limb from its position. As dark came on they hoped to escape then unseen by the enemy, but before the sun was down the enemy with their shells set fire to the mill, the light from which delayed their escape still longer. I really do not see how any position could be more trying than this. It equals, in thrilling interest, anything I ever read or heard of in Indian warfare.

Danger was all around them. They were unable to help themselves or get help from others, and even night did not conceal them from their enemies. But at length the mill burned down, and all came safe from the very jaws of death. Capt. Edmundson, with several of his men, succeeded also in recovering the body of poor Parks. His life would have been saved, and the rest of the company freed from all danger, if Gen. Jackson's order had been received in time. His order was to leave the mill when the workmen left the dam—before daybreak. But this order was not delivered to the captain in time. It is peculiarly sad to lose a life which might have been saved—but I hope he was prepared, and certainly, as far as this life is concerned, death met upon the utmost verge of our State, in an effort to defend it against the invader, is full of glory

After two days more, enough of the dam was destroyed to turn off the water, and we were glad to turn our faces towards Winchester. Our whole brigade was in a very critical position. Look to the map, and you will see Williamsport in a bend of the river. On the left side of this bend is a smaller one. Just at this point is the dam, and within this peninsula, not over a mile and a half wide, we lay all the time. From both sides, therefore, we were exposed to the enemy's guns, and only avoided them by moving about frequently from place to place, spending our nights generally in the woods, close to the river, and during the day returning to the open fields to cook our food. From this funnel, however, we escaped on Saturday morning, and reached our old camp on Sunday night.

I wrote to you that I had seen ———. My conversation with him on the subject of religion was very gratifying. It is glorious news to hear of other similar cases. I will see as soon as possible, and also Mr. ———. On our march up from the Potomac I fell in with ———. He introduced the subject of religion, which, of course, was a most agreeable topic. It was the Sabbath, and much did our minds need every help to keep our thoughts in the right channel. I will seek to have further intercourse with him.

I received recently from the Central Presbyterian office some Testaments, $10 worth, the amount of money on hand for our regiment. These I will sell, or give away, as seems proper. *Testaments are more needed here than guns or powder.*

Your affectionate son.

Young Parks, who was slain, was a worthy member of the Presbyterian church. His body was brought to his native place, and interred in the midst of an immense and sorrowful assembly.

The persons indicated by the blanks towards the close of the letter are young men who left home destitute of all religious concern, but who have become awakened, or hopefully pious, since they entered the army.

On New Year's Day, 1862, they left Winchester, and the following letter gives a vivid picture of their march:

Bath, Morgan Co., Jan. 4, 1862.

My Dear Father: I wrote you a line just as we were leaving Winchester, saying that we expected to march to Romney; but we were mistaken. You will see where we are by referring to the map. We have been on the march since the first of January, at 2 o'clock, p. m., but have come only about forty miles. It has been the worst march in every respect we have ever taken. The roads were so bad, and the wagons and horses so poor, that it was impossible to go more than ten miles a day. Our company was separated from its wagon with all its baggage and provisions, on Thursday, and we have not seen them since. By sending back men to meet it, enough food has been brought to keep us from starving. But our blankets we have not seen for two days and nights, and our tents have been sent back to Winchester to relieve the wagon of its load. To make our condition still worse, the weather has become very wintry. Thursday night we did not sleep at all—only nodded for a few moments around the fires.

Our company was with the general's wagons, and behind us was a long train, whose drivers were all yelling at, and cursing, and beating their horses. We could only advance a few hundred yards at a time. When one wagon stalled, all behind it had to wait until it could move again. We were stopped in this way repeatedly, but kept straggling on from daylight until 11 o'clock at night. We were then stopped for so long a time, that we kindled large fires and prepared as best we could to remain until morning. But at 2 o'clock, a. m., General Jackson sent us an order to push forward to him, a mile and a half in advance, if possible. We started, but had not gone a fourth of a mile when we were forced to wait until morning enabled the men to get a wagon before us out of a mud-hole. By daybreak we were up from our fires and working on.

After getting to the general, he told us to march with our regiment. We did so, but still met with so many delays that we made no better progress. Just after dark, while we marched on, the snow commenced falling very rapidly. You may imagine that a dreary prospect was before us. We had eaten nothing since morning, our wagon was several miles before us, we had no shelter for the night, and not even a blanket to protect us from the snow and the cold. We have seen some hard times, but this was the worst of all. Several wagons lay along the roadside, broken down; and one, with its team and all its baggage, with a soldier on the top of all, pitched over and rolled down a bank twenty feet long. None however was injured. We at last came to our camp-ground, and amid the driving snow and piercing cold, the men began to collect wood for their fires, and to seek shelter under the bushes. C—— P—— and I, with the captain's permission, returned to a barn a mile back of us, and found a bed in the hay and fodder.

We slept pretty well, but were glad to leave at daybreak. We found the snow only an inch or two deep, but it was freezing cold. We joined the regiment just in time to march with it. I got my breakfast at a house on the roadside. When we got within a mile or two of this place, we halted while General Jackson reconnoitred to see how he should drive the Yankees away. At length we moved forward, but the fleet limbs of the enemy saved all but twenty. We entered the town therefore with no loss of life, and are quartered tonight in rooms which were occupied last night by the enemy. They were only, I hear, some six or eight hundred strong. We are in one of the houses of the Berkley Springs. This is a happy close to a most dreary march. So now let the memory of the past only stimulate to warmer gratitude for our safe deliverance from danger and hardship, and give us stronger confidence for the future. The Hand that has helped will continue to help; and now, with a happy goodnight to you all, I close my letter to enjoy a good night's rest in a house by a fire.

Your affectionate son,

Hugh.

At a well-known period in the history of this war, he wrote to his father thus:

February 5, 1862.

There is but one feeling with us—that of perfect devotion to Gen. Jackson. With him we are ready to go anywhere, and to endure anything. But if he is to be run down, our spirit is utterly broken, and we can never re-enter the service with cheerful hearts. But I trust his resignation will not be accepted, and if so, all will be well again, and our noble commander will come forth as triumphantly from the assaults of Southern *friends* as he has done from the bullets of Northern enemies. The Government must know how essential he is to the success of the Southern cause.

The year for which he had enlisted was approaching its termination, and the question of re-enlistment gave him much concern. He was not long undecided. The following letter to his father explains his views on the subject:

Winchester, March 4, 1862.

Yesterday the order came very unexpectedly for each captain to muster his men for re-enlistment. We had to decide the question during the day. Few were prepared to decide so important a question on so short notice. After no little anxious thought, with prayer for divine guidance, I decided to re-enlist. Some of the reasons for doing so are these. Although my year expires in June, I consider it my duty to remain in the army until next fall, when the Seminary term commences, and so far, as we can now see, there would be no better reason for leaving the army then than exists now. The condition of our country must become, during the summer, better or worse. If better, Gen. Jackson says my reasons would be sufficient to secure me a discharge from the service to return to the Seminary. If worse, I wish to remain where I am.

I need not say how very important it is for the preservation of our army that as many of *us* as possible should stand firm in our places, resolved never to give up the cause we have espoused. In doing this, everyone must sacrifice a great deal. In my own case it cost me a great struggle, for it removes far off the most cherished object of my heart. The ministry is still before me. On it my best affections fasten, and in it are wrapped up my brightest hopes. Nothing, therefore, could give me greater pain than to have any barrier placed between me and the ministry, or to have any veil cast over the hopes connected with it. But yet there are good reasons for my remaining in the army.

It has been to me a school which I much needed, and from it much has been learned that was almost essential to my success in the world, and which could scarcely have been learned anywhere else. Three years spent in the army, if I am spared, will do much to fit me for the ministry. Besides, how is our army to be supplied with religious reading? We have very few chaplains. Unless, therefore, there are some who will be glad to receive and distribute Testaments and religious books, this work will be woefully neglected, and the results must be disastrous. I have sought to do a little to supply this want—little indeed it was— yet, wherever the good word of God falls, we may hope for fruit unto eternal life. And if the plan suggested in one of my recent letters, to get permission, without a regular license from Presbytery, to act somewhat in the capacity of chaplain, in the absence of a regularly licensed minister, could be carried out, it would give me more liberty, and enable me to do more good.

With such views as these, not without hesitation, I admit, my course has been chosen. I regret that time was not allowed me to consult you more fully, but in your last letter, you threw the responsibility of deciding entirely on me. I hope that it is for the best.; My mind and heart are with you all at home, yet free from anxiety, because God is with us all.

To His Sister, Mrs. M'Crum

Let me hear how the Seminary prospers. I cannot be there, but still I am anxious to hear how many are there. The war has put a great barrier across my path, but one which cannot be avoided. It must be crossed. If I get through safely, I shall enter upon the work of the ministry with unspeakable delight. I long to spend my life in the work of saving souls, and to be kept back now when just on the verge of commencing my work, is like being kept from home when it is just in sight. But I may do more good here than in the ministry. I bear my delay therefore, with patience.

There were many in the Confederate Army whose views and spirit were substantially the same. There were twelve or fifteen in the company to which he belonged, and the influence they exerted was eminently useful.

Winchester, March 7, 1862.

My Dear Father: Your letter, with mother's, came yesterday This was a real feast to me, and I reply at once.

The army and the community here are still kept in painful suspense, as to what is to be done. The impression is general that the place will be evacuated, and some of the citizens are already leaving. But no one knows what is to be done. The soldiers only have orders to be ready to move at any time, but when, or in what direction, is wholly unknown to us. My own impression is, that Gen. Jackson will fight, unless they come in overwhelming numbers. Charlestown is their chief point of rendezvous, and if they move from there towards Winchester, a force from Leesburg can easily fall in their rear, by the help of which we could hope to defeat them. And if, as you remember, Gen. Jackson drew up his brigade of four regiments, last summer, and watched more than an hour for Patterson's whole army to advance to the attack, we may expect him to dispute the enemy's advance now. But whatever comes, may we be ready to meet it. The only way to have any true peace of mind is just to be ready for anything, so that, come what may, we shall be prepared to bear it. It is not however, anxiety for myself that breaks my peace. Learning, through your letter received yesterday, that you had thrown the responsibility of volunteering on T., gave me more anxiety than anything of a personal nature that has occurred during the war; yet it may be best for him. So far as this life is concerned, it is far better that every Southern man should die, resisting the Northern invader, than bow his neck to the cruel yoke he seeks to impose upon us. And as to our eternal interests, the only way to secure them, is by faithfully following the path of duty. And what duty can be more imperative or sacred than resistance to the fanatical power which now rules the North, and seeks to subjugate or destroy us? The path of the soldier, therefore, full of temptation and danger, may become the way of life to many. The instances of this among our Lexington boys, should encourage all to hope for the best.

To His Mother.

Your letter was a treat to me. The expressions of affection, and the accompanying prayers for me, are grateful to the heart. You expect us to move forward very soon, either to another great battle on our own soil, or to invade that of our enemies. Of course, I cannot tell what a day may bring forth, but I see no reason to expect a great battle so soon. I am ready, I hope, for anything. I do not feel like turning my face homeward, however, until all at home are relieved from fear of the enemy. I wish to return to enjoy with you the pleasures of home in peace, and not to share the anxieties which now distress you. Let us only bear up with Christian firmness, and fight with courage, trusting in God, and we may hope for a speedy close to the war. "Thank T. for the prayer with which he closes his letter to me. O! if he were a Christian, how much more willing I should be to die.

Mrs. Gen. Jackson arrived yesterday She came to headquarters just as Bishop Johns was about to begin evening worship. Her arrival occasioned some excitement. She looks very well. I had the pleasure of speaking to her after the service had ended. Her face, as always, seemed like sunshine.

Bishop Johns preached for us two very good sermons. They were simple, earnest, faithful proposals of Christ to his hearers. I enjoyed them both very much, and hope they did good to all. Much love to one and all, but especially to you, my devoted mother, from your son,

Hugh.

To His Youngest Brother:

The recent disasters, and especially that at Fort Donelson, have not discouraged but aroused the army, and they are more anxious to do something to redeem our cause than ever. I am glad that the same effect has been produced among the people, many of whom ought to have been in the army long ago. No man ought to permit himself to be drafted. It is my intention now to remain in the army. Although you are not yet seventeen years of age, I wish you could be here. But, T., I am afraid to see your life in so much danger. I should tremble far more for you than for myself. If I am killed, I have a good hope, that I should at once enter Heaven, and be happy forever. This hope cheers and animates me at all times, so that while death walks on every side, no tormenting fears arise. But alas! how different with those, who, unprepared for death, meet it on the field of battle. I have heard such men cry to God for mercy in the midst of the battle, when their cry seemed louder than the roar of the cannon, and certainly pierced the heart with keener anguish.

How then could I endure to see you placed in danger of such a fate? Will you then, at once, seek preparation for death, so that whether it meet you at home, with everything to promote your bodily comfort, or amid the horrid carnage of the battlefield, it will be without terror? Why not, at once do so? Why wait one day, one hour longer? Everything calls you to decide quickly for God and against sin. Every day you live, out of Christ, sin is binding you more and more firmly in its fetters, and may thus hold you as its captive forever. I beseech you therefore, to break off from every form of sin. Tear yourself away from it by fleeing at once to Jesus Christ, the only Saviour from sin and death. Do you never feel anxious to be a Christian? When you sit in your room at night, with your Bible at your side, does something never whisper to you—open, read, obey that book, that you may be happy forever? I know it does.

This is the Spirit of God, speaking to you. Heed its voice—search the Scriptures, and you shall find eternal life. I wish I could write more to you, but I cannot today. My prayers follow you day and night. But even this will avail nothing, if you will persist in rejecting the Saviour. The question of life or death, salvation or eternal destruction, must be decided by yourself.

The only reason why sinners are, lost is, that they 'will not come to Christ, that he may give them life.' It is their own fault. How will you decide? Decide at once for Christ, I do beseech you. Your fond brother,
Hugh.

To his mother he writes:

> You have, no doubt, seen the Message of President Davis to Congress on the recent victory. It is the most becoming and beautiful thing of the kind I ever saw. It displays joy and gratitude, but no exultation nor boasting. It is the language of a man who feels his need of divine help—appreciates our danger—feels our sorrows—and rejoices in our good more than in his own. How despicable do our enemies appear in the light of this Message.
> If this Message be, as I believe it is, an exponent of the feelings of the Southern heart, it is even more cheering than the victory which called it forth. If we do not now forget the source of our power, and who it is alone that can give us the victory, we may be assured that our God will not leave us to the will of our enemies, but will rid us of them forever.

Thus, pure was his piety, and elevated was his patriotism. His thoughts and his prayers were given habitually to his God and his country.

Early in the spring of 1862, General Jackson was compelled by greatly superior numbers to abandon Winchester and move slowly up the valley. The following letter to his father describes the Battle of Kernstown, the first that was fought after the evacuation of Winchester.

> March 29, 1862.
> My Dear Father: We moved from Strasburg in the morning expecting after a slight skirmish, to spend the evening in Winchester. With merry hearts we marched on. After seeing the general's wagons safely across Cedar Creek, our company went ahead more rapidly. (His company was bodyguard to General Jackson.) The roar of cannon soon proved that there was some obstacle in our way. About noon, it was ascertained that we should have a battle. This had been so little expected that many had left their guns and cartridge boxes in the wagons. I bor-

rowed cartridges from others, and went on. Our whole force could not have exceeded 3,500. Our company marched to a point within six miles of Winchester, and then turned into the fields on our left in search of our Regiment. After going nearly a mile, we reached it just in time to move with it to a new position further to the left. As we moved from the woods, the enemy's artillery opened fire upon us. Their shells passed very near us, but no one was struck. Some of the shells fired at us, struck the ground and rebounded, forming a graceful curve, and leaving a track of smoke behind them, exploded like rockets, thirty feet above our heads. But for the danger, the scene would have been beautiful.

Our artillery passed beyond us, and to our left, drawing the enemy's fire from us to themselves. During the cannonading, we lay quiet, some talking and even laughing, while others were silent and thoughtful. We were soon ordered to march beyond the artillery. The crack of the rifles and the whistling of the balls, soon told us what we must now expect. Soon volleys of musketry seemed to shake the hills with their incessant roar. I could but wonder how anyone could escape. But our Liberty Hall boys moved forward at a quick step to the brow of a hill where the enemy were in full view. From this point we continued to fire about an hour. I do not remember to have seen a man near me struck, although I saw the blue-coated enemy lying dead and wounded, and now and then others would fall. A regiment on our left, perhaps the 37th, saw the enemy trying to reach a stone fence, and starting, reached it first. From this position they poured a deadly fire into their ranks, which together with our fire on their flank, soon forced them to retreat. We exulted for an instant, but they soon renewed the fire from the top of a hill.

Our men were nearly worn down by constant exertion against men who were reinforced every few moments by fresh troops. They succeeded at length in getting on our right, and threatening to cut us off entirely from any way of escape. We therefore retreated, loading, and firing on them as we ran. Once, when I looked back, I saw the old "stars and stripes" waving over the ground we had just left. This vexed me more than anything else during the day. A party of us presently halted and fired into a party of them. They scattered like a flock of partridges. A little while after this, I was out of sight and saw them no more. Morrison and Lyle (their captain and 1st lieutenant), were with me just before we stopped to fire this last time. I did not see them again. They went too far to the right, and fell into the hands of the Yankee cavalry. If taken to Winchester, they will find warm friends.

If we leave behind us when forced to retreat, as true and loyal Virginians, as are the people of Winchester, the Yankees may march through the whole land, and yet accomplish no more towards our subjugation, than the arrow which pierces the air and leaves no trace behind. Our loss in killed, wounded and prisoners will be a little over 400. The Yankee papers acknowledge that they had 8,000 men engaged, and 350 killed and wounded on their side. These numbers may, with truth, be doubled. One of their colonels, and fourteen of their captains and lieutenants were killed. Our soldiers are not discouraged in the least. Our confidence in General Jackson is undiminished, and we will follow him with as much enthusiasm as ever. I most firmly believe that God is on our side, and on this, as an immovable rock, we can rely

Your affectionate son,

Hugh.

After the battle just described, General Jackson fell back slowly up the valley, with only about 4,000 men, in the face of the enemy numbering at least 20,000. On reaching Harrisonburg, he turned to the left, leaving the great road leading from Winchester to Staunton in uninterrupted possession of the enemy. Neither friends nor foes knew where he had gone. The former, under the impression that he had abandoned the valley, were much alarmed, and the latter, unwilling to return or to pursue him, and afraid that if they continued on towards Staunton, he might fall upon their rear, concluded to take formal possession of the village of Harrisonburg, and there pillage and burn, and play the vulgar tyrant in general, so as fully to let our people elsewhere know what they had to expect if subjugated, and thus fire them with a fiercer spirit of resistance. The sensitive and refined heart sickens at the recital of their brutalities.

Jackson encamped for a short time at Swift Run Gap, in a gorge of the Blue Ridge, nineteen miles from Harrisonburg. He then crossed the mountain, to Meacham's River in Albemarle, thence recrossing at

Rockfish Gap, hastened on through Staunton, towards the Alleghany, to pay his respects to Milroy at McDowell.

The march from Swift Run Gap to Meacham's River, the most laborious and painful they had ever taken, is thus described in a letter to his father:

> We are in Albemarle County, eleven miles south of Meacham's River. Yesterday and last night we made the worst march we have ever taken. Our wagons started about 7 o'clock in the morning, but could not go over eight miles during the day and night. The troops were behind, and dark found us only two or three miles from the camp we left in the morning. The remainder of the distance we came after nightfall, wading much of the way through mud and water, ankle and sometimes knee deep. This is no exaggeration, but a simple fact. The men became perfectly reckless, and plunged into mudholes and ponds of water with a yell or a laugh. We passed a camp on the wayside, and instead of finding our wagons there, were told that they were three or four miles ahead.
>
> We complained some, but pushed on. Most fortunately we had sent on a man from each mess, to build fires and prepare supper for the rest. The thought of fire and supper cheered many a heavy heart, and when, between nine and ten o'clock, we reached our camp, shouts of laughter echoed through the woods. Everyone had an Iliad of woes to recount, spiced however, always with something ludicrous, and we all made merry over the toils and mishaps of the way. Today we have remained quiet, waiting for the troops behind to come up. Tomorrow morning, we leave to go east—as some say. But where we are to go, for what purpose and with what result, no one knows. If God be our guide, all will be well.

On the same march he adds:

> It pains me to leave the valley, yet it did me good to get into Albemarle. How pleasant it would be to spend a week or two in Charlottesville, my native place. But I do not expect this. We hear that the people of Rockbridge are becoming alarmed. It would be painful to have all communication with home cut off. But this, and even worse can be borne, provided we can only repel the invader. If his unholy feet should ever touch the soil of Rockbridge, I sincerely hope that the undefended citizens will

remain at home. It is useless to run away. Yes, let them remain in their invaded homes, calmly. but firmly refusing to yield any obedience, or show any favour to those who thus come to rob and to ruin them. When I can do nothing else for my own dear home, and the loved ones there, I can pray that God would give them courage in the face of their foes, and submission to his holy will.

These fears were groundless as to his home, and the sorrow he felt at leaving the beautiful valley in which that home stands, was soon removed, for they did move the next morning, to pass, as we have seen, to Staunton, and so to the northwest.

In a letter, written at Franklin, in Pendleton County, he refers briefly to the battle with Milroy at McDowell, and to their situation at Franklin.

Our brigade was not in the battle. It was fought at great disadvantage on our part, but victory, at length, rewarded the resolute bravery of our troops. They fought as if resolved never to surrender. As we marched to the field after the battle, we met many wounded, who cheered us on, boasting that they had got the field at last. We hear good news from Williamsburg. May the power of the enemy soon be broken, and their armies scattered to the four winds.

The enemy now took position before us, and we were brought forward, confident that a battle was at hand. Now, our regiment was in front. Several companies were sent forward as skirmishers. These were met by the skirmishers of the enemy, and a brisk fire began, which is usually the initiative to a general engagement. One of their shells, aimed with great precision at a point at which Gen. Winder, Col. Ronald and several of us were standing, fell within four feet of me and exploded, covering me with earth. But, 'no one was hurt.' My escape was wholly providential. How gracious has been God's care of me. Oh! that I could thank him and love him as I ought.

Yesterday, we remained quiet, observing the morning *as a Sabbath*, having religious services in several regiments, and in the afternoon moved back several miles to this point. (When a Sabbath as such was lost, Gen. Jackson's rule was to observe the first quiet day he could command, as a Sabbath.) We have been pursuing the enemy down a ravine, in which they can choose many positions, from which they could only be dislodged by storm at the point of the bayonet, and through a country which produces nothing but maple sugar. Not one acre in a thousand can be cultivated. We are on the march again, and *en route*, I think, for Harrisonburg. We are all fatigued and our feet are sore. Otherwise we are well.

They hurry on, and the next we hear, is that having spent the Sabbath as a day of rest, at the Augusta Springs, they meet the enemy. He says to his father:

> We are in Front Royal. The enemy fled in haste yesterday afternoon. Several hundred were taken prisoners. Few were killed on either side. Captain Sheets was killed while scouting round the town. I would not have lost him for a thousand Yankee prisoners. We took the enemy here by surprise. Two Yankee trains, heavily laden with commissary stores, arrived from Alexandria just in time to fall into our hands. There were, I hear, several thousand barrels of flour and several hundred sacks of salt, with many other valuable articles. We move this morning towards Winchester, distant nineteen miles. The force of the enemy here is not known. But from what we hear, it does not exceed 10,000. Tom (his youngest brother), was left at Harrisonburg, completely worn out. Many of the boys are broken down. H. M. could not keep up with us, yesterday. He is well, but footsore, and much wearied. We marched twenty-five miles yesterday, and can do the same today, if thereby we can only drive out the invader. Send my clothes as soon as possible, as I am much in want.
>
> Warmest love to all. I hope soon to date a letter to you from Winchester."

This hope was soon realised, for his next is dated

Winchester, May 27, 1862.

My Dear Father: General Jackson has gained a complete victory over Banks, putting his army to utter rout, and capturing several thousand prisoners. This brilliant success began at Front Royal on Friday afternoon. Saturday morning our army pushed on towards Winchester by two routes. A part of General Ewell's force moved directly towards this place. The rest, together with General Jackson and his army, turned to the left towards Middletown, situated five miles from Strasburg and thirteen from Winchester. Banks, with about 8,000 men, had been at Strasburg, expecting us to come directly down the valley. On Friday night he heard what had occurred at Front Royal, and on Saturday morning made a hasty retreat towards Winchester. But our forces came into Middletown as his were passing through, and cut his army into two parts, forcing the smaller portion to hasten back to Strasburg. They burned the bridge over Cedar Creek, to prevent our pursuit. What became of them I have not heard. It is reported that many of them were captured, and the rest, I hope, are making all haste towards the Ohio River. We, at once, turned to pursue the other and larger portion of his forces. Ashby's cavalry charged up the road towards Middletown, as Banks passed down, and at once a panic and a rout ensued. Some of the enemy's cavalry were killed, but the most of them threw themselves from their horses and fled. Almost an entire regiment was so frightened that they could make no resistance. As we pursued the enemy, the road was lined on either side with wagons—many left without horses—others upset, with their contents scattered in all directions, and towards evening we found dozens of wagons on fire. We did not halt as night came on. The Yankees at length became somewhat stubborn, and hiding themselves on the roadside, fired on our men as they passed. To be ambushed thus in the dark was fitted to throw our men into confusion. And to some extent it did so. But skirmishers were sent in search of them, and while they fought the enemy in the bushes, order was restored to the ranks. They at length gave back, and we moved on. We fell into an ambush several times, but General Jackson seemed determined not to be stopped, and we pushed on until three o'clock in the morning, when we lay down on the roadside, a mile and a half from Winchester, and rested until the day broke. We rose, shook the dew from our limbs, and moved forward. I saw General Jackson ahead, watching the Yankee skirmishers, and sending some of our men to meet them. In a few moments firing commenced. The 27th Virginia, under Colonel Grigsby, drove in the enemy's skirmishers, and took the hill on which they were posted. The cannonading soon became brisk. The Yankee sharpshooters did us ranch more injury than their artillery, killing two of the Rockbridge battery, and wounding most of the eighteen who were wounded during the battle. Once our artillery were compelled to yield a little, but in a short time our infantry advanced to meet that of the enemy. The tide now turned in our favour. The enemy broke—our men advanced with loud cheers—then they rushed forward, driving the excited foe before them. 'Forward,' was now the command to the whole army, and in a few minutes, we were rushing through the streets of Winchester, amid the most rapturous cheers of the citizens, who had sought shelter from the balls in cellars and elsewhere, but now they ran forth frantic with delight. We paused long enough to shake hands with acquaintances whom we happened to see on the wayside.

Many of the frightened and retreating foe dispersed themselves through the town, begging the people to shelter them in their houses, kitchens, or even stables. The prisoners may be numbered by thousands. The rout was more complete than that at Manassas. Most of our troops were worn down, and stopped five miles above Winchester. It would make your blood boil to hear of the insolence and cruelty of the enemy practiced on the people of Winchester, from General Shields down to the lowest Dutchman that wallowed in the streets. But the crowning act of all was their setting fire to the town. One street was in a blaze when we entered, and a large building in the heart of the town, filled with medicine, was fired, but happily extinguished. So long as their sentinels dared to remain, no one was permitted to attempt to extinguish the fire. These are the friends who come only to protect us, and to seek a more permanent union with us. Deliver me from such friends.

We have already learned that Capt. H. R. Morrison and Lieut. John Lyle were captured at the Battle of Kernstown. They were immured in a dismal prison at Fort Delaware, where for about five months they endured much hardship. When the offices thus made vacant were filled, the company conferred the captaincy on the subject of these sketches. On his election, he wrote to his father as follows:

> The result surprised me greatly I had hoped for nothing higher than the lieutenancy, and was not confident of that. But the question was decided in my favour, and with much fear I accept the position. I do not expect any increase of happiness, but an increase of responsibility, leading to much perplexity and

toil. The care, the kindness, the ceaseless effort called for, will greatly increase my need of help from the grace of God. To this source I look, praying that by example and by effort the men may become good soldiers and good Christians. I ask that all at home will pray that I may be fitted for the position I now hold.

On the same subject he writes to his brother Henry:

> Promotion in itself brings neither peace nor happiness, and unless it increases one's usefulness it is a curse. An opportunity is now afforded for exerting a wider influence for good, and if enabled to improve this aright I shall then be happier than before. My life is now given to the army, and will be spent in it, even to the end of the war. But if my life is spared to see the end, and we are successful in our struggle, it will be the delight of my heart to spend the remainder of it in the work of the ministry. I am not fond of the army. Indeed, many things in it are hateful to me; but nothing is so much so as the invader of my native soil.
>
> Tom has joined our company recently. I feel most anxious about his soul. This is now more than ever under my influence and in my hands. This thought makes me tremble. I can only pray that God would visit him with His grace and save him. Let us never forget him in our prayers; for it may be that while you pray, he is exposed to all the dangers of the battle, or possibly just on the verge of eternity. If unprepared, how sad will be his end. The thought is dreadful. Let us trust in God, and be instant in prayer.

The next battle in which he participated was that near Harrisonburg and at Port Republic.

> Brown's Gap, June 11, 1862.
> My Dear Father: General Jackson has fought two more very hard battles; defeated the enemy both times, drove him as far as he wished, and then extricated himself and saved everything from the trap set by the enemy to catch him. Our regiment was not in the thickest of either fight, and no one of our company is hurt, though the balls have made holes in some of their clothes. Our army had fallen back to Port Republic, and we hoped to rest for several days, and prepare for another campaign. With these thoughts, we were lying in our camp, on Sunday morning, the 8th instant. A bright sun made all around look beautiful and

cheerful. We were expecting soon to meet for public worship, and to spend the day in calm and holy communion with God and his people. Suddenly, artillery opened fire within sight of us. The enemy had come up the south side of the Shenandoah, and were trying to destroy the bridge at Port Republic, which was our only way of escape, if the enemy pressed upon us.

Their cavalry at the same instant had dashed into Port Republic, seized Major Crutchfield, of General Jackson's staff, and the general himself had to run fast to slip them. They had a piece of artillery in Port Republic. He passed near, and gave them *some order*, and dashed on to our camp, ordered the long roll to be beat, and in an instant, we were pushing down the road. Our infantry pickets had now cleared Port Republic of the enemy, retaken Major Crutchfield, with the guard over him, and captured that piece of artillery. Our artillery was already in position, firing at the enemy across the Shenandoah. We came up just in time to witness the beautiful scene. The Rockbridge and Alleghany batteries fired with great accuracy, and every shot told with wonderful effect. The enemy were in the open bottom, we on a commanding bluff. They were soon thrown into disorder, and ran off in a hurry. We saw them, their guns glistening, their flags and all, and it did us good to see them in such a hurry to get out of our country.

We remained where we were to guard the position; but it was soon evident that the main army of the enemy was advancing from Harrisonburg. This was only a feint to attract our attention, cut off our only way of escape, while their main force advanced from the other side to crush and seize our whole army. This was their plan. One part was already foiled, and in a wink General Jackson was moving the rest of his army to check their advance from Harrisonburg. The artillery soon opened, four or five miles from us. It grew faster and louder, till there was an incessant roar, which made everything quake. It was more incessant, louder, and continued longer than any other cannonading I ever heard. It lasted from 10 a. m., to 3 p m., which, with the cannonading near us in the morning, made the fight with artillery alone continue over six hours on that day.

The report came to the infantry that our forces were falling back, and we received the order to withdraw from our positions. This, however, was soon countermanded. We remained in our places, and from the sound we could tell that the enemy were giving way. How earnest was our prayer that God would grant us complete success, and our prayer was answered beyond our highest expectations. The enemy were driven back five or six miles, and after dark we were recalled to camp, back of Port Republic, to hear more particularly of one of the hardest battles of the war, in which an inferior force, retreating, and attacked by one larger and fresher than itself, yet rallied so rapidly, and resisted the enemy so bravely, that he was compelled to give back and retreat. It was one of our most wonderful victories. But our work was not yet done. We must attend to the force on the south side of the river. The morning dawn found us marching on a foot-bridge constructed over the south branch of the Shenandoah, and down the south bank of the river. General Jackson, as usual, was leading us.

It was venturing a great deal to attack this force of the enemy They were not so numerous as we, but there were at least two, and, I believe, three brigades of infantry, besides cavalry and artillery. We must fight them too, in a narrow bottom, between the river and the mountain. And if the enemy towards Harrisonburg should return, they could take the first position we had on Sunday morning, and compel us to yield. But 'nothing venture, nothing win;' so we go ahead. We saw the effects of our fire the day before. Dead and wounded Yankees lay along the road, and the trees and houses were badly torn by the balls. This was but the ante-chamber. We would soon enter upon more horrible scenes. Our regiment, with the second, passed under the fire of the enemy's cannon into the mountain side.

We climbed back and forth over ridges and through the thick tangled brush, till we were worn out. We were once very close to the enemy's cannon on the mountain side, and thought our duty was to charge it. But no, we must march back, while General Taylor's Louisiana brigade advanced to this work. They did it nobly; took the enemy's battery, though they were forced to give it up; but it was retaken, however, afterwards. We marched to the rear, and were left there till we heard the shouts of our boys in pursuit of the enemy. The issue of the day long hung in doubt. Our men were several times repulsed, and the cheers of the enemy, with the evil reports of some of our own men, made us fear the worst. But we put our trust in God, and felt confident of success. Soon our hopes were realised. The enemy was in full retreat, which became in a few minutes a perfect rout. Eight or nine pieces of artillery, almost if not all they had, were taken.

Their ambulances, with their loads of wounded, were left to fall into our hands, and hundreds of men and arms were captured. The work was well and completely done. We pursued them seven or eight miles. But the enemy were on our side, and if we followed farther, they would shell us as we returned. We came back, therefore, in the woods, on the mountain side, to conceal us from the enemy, who were now on the opposite bank of the river, then struck a road leading to the turnpike across Brown's Gap, and at one o'clock that night I dropped my weary limbs on the top of the Blue Ridge, at the corner of old Albemarle. We had now escaped the enemy's reach, and left both portions of their army defeated. We are now in a position where we can rest in safety, or move in any direction we choose. The enemy have not crossed the river at Port Republic. General Jackson had the bridge burned to prevent them from getting behind and pursuing him.

I consider these two victories by far the most wonderful he has gained. The enemy formed a concerted plan to catch and destroy our whole army. General Shields had sent two brigades of his division up the south bank of the Shenandoah. He, I think, joined Fremont in the Valley, and was in the fight on Sunday. General Tyler commanded them on Monday. Their whole plan was foiled, all of our baggage was saved, both portions of their army driven back, and much of their artillery, with many prisoners, was taken. In the management of this affair General Jackson has shown great skill; while at the same time Providence has aided him in a most wonderful manner. Had the enemy returned from Harrisonburg three hours sooner, they would almost certainly have compelled us to retreat with great loss, and turned our victory into a defeat. But God guides our general, and enables him to venture much, to run great risks, and yet to gain the most brilliant successes. Let praise be given to His great name for His recent favours to us.

You have heard, of course, of Colonel Ashby's death. He was killed in a heavy skirmish near Harrisonburg, on Friday evening. A most noble sacrifice to our holy cause. It is felt by us all as a personal affliction. The sun shines brightly today, and all is cheerful in camp.

After this battle, they rest near Wier's Cave for a few days, and he writes to his mother thus:

> We are today near Wier's Cave, and encamped in a beautiful grove, greatly enjoying rest in the shade. Yesterday afternoon a party of us visited the cave. It was a delightful recreation, especially to those accustomed to the hard service of the soldier. It made us feel as though it would be possible once more to lead a quiet and civil life, and take part in the pastimes which make such a life happy. We then took a roll in the Shenandoah, and returned to camp clean and in good spirits. A good night's sleep has almost prepared us for another of General Jackson's tremendous flank movements. Our present encampment is too pleasant for us to expect to remain in it long, and we confidently expect the order to march very soon; but in what direction, or to what point, no one can tell.
>
> All are willing, however, to go wherever General Jackson bids; having implicit confidence not only in his integrity and fearless courage, but also in his skilful generalship. His recent success has greatly increased our admiration for him. The campaign was splendidly conducted. He not only extricated his whole army from a trap skilfully set for him, but defeated one portion of their army, holding the other in check at the same time, and on the next day utterly routed the second portion, capturing nearly all their artillery, five or six hundred prisoners, bringing all off safely before me first could sufficiently recover from the shock to attack us. Yes, the whole North-Western army conspired to catch and destroy our general and his troops, but it signally failed. It is true, at one time they had surrounded us. In their own favourite language, they 'had us in the bag;' but then they had no man brave or skilful enough to tie the bag and hold us in. My warmest love to all at home. How I long to see you.

He wrote to his father, urging him to visit the army:

> I think you will enjoy the visit, and you know it will be a rich treat to me. I greatly desire to see you again. Nothing, certainly, but a clear and strong conviction of duty, within approving conscience, could keep me contented in this painful separation

from the dearest earthly objects. But when death comes near, as it does so often here, it brings the Christian so near to God and heaven—the centre around which he hopes to meet those he loves best—that he almost forgets his temporary absence from earthly home and friends. The parental threshold, and especially the family altar, are certainly very dear, but our true home is in heaven.

Our company still acts as bodyguard to the general. Our situation is very pleasant. We are relieved from many things that used to annoy us; and a fine band often regales us with its music. We have also some leisure time for reading such books and tracts as we can get, and for enjoying the society of each other and of friends from a distance, who frequently call on us. I sometimes fear I shall not only become contented, but even pleased with this mode of life. I used to wonder how one could choose the life of a soldier. I thought its dangers and hardships would make it irksome in the extreme. But we quickly become accustomed to these things, while the excitement of an active campaign imparts pleasure, which is much enhanced by a firm conviction of the justice of the cause for which we struggle. I feel now that if taken back to my former quiet life, it would be, at least for a time, somewhat irksome. And, indeed, did not the ministry, with its most blessed work, hold the supreme place in my heart, I could be a soldier for life.

But as my former desire to preach has not been weakened, but rather increased by my experience in the army, I am exceedingly anxious to close this life and enter upon that. When I shall be gratified, I cannot tell. God, who has manifested himself in the storm which has broken over our country, and now rages around us, must bring us peace again. If he does not, men on both sides will become worse and worse, and war cannot end. The humble prayers of God's people can do much more to end it than all the bullets and bayonets of our soldiers. And while it lasts, the former alone can make the latter successful.

If you come to see us, bring us some tracts and testaments. I can readily find persons who are more than willing to receive them. Anyone would be surprised to find how welcome he will be on a visit of Christian love to the tents of the soldiers. They will listen to his words, and thank him for any manifestation of love for their souls. I wish I could do more of what conscience bids me do, and what I know there is so much joy in doing. Why should so little be done in the army for the eternal interests of the men? Chaplains are scarce, and the few who are here are so restricted in their salaries that they cannot defray expenses.

I hope and pray that your visit here may not only gratify the longings of a son's heart, and the wishes of many true friends, but also do much to excite Christians to greater activity and awaken the impenitent to a sense of their sin and misery If Christians were only as prayerful and active as they should be, how much good might we not expect to result. Nearly one-half of our company are professing Christians; and in our regiment I know there is a very strong religious element, which, if active, might restrain much sin and promote very much the cause of Christ.

Several letters have just been received from various members of our family. They are a rich treat. These are visits from those I love, which revive my spirit when drooping, and heighten my joy if they find me happy Your contemplated visit to brother George will be very delightful. I am sure it has been a source of joy to our Synod to welcome back some of the loyal sons of Virginia who have fled from the land of tyranny and oppression.

When you have an opportunity, remember me, with great affection to the professors in our Seminary; and to any other friends with whom you may meet.

                Your affectionate son,

                              Hugh.

To His Sister, Mrs. M'Crum.

Our life, at present, is so much better than it has been for several months that we are having a delightful time. It is true, the sky is our roof, and the earth our bed, but then it don't rain, and we are not marching; and when a box comes in from home, we live and feel like princes. I am sorry that father could not visit us, but hope he will still do so. He will feel quite at home at General Jackson's headquarters, with the general and Dr. Dabney. The latter is very busy, but preaches whenever he has an opportunity. I heard him last Saturday, then twice on the Sabbath, when about two hundred soldiers received the sacrament of the Lord's Supper at his hands. This was a spiritual feast indeed. The religious element in our company is very strong; sufficient, I hope, to control all other elements, and give tone to the whole body. We hold a brief meeting every night, just after roll call. The man whose turn it is stands up, while the rest stand around him. He reads a chapter, sometimes sings a hymn, then leads in prayer. There is some profanity, but this is lessening.

Why should not the army be a school for the reformation of the wicked? Such it has proved to J. W and J. R. They are now perfectly sober men and good soldiers. I am much gratified at the accounts I receive of your prayer-meetings held in our behalf. The prayers of those at home greatly strengthen and encourage us in the army. I will endeavour to remember you all at your hours of prayer. Yet we are so drawn about from one place and employment to another that I have scarcely a moment for connected, sober thought. As for instance, today I have been soldier, cook, and *washerwoman*. Around me, as I write, some are cleaning their guns, others are putting away the remnant of our dinner, some are washing plates, and some are trying to sleep. I am sitting on my knapsack, with a tin pan as my writing desk. I write a sentence and have to stop to do something or to talk to someone. Yet amid all this commotion my thoughts keep their direction homeward. Like the needle, they may be changed a little by the objects near me, but they soon turn again towards the home circle and hover around the much-loved place.

I saw —— as I passed through W lately, dressed out in a fine suit, A man in fine clothes now is an offence. But *he* is excusable, as he is not fit to be in the army.

They were not permitted to remain long at their delightful encampment near Wier's Cave. They crossed the Blue Ridge at Rockfish Gap. On reaching Charlottesville he became very unwell, so much so that at the earnest persuasion of friends and with the consent of the surgeon, he determined to leave his company under the command of Lieut. G. B. Strickler, and made a very unexpected visit to Lexington. His health was not seriously impaired, but his flesh was wasted and his strength exhausted by the toils and privations of the preceding three months. Within a less period than that he had marched four hundred miles, and been engaged in five battles, besides several combats. When he left his company at Charlottesville, he was wholly ignorant of its destination; but soon after reaching home, he became convinced that the army was on its way to Richmond. He was, with great difficulty, induced to remain until the tidings came that the fighting around Richmond had actually commenced. Then neither friends nor physicians could prevail with him to remain another day.

When he heard of the part his company acted in the famous charge at Gaines' Mill, under the command of Lieut. Strickler, he became greatly excited, and said: "All the money in the world could not compensate me for the pain I feel at not being with them. But if they only conquer, this will moderate my sorrow;" then hurrying away, he reached the field just in time to discover that they *had* conquered. The first of that series of memorable battles, that at Mechanicsville, was fought on the birth-place of his father, and that at Ellyson's Mill in full view of the cemetery where the remains of his ancestry had been buried for more than one hundred and sixty years.

"I fought," said a descendant of the same ancestry, and of the same name, "in sight of my father's grave." Well might he have added, they have not only invaded my native State, and sought to rob us of our homes, but their missiles of death have broken down the enclosure, and ploughed up the earth around and over the graves of my fathers. Some of those ancestors were among the brightest ornaments of the old Hanover Presbyterian Church, under the pastoral charge of Samuel Davies.

In that desperate fighting, the youngest brother of Captain White—so often written to or mentioned in these letters—a youth then not seventeen years of age, took an active part. No language can express the emotions kindled in the heart of the father by the thought of such fighting, around such a place, by such a boy. And the tear starts now at the remembrance of that venerable mansion, in which the founders of the Presbyterian Church in Eastern Virginia were wont often to meet for consultation and prayer, now all riddled with cannon balls, thrown in part, no doubt, by Presbyterian hands. "Father, forgive them, they know not what they do."

During his visit to his friends, he wrote to his aunt, Mrs. Hutchinson, of Monroe:

> You will be surprised to receive a letter from me written at home. I rejoiced to find myself in the warm embrace of my mother, on Sunday night. Two days before, I was with the army on its march through Albemarle, with no idea of leaving, though I was much reduced in strength by sickness and the hard service

of several months past. Brother James, who was with us for several days, urged me to stop, and readily securing the surgeon's permission, I yielded and came home. The joy of getting here, and the rest of a few days, have refreshed me very much, and I hope soon to return to my place in the army. It is really painful to be absent, to be lying at ease here, in the lap of luxury, while others, my comrades, are bearing the burden of the service, or perhaps struggling with our enemies. I would not remain at home now, for any consideration. Our army seems to be making its way to Richmond. The great struggle there must come off soon. McClellan cannot abandon the effort without a battle. The people of Richmond are calm and full of confidence, resulting, I believe, from their trust in God. How I long to see our army burst the chains which bind our State, and set her free once more.

Gen. Jackson's efforts in the valley, his terrible blows upon the enemy, falling so fast and with such slaughter, have stunned and driven thorn back, while the people have regained their confidence and cast their fears away. We hear that Fremont and Shields have left the valley for Eastern Virginia. If this be true, the upper valley will be free from their hateful presence. But unless we can whip them badly at Richmond, this part of the State will still be exposed to their ravages.

During the same visit, he wrote to his brother Henry:

All the delights of home cannot make one rest satisfied when a battle is imminent which may decide the fate of his country, and in which his comrades will take part. I wish the battle at Richmond could take place at once, but would be very sorry to be absent. Not that I have become indifferent to cannon balls or fond of danger. Safety is more to my taste, but you understand my feelings. I only hope and pray that Gen. Jackson may be as richly blessed at Richmond as he has been elsewhere. I do believe that God has him in His special favour, and guides him in all his course. Otherwise he could not run such risks in safety, and gain the most brilliant successes, when circumstances make defeat and ruin seem so inevitable. May the same divine hand continue to preserve and bless him.

He adds:

I long for the time when I can enjoy the pleasures of home in peace. But for the present, my duty and happiness are in the army. God bless you in your glorious work, as a minister of the Gospel.

On another occasion he writes to the same brother:

Rest satisfied therefore that duty bids you stay at home; mine is to remain in the army, and I am willing to do it for the glorious cause in which our young Confederacy is engaged. If we give up, everything is lost. If we struggle on, endure hardships, exert our utmost strength, and put our trust in God, who has so far been very gracious to us, we may hope after a while to taste the most blessed fruits from these present distresses.

My chief source of sorrow is, that I can do so little, or rather that I do so little for the cause of my Saviour. Father seems to think the army a glorious field for usefulness. To him, doubtless it would be. But what have I done? I hope my influence for good has been felt in our own company—but to how little extent! I can only look to God to give me the heart to work, and then open up paths of usefulness for me. If I really wish to do good in the world, it must become a subject of constant study, followed by ceaseless effort. I am very glad to hear that you are so comfortably situated. You have nothing now to hinder you from doing much good. May God grant you this great privilege. It is a pleasing subject of thought to me, especially on the Sabbath, that father, two brothers and a cousin are all preaching the gospel. I do not forget to pray for you. May I soon be permitted to join the number, and give my energies to the same good work.

Having reached his post just after the defeat of McClellan, he wrote to his father from below Richmond:

Below Richmond, July 3, 1862.

My Dear Father: I sent word to Dr. Brown this morning, who had promised to forward the news to you all, that all of my company were safe. This is due only to the merciful protection of God. They have been in two of the most important and bloody battles fought during the past week—on Friday and Tuesday. The fighting was desperate, and their escape is very wonderful. T. was in the battle on Friday, but has fallen back sick.

Yesterday and today a calm has rested on the bloody field, broken only by an occasional discharge of cannon, heard afar off in the direction of James River. The enemy is on the banks of the river, if he has crossed, as is the report. Their army must be greatly weakened and demoralised. Many of the prisoners represent their soldiers as broken-spirited, rebellious, and ready to desert. Yet McClellan still has a large force, and if reinforced by Shields and Fremont, may attempt to move up the south side of the river. But he can never have so fair a prospect of taking Richmond as he had before. He possessed every advantage in the late battles. He had worked hard for twelve months, had raised an immense army and equipped his troops in the best manner possible. He came within sight of the great prize, and fortified himself strongly in the faces of our men.

We made the attack on his own positions, drove him from every one, capturing thousands of his men, nearly one hundred pieces of artillery, and killing two of his men to the loss of one on our side. Ought not this to be regarded as decisive? Can they ask any fairer, fuller test? The truth is, their soldiers are not actuated by the spirit which animates ours. They can make a grand show, blow their trumpets, and bluster about their flag, but are quick to choose between defeat and death. Considering what they have at stake, the former is far the better of the two. But it is not so with us. Our earthly all is at stake.

Best love to all at home. I feel far better contented now that I am at my post again, although my heart longs to be at home in peace.

    Your affectionate son,

                  Hugh

And when the army moved nearer to Richmond he wrote as follows:

              Glenwood, July 14, 1862.

My Dear Father: T. and I have been as much at home for several day's past as we could be anywhere, except in Lexington. Our brigade is encamped on uncle Hugh's farm, within a few hundred yards of his house, and I have been permitted to spend my nights and take my meals here. I found T. here, and he remained until yesterday, when he obtained leave to make a short visit to our relatives at Hilly Farm in Hanover. His health has improved, and though not firm enough to endure a severe campaign, he is comparatively well. I think he had better remain with us and make a third trial of his strength. If he breaks down again, he can then apply for a transfer to the cavalry service. This I am very reluctant for him to do, unless it becomes necessary. My own health is perfectly good, and I am fattening and strengthening daily.

I had much pleasure in seeing my relatives in and around Richmond. Uncle Hugh and Aunt Ann have been very kind, doing, indeed, just what makes me feel most happy—making me feel perfectly at home.

Yesterday I went to Richmond in Uncle Hugh's carriage, and had the pleasure of hearing Dr. Hoge preach. I enjoyed the service greatly. Gen. Jackson was present, and immediately after the benediction, all eyes were turned upon him, and the crowd gathered uncomfortably close about him. The general seemed uneasy, really appeared confused, pushed for the door, and vanished almost in an instant. I could but smile to see him fairly conquered and made to run.

I see in this country no such ghastly figure as famine, which many seem to think walks abroad, making all the people as ghost-like as itself. Nor is disease as prevalent as was expected. Though we are near the Chickahominy Swamp, we are on its south side, and the atmosphere is as pure, while as delightful a breeze is now stirring, as I ever felt in the mountains.

    Your devoted son,

                            Hugh.

To his aunt, Mrs. H.

With mountain barriers all around you, I suppose you feel quite safe from Northern bayonets.

The token of remembrance, enclosed in your letter, took me quite by surprise. I, of course, thank you most heartily for it, and accept it as a new evidence that you still remember me with affection. In this view I prize it highly. But do not imagine that the war has impoverished me. This it cannot do. I had nothing before the war, and hence I am entirely safe in this respect. I have neither houses nor lands nor money to trouble me, and if it were not that my friends are terrified for their own safety and that of their goods, I should be as independent and free from apprehension, as the wild Indian who calls all the hills his own. But though I have been thus far full of hope, and perhaps more cheerful than was proper, in a time so full of suffering, yet I confess that the late success of the enemy in the west has saddened, though it has not disheartened me. But I will not censure, lest I betray my ignorance. It is much better to provide for the future than to grieve over the past. And if reverses destroy that self-confidence in which we had wrapped ourselves, and lead us to gird on afresh the weapons of war, they may prove a blessing in the end. I am exceedingly anxious to remain in the army until the struggle is over. If conscience would permit, most gladly would I enlist for the war. But if the pulpits are vacant, the country is lost. I must therefore, if possible, return to the Seminary in the fall. I will remain, however, in the army until that time, and if the skies are any brighter, and I am alive, I will resume my course of preparation for the ministry In this work I desire to live and die.

I see something in the camp to admire, and something to censure, but, in the main, my belief in the doctrine of total depravity is confirmed and strengthened. I am glad, however, to say, that in our company I can see no increase of any form of sin. Only one or two ever swear, and I have never seen one intoxicated. The Bible is the constant companion of nearly all, and several, I think, would make a profession of religion if the opportunity were offered.

On another occasion he writes:

We are cheerful. But this does not arise from forgetting our homes, nor from indifference to what is to come, but from a calm purpose to meet and bear the worst. There are rumours of peace. Should the North return to reason, their mad career be checked, and peace smile upon our Southern Confederacy, it will be another of the wonders which God is working in the world at this time. Nations crumble in an instant, and from their ruins, others arise as quickly. May a merciful God work this miracle of deliverance for us. God only can do this, and send us back to the peaceful pursuits of civil life. It would give me great joy to carry out the cherished plans of my life which are now suspended. I wish to preach the Gospel. Any other occupation would be pursued only as an affliction. Yet other pursuits are inevitable now.

He was ever considerate, in a remarkable degree, of his mother's comfort. One of his chief sources of anxiety at the approach of a battle, was that she might be prepared for her sad share in its results. He would write to her beforehand, to prepare her for it. On the eve of one of the most desperate of the eight battles, in which he bore an active part, he wrote her a letter full of the tenderest filial love, and expressive of the strongest faith. He concludes this letter in these words:

Mother, don't be anxious about me. I have a sweet assurance that my soul is safe, and as to my body, that is only dust.

And then when the battle was over, his first effort was to find time to communicate the intelligence of his safety to all at home; and a form of expression, he used on such occasions was this:

May the anxious heart of my devoted mother now be comforted.

Truly, his was the heart, and the tongue, and the life, of a devoted son.

To a friend and classmate:

Your letter was received yesterday, and read with pleasure and profit. The account you give of your religious experience agrees so well with my own that I could but feel the warmest sympathy for you in your struggles with unbelief and fear. Yes, when sin separates us from God, heaviness and gloom must oppress us. We would give the whole world, were it ours, for one smile from our Heavenly Father's face. But while we thus suffer, Jesus stands with open arms to receive us, if we will but trust ourselves in his hands. It is unspeakably precious to exercise trust in God—in his grace, his power and his promises. The little child, when frightened, flees to its mother's arms, and in a moment, its fears are gone, and it sleeps securely on that mother's bosom. Thus we, timid children, of little faith, should flee to Christ.
Why may we not do this at all times? Unwillingness to do it is alike displeasing to God, and disquieting to us. Christ has endured the wrath of God due to us for sin. How bitter was

the cup he drank for us? Yet he drank it all. He endured the curse for us, so that we have no part of it to endure. Then let us neither doubt nor fear. We cannot make ourselves holy. Sin is all that we can call our own. Holiness is the gift, the free gift of God, through Jesus Christ. Let us accept that gift, and all the powers of earth and hell cannot prevail against us. Agreement in these great matters unites us tenderly together. Therefore, write about them, and we will endeavour to prove helpful to each other in *this* warfare.

To the same:

The recollection of the scenes passed at college is pleasant, and yet there are mingled with it some things which cause no little sorrow. It is the thought that days, and weeks, and years arc flying away and hurrying us on to the judgment, while I am doing so little to prepare for that great day. You seem to utter the language of my heart when you mourn for the deadness of your own. 'I hear, but seem to hear in vain.' I try to pray, but my lips refuse to utter the language, because I lack the spirit of prayer. How often do I rise from my knees mourning over the solemn mockery which I have been rendering to God under the pretence of worship? I cannot conceive of a worse condition than that in which my soul sometimes is. But yet it is all my own fault when our heavenly Father hides his face. We know that our Saviour sympathizes tenderly in the sufferings of his people. We know that he felt keenly when he found the disciples whom he had taken with him to watch 'heavy with sleep.' So, he feels for us when we are pierced with anguish on account of 'the sin that remaineth.' And, blessed be God, there are times when the love and sympathy of Christ are sweet to our taste—when standing beneath the cross, and looking up to the Lamb of God, we can say '*our Saviour*.' Such moments are rare; but yet one half hour thus spent in the morning, sheds a fragrance over the whole day. How I long to reach that state in my progress when this sweet sense of my Saviour's love shall abide with me forever. But we have need of patience, for such attainments are not made in a day. And yet by 'patient continuance in well doing'—by committing our souls into his hands and waiting upon him, we may make great and rapid progress in the divine life. The anniversary of my public profession of faith in Christ is fast approaching, and I feel somehow a reluctance for it to come. There are so many sins which I ought to have overcome, and so many opportunities for doing good which I did not improve, that I am filled with fear and shame. But hope cheers my drooping heart when I look up to that arm which I know is able to destroy sin where it remains, and to perfect good where it is begun.

In Christ 'all the fullness of the Godhead dwells.' Let us come to this fountain and receive this blood of purification into our souls. This is the only true preparation for God's service, either in the ministry or out of it. I shall do what good I can in my present line of life, yet the infinitely higher interests of the church open wider and more blessed fields of labour.

In illustration of the purpose just expressed of seeking to do good in every line of life, it may be stated, that from a very early age he sought to be useful to the coloured people—beginning with his father's servants. This people were greatly attached to him. He was at home but twice after entering the army, and that for a very short time. And yet the usual portion of each Sabbath at home was spent in the coloured Sabbath School. Many of these people manifested the deepest sorrow when they learned that they should see his face no more.

One good old man, a member of the same church with himself, said to his father with many tears, "I am very sorry he is gone. But you may be *sure* that *he* is in heaven." His manner of approaching this class of people, or of encouraging them to approach him, was so open, frank, and cordial, that they were always pleased to meet him. He often said, "It pains me to know—as I am obliged to do—that if this war lasts long, the coloured people will be the chief sufferers."

The mother of a young man belonging to the army called at the Lexington parsonage to inform her pastor that her son seemed much interested about his soul, and, indeed, she hoped he was a Christian, and would embrace the first opportunity to connect himself with the church; and then, weeping as she spoke, added:

Your son Hugh has been very kind and faithful to him. As he did not belong to his company, and as he could not easily see him, he wrote to him; and soon after he went over to his camp, asked him to walk with him. They went together into a grove, a considerable distance from the camp; and, after conversing fully with him, he proposed that they should unite in prayer; then, kneeling at the root of a tree, he prayed for the soul of my son, and now I hope he is a Christian.

They were members of the same congregation at home, but in the army, one was a private in the ranks of one company, and the other was the captain of another. Yet, unmindful of the difference in their military rank, intent only on the good of the young man's soul, he sought him out, then sought a retired place in a distant grove, and there, with the heavens above and the damp earth beneath their bended knees, he called on God to save his friend.

At the close of a prayer-meeting in the lecture room of the Presbyterian Church, the congregation were reminded of the near approach of their stated season of communion, and any who might desire to connect themselves with the church on that occasion were requested to make their wishes known to the pastor. As the audience dispersed a gentleman was observed lingering at his seat. It was a soldier who was at home on sick furlough. As the pastor approached, he took his hand and said:

> I had hoped to connect myself with the church at the next communion, but I shall be compelled to return to the army before the time arrives. Your son, Captain White, had two conversations with me at different times, when we were marching together, in reference to my soul, and my purpose has been fully formed for some time to join your church. I am very sorry I am obliged to leave.

These are instances selected from among many which illustrate his fidelity in seeking the salvation of the souls of those with whom he came in contact. During his last brief visit at home, there were a number of sick and wounded soldiers in Lexington. With some of these he had no personal acquaintance; but it is believed that he visited, conversed, and prayed with most or all of them. It is well remembered that he more than once left the most attractive company to perform a service of this sort. He was remarkably free from what Dr. Johnson calls "a whining pretension to goodness." He seldom or never spoke in the presence of others of his religious emotions. If he did so, it was ordinarily to those like-minded with himself, and at times and in places deemed appropriate to a theme so delicate and so sacred. In such society and in such places, he was judicious, but communicative. Many of his letters evince how freely he could pour out his heart to a friend whom he knew and loved.

Discriminating between mere talk about himself and words fitly spoken in defence of the truth and Author of the gospel, he was ever ready to avow his love for that truth and his veneration for its Author, as well as his fixed aversion to everything mean and wicked. His gentleness and modesty never degenerated into pusillanimity, nor his piety into fanaticism. He well knew how to be habitually cheerful without being frivolous, and how to commend true religion to the cultivated, natural taste of irreligious men, so as to secure their respect, if he could not their allegiance, to the Saviour he so much loved. The consequence of this was, that if, during his life in college, he entered a room filled with the gayest students, provided only they were gentlemen, he was received with gladness; and although his presence effectually restrained every form of vicious excess, it never diminished the harmless vivacity of the party God graciously taught him at an early age that important, yet rare and difficult lesson, how to be at once the cheerful companion and the consistent and useful Christian. If that was said in his presence which he regarded as untrue or wicked, he ordinarily dropped the conversation abruptly, and expressed his dissent by silent sadness, rather than by a bold and ill-tempered resistance.

An intelligent gentleman traveling with him in a stage coach, became the silent but interested listener to a conversation between him and a man much older than himself, in reference to the main point then at issue between the North and the South. The man, though a Virginian by birth, had sold and *pocketed* his servants, then gone to Illinois and turned abolitionist. All this leaked out in the course of the conversation. "And when this discovery was made," said our informant, "with a countenance expressive of the deepest sorrow, blended with the profoundest contempt, he at once became silent, and refused to hold any further intercourse with his misguided and unprincipled fellow traveller." His course would have been somewhat different, but for the disparity in their ages.

This sketch of his character will explain in part his singular usefulness among persons of all descriptions.

We left the subject of these sketches enjoying the hospitalities of his friends in and around Richmond, after the signal defeat of the invader. But such enjoyment was of short duration. The enemy, under the command of a man by whom the defeated McClellan had been superseded, now sought to reach Richmond by a more circuitous route. Their new commander, "with great swelling words of vanity," protesting that so far in this war he had "only seen the backs of his enemies," and "only sought repose in the saddle," reinforced by the shattered remnant of his predecessor's defeated forces, was moving in the direction of the Central Railroad, aiming to reach that road at a point some sixty or seventy miles west of Richmond. The Stonewall Brigade was ordered to move towards the same point. They accordingly left their pleasant encampment, and passing through Louisa, made a stand in Culpeper. During the brief period of comparative quiet now enjoyed, he wrote as follows:

To his sister, Mrs. Dr. Wade.

Madison County, July 23, 1862.

My Dear Sister: Mr. Hilton, of our regiment, starts for Christiansburg tomorrow, and right glad I am to drop you a line of congratulation upon the new light which has recently appeared in the west and in your house. Another star has risen to give light to the world—another child to gladden the heart of its mother—another niece to amuse and delight its uncles. And this is your daughter and my niece. It is a real pleasure to turn away one's thoughts from the war, with its scenes of deadly strife, of bloodshed and destruction, to the quiet pursuits and joys of the home circle. I never felt happier than when I sat down recently at home, where no clash of arms could be heard, and where all was peace. I hope it will not be long until I can see and play with the little ones of your house.

But our faces are now turned towards Washington, and although we are idle now, I hope that our generals are only preparing for an advance. If invasion is feasible, we ought to try it, that the burden of the war may be laid upon the homes of our enemies, to teach them how sore a thing it is when it comes to our own doors. If we remain idle after our victories, it only requires a short time for the Yankees to recover from their defeat and panic. They are well-nigh frightened to death for a while, but if we leave them in possession of all their cities and their homes, they feel secure, and soon create a new excitement in favour of the war, and push forward the poor Dutch and Irish to fill their broken ranks. If the men refuse to volunteer, they can be forced out, and we may soon expect to see another immense army gathering around us. But they have been thoroughly whipped at Richmond; their effort is seen to be foolish by their own people; and without doubt we shall ultimately be free.

When our army came back to Richmond from the lower Chickahominy, we had a delightful time with friends and relatives. Among others I saw Wm. S. White, Jr., whom I had not seen since he left Lexington, some eight or nine years ago. He fought bravely at Bethel in the beginning of the war, and at Ellyson's Mill he fought under very affecting circumstances, working at his gun for hours in full view of the graves of his sires. What could inspire a man with higher, holier courage than the sight of such a place at such a time?

I also saw another cousin, George A. Jones, who was so badly wounded in one of the many battles around Richmond. He seems to be comfortable now, and doing well. But I fear he is yet to suffer more than he anticipates. It is thought by some that the ball is yet in his foot, although the surgeon thinks that it inflicted the wound without permanently entering. Aunt M——, his mother, is quite well and cheerful, greatly delighted to breathe the pure Southern air, untainted by the presence and the breath of our cruel invaders. Their family suffered from the depredations of the enemy only to the amount of one thousand dollars, which was so much less than many of their neighbours suffered, that they estimate that as nothing.

T—— paid them a short visit at Hilly Farm, and was much pleased with all he saw, and especially, I think, with all he *ate*. He feasted on peaches, pears, apricots, &c.

We saw Aunt E—— also. Her home near the eastern extremity of Broad street, is very comfortable. She has been greatly troubled and excited by the Yankees, but now *laughs all over* at the way they have been driven off.

Give my warmest love to Cousin H—— and all the children—they are too many now to mention all by name. T. would write, but he has so thoroughly exhausted himself by writing four full pages of foolscap to father, that it is impossible.

Your devoted brother,

Hugh.

Soon after the writing of the foregoing letter the Battle of Cedar Run occurred. In this he bore an active part, but so rapid were the movements of our army after this that he failed to write a full description of that memorable engagement, from which he and his youngest brother, so often referred to in his letters, escaped unhurt.

All that he wrote respecting this battle may be found in the following hasty sketch to his father, written near Gordonsville, August 13, 1862:

> My whole company passed safely through the recent battle in Culpeper. The favour of God to us calls for the highest praise. O, that we could all learn to lean upon and trust him at all times.
>
> I was greatly pleased with the behaviour of my boys in the fight. The loss in our brigade was only twelve or fifteen killed, and as many wounded. This is very surprising, as we advanced through .an open field upon the enemy, who fought under the cover of woods—at least they were driven to this position from the open fields, and were soon driven thence also. The pursuit was very short, for night soon covered all the field with darkness. Several pieces of artillery were taken, together with four or five hundred prisoners, while the enemy were driven entirely from the field, leaving their dead and many of their wounded in our hands. We slept that night just where the enemy's cannon had been placed, and expected to awake at daylight to follow up the pursuit.
>
> During the night a brilliant cannonade was kept up for several hours. As Gen. Jackson could not push on after the Yankees himself, he was determined to make the shells follow them. We stood and observed the scene with great interest. We could see the flash of our cannon, sometimes the bright track of the shell, and then the bursting of it. The shells were poured all through the woods into which the enemy had run, and we hear from prisoners taken afterwards that they did them much harm. They made a feeble effort to reply to our guns, but with no effect.
>
> As one or two of their shells fell within our brigade, we concluded to move our beds a short distance and then slept until morning. Why we did not pursue the enemy I cannot understand, unless the report that Burnside was trying to cut us off at Orange Court House, was true. But this is certain, we have met the boastful outlaw, Pope, and whipped him thoroughly, and this, I trust, will discourage the Yankees still more, and fill our hearts with more lively hope and confidence in God.
>
> We lost our Brigadier Gen. Winder. He was struck in the side with a shell and died in a few hours. He was a most gallant sol-

dier, and by his admirable discipline, was not only keeping the Brigade efficient, but was making it better, I think, than it ever was before. His last words exhibited a noble spirit. 'Tell my wife and children,' he said, 'that I died like a brave soldier.'

Our loss in the 2nd Brigade was very heavy. The 'Dixie Greys,' from Roanoke, were almost destroyed. Our total loss is over a hundred killed, and several hundred wounded.

The scene on the battlefield was more like the pictures of battles than any I had ever witnessed. As we, on the left, moved forward and gained the top of a ridge before us, we could see the line of battle extending around to the extreme right, all along which the smoke rolled up in great clouds, and fire from the two sides flashed fiercely at each other. I did not have time to look long at this scene, for a little smoke, and some fire too, nearer at hand engaged my attention.

T. and I were separated from our regiment towards the close of the fight, but found it after the fight was over. The colonel had recalled it to form in line of battle. I did not know of the order until we were so far ahead that I was unwilling to go back. The Yankees were running, as they only can run, and the rest of our army were in hot pursuit of them. We fell in with another regiment, therefore, and went ahead. T., J. M., and Willie Preston, fought much of the time right at my side, and deserve great praise. T. was left at the camp near Gordonsville, sick, when we started to Culpeper, but expecting that we would have a fight, came on to take part in it of his own accord.

I hear that our boys, captured at the Battle of Kernstown, are now at home. This is delightful news. Give my love to them all, especially to Morrison. Write soon to

    Your affectionate son,

                Hugh.

The Second Battle of Manassas, in which he fell, was now near. The rise of the Rappahannock separated them from their wagons and their rations. They consequently suffered very severely, for two days, from hunger. During this time, he wrote the last letter that ever issued from his pen. It is dated "Banks of the Rappahannock, August 24, 1862," and is as follows:

My Dear Father: You are all no doubt anxious to hear from T. and myself. We have not had another battle, though there has been' some sharp skirmishing, and the roar of artillery has been almost incessant for several days past. We have moved some distance up the bank of the Rappahannock each day, halting occasionally to throw shells at the enemy and receive some from them. We have had their shells to awake us in the morning, keep us uneasy during the day, and scarcely to allow us to sleep at night. They have sometimes split the trees under which we were lying, but we have thus far escaped without injury. General Stuart has just captured three hundred prisoners, destroyed a large number of Yankee wagons, bringing off the horses, and found the trunks of General Pope and thirty other officers at a railroad station. He took a fine uniform coat, marked 'General John Pope.' Our major saw this coat.

We thus annoy the Yankees a little, though it costs us hard service and allows us little to eat. But our wagons have just arrived, furnished us abundantly with bread and bacon, and we are all right once more. The Yankee artillery still continues to roar, but all are as merry in camp as if the enemy were a thousand miles off. It is wonderful how indifferent men can become to the most horrible scenes. T. is now behind the army, sick with the jaundice. He is able to go about, and I have just heard that he was with a citizen, making his way towards Gordonsville. He has the surgeon's permission. I deeply regret that I did not see him again, and furnish him with more money before he left. He must be transferred to the cavalry, for he cannot stand the infantry service.

The order has just come to cook three days' rations, and it is probable that we shall move forward in the morning. But no one knows.

This has been very little like the Sabbath. With spirits saddened by hunger and fretted by the constant roar of artillery, we have been kept in an uncomfortable frame of mind. The busy preparations for tomorrow prevent any enjoyment of the Sabbath. However, Dr. Stiles is to preach to the brigade this afternoon, and I hope to hear him. It requires a great struggle to keep the busy scenes around me from driving all devotion from my heart. They ought to have a contrary effect. I ought now more than ever to seek my strength, my happiness, my all, in God. How could I live without him? With him no storm can disturb my peace, no danger can come nigh, no harm can befall which will not do me good.

I feel greatly relieved at T.'s absence. I hope he may not return until the shock of battle I see approaching is past. I can but feel confident that all will be well when it does come. God will give us the victory, and enable us to crush the infamous man who now leads 'the grand army of the glorious Union.' When Lincoln presides, with Halleck as military chief at Washington, and Pope as the first commander in the field, how can they triumph over our leaders, who are as distinguished for their piety as they are for their bravery and skill.

I send you three hundred dollars. Of this I wish you to appropriate one hundred dollars for T.'s outfit for the cavalry, one hundred to be held subject to my order, and one hundred as a donation to the Confederate States Bible Society and our committee for the publication of religious tracts and books.

Give my warmest love to all at home. You are constantly in my mind and firmly engraved upon my heart. Write when you can to your devoted son,

Hugh.

The tone of this letter differs from all his former letters. It manifests a strong presentiment of the terrible conflict in which he so emphatically predicts that our army was to conquer, and in which, though unknown to himself, he was to fall. The satisfaction he expresses at the absence of his young and much-loved brother, almost warrants the supposition that he expected to fall. Alas! alas! he never heard from us more, nor we from him until the sad tidings came of his death.

Nothing is better known than the rapid and prolonged march of the Stonewall Brigade, and others under Jackson's command, for the purpose of getting into the rear of the enemy. In this they were successful. They marched sixty-two miles in two days—the 26th and 27th of August. Gen. Longstreet sought to unite with Gen. Jackson, but was delayed by encountering the enemy on the way, and thus, for two days, Jackson, with a very inferior force, held the army of Gen. Pope in check. During these two memorable days the issue was still undecided. The fighting however, was desperate, and some of Virginia's noble young sons perished. Among these were Henry R. Paine, of the Rockbridge Artillery, and Wm. C. Preston, of the Liberty Hall Volunteers, both natives of Lexington, and both highly distinguished for their accurate scholarship, their consistent piety, and their indomitable courage.

When the approach of night closed the conflict on Friday, the 29th of August, Colonel Baylor, acting brigadier of the Stonewall Brigade, sent for Capt. White, and proposed that a prayer-meeting should be held at his quarters. This proposal met a prompt and joyous acceptance, and the young captain conducted the meeting. On the ensuing morning, Gen. Lee, reinforced by the arrival of Gen. Longstreet, renewed the attack, and then came one of the most desperate and sanguinary conflicts on record, which ended in the total defeat of the enemy. But to the counties of Augusta and Rockbridge, the victory was dearly bought. The former lost her loved and honoured Baylor, the other her brave young Captain Hugh A. White. On Friday night these officers mingled with many of their comrades in prayer and praise, and on Saturday afternoon, they passed almost at the same instant, from the carnage of the battlefield to the purity and peace of heaven. As fellow-heirs of the grace of life, they were lovely in their lives, and in their death, they were not divided.

The Sabbath and the sermon spoken of in the preceding letter, were the last our dear boy ever heard or spent on earth, and the prayer-meeting conducted by himself in the tent of Colonel Baylor, on the night preceding his death, was the last he ever attended. As the last charge was made, when the issue of the desperate struggle was extremely doubtful, and when it was rendered more so by the fall of acting Brigadier Baylor, who was bearing the colours of the 33rd Regiment, our brave young captain rushed forward, seized the colours as they fell, waved them in view of the brigade, advanced in front, until clouds of smoke hid him from the view of his own company and of his comrades-in-arms, when he fell, and was found by his company as they advanced in pursuit of the retreating foe. It is not known that any human eye saw him fall, or whether he spoke or even breathed after the murderous missile entered his breast. But we needed no dying words to assure us of his safety. We needed no other farewell than that contained in the preceding letter.

A dear friend—herself afflicted much in the same way—wrote thus to his mother:

> May the tender Jesus who said, 'Weep not' to his own mother in the extremity of her sufferings, say the same to you, dear friend. What need have we to look away from the surroundings of our dear ones' deaths, to forget the battle and the blood, and all the awful circumstances through which they passed into,

the pure presence of God. Think of it—the exchange of the boom of cannon for 'the harpers, harping with their harps'— the shrieks of furious enemies for the hallelujahs of angels—the fierce onset for the 'Come, ye blessed of my Father'—the madness of war for the boundless peace of Heaven. These were the exchanges your precious boy made when he breathed out his life into the hands of his Saviour. For himself, he felt nothing but a holy joy, as our Willie did, and if he turned his thoughts to the anguish of his father and his mother at his loss, it must have been with the triumphant assurance that the trust in Jesus which they had taught him, and *which was strong enough for him to die by, was also strong enough for them, to live by.*

✶✶✶✶✶✶

Note:—Wm. C. Preston, son of Col. J. T. L. Preston, of Lexington, Va., who fell in the same battle.

The following extract is taken from a sketch of his life and death, published in the Central Presbyterian:

"'Don't distress yourselves about me, boys, I am not afraid to die,' he said to his comrades, as they pressed anxiously around him. There spoke the considerate friend—the chivalrous young soldier—the fearless Christian. Of the few remaining hours of his life, little is known. Thus, much we are permitted to know. His beloved Captain, Hugh A. White, was with him on the morning preceding his death. Turning to the surgeon, Willie asked if it was possible for him to survive; he received a negative answer. 'Could you get a letter to my father?' he asked of Captain White. Upon being reminded of the difficulty, he acquiesced and said: 'Then I will deliver my messages to you.' These undelivered messages are forever sealed up in the bosom of the noble young leader, who fell, instantly killed, a few hours later." Thus, let the names of these martyrs in the cause of their country go down to posterity together.

✶✶✶✶✶✶

You are an honoured mother to have reared such a son for immortality. He did not need long years to fit him for a life with God, and if he has gotten home the soonest, without the toilsome march, you will not think *that* cause of sorrow, dear friend. If he could lean from the heavenly heights today, would he not say something like this: 'Precious mother, there is no need of tears for me. I had all the happiness earth can give. I had a sweet, beautiful life with you all, and without the trial of any grief, am translated now to the full possession of the bliss of God's redeemed. Rejoice in my joy.'

His dear father and you have my tears and prayers. What have I else to give?

Yours in like faith and sufferings,

M. J. P.

From a large number of letters written to his family and friends, it is deemed advisable to insert extracts from only three. All these relate chiefly to the time and manner of his death. As to the slight discrepancy which appears in two of these accounts of the posture in which he was found, it is sufficient to remark, that one saw him before and the other after he had been turned from the posture in which he fell.

The first of these extracts is from a letter of General Thomas J. Jackson to Rev Dr. Dabney. The general says:

> In the Second Battle of Manassas I lost more than one personal friend. Among the number was Capt. Hugh A. White. We were members of the same church, and had been co-labourers in the same Sabbath-school. His Christian labours were not confined to times of peace. In the army he adorned the doctrine of Christ, his Saviour. When Testaments or other religious works were to be distributed, I found him ready for the work. Though his loss must be mourned, yet it is gratifying to know that he has left us a bright example, and that he fell, sword in hand, gallantly cheering on his men, and leading them to victory in repelling the last attack of the enemy upon that bloody field.
>
> Very truly your friend,
>
> T. J. Jackson.

The following extract is from a letter to his brother from one who served with him as. first lieutenant, and who succeeded him as captain, and who was wounded on the previous day:

> Dear Sir: I have endeavoured to procure all the particulars of your brother's fall, but have only partially succeeded. Many saw him just previous to his death, and several very soon afterward, but I can find no one who saw him in the interval between the time when he was struck and when he expired, if there was any. The reason seems to be this: Immediately before he was shot, the brigade had been ordered to charge, but had not proceeded

far before it was thrown into considerable confusion, partly by obstructions in the line of march, but principally by the fierce resistance of the enemy; and it was just at this juncture, when companies were separated from their regiments, and officers from their companies, that your brother, eager to meet the foe, and undismayed by the circumstances which had produced a temporary confusion in his regiment, having advanced far to the front with his sword in one hand and his hat in the other, calling on his men to follow him, *fell* unobserved near the spot already hallowed by the blood of the gallant Colonel Baylor. Before his fall, and probably at the moment the fatal missile entered his noble bosom, he was bearing the standard with which Colonel Baylor fell while leading the brigade to the charge.

But although on account of the confusion, his death was unobserved, his presence was soon missed, and a member of his company, fearing he had been injured, proceeded to look for him, and soon found his body. He was lying on his face, resting it in his hands, and his pistol and his unsheathed sword lay by his side.

He was afterwards 'buried on the field' by a few of his little band, assisted by some friends from other companies.

Thus, fell our beloved captain, mourned not only by the company that had followed him so long, but by every soldier who knew him. We loved him not only as a soldier, but also and especially as a Christian gentleman. As a soldier and officer, he was a model; to his company he was exceedingly kind, but his kindness never assumed the form of partiality. He was just. In the camp he devoted himself exclusively to the promotion of its interests, temporal and eternal. In action he was perfectly fearless, yet his courage was controlled by a sound discretion. On such occasions he was possessed with a peculiar enthusiasm—an unconquerable zeal and determination to meet the foe, and consequently he was always seen among those gallant spirits who go farthest in the direction of the foe. His command never was '*go on*,' but always 'come on.'

As a Christian gentleman he was also a model. Such earnestness of disposition—such nobility of soul—such sublimity of purpose—such humility—such devotion to Christ's cause, not inducing noisy demonstrations, but those quiet, irresistible movements, which are like the silent flow of deep streams. How rare

are such characters! I have never known one as young as he, so faultless. His piety was active—a real living principle whose movements and influences were seen and felt, not only by his fellow Christians, but also by all who came in contact with him. His efforts to secure the salvation of his company were unceasing, and to compass this end he was much in prayer, and abounded in good works., As often as circumstances permitted, he distributed religious reading—tracts, newspapers, memoirs, &c.—among his company and sometimes in the regiment. It was also his custom, as occasion offered, to assemble his company nightly before the door of his tent for religious services. We deeply mourn his loss, and feel that his place can never be filled. But

Though lost to sight, to memory ever dear.

It gives me unspeakable pleasure thus to bear testimony to the inestimable worth of your noble brother.

Your friend,

G. B. S.

The last extract is from a letter to Rev. Dr. Brown, of Richmond, from one who, at the time, belonged to the Rockbridge Artillery, but who was soon after promoted to a place on Gen. Jackson's staff. Dr. Brown published this extract in the Central Presbyterian. The writer says:

The 'Stonewall Brigade' received the attack well; was flanked by a strong body of the enemy, fell back a few rods, changed front and again advancing, drove the enemy with great slaughter from the field and the cover which they sought. The result to our dear old brigade was fearful. Col. Baylor, commanding, was mortally wounded, and O! how sad I am to tell you, that our dear friend, Capt. Hugh A. White, of Lexington, the noblest of soldiers, fell pierced through his body, when in advance of the brigade, with hat and sword in hand, calling to his men, 'come on, come on.' I have seen no one myself who saw him fall. Just after this success of our brigade we advanced with our battery to cover their advancing columns. The ground was strewn around with the gallant, dearly loved veterans of our old Stonewall Brigade. Beyond was the long line of blue-coated hirelings, who paid for their crime with their life's blood.

I stood leaning against my gun, waiting for orders and watching the tide of battle as it steadily receded from me. Soon one of the Liberty Hall Volunteers came up, and, with tears rolling down his cheeks, told us his brave captain was lying there in front of us.

I ran forward, and there, *too true*, was my best, my noblest friend, with his sweet, lovely face upturned, his eyes gazing upon that world where his spirit had gone, and his body in its last, long sleep.

His sword had been already taken away. I found and took off his Bible and several letters. It was indeed heart-rending as we gathered around. Dear, *dear* Hugh, the purest, the truest, the best of us all. May we of his companions who are spared, live to love and serve our God more and better, and die to meet him in our home above. What a blessed ministry did we anticipate in his! How full of the promise of usefulness were his amiable, attractive qualities, his accurate and increasing attainments, and his quiet, yet earnest, active piety. But I must say no more, though of this subject my heart and head are full. Our victory is great. Again, let us turn to God—may his goodness lead us to new repentance and obedience.

J. P. S.

Robert Fairfax

A Sketch of the Life of Randolph Fairfax

By Philip Slaughter

RANDOLPH ENLISTS IN THE ROCKBRIDGE ARTILLERY

During the vacation, the university was converted into a military school, and Randolph passed from the groves of the academy to the *campus martius*. In the meantime, the Battle of Manassas was fought, and then the university became a hospital. Randolph assisted in receiving and nursing the wounded soldiers, and could no longer resist the call to the field of battle. He repaired to Manassas Junction and enlisted, as a private, on the 12th of August, 1861, in the Rockbridge Battery, then commanded by Captain (now General) Wm. N. Pendleton, and afterwards by Captains (now Majors) McLaughlin and Poague, and more recently by Capt. Graham. For our knowledge of his career as a soldier we are indebted chiefly to the familiar letters of himself and his messmates, from the camp-letters, written upon scraps of paper in pencil, and with the off-hand freedom of a family correspondence. Randolph's letters contain a continuous description of Jackson's wonderful campaigns, as they appeared to a boy of 18 years of age in the ranks.

This is a point of view from which we do not often look at the evolutions of armies. This fact, by itself, invests these letters with interest. We shall reproduce copious extracts from them, because they add something to the materials of history, and are fitted to do good, by their moral and religious tone, their glowing patriotism, and the spirit of contentment and cheerfulness which they breathe in the midst of the severest trials to which a youth so gently nurtured could be exposed.

His letters, too, hastily as they have been penned, are characterized by a vein of strong common sense unusual in one so young, and by uncommon sagacity in speculating upon the probable objects of movements in the army; from August 12 to October '61, they describe his first impressions of Manassas Junction, which anyone who visited it during the winter and fall of '61 would recognise; his walk to Centreville in a drenching rain over the late battlefield, and his enlistment in the Rockbridge Battery; enumerate his messmates, among whom are Kinloch Nelson, Jim Garnett, L. Macon, L. Blackford and "other nice fellows."

His visits to his old friends of the 17th Virginia; his pleasure at hearing the familiar voices of Bishop Johns and the Rev. Mr. Walker on two successive Sundays; his experience in cooking; his amusement "in seeing ———, with his sleeves rolled up, washing dishes and making up bread"; make light of the so-called discomforts of camp-life; describe a review of the Virginia troops and presentation of flags by Governor Letcher—a review of the Stonewall Brigade by Generals Johnson, Beauregard and Smith, in the presence of two members of the English Parliament, Sir James Fergusson and the Hon. Mr. Burke—the concentration of troops at Centreville, and the construction of breastworks—the marching and countermarching to Fairfax Court House and Centreville—the picketings at Mason's, Munson's and Upton's bills; rejoice in the open air and active life; and express the opinion that with a little precaution, suggested by common sense, a soldier, if he has a good constitution, ought to be more healthy than other men.

He represents his experience of camp-life as very pleasant so far, and he has no desire to be an officer.

> My situation is the more desirable of the two. I have none of an officer's cares and responsibilities; I have as agreeable companions as I have ever had at school or college; have as many privileges as I desire, and live as well as most officers, and better than many. The additional honour is very little in my opinion, as my experience has shown me that epaulets are not always criteria of merit. The attraction of office would not induce me to give up the agreeable society and companionship, and light duty of my present situation.

He then bewails "the desolation of Fairfax, where barren fields, dilapidated houses and old camp-grounds testify to the ravages of war"; and concludes with the lamentation: "I am afraid poor old Alexandria will never raise her head again."

The summer holidays, and drills, and dress-parades were now past, and he was called to look at the more serious features of "grim-visaged war." Jackson had been assigned to the command of the Valley, and had taken leave of his old brigade in a characteristic speech, concluding with the now historical passage:

> You were the first brigade in the Army of the Shenandoah, the first in the Army of the Potomac, the first in the 2nd Corps, and the first in the affections of your commander.

Jackson's command consisted of his old brigade, some thousands of militia, and Ashby's cavalry. In a letter dated the 12th of November, Randolph says:

> Last Friday we marched from 6 a. m. to 7 p. m., stopping only to water the horses—marching 25 miles, of which I walked 22; slept that night in a barn—next day crossed the Blue Ridge in a drenching rain. Many of the men were drinking and disorderly—reached Berryville that evening, and were quartered in the Court House. I and three friends were hospitably entertained by Dr. Kownslar, and actually slept in feather-beds without taking cold. We started the next day (Sunday), just as the church-bells were ringing, and marched to Winchester.

November 24th he writes:—

> Our camp is prettily situated among some cedar knolls near Winchester, and is occasionally enlivened by the presence of the ladies.

He speaks of the hospitalities of the Williamses and the Bartons, both of whom had sons in the battery. He says:—

> I can hardly realise that this is Sunday, so different from the Sundays of former days. How little did I think last year, when I was enjoying those delightful Sundays at home, that I should ever spend one in such circumstances. There is, unfortunately, too much truth in the saying, 'There is no Sunday in war.' But Sunday here is perfect enjoyment to what it was at Centreville, where the chief difference between it and other days seemed to be absence of drills. Yesterday was my nineteenth birthday, and it makes me quite patriarchal to think of it.

The Winter Campaign to Bath and Hancock

We continue our extracts from Randolph's correspondence, January, 1862:

> Leaving Winchester on the first, and marching about thirty-two miles, we reached Bath on the 4th, and driving the Yankees out, followed them to the river. That night and most of the following day our battery was engaged in firing at the town of Hancock, on the other side of the Potomac, and at the Federal batteries. I suppose our movement was a feint to cover Gilham's operations towards Capon Bridge. During this trip my patriotism was put to a severe test by marching through the mountains over the icy roads as smooth as glass, bivouacking at night in the snow, and rolling the heavy guns up the slippery steeps by day. On the day we left the Potomac we marched from ten o'clock in the morning till twelve at night, and only made seven or eight miles. Even then we did not reach our wagons, and had to *sit* around our fires one of the coldest nights I ever felt. The next day we overtook our wagons about sundown, and pitched into a good supper which our cook had prepared for us, having been without food, save a morsel by the way, for thirty-six hours. Three roads meet here, leading to Romney, Winchester and Martinsburg, either of which we may take.

Jackson took the road to Romney. and in the meantime, Randolph, being determined to re-enlist, got his first furlough and visited his family in Richmond. When he returned to the field his command was encamped at Cedar Creek, about two miles from Strasburg, Jackson having evacuated Winchester and retired from the Valley.

The following is his account of the Battle of Kernstown:

> On the 22nd of March, much to our surprise, we took up the line of march towards Winchester. I suppose the object of the move was to keep Banks' force in the Valley. We met the enemy at Kernstown. The battle began about two o'clock and raged fiercely until night. Our force was not more than 3500 infantry, cavalry and artillery, while that of the enemy was more than 10,000. On our way to our position our battery had to cross a wide, open bottom exposed to the fire of the Yankee artillery. Several shells exploded near us, disabling one of our guns. Just before we got into position a shell passed through one of the wheel-horses of our third piece and into the other, where it exploded, tearing off the legs of the driver and the foot of a man walking by the gun. It was a horrible sight to see the

mangled horses and men being helpless on the ground. We got into position about three o'clock, and were firing until it was nearly dark.

The infantry had by this time fallen back nearly to our position, and our guns were turned to pour canister into the Yankees so soon as they should appear on the edge of the woods. The position was unluckily a bad one, as they were able to come too near under cover of the woods. Consequently, our fire was not so effective as it otherwise would have been, although we learned afterwards that it was very destructive. The Yankee captain, Schriber, says in his report that 'the Rebels advanced their heavy battery (that was ours), which threw some well-directed shots in our (Yankee) battery and our cavalry and infantry on the slope of the hill, soon rendering it evident that the Rebel battery would have to be taken.'

This explains the advance of the Yankee infantry on our flank. The Yankee captain further says that 'the canister from our battery strewed the ground with dead and dying and broke the infantry that was charging us.'

Our drivers being raw hands, we were so long limbering up that two of our men were wounded, one of our horses struck in three places and his mate in one. In this state we drove off the field while the Minnie balls were flying at a most uncomfortable rate, and succeeded in getting our piece into a little hollow in the woods, where our worst wounded horse fell dead. Discovering that we were now between the lines, our lieutenant ordered us to cut the traces and make the best time in getting away, which we did in Bull Run style. I hated mightily to lose our old piece. It was one taken at Manassas, and one of the best of our six-pounders. It is some consolation to think that we got it off the field, and only left it when our horse was killed and there was no time to put in another. I have great reason to be thankful to God for my preservation, and that of my friends. My only trust in such times of danger is, that I am entirely in God's hands, and He will preserve me until His own good time. Our piece was the last to leave the field.

I escaped with a bullet-hole through the skirt of my coat. Our men acted very gallantly. One of our mess received a letter from his father, Mr. —— ——— of Winchester, saying that the enemy's loss, as estimated by a person who visited the hospitals, was 800 wounded and 500 killed; while our killed, whom Mr. —— helped to bury, numbered 85, and our wounded in the enemy's hands 92. Our total loss in killed and wounded was about 425. I am told that the Battle of Kernstown is considered in Richmond a victory, and I suppose it was, since we inflicted a heavier loss than we suffered, and gained our object in keeping their large army occupied by our small one. Our army has been increased in numbers since the battle, by recruits and drafts from the militia. The night after the battle we encamped about four miles from the field, and leisurely began our retreat the next day about ten o'clock, eating our dinner at Cedar Creek, and then marching to our old camp-ground, about two miles above Woodstock. The Yankees are at Edinburg on the other side of the river, and our guns are sent down every few days and have artillery duels with them.

Jackson soon resumed his retreat up the Valley, and reaching Harrisonburg, turned towards the Blue Ridge, and crossing the Shenandoah, took his position in Elk Run Valley, near Swift Run Gap. Here the troops were exposed for several days to heavy rains without tents. On the 16th of May, Randolph writes from the foot of Shenandoah mountain, whither Jackson had gone to meet Milroy advancing from towards Monterey:

> Since my last letter, we have been constantly moving. In two weeks, we have been in the counties of Rockingham, Albemarle, Augusta, Highland, and Pendleton, crossing the Blue Ridge and Shenandoah mountains twice, and have fought a battle on the western slope of Bull Pasture mountain, at McDowell. From the nature of the ground artillery could not be used on our side. While the battle was proceeding on the top of the mountain, we were in camp on this side. The fight began just before sundown and lasted until nine o'clock. Our brigade marched up the mountain just before the fight commenced, and was then marched back about five miles to camp to cook. It was again sent for, and the firing ceased just as wo reached the top of the mountain the second time.
>
> This movement of Jackson's was a great surprise to the Yankees, who left behind many tents and stores, and destroyed more. There are so many gorges and defiles in these mountains that the pursuit of the enemy must be slow and cautious, or our vic-

tory would have been more fruitful. I think it probable our next destination will be Harrisonburg, where, uniting with Ewell, we may, by God's blessing, drive the Yankees out of the Valley.

I was much pleased with a sermon preached for us last Monday by Dr. Dabney—the day set apart by Gen. Jackson as a day of rest and thanksgiving. The services were held within hearing of the enemy's guns and were impressive. Dr. Dabney's view of the war was that it was a visitation of God upon us for our sins, and that it would not cease until the purpose of God was accomplished—that is, until our people repent and turn to God; or else it may cease for a while, and when our cup of iniquity is full, more terrible punishments may come upon us. He also said, that God sometimes uses a more wicked instrument to punish a more innocent one, but that the punishment of the more wicked instrument would surely fall sooner or later, with terrible vengeance.

He spoke of the Babylon of the North, and predicted its downfall and destruction. His view is, that nations, as they cannot be punished in the next world, are punished in this for national sins—a view I think entirely coinciding with the Bible. I think the fate of the country is now in the hands of the praying people, and though I cannot see how or when, I believe God will certainly answer the prayers of His faithful people in the land. I believe I have not told you of the new discipline of our army. We have come to be veterans—have no tents, carry our knapsack and blankets, never ride on caissons, obey orders implicitly without inquiring the why or wherefore, and, in case of necessity, can live on half rations and not think it anything remarkable. When expecting a fight our rations are six hard crackers and a quarter of a pound of pork a day.

Pursuit of the Yankees to the Potomac

Randolph's anticipations were realised: Jackson went in pursuit of the Yankees in the Valley. In his next letter, dated 27th May, 1862, our young friend says:

Last Friday we made a forced march from Luray to Front Royal, a distance of twenty-seven miles; surprised the Yankees stationed there (two regiments with cavalry and artillery), took the town, with a large amount of quartermaster and commissary stores, and about 700 prisoners and two pieces of artillery. And all this with the loss of only two or three killed and wounded. The Yankees left in such a hurry that they did not have time to burn two fine bridges which they had just built across the two branches of the river at that point. By a strange coincidence one of the Yankee regiments was the 1st Maryland, who came into contact with our 1st Maryland, who completely routed the Yankees, chasing them through the town, and taking their camp and colours and a good many prisoners.

Nearly all the remainder of the regiment, with their colonel, lieut.-colonel, major, and many captains, were brought in that night by the cavalry. The next day we marched on towards Winchester, and then struck off to the left to get into the Valley turnpike at Middletown and cut off the Yankee forces at Strasburg. We captured at Strasburg many prisoners, and a large amount of medical and other stores, and I have heard a battery of six guns, that was escaping by a by-road to Moorfield.

This last I am not quite certain about. Our cavalry also captured almost the whole baggage train of the Yankees, consisting of hundreds of wagons. Pushing on all that day and all night without the least rest, driving the Yankees before us, we reached Winchester a little before daybreak. Here the Yankees made a stand, and while we attacked them in front, Ewell's division attacked their left flank, on another road. The battle began at early dawn and lasted about two hours and a half, when by a general charge our men drove the Yankees from their position, completely routing them and chasing them at a double-quick through Winchester. Such a rout has not been since Manassas; arms, knapsacks, blankets, and all sorts of accoutrements, were strewn along the route of their flight.

We pressed them for five miles beyond Winchester, but the broken-down condition of our troops compelled the infantry to stop. The cavalry continued the pursuit. It is impossible for me to form an estimate of our captures. I know that our loss is small, and the number of our prisoners must be near 3000; the amount of stores, ammunition, &c, is very large. We were exposed to a hot fire from some sharpshooters behind a stone wall, as well as a heavy artillery fire. Poor Bob McKim and another were killed, and we have sixteen wounded. It is only through the blessing of God that none of us were hurt.

Our passage through Winchester was perfectly glorious. The

pavements were crowded with women, children and old men, waving their handkerchiefs, weeping for joy and shouting as we passed at double-quick. Our troops were loaded with Yankee plunder, and rigged out in Yankee clothes to such an extent, that an order forbidding it was issued, lest it might lead to firing on our own men. Most of our spoils fell to those who lagged behind, as those in front had no time to stop.

Among other things captured was a wagon load of lemons and one of cake. The lemons were reserved for the sick, but the cakes were disposed of in short order. Among the spoils I have seen two Yankee breast-plates that so much has been said about. They were of different patterns; one a simple steel plate, and the other had points and came down over the hips. Unfortunately for the owners they had no plates behind, where they were most needed. We are now resting. Yesterday was observed as a day of thanksgiving. It is impossible to tell when or where will be our next move,

On the very next day after this letter was written, the old brigade, with Carpenter's and McLaughlin's (the Rockbridge) batteries moved towards Charlestown. While our forces were finishing up their work on the Potomac, intelligence was received that Shields was moving from Fredericksburg, and Fremont from the west, with a view of concentrating in Jackson's rear, and cutting him off with his prisoners and spoils. Accordingly, our army began to fall back up the Valley on the 30th of May. Ewell had been sent to hold Fremont in check at Strasburg, and the retreat continued to Harrisonburg, with a caravan of prisoners and booty in front, and the eagle-eyed Ashby guarding the rear.

The Battles of Cross Keys and Port Republic

The stirring events immediately succeeding, we will allow our young soldier to tell in his own words:

> Camp near Port Republic,
> June 14th, 1862.
>
> Dear Mama:—I have already told you how completely we were surprised last Sunday. We were all lying quietly in camp, expecting to have a day of peace and rest, when we were startled by the sound of cannon in our front. A scene of the utmost confusion ensued. The wagons were packed, and our pieces hurried

forward as fast as the horses could be hitched. We took position on a commanding hill, opposite Port Republic, from which we could see the Federal columns coming up the road on the other side within easy cannon range. After a brisk cannonade, we drove them back in confusion. Our position was such that they could not bring their cannon to bear upon us, so that all the firing was on our side—a kind of fighting which we all agreed was decidedly the most pleasant we had ever tried.

This was the advance of Shields' army consisting of three or four regiments which had pushed on rapidly. It is said that Gen. Jackson, whose headquarters were at the Port, was informed of their appearance only a few minutes before they had actually posted their guns around the town, and he narrowly escaped being taken prisoner. The general had just crossed the bridge, when he saw a Yankee gun come down the road on the opposite side and take position so as to command the entrance to the bridge. Taking it for one of our guns, he called out, 'Limber up and come over, or the enemy will get you.' The Yankees looked surprised, and then turning their gun upon the general, informed him of their true character by firing a shot at him. One of our pieces happening to arrive at the time, and putting in two well-directed shots, compelled the Yankees to abandon their piece, which was afterwards secured by us.

Soon after this little affair we heard cannonading to our rear, which was the opening of the battle between Fremont and Swell's division, our rear-guard. The battle raged all day, and we anxiously listened to every shot to tell by the sound which side was gaining ground. The suspense was awful, for we knew that if our forces were driven back our retreating army would be assailed by the force in our rear, and probably be cut to pieces. Towards evening, to our great joy, we could hear the report growing more and more distant, and we soon knew that the enemy had been repulsed. I understand that our centre was posted upon a strong hill, which the enemy attacked in front. They led regiment after regiment to the charge, and were as often driven back by murderous volleys.

Only a part of our force was engaged in this fight; our brigade and General Taliaferro's were kept to guard the bridge, and some others were held in reserve. That night we were brought over to the east side of the river to camp, fully expecting to return and attack Fremont with our whole force in the morning. But, to our surprise, we were led against the enemy on that side, while the remainder of our forces, who had held their position during the night, were drawn back to our support, and the bridge burned to keep the enemy from following.

Some blame Jackson for not attacking Fremont instead of Shields. But I think he pursued the wiser course. If we had attacked Fremont and been defeated, there was no safe way of retreat; and no general should go into battle without providing a way of retreat in case of defeat. In the Monday's fight with Shields, we had about five or six thousand. The enemy's force was about eight thousand. The battle began soon after daylight, and after a long cannonade, chiefly by the enemy; during which time our right wing moved around through the woods so as to flank the Yankee position. Our left wing, consisting of our battery and some pieces from other batteries, with several regiments of infantry, advanced to the attack. We were met by almost the whole force of the enemy, and, after a hard struggle, we were compelled to fall back.

It seems that our advance was made too soon, so that instead of having our right wing operating in conjunction with us, the enemy were able to meet us with an overpowering force, and drive us back before our right was ready to attack. Our battery was posted in an open wheat field, exposed to fire from infantry and artillery. We could see and hear the balls cutting through the wheat on every side; but, strange to say, we escaped with but few casualties. Nothing but the mercy of God kept us from suffering severely. As we drove off the field, I thought the day was lost; but soon we heard the firing on our right, and our wing returned as soon as the regiments could rally. The complete rout of the enemy soon followed, and five splendid guns and five hundred prisoners were taken. And all this was done in sight of Fremont's army, which just then appeared on the heights on the opposite side of the river; but too late, as there was an unfordable river between us.

Our army was drawn back to Brown's Gap by an old mountain road, the knowledge of which was the key to our whole success. For had we been forced back by the same road we came, we would have been shelled to pieces by the Yankee guns on the opposite side of the river, just as we had shelled them on this day. Our cavalry followed the enemy for ten or twelve miles and came up with the baggage-train; all of which would have been captured, some think, if poor lamented Ashby had been there to lead them. I have not been able to ascertain definitely, but I think our loss could not have exceeded 500 wounded, though I see a newspaper exaggerates it to 500 killed and 1000 wounded. I think that papers that print every idle report they hear are the curse of our country. Fremont has fallen back to New Market, and we are resting.

Yesterday, June 14th, by special order, services were held in the regiment, giving thanks for our victories and prayers for further blessings. I heard a delightful sermon from Dr. Dabney yesterday evening, and another this morning. This evening the sacrament of the Lord's Supper is to be administered, and I hope I may be able to attend. It is such a comfort and a great cause for thanksgiving to have such a Christian as Jackson for our general. I have known him, when obliged to fight or march on Sunday, to set apart another day for rest and divine service. And when other generals would have continued marching, I have known him to lie by and rest on Sunday. No wonder the blessing of God attends his army in such a signal way. I thank God for the glorious success, as He alone can be considered the author of it. I also thank Him sincerely for my preservation during the fight.

Jackson's on to Richmond

Jackson now flew swooping down from the mountains like an eagle upon McClellan's rear on the Chickahominy, and in co-operation with Lee, won the series of brilliant victories around Richmond which have made the names of Coal Harbor, Gaines' Mill, and Malvern Hill historical. The battery to which our young friend belonged was held in reserve until the bloody fight at Malvern Hill. He writes:

> For an hour, we were exposed to the heaviest artillery fire I ever saw. Shot and shell seemed to pour over in one successive stream and burst in our midst. We lost two killed and ten or twelve wounded in our company. I was struck by a piece of a shell on the collar-bone, but fortunately received from it only a bruise, which put me on the disabled list yesterday. It was only through God's mercy that our loss was not greater. Numbers were struck by fragments of spent shells, which did no serious

injury. The poor 17th, of Alexandria, I hear suffered severely. Hector Eaches, Charlie Whiting and Colonel Marye were taken prisoners. We drove the enemy step by step, capturing many prisoners and much artillery. I pray that God will continue to prosper our armies until our enemies are entirely overthrown. Don't trouble yourself about my promotion. I am content where I am, and perhaps it is best for me to remain where I am. I would not feel right in accepting a position that would take me out of active service. God again in His mercy has preserved me, and none of my friends were severely hurt; for which, and His other mercies, I owe Him a life of gratitude, and pray for grace to lead it.

After three days' leave of absence, which he spent with his family in Richmond, Randolph joined his battery at Gordonsville, and writes on the 7th of August:

Judging from appearances, both sides are gathering their forces for a decisive struggle. I have no doubt of the result, if the Yankees will only fight us.

His next letters of the 11th and 13th of August give an account of Jackson's advance into Culpeper, and the Battle of Slaughter's Mountain. He says:

Three pieces of our battery were under a very hot fire, but it sustained no injury. General Winder, our brigadier, was standing by one of our guns when he was struck. His death is a great loss to us, as he was one of our first officers. Major Andrews, chief of artillery of our division, was severely wounded and fell into the enemy's hands. Our brigade fought splendidly, and was complimented by General Jackson, who said they had always done well, but this time gloriously. A panic is said to have seized some of the troops, which exposed the flank of some regiments and led to disorder and loss. Our victory was complete. The enemy asked for a flag of truce to bury their dead.

The force engaged on our side was the 1st, 2nd and 3rd brigades, one brigade of Ewell's and several of Hill's, which came up during the fight. We were surprised at our fall back to Gordonsville after our victory. But Jackson has some plan in his head. After again leaving Gordonsville to advance on Pope, we met with no obstacle until we reached the river. The long siege-guns of our battery were engaged in an artillery duel with the Yankee batteries on the other side of the river. After several days' skirmishing and unintelligible manoeuvres, we crossed the river at another ford without any opposition. We then marched day and night, reaching Manassas Junction on the 30th day, taking the Yankees by surprise. It is wonderful how successful Jackson is in his movements. We effected a march along the entire flank of the enemy and reached his rear without his knowledge. Just after reaching Manassas we saw a brigade of Yankees sent from Alexandria to check the supposed cavalry raid, filing down the opposite hills. They advanced in beautiful line of battle up into a semicircle formed by our infantry and artillery concealed in the valley, until our artillery opening upon their flank and rear, they discovered their mistake and retired precipitately. If I may presume to criticize, it seems to me that if we had suffered them to advance further and then closed upon them with our infantry, we should have captured the whole lot; but as it was, we took many hundred prisoners. At Manassas Junction a large amount of stores were taken and destroyed. That night we marched by the light of the burning depot and cars in the direction of Sudley Church.

We had now been marching three days and three nights, with only about four hours' sleep during our march. Nothing but exhilaration at our unwonted success kept us up. Here we were at Sudley Church, with about 20,000 men, with Pope in our front, and a large force advancing from Alexandria on our rear. Well might the Yankees think they had us in a trap! But we privates, with entire confidence in our generals, were in blissful ignorance of our danger. For two days, by manoeuvring and fighting we kept them back, until about the middle of the second day we saw the long-expected Longstreet advancing on our right. At one time we were completely cut off, and four successive couriers from Longstreet to Jackson were captured, but the fifth got through with the glad tidings of his approach, and Jackson is said to have grasped his hand in joy at his coming.

The next day (Saturday) about three or four o'clock the enemy attacked us, and were driven back at every point. We had a splendid view of the battle from a hill on which our battery was posted. It was the grandest sight that I ever saw. Artillery was blazing from every rise in the valley below, shells bursting in every direction—batteries and horsemen galloping over the field in pursuit; while away off on our right we could see the long line of Yankee infantry drawn up to oppose Longstreet, and sheets of smoke bursting from their guns. Soon a cloud of smoke enveloped the plain, and we could only hear the successive roar of artillery and rattling of the musketry, gradually becoming more and more distant. I don't think I ever saw such a disproportion in losses—ours being comparatively light, theirs very heavy.

The Rockbridge Battery accompanied Jackson on the march to Maryland from Manassas, and on his return to Martinsburg to clear out the Yankees in our rear, and which resulted in the capture of Harper's Ferry, with valuable stores and munitions, and 11,000 prisoners. The gun to which Randolph belonged, with two regiments of infantry, was left in Martinsburg as Provost Guard, and was sent while there to destroy a bridge near North Mountain Station. Finding the Yankees in too great force for them, they only tore up the railroad track and returned to Martinsburg. In a letter from that place, dated September 14th, he says:

> The prospect of a little rest here is truly delightful. We have now been more than a month without a change of clothes; either marching or fighting nearly every day, and sleeping without shelter. We have been reduced to a degree of raggedness and dirt that is scarcely tolerable, and the worst of it is we have no chance of getting our baggage, which was left at the Rappahannock.

In the same letter he speaks of the good conduct of our troops in Maryland—the strictest discipline having been maintained. In reference to the sentiments of the Marylanders, he says:

> There are numbers of the people who would receive us gladly and avow their sympathies for the South, were they assured that we would keep possession of the State.

His Last Letter

On the 3rd of October, 1862, he writes from camp near Bunker Hill:

> The army is now resting and being re-organised. It is unfortunate that we could not have continued active operations; but it

is impossible. The men are ragged and barefooted, and the ranks so reduced by straggling that we could only bring half our force into the field. It is shameful. There was not half of our army engaged in the Battle of Sharpsburg. The scoundrels were straggling over the country and eating out the hospitable farmers on their way, while their comrades were beating back McClellan. I don't think we could have had more than 40,000 men engaged at Sharpsburg, and yet we repulsed the enemy. But as the more we drove them back the better their position became on the slopes of the mountains, it was clearly our policy to fall back.

On the 20th and 22nd of October, 1862, Randolph says:

> We have been transferred to the regiment of Col. Thompson Brown, which constitutes the Reserve Artillery of Jackson's Corps. We have thus dissolved partnership with the old First Brigade, and we are all sorry to part with old friends, and dissolve a connection which has existed from the beginning of the war. We have now two splendid twenty-pound Parrots. Such heavy guns are generally held in reserve. We think that our general intended the change to relieve us from the active service in which we have always been engaged.
>
> Gen. Jackson paid us a high compliment at dinner at Mr. Dandridge's, and said we deserved to have rest. The monotony of our present camp life is relieved by drills, guard duty and cooking, and now and then diversified by a corn-detail, when we have to go ten or fifteen miles and shuck out a wagon-load of corn. I happened to be on a corn-detail during the late snowstorm, and we had a terrible time of it working in the cold driving snow without gloves.

After a march of fifteen days, the Rockbridge Artillery encamped near Port Royal, on the Rappahannock River.

He says, Dec. 7th:

> The weather now is intensely cold, and I am afraid many of our poor soldiers are suffering. Oh, how I wish that this cruel war would cease! I think when peace is declared I shall be like a man just released from prison, or a condemned criminal just receiving his pardon. May God bless you and keep you all."

His last letter, which was found in his pocket after his fall, was written to his mother on the 11th of December, the day after

the Battle of Fredericksburg opened;
Remembering your injunction to write immediately after every battle, I hasten to obey it, and relieve you of any anxiety on my account that may have been awakened by the engagement of yesterday at Fredericksburg. We were on picket near Port Royal, and, although eighteen miles distant, distinctly heard the cannonade; it was the most continuous and rapid I ever heard, lasting from four o'clock till sunset, I think the enemy must have been repulsed once or twice, but at last succeeded in crossing the river, and now have possession of Fredericksburg. They are, however, no better off than they were before. We have heard firing again this morning, up the river, but don't know what it is.

The day before yesterday we had an affray with the gunboats on the river below. Our battery was sent down, with the long-range guns. We only succeeded in getting five or six shots at a boat passing up; but our 26-pounder, with a Whitlock gun, had a sharp duel with five gunboats above. The engagement, I believe, was harmless on both sides.

This was the last letter Randolph Fairfax ever wrote. On the very next day, as the sun went down, amid a storm of roaring guns and shrieking shells, he fell by the side of the gun he had served so well, and

*Death lay upon him like an untimely frost
Upon the fairest flower of all the field."*

Berkeley Minor, one of Randolph's most intimate friends, in reference to the Battle of Fredericksburg, says:

The company never behaved better than on this occasion. I speak of my own personal knowledge of the second section, that is the two twenty-pound Parrots, with one of which Randolph and I worked, as the first was placed in a different part of the field by Major Pelham. Lieut. Graham had command of that section, and was highly complimented by Major Pelham. Our section was under the most tremendous fire that any of the company had ever witnessed. We were in position about two hours only, but were under fire long before we got into position. The fire was most terrible about sundown. Then it was that our dear friend fell. We had ceased firing for a while, when

Gen. Jackson rode up and ordered all the guns to be shotted and fired simultaneously, and continue firing as fast as possible. This, it appears, drew the fire of almost all the enemy's guns in range upon us. Such a shower of shot and shell I never saw before and hope never to see again. This lasted until daylight was gone. After dark we brought off our guns.

E. Hyde says:

The piece of shell which was the cause of Randolph's death, entered the corner of the left eye, killing him instantly.

T. McCorkle, who was at the same gun with Randolph, says:

That same shell, of which a fragment struck Randolph, badly wounded Lieut.-Colonel Coleman and Arthur Robinson, of Baltimore. (Gen. Jackson had left the place where it exploded, a few minutes before. Lieut. McCorkle was near the same gun, but was not killed until shortly afterwards. Thomas McCorkle and Berkeley Minor bore Randolph's body off the field, and that night he and Lieut. McCorkle were buried together by their weeping comrades, not very far from where they fell.

★★★★★★

Note: Lieut.-Colonel Coleman and Arthur Robinson later died of their wounds. Coleman was Professor of Latin at the University of Virginia, and Robinson of the best blood of Maryland. Both were Christians, and died full of hope.

★★★★★★

Lancelot Blackford, who communicates these facts, says:

Few of the victims of the war have been committed to the earth on the field of glory, with more genuine grief than that which attended the interment of these two young heroes, on Saturday night, the 13th of December, 1862.

www.ingramcontent.com/pod-product-compliance
Lightning Source LLC
Chambersburg PA
CBHW030216170426
43201CB00006B/109